Hollywood Fantasies of Miscegenation

Hollywood Fantasies
of Miscegenation

SPECTACULAR NARRATIVES OF
GENDER AND RACE, 1903–1967

Susan Courtney

PRINCETON UNIVERSITY PRESS

PRINCETON AND OXFORD

Published by Princeton University Press, 41 William Street, Princeton, New Jersey 08540

In the United Kingdom: Princeton University Press, 3 Market Place, Woodstock, Oxfordshire OX20 1SY

Library of Congress Cataloging-in-Publication Data

Courtney, Susan, 1967–
   Hollywood fantasies of miscegenation : spectacular narratives of gender and race / Susan Courtney.
      p.   cm.
   Includes bibliographical references and index.
   ISBN 0-691-11304-1 (alk. paper) — ISBN 0-691-11305-X (pbk. : alk. paper)
   1. Miscegenation in motion pictures.   I. Title.

PN1995.9.M57C38 2004
791.43'6552—dc22

2004044320

British Library Cataloging-in-Publication Data is available

This book has been composed in Sabon

Printed on acid-free paper. ∞

pup.princeton.edu

Printed in the United States of America

10 9 8 7 6 5 4 3 2 1

In memory of Michael Rogin

Contents

Illustrations

Preface

THIS is a study of fantasy bound up with many histories. In it I propose that representations of miscegenation have had a far more integral place in the history of American cinema than we have yet to fully recognize. They offer particular insight into cinema's role in the intertwined productions of race and gender in twentieth-century culture and into the role of racial and sexual fantasy in shaping the form and content of Hollywood cinema itself. The book thus reads film history in the context of wider cultural history in an attempt to shed new light on a series of longstanding questions.

While my methods are heavily indebted to feminist film theory and criticism, I join recent efforts to expand that field in two ways: by interrogating the coproduction of gender and race throughout the history of American cinema; and by tracing a series of pivotal moments in that history, some of which substantially complicate earlier formulations about classical cinematic formations of identity and difference. As any number of conference panels and book jackets now make clear, I am by no means alone in feeling the need both to historicize theoretical discussions of this sort and to expand the feminist theoretical field to attend to forms of difference beyond, but often intimately tied to, categories of gender and sex. The book thus investigates what a growing number of cultural critics have come to see as the virtually indissoluble connections between constructions of race and gender, seizing a history of Hollywood fantasies where those connections are especially visible, and relentlessly visual.

Beyond, but undoubtedly central to, the intellectual histories that drive this project are my own history and the history of the book's writing. Looking back, I trace my desire to make feminist film theory grapple with the centrality of race to gender not only to my having come of age as a scholar within a tradition of feminist film theory increasingly critiqued for its sometimes blinding whiteness but also to having grown up in often mixed, usually self-segregated public schools in and around Oakland, California—first as the daughter of a young, white, working-class single mother and then, after a marriage that lasted a good while, in an upper-middle-class nuclear family more of the kind I had long dreamt about. Especially in the adolescent years of this second phase of my childhood, I often felt the expectation, from others and myself, that I should behave not just like a "girl" (which meant, by definition, a straight one) but like a "white girl." While I was mostly oblivious to the cultural forces in play with each of those terms, at some level I knew full well that they could be fused in powerful, demanding ways. This is not surprising, I see now, since being white and being female were perpetually linked in so many of my routine experiences of access, conflict, and pleasure.

As a young white woman in graduate school, I found the academic-sounding interests with which I had just begun this study suddenly vivid, and present, when Hollywood's favorite fantasy/nightmare of miscegenation—as canonized in D. W. Griffith's *Birth of a Nation* (1915)—returned with a vengeance in the media frenzy surrounding the murder of Nicole Brown Simpson and the investigation and trials of O. J. Simpson.[1] While the national obsession with the case was marked from the outset by an awareness that the flooded field of representation was itself tremendously overdetermined (brought home, for example, by the news that the celebrity suspect's photo on the cover of *Time* magazine had been darkened), it nonetheless also was marked by a profound failure to seriously confront the representational hysteria.[2] The public opinion polls that became a media staple continually insisted that we should make sense of the whole phenomenon along black and white lines of reception and belief; but all those polls seemed able to tell us (again and again) was that the fantasy of a black man beating a white woman, to death, was intolerable to African Americans and maintained its cultural staying power in the white imagination.[3]

In that same period, with the need for more complex ways to understand the history of miscegenation in popular American culture so apparent, the still critical role of cinema in that history also became vivid for me once again in the *lack* of response to Hollywood's 1995 update to Griffith's 1915 blockbuster. Watching *Just Cause* rehash images of a white woman brutally battered at the hands of a black man among a racially diverse crowd in Emeryville, California (adjacent to Oakland and Berkeley), I was dumbfounded by the voraciousness of this particular return of the fantasy of the black rapist-cum-murderer, and by the virtual silence on the topic inside and outside the crowded theater. Whereas the Simpson phenomenon provoked a range of critics—thoughtful and unthoughtful, male and female, black and white, and so forth—the audience in Emeryville seemed to consume the Hollywood film without any visible or audible signs of resistance. What did it mean, I later wondered, that even as one could hear murmurings of racial resentment between members of the audience, we all appeared to take in the racist screen images without contest?[4]

While these events signaled the continued relevance of my subject, it became all the more vivid with my relocation to a job at the University of

South Carolina, Columbia. In the course of my first semester, news surfaced of the state's being one of the last two in the country to still have a ban on interracial marriage, even though all such laws had lost "real," enforceable effect since the Supreme Court deemed them unconstitutional in 1967.[5] While previous objections to this clause of the state constitution had apparently fallen silent for political reasons, at least one legislator now pushed for the necessary referendum required, and ultimately passed, to repeal it. When the legislature passed a provision to "let voters decide whether to remove [the] archaic ban," coverage in the local paper gave pause.[6] Amid dozens of "archaic" comments from legislators who voted against giving voters the choice to remove the symbolic ban, comments that invoked virtually every racist discourse ever peddled (God, blood, racial purity, and the separation of species among them), the most astounding came from a Democrat from Cherokee County. As quoted and paraphrased in the front-page story: "It mystifies [Representative] Phillips that people of different races would want to marry. The attraction of white women to black men especially puzzles him. 'I don't know what prompts it. Is it the athletics in the blacks? Or is it just curiosity?'"[7]

In part I feel ashamed to even reprint this quotation here, hesitant to dignify such utterances with further publication, and loath to invite my readers to interpret them too quickly as indicative of a singular blanket of archaism across what I experience, in fact, to be a complex and conflicted state of racial fantasy and belief. That response of mine is similar to one I sometimes have in the classroom when I watch *The Birth of a Nation* and related films with my students, yet another time. Obviously such texts require attention, despite their "archaic" place in the histories of film and American culture. And yet, as I hope will soon become clear, my intention is neither to simply drum up the most outrageous miscegenation rhetoric I can find nor to privilege its most "real" instantiations. Certainly I *am* concerned with the interracial marriage referendum in my new state, as I am with the Confederate flag controversy here, and with subsequent legislation that declared an official state holiday honoring Martin Luther King Jr. only by also officially sanctioning Confederate Memorial Day in one and the same bill. At the same time, I am also deeply concerned about recent anti-immigrant and anti–affirmative action legislation in my "native" state of California. Indeed, I have centered this book around Hollywood texts in part to interrogate the proliferation and function of related representations that circulate within and between counties as seemingly distant as Alameda, California, and Cherokee, South Carolina. Nevertheless, living now where I do—with the most overtly conservative public discourse on race I have ever experienced in daily life, and a community of students with whom such matters often feel all the more vital to understand and negotiate—has brought a new kind of presence to the history and consequence of my subject. Now a white girl from California in the South, living in the actual place everyone, everywhere, has been invited to imagine as "home" to *The Birth of a Nation* no less, I am still utterly convinced that we have yet to fully take stock of the form and function of such cultural fantasies, and all the more attuned to the manifold social and psychic realities they can expose, deny, assert, and resist.

Acknowledgments

I DEDICATE this book to the memory of Michael Rogin because I cannot imagine it without him. Reading his work was profoundly inspiring from the earliest stages, and the responses he gave to my own were always exhilarating like no other. I hope to honor here in some small way the passionate intellect he shared so generously, as critic, teacher, and friend.

I am also humbled, and delighted, to thank many other remarkable people who helped me write this book. At the top of this list is Patricia Reilly, for she not only knows each of its arguments, struggles, and triumphs like no one else but actually has seemed to feel the pleasures of the process, and the pain, almost as deeply as I have. I do not have enough space to thank her for all her gifts to me (as friend, interlocutor, editor, cook, expert shopper, etc.), but I do want to thank her publicly for helping me, time and time again, to see what works, what does not, and how I might move from one to the other.

I am deeply indebted as well to my extraordinary teachers at Berkeley, each of whose influence is distinctly evident for me in the pages that follow. Here I thank Carol Clover, Tony Kaes, and Kaja Silverman, as well as Mike Rogin, for showing me in all kinds of ways how to be a better critic, a better historian, and a better theorist than I ever could have been without each of them. I am also tremendously grateful for, and repeatedly moved by, their long-term and long-distance commitments to me and this book.

Generous, exacting readings from several others have also been vital. Tom Gunning and Linda Williams read the manuscript at both early and late stages and responded with precision, recognition, critique, and passion that I am still learning from, and that I value most dearly. Charlie Musser and Matt Bernstein also offered extremely important, helpful feedback. Deep thanks also for crucial readings and discussion of various (and sometimes multiple) pieces along the way to Greg Forter, Pamela Barnett, Jacqueline Stewart, Bob Bohl, Dan Streible, Jennifer Culbert, and Kate Brown. And for more fleeting but sustaining encounters I very much remember (even if others might not), thanks to Richard Dyer, Valerie Smith, Adrienne Davis, Amelie Hastie, Mark Williams, Herman Gray, Constance Penley, Lynn Joyrich, Charlene Register, Mary Desjardins, Elena del Rio, Anne Nesbet, Mark Sandberg, Eric Smoodin, Marilyn Fabe, Russell Merritt, Jane Gaines, Thomas Elsaesser, Krin Gabbard, and Patricia Welsch.

Thanks also to the editorial board at *Genders*, Ann Kibbey and Thomas Foster in particular, for helpful responses to an earlier portion of chapter 4, published there as "Picturizing Race: Hollywood's Censorship of Miscegenation and Production of Racial Visibility through *Imitation of Life*," *Genders* 27 (1998).

Institutionally, I have enjoyed two phenomenally supportive department chairs, Steve Lynn and Robert Newman before him; a program director in Ina Hark who always believed in this project; and research support from the Office of the Vice President for Research, the College of Liberal Arts, and the Department of English, all at the University of South Carolina, Columbia.

For assistance with the book's research and production, thanks to the staffs of the Margaret Herrick Library (especially Sam Gill, Barbara Hall, and Faye Thompson); the UCLA Film and TV Archive; and the Library of Congress. Closer to home, I fear I would not have survived all the cite checking and indexing if it were not for so many excellent research assistants over the years, including Anne Goebel, Susannah Clements, Rosina Marini, Michelle Reed, Ladka Khailova, and Todd Kennedy. Thanks, too, to Susan Swartz for a wonderful year of meticulous work in the library. And most of all, I am grateful to the excellent staff at Princeton University Press. My editor, Fred Appel, has seen this project through a long and at times quite challenging process, always with a calm and sharp focus on the best interests of the book-to-be. And Kathleen Cioffi and Dimitri Karetnikov were wonderful as the book made its way through production.

As for the rest of the life that makes the book, I am blessed with many wonderful colleagues, students, and friends in Columbia who make life and work here such a pleasure. I cannot possibly include everyone who matters on this list (there is that much pleasure here!), but I can start: Greg Forter, Pamela Barnett, Agnes Mueller, Nicholas Vaszonyi, Leah Vaszonyi, Nina Levine (and all the regulars at Club Levine), Dan Streible, Teri Tynes, Laura Kissel, Ed Madden, Bert Easter, Rebecca Stern, Dianne Johnson, and Julie Hubbert and Co. In places and times more distant, but never forgotten: Mari Balestrazzi, Amy Zilliax, Rob Miotke, Kath, Keith, and Hannah, Amy and Gwen Albert, and Carol Jameson. Believe me, you all helped.

Last, but in many ways first, there is my family. Much love to all the Courtneys, Guttersons, Bohls, Williamses, and Kepleys, and to Grandpa George. Thanks especially for learning to ask questions other than "Is it finished?" and for celebrating other triumphs, large and small, along the way. For me the completion of this book also calls up the memory of my father, LaMar Courtney, who helped me see myself as someone who could write it. I also want to single out my mother, Laura Courtney, for affirming me since before I can remember with forms of love I am still learning to appreciate.

And in the most vital here and now of my everyday life, my deepest love and gratitude I share with my husband, Bob Bohl. His love, insight, humor, patience, editing, laundry skills, and abiding commitment to good food and drink—not to mention his willingness to watch most anything—were vital from beginning to end. And this last year and a half I literally could not have done it had he not been taking such loving care of our daughter. That this book's last push, as it were, coincided with Chloe's entry into our life is utterly in keeping with how connected our joys at home have been to this work.

November 2003

Hollywood Fantasies of Miscegenation

What Happened in the Tunnel and Other Open American Secrets

The Interracial Screen Kiss

A recent cover story in *Jet* entitled "Is It Still Taboo for Blacks and Whites to Kiss in Movies?" helps me articulate two apparently simple but persistently significant characteristics of this book's subject: its particular forms of cultural familiarity and spectacularity, both of which function (paradoxically) to keep us from thinking about what the filmic representation and repression of interracial desire can mean. The first of these is evidenced by my strong, if unsubstantiated, memory upon discovering the cover at the grocery store of having seen others like it at checkout counters past. That this sense of familiarity is not simply that of an author's with her subject is further evidenced by the most recent waves of films that feature, and loudly contemplate, interracial couples (e.g., *Far from Heaven* [2002], *Monster's Ball* [2001], *Bulworth* [1998], *Jackie Brown* [1997], *Lone Star* [1996], *One False Move* [1992], *Zebrahead* [1992], *Jungle Fever* [1991]). Our cultural familiarity with such representations predates these films and is certainly tied as much to the extensive legal, extralegal, political, economic, and familial histories of "miscegenation" in the United States, as to the extensive history of interracial fantasies throughout American popular culture and its cinema.[1] What I am calling cultural familiarity might also be described as a sense of cliché, or "obviousness," that clings to them.[2] To say this is to suggest that to the degree such fantasies have become cliché, the ideologies sustained with them remain obstinately obscured.

The simultaneous sense of our collectively knowing and not knowing about this subject is demonstrated by the story that lies behind *Jet*'s inquiring cover. Apropos of checkout stand literature, and of *Jet*'s particular interest in black celebrity, the story effectively consists of a star-oriented list, with pictures, of contemporary black actors who have and have not kissed whites and in which films. The "still" of the title's question is given no historical context; there are none of the expected references to first or forbidden interracial kisses in film and TV history, and scant attention is paid to the politics of the filmic "taboo." The most direct answer to the title ambiguously asserts: "If it's still taboo, they [Lau-

rence Fishburne, Whitney Houston, and Lela Rochon ha]ve all committed the forbidden act."[3] Perhaps because the structure of the question
wants a "yes" or "no" that is not forthcoming, the most interesting complexities hinted at are not acknowledged or pursued.[4]

I begin here not because I expect critical analysis in the checkout line
but because this example so resonates with the popular screen productions that preoccupy this book; and because, until recently, the academic
world, certainly in film studies, has been a good deal like the reader constituted by the article in *Jet*: we knew such couples signified a lot, we did
not take much care to consider exactly what.[5]

Certainly that state of academic affairs has changed considerably in
recent years, as is attested by the growth of scholarship in history, literature, and a range of critical "studies" (e.g., legal, cultural, American)
interrogating "border" crossings, breeches of "the color line," and the
like.[6] Such scholarship, much of which has emerged in the course of this
book's writing, signals increasing awareness that representations of interracial desire and sex have much to teach us about the erection and
transgression of racial categories. In a short but provocative essay, Nick
Browne declared as much about Hollywood film in particular, arguing
that "the ideological centerpiece of American popular representation of
racial relations" was a certain "constituting prohibition"—"no nonwhite man can have sanctioned sexual relations with a white woman"—
that effectively "constructs parallel racial worlds and puts a boundary
between them."[7] Interrogating open transgressions of such boundaries
via blackface, Michael Rogin proposed in a different vein, borrowing
from the lyrics of an Al Jolson song, that the figurative couple "Uncle
Sammy and My Mammy" is fundamental to the cultural production of
white American identity.[8] The project at hand pursues these and related
issues that emerge when one recognizes that a whole range of interracial
pairs, triangles, and quadrangles have perpetually served as key sites of
American cinema's mutual constitution of race and gender, and of continuous, shifting relations among these and other categories of identity
and difference.[9]

The bookend-like "classics" near the historical extremes of this study,
The Birth of a Nation (1915) and *Guess Who's Coming to Dinner* (1967),
make it apparent that to imagine an interracial couple in popular American cinema has always meant to imagine identity in ways that put into
alignment, and utterly bind together, a series of identity categories.[10]
Birth begins with highly patriarchal and bourgeois depictions of family
and home that are then threatened and restored in explicitly interracial
terms that in turn give birth to the white supremacist and decidedly phallic nation finally celebrated. In *Guess* the alignment moves in the opposite direction. With its "How would you feel if *your* daughter . . ." prem-

ise, the film takes us from the public space of a crowded airport where the young lovers are first spotted to the private, patriarchal space of Tracy and Hepburn's modern mansion and, ultimately, to the titular dinner table of the film's final shot—here figured as the last stand and absolute core of all social relations. In any number of permutations, with an assortment of functions and outcomes, and despite common assumptions that they are simply "about race," Hollywood fantasies of miscegenation thus invariably bind together multiple registers of difference, necessitating interrogation of that very binding despite, and because of, the excesses of cliché that also often accompany this process—excesses that drip and bleed from *Guess* and *Birth*, respectively.

While the chapters that follow attempt to map the crowded intersections of difference thus embedded in, and negotiated through, American screen fantasies of miscegenation, I should clarify from the outset the primacy of race and gender for this project.[11] For the inextricable join between these categories in popular American cinema is perhaps nowhere more visible than in texts that fantasize interracial desire.[12] And here we arrive at the second point I take from *Jet*'s cover story, more specifically from its images, and that is the spectacular quality of my subject.

The cover is filled by four stills of interracial embraces (not kisses) from four contemporary films.[13] The story within is also photo-filled, with thirteen more illustrations, nine of which are explicitly intimate. The text asks, without really answering, the title's question. But the sheer volume and repetition of images—mostly close-ups and medium shots of couples holding and touching each other, in compositions that emphatically juxtapose light and dark faces, arms, and hands—insist that even if interracial desire is not categorically taboo (there are seventeen images after all), it is nonetheless a sight to behold.[14] Even so, despite all this exposure, the sight of interracial kissing itself is mostly withheld, even in the photos from films that the text reports include it.[15] Nevertheless, whatever the identities of individual readers attracted by the cover, and however they might interpret the ambiguous messages about the subject (something "still taboo" for better or worse? a liberating sign of changing times? a titillating transgression?), all are invited by the serial repetition of seventeen photographs to consume it as an immanently visible one.[16] Like the publicity still that covers the front of the videotape box for Spike Lee's *Jungle Fever*, a close-up of interlaced white and black fingers, the details of photography and layout in *Jet* produce the interracial screen couple as an iconic image that presumes to signify instantly, transparently. In fact, such representational details produce the complex and ambiguous subject *as if* its meaning were transparently visible.[17]

What is more, these images produce race and gender as themselves visible categories and insist upon the certainty of each in part by drawing upon the visual codes of the other. The repeated juxtaposition of contrasting skin tones draws attention to skin color in ways that reaffirm the notion that it is a natural, "obvious" signifier of "race."[18] And visual codes of heterosexuality and gender also permeate the depictions of bodily posture (the men often hold protectively as the women cuddle under and wrap around them), hair (shortly cropped vs. long and "soft"), and states of dress and undress (floral prints, bridal gowns, plunging necklines; suits, athletic and military garb). In combination these images make especially clear that if the possibility of sexual "mingling" across racial lines always implies the potential dissolution of those "lines" and the categories and social structures they enforce, then such destabilizations of race are partly grounded by the rigid conventions of gender identity and heterosexual romance also on display. Conversely, on the occasions when those conventions seem less absolute (e.g., when couples are dressed or undressed similarly), lighting and casting often produce differences of skin tone and hair as *more* visible. This kind of interplay, wherein temporary transgression of one register of difference is negotiated or stabilized through the reassertion of another, is a regular feature of interracial screen fantasies, providing unique opportunities to interrogate such simultaneous, but shifting, coproductions.

Two contemporary films explicitly comment on the familiarity and spectacularity of popular fantasies of interracial desire, one largely suggesting and the other all but insisting on their cinematic histories. In Spike Lee's *Jungle Fever* the camera suddenly aligns itself with an unidentified gaze from an apartment window that (mis)sees a playful lovers' quarrel on the street below as a black man's assault of a white woman; this look of white surveillance quickly results in the black man's harassment and near beating by police. The combination here of the camera's pronounced alignment with an invisible witness (the only such shot in the film), the instantaneous judgment that presumably leads to the phone call to the police, and the police's arrival with blinding lights (and guns) immediately pointed at the accused emphatically places the scene in a history not only of lynching and police brutality but also of vision and visibility. Indeed, the view from the window Lee momentarily forces us to occupy is in part the product of a history of white vision that cannot be read apart from the history of American cinema.[19] And insofar as this is the moment that makes Flipper Purify (Wesley Snipes) turn away from his white lover (Annabella Sciorra), the overwhelming force of that white gaze and the blinding violence it portends are pivotal to the film's final rendering of what the relationship between the black man and the white woman signifies. For this is the encounter that makes Flipper flip back, so to speak, to his black family and neighborhood to purify himself and the young (light-skinned) black prostitute he protectively embraces in the film's final shot.[20]

In Warren Beatty's *Bulworth* the spectacular status of a very different interracial couple is also unmistakable, and its familiarity is called out. When a powerful white male senator (Beatty) finally goes public with his desire for a black woman (Halle Berry), a circus of reporters' flashing cameras literally renders their kiss a mass tele-photo event. While the film's politics are debatable, it speaks one cinematic truth for this book in the implied assertion of a knowing bystander, played by Amiri Baraka. Admonishing the gathered spectators who stand agape at the spectacular interracial kiss, he asks, "Why are you looking like you haven't seen this before?!" Reading "this" not simply as the sexual encounter of a white man and a black woman—that most disavowed but institutionally sanctioned miscegenetic encounter in U.S. history—but also as the production of miscegenation fantasies for our viewing pleasure, this book confirms that viewers of American cinema certainly *have* seen it before, or at least have been sorely tempted, whether or not we remember it. And when cinematic energy has not been expended on showing "this" to us, it has been spent in equally meaningful ways on withholding it from view.

TUNNELING BACK: THE MISCEGENETIC BIRTH OF A NATIONAL CINEMA

Perhaps the most striking evidence of Hollywood's preoccupation with the subject is the fact that the most long-beloved origin story of classical Hollywood cinema itself depends upon a relentless fantasy of miscegenation. For it is the ostensible fear of black men raping white women that not only sets the narrative of *The Birth of a Nation* in motion but increasingly fuels much of the cinematic form that caused an earlier generation of film historians to celebrate the film as the "birth" of Hollywood cinema, and to crown its director, D. W. Griffith, as that cinema's honorary father.[21] Identifying the desire it strives to eradicate, but upon which it ironically depends, in one of its intertitles the film names miscegenation, like a kind of shadow title, the "blight [of] a nation."

But the mixed origins of American cinema can be traced back further to a host of early short films, beginning at least with Edwin S. Porter's *What Happened in the Tunnel* (1903). And ongoing Hollywood preoccupation with the subject is evidenced not only by a wide range of films produced in each subsequent decade but also by the industry's explicit prohibition against it for nearly thirty years. With a clause inherited from the guidelines known as the Don'ts and Be Carefuls (1927), the Production Code forbade the depiction of "miscegenation (sex relationships between the white and black races)" from 1930 to 1956. Interrogating such striking appearances and disappearances, this book attempts to understand miscegenation as variously defined and denied by popular American cinema itself, focusing on fantasies of black and white sexual relations when appropriate but also considering related fantasies of desire between whites and Native Americans, Asians, Mexicans, and a range of typically unspecified islanders. In analyzing such a range, I aim to discern how such fantasies are depicted and modified throughout the larger historical period, and to what ends.

I do not attempt a comprehensive treatment of this history. Rather, I read pivotal clusters of popular films, censorship documents, and related cultural material at a series of punctual moments. In the process, my readings are guided by two primary concerns. The first I have come to think of as the musical chairing of popular Hollywood (and pre-Hollywood) fantasies of miscegenation: the arrangements and rearrangements of players and interracial scenarios that invite us to consider how perpetually shifting and recurrent paradigms are revised and resurrected over time. The second focuses on matters of cinematic form, interrogating how conceptions of gender and race have been mutually produced and negotiated through filmic articulations of vision, visibility, voice, and cinematic space. The ways in which these two conceptual paths repeatedly converge in turn lead me to propose that particular interracial scenarios in particular historical periods reflect not only historically specific ideological concerns but also specific filmic mechanisms for (mutually) constituting race and gender.

A look at *What Happened in the Tunnel* is instructive here. In this short comedy a white woman and her black maid respond to a white man's persistent flirtations with the white woman (fig. I.1) by trading places with one another as their train passes through a tunnel. When the train emerges into the light, the man who has moved in the dark to kiss the white woman finds himself kissing the black woman instead (fig. I.2). The film ends with the women's laughter as the flustered kisser pretends to read his newspaper (fig. I.3). The first interracial screen kiss is thus staged as a kind of spectacular secret exposed, an "attraction" advertised by the title that dare not name it but sets us up to want to see and know it.[22] That we do only fleetingly, that we are denied the critical moment within the tunnel itself and experience more its aftershock than its occurrence (the man pulls away almost as quickly as they come back into the light), further toys with our pleasure in interracial screen fantasies, as Jane Gaines and Sharon Willis have both suggested in different contexts, as one of seeing/not seeing, knowing/not knowing their conditions and implications.[23] And for good reason: if we extend our contemplation of the scenario much is exposed, even by this shortest of films.

Most significant, perhaps, is *Tunnel*'s open display, albeit fleeting and significantly qualified, of the very interracial sexual encounter that will be most avidly disavowed for many decades to come, namely, that between

FIG. I.I. *What Happened in the Tunnel* (1903). Library of Congress, Motion Picture, Broadcasting, and Recorded Sound Division.

FIG. I.2

FIG. I.3

a white man and a black woman. For, as we will see, the future suppression of this interracial pair, and thus of the legally sactioned history of sexual exploitation under slavery it might threaten to evoke, combined with its replacement by the far more popular and enduring Jim Crow era fantasy of the black rapist, will profoundly shape and obscure the meaning of "miscegenation" in dominant American cinema, and American culture, for the better part of a century.[24] While later chapters will consider how such a profound restructuring of popular memory and fantasy occurred at the movies, here it pays to consider how even this momentary flash of racial-sexual history is filmically negotiated in 1903 before being more forcibly denied.

Lasting no more than a minute all told, several seconds of which feature a black screen, even this very short and relatively simple film foregrounds the routine complexity of interplays between multiple orders of difference in film fantasies of miscegenation, as well as cinema's capacity to position and reposition the spectator in relation thereto. Most obviously, the blackout experienced by the onscreen passengers is also experienced by the film's spectators, a reminder that we, too, are subjected to the machinations of an apparatus that locates us in space, time, circuits of desire and identification, and the looks that enforce and subvert such relations.[25] And in this case that positioning has been much debated. Several feminist critics have seized upon *Tunnel* as evidence of resistance to patriarchy (the women laugh at the man) and/or of its restoration (the women are defined as spectacle, despite and beyond their laughter), often noting the intersection of these with the film's racist humor.[26] Jacqueline Stewart reads it also as an example of early cinema's registration of black mobility into formerly "white" spaces in the period and white anxiety about that movement.[27] And Jane Gaines has recently prodded us to pay more attention to the importance of sexuality in this film: "There is room here to consider the acceptance or rejection of the heterosexual kiss as a position equal in importance to race or gender. Wanting to be or not wanting to be kissed may override everything else" (90). My contribution to such readings is to insist not only that we need them all but also that if we read *Tunnel* as negotiating anxieties about the simultaneous instability of multiple orders of difference, we can develop our understanding of how it intricately binds those orders together, negotiating potential breakdowns of one through the strictures of the others.

As its critics have observed, the film's racial joke depends on visual codes that direct the spectator how to read the women as (proper and improper) spectacle.[28] It is because the black woman is inscribed as not properly a "woman," as anything but the object of this man's desire, that the racial divide is so rigid in the first place.[29] This is enforced even before the joke through the direction of the man's attentions and the representation of the women. The white woman, first centered within the shot as the recipient of the diegetic male look, wears a dark, high-fashion hat and dress with an elaborate collar that frame her face to be seen. The black woman, wearing a mostly white maid's uniform, is obese and very dark. Displayed in this fashion, her facial features almost disappear in the composition, and she is visually marked as "other" than the white man and woman, who are more visible and visually joined.

At the same time as the film's racism thus depends upon conventional terms of sexual difference and heterosexual (male) desire, these women—traveling alone, pulling such a trick, and enjoying their laugh at the man—clearly signify female movement and transgression of male control.[30] But, in a reversal of the gesture whereby the film manages racial chaos through conventional orders of gender and sexuality, we can also read the racial joke and its assumptions as the sanction and the limit of the women's transgression. They travel without men, but with an evident racial and class order of mistress and maid that makes them appear as a "proper" female couple. And their switch and laughter can also be read as in part complicit with the assumption that the black woman is not a proper object of desire for a white man.

Hence, in this earliest film fantasy of miscegenation, we find a structure that at once allows for the expression of anxiety about the unstable state of dominant racial and sexual affairs but also offers, in its dovetailing of said affairs, means of negotiating its multiple anxieties. If there is one thing that binds together all American film fantasies of miscegenation, this is it. Throughout this book I aim to interrogate the ways in which race and gender, most vividly, are thus repeatedly defined and redefined through one another in such texts—in a host of different ways, at different moments, in response to a host of particular and ongoing worries and pleasures.

HISTORY, FANTASY, AND FILM

Even this introductory glance at the project's main concerns should make it evident that the racial and sexual logics at work throughout the texts under examination, and already in *What Happened in the Tunnel*, are not unique to the cinema. Fantasies of miscegenation, and the desires and relations they articulate, have a much longer and wider history than cinema itself. While this study cannot attempt to address all of that history—including extensive rhetorics of miscegenation in the law, literature, science, and so forth—we must keep it in mind in order to discern the particular ways cinema inhabits and shapes that larger cultural landscape.

The complex relations that can obtain between American cinema's investments in miscegenation and those beyond it are suggested in part by the way *The Birth of a Nation*'s title echoes the first antimiscegenation statute in the United States. Passed in 1661 by the Maryland General Assembly, that statute deemed intermarriage between white women and black men "the disgrace of the nation."[31] Yet, although this originary law and Griffith's film both imagine sexual union between blacks and whites as tantamount to the ruination "of the nation" itself, the former targeted quite a different relation than those that made it to the screen. While *Birth* is fixated on a fantasy of newly freed black men chasing upper-class white women in the reconstructed South, the Maryland statute addressed intermarriage between black male slaves and white female servants.[32] Indeed, it capitalized on that relation by declaring that a white woman who married a black man "was to serve the master of her husband, and all her children were to become slaves." In other words, as one legal historian explains, "What the Maryland miscegenation statute did . . . was to insure the slaveholders the right to keep in bondage both parties of a miscegenous marriage as well as their children. This property aspect of the Maryland statute quickly spread to the other states. According to some historians it became a practice of plantation owners to encourage their slaves to marry low class white women in the hope of gaining more slaves."[33] This juxtaposition of a legal and a filmic treatment begins to demonstrate that even when the rhetoric is similar, the two spheres of discourse can function quite differently. Whereas miscegenation law so often works to protect and fortify white male property, dominant filmic treatments of miscegenation typically work to fortify and protect white male identity.[34] And while such projects certainly overlap (the law keeps boundaries of "whiteness" and "maleness" intact, and cinema legitimates systems of material privilege), American cinema's ongoing concern with miscegenation is more squarely devoted to negotiating the *psychic* colorations, if you will, of identity and desire.

At the same time, without forgetting the very real and often brutal social histories that have given rise to, and resulted from, dominant cultural fantasies of miscegenation, it is nonetheless also relevant that significant portions of that history have also taken place within the field of representation. The rhetoric of miscegenation that sought to legitimate lynching was targeted by Ida B. Wells already in the late nineteenth century as itself a misrepresentation. As Hazel Carby quotes and paraphrases her, Wells argued that "the association between lynching and rape was strictly a contemporary phenomenon. . . . there was no historical foundation for that association, since 'the crime of rape was unknown during four years of civil war, when the white women of the South were at the mercy of the race which is all at once charged with being a bestial one.'"[35]

The "bestial" image of black men appears "all at once" when other attempts to justify black disenfranchisement had failed. As Carby vividly writes, "The cry of rape was an extremely effective way to create panic and fear . . . the charge of rape became the excuse for murder" (308). While the reported (real) violence sparked by Hollywood fantasies of miscegenation has fortunately never approximated anything of the catastrophic magnitude of lynching, these texts have nonetheless long fed and solicited anxieties, desires, and beliefs of considerable consequence. This book thus interrogates popular cinema as a unique form of history in its own right, as a record of dominant fantasies consumed in the course of everyday life by whites and people of color alike.[36]

Focusing on the status of miscegenation *fantasies* in this project for a moment, a final consideration of those lurking outside the cinema can better attune us to reading the filmic versions in which we will soon enough be immersed. Useful here is Ruth Frankenberg's *White Women, Race Matters: The Social Construction of Whiteness*, a book which "begin[s] . . . an inventory of whiteness as a subjective terrain" by analyzing interviews conducted with thirty white women in the mid-1980s on their attitudes about race.[37] From a chapter on these women's ideas about interracial sexual relationships, two interviews are especially relevant here. The first is with a woman given the pseudonym Chris, in her early thirties at the time, speaking of her middle-class upbringing in an all-white community on Long Island:

> CHRIS: The Black boys—I was just scared to death of them, figured they wanted to be sexual with me.
> FRANKENBERG: Why did you feel that?
> CHRIS: I think, a stereotype I'd learned.
> FRANKENBERG: Where from?
> CHRIS: Books, TV, *To Kill a Mockingbird*, we studied it in school a lot. . . . [We learned] that there were parts of the country where things aren't so rosy—the South, that had slavery and the thing that happened there all the time was that Black men wanted to rape white women. (79)

In a strikingly conscious manner, Chris openly attributes the "stereotype" of the black rapist to cultural representations, seeming even in her list of sources to conflate those with her "education" proper. Yet as soon as she acknowledges the effect of this representational saturation, she disavows it by projecting the fantasy onto an alleged history of distant "parts of the country . . . the South." Chris's divided belief in the myth of the black rapist—her knowledge of its being a pervasive, influential construction and her disavowal of her own investment in that construction—is indicative, I think, of the wider status of such fantasies in dominant

U.S. culture. Even when we as subjects of that culture, especially "we" white subjects, can begin to recognize where they come from, we do not seriously admit the degree to which they have invaded us.

It is this invasion of American subjects by cultural fantasies of miscegenation, and the forms they can take on within and among us, that is this book's deepest concern. Because popular cinema is such a ripe site for analyzing collective belief, it offers an ideal set of texts for such a study. And Frankenberg's interviews with real people not only confirm the power of popular media to disseminate such fantasies but highlight the complex and contradictory ways we can internalize them.

Chris's singling out of To Kill a Mockingbird is particularly suggestive. For the only text she names as a source for her belief in the myth of the black rapist is one whose narrative seeks to expose and critique that myth. Although the visible majority of white townspeople in the novel and the film are quick to believe Mayella Ewell's charge that Tom Robinson raped her, the extended courtroom scenes prove Tom's innocence and go so far as to suggest that Mayella's white father is the true abuser. And yet, defying the logic and purpose of this narrative, Chris remembers the myth and forgets the critique. Certainly Mockingbird gives her the means to do so insofar as the jury convicts Tom despite his innocence, and he is shot to death when he tries to escape. Nevertheless, still striking is the degree to which the accompanying critique of that chain of events disappears from Chris's account of the representational education that taught her "that Black men wanted to rape white women." This suggests that what makes these fantasies is in part their ability to supplant and reconfigure rational logics of classical narrative with the often blatantly fictional and contradictory maneuvers of the psyche and representation.

Such forms of contradiction are further suggested by another of Frankenberg's interviewees, a white woman raised in Alabama in the 1930s:

GINNY: Black people would ride in the back of the bus, had different restrooms, and couldn't eat in the same cafeteria as a white person. When I went into town with my husband to buy my kids some clothes—it's funny, I guess you're raised like this—if you see Black people touch anything, you won't buy it. I don't know why.

FRANKENBERG: Because that's how you're raised?

GINNY: Yes. But since I've got older and especially since I've come to California, I always—never taught my kids that. I said I didn't want them to marry into it, you know what I mean. But as far as being friends, I've had Black people in my house. . . . To me, they're like me or anyone else, they're human. (96)

Recognizing the contradiction between Ginny's simultaneous insistence on sameness ("they're like me or anyone else") and difference ("I didn't want them to marry into it"), Frankenberg interprets it to mark a "shift [in a racial boundary that nonetheless] remains intact: from a position of full avoidance of shared space, Ginny will now allow Blacks into the house and into the friendship circle, but not into the family and not into the bodies of family members" (96). After examining such overtly sexual anxieties about interracial contact, Frankenberg concludes that the idea of interracial relationships threatens boundaries of race, culture, and, "more than that," the economic hierarchy that depends upon those boundaries (100).

While Ginny's racial-sexual phobias certainly do work to shore up economic hierarchies, in our context the complexity of her utterance begs further analysis. What seems missing is attention to the fact that the stakes of her narrative are not simply cultural and economic but also fantasmatic. The continuing fluctuations of uncertainty and contradiction ("I always—never") seem to mark it strikingly as an eruption of unconscious desire—an eruption that only makes sense if we listen to the contradiction, the mistakes, the certain uncertainty it repeatedly trips over. Because Ginny's text seems to operate more by the illogic of a transcribed dream than by the rules of rational thought, it seems appropriate to dissect and rearrange it to pursue the relations between her segregation memories and interracial phobias.[38] For there are distinct echoes between her analysis of shopping and her conception of white woman as sexual commodity: "I didn't want them to marry into it." "If you see Black people touch anything, you won't buy it." Ginny, mother of a white daughter, implicitly links these statements herself when she describes a white woman she knows who married "into the Black" and had a child in that marriage and now "she can't go with a white guy" (96). To marry "into it" is to touch what black people touch and to be touched by "it," to become spoiled goods in a white sexual marketplace.

Yet these echoing details suggest an even greater horror. To marry "into the Black" is to lose that inexplicable distinction ("I don't know why") that kept *them* at the back of the bus, in different rest rooms and cafeterias. This distinction and the hierarchy it works to maintain seem all the more tenuous when we read the clues in Ginny's speech elsewhere that mark her lower-class background (89, 96). To keep your child from marrying into it, as Frankenberg claims, is to keep the distinction alive and certain. Further, the social and economic reasons underlying racial difference are obscured precisely by being displaced onto an even deeper psychosexual layer of racial beliefs.[39] In Ginny's narrative the shift from shopping to marriage facilitates a restructuring of racial knowledge, such that the reason for segregation—the fact that racial difference and separation worked to secure social and economic hierarchies—becomes forgotten and is supplanted by the "self-evident" belief in the miscegenation taboo: she cannot explain why you don't buy what black people touch ("I don't know why"), but she assumes there is no need to explain why you don't want your children to marry into it ("you know what I mean"). As racial ideology is mapped onto the sexual, its "reality" is thus firmly implanted and secured at the level of psychic belief.[40] Only by recognizing this kind of displacement of the social apparatus of racism onto the fantasmatic, and the kinds of affective investments in often contradictory and irrational beliefs it facilitates, can we begin to understand how Ginny and the dominant white culture of which she is a part can come to speak and believe such an open contradiction as, in effect, "they're just like me or anyone else, they're human; they're nothing like me, they're not human."[41]

Without a doubt, Ginny is not alone in having "forgotten" whatever explanations she might have once known about race, segregation, and interracial contact. Indeed, the racial-sexual fantasies and beliefs imparted to her in the South in the 1930s seem quite close to the ones that Chris "studied in school [and out] a lot" on the East Coast in the 1960s. Moreover, I think we have only just begun to understand the degree to which such psycho-logics structure dominant American fantasies of race and sex. At the very least, these white women's words strikingly illustrate the constancy and strength of dominant miscegenation fantasies, and their dissemination throughout the United States throughout the twentieth century.[42] In addition, they would seem to call our attention to the ways in which the social, cultural, and economic hierarchies held in place through the fiction of racial difference are in fact installed in us, produced and reproduced, through sexual fantasy. While Frankenberg's project is a welcome attempt to begin uncovering such relations in the white imagination, it also implicitly reveals the need to pursue that project in the field of representation, a field uniquely devoted to the production of cultural fantasy. For only through such examination can we begin to see, and remember, the meanings behind fantasies of miscegenation that are in many ways still as "obvious" in our national unconscious as in Ginny's. Because of Hollywood's unique contribution to the production of such "obviousnesses"—its powerful mechanisms for inviting spectators to desire, identify, and believe—it is to that cinema that I now turn.

OUTLINE OF THE BOOK

This book is divided into three parts, interrogating dominant American screen fantasies of miscegenation before, during, and after the Production Code's express refusal of them. Chapter 1 considers a variety of short films from 1903 to 1912 that flirt with interracial desire, most of which were directed by D. W. Griffith at Biograph. Proposing that these films mark a transitional phase in the development of classical modes of constructing gender and race, as well as a significant backstory to *The Birth of a Nation*, I analyze the ways they regularly subject not only women but also men and the spectator to states of intense vulnerability. I then consider how such representations were transformed into the now "classic" spectacles of white female suffering, an investigation that continues in chapter 2. There I begin with the inflamed contemporary rhetoric that surrounded black boxing champion Jack Johnson, arguing that the popular fantasy of a black man beating a white woman was a direct effect of the repression of the fantasy of a black man beating a white man. I demonstrate how this process is cinematically elaborated in *Birth* to produce a transcendent form of vision for its white male protagonist that is systematically differentiated from forms of white suffering Griffith now confines for the most part to female bodies, and from a form of black male looking he insists is utterly carnal. It is the fusion of these forms, I propose, as well as the familiar ideologies they perpetuate, that gives rise to the film's new "nation," its privileged white subject, and a filmic spectator modeled after him.

Turning in the second part to the Production Code's prohibition, I argue that although Hollywood's was not the only such ban, its forms and effects were considerable and unique: it shaped not only who could be imagined doing what with whom but also how spectators would be cinematically trained to read "race."[43] Chapter 3 offers a cultural context for, as well as a history of, the Code's miscegenation clause and selectively surveys the files of the Production Code Administration (PCA) to decipher what the Hollywood censors did with it. Reading their often confused and contradictory interpretations of a seemingly specific ban on "sex relationships between the white and black races," I argue that the PCA was ultimately complicit with the reduction of questions of "race" in U.S. culture to issues of "black" and "white," and that it helped to construct those identities in increasingly visual terms. Chapter 4 expands this argument through case studies of two tremendously popular films from roughly the beginning and near end of the Code's strict ban, *Imitation of Life* (1934) and *Pinky* (1949). Reading these extraordinary PCA files and the films that eventually emerged, I argue that with the help of the miscegenation clause classical Hollywood cinema gradually shifts the location of racial meaning from invisible discourses of "blood" and ancestry to visual discourses of skin, color, and cinema itself. And these racial projects, it becomes clear, thoroughly depend upon classical cinematic mechanisms for producing sexual difference as well.

In the last part, chapter 5 considers the surge of miscegenation films in the 1950s, following the dismantling of the Production Code's ban. Interracial tropes examined in earlier periods return with a vengeance in attempts to fortify increasingly beleaguered white male subjects facing increased demands for racial justice and a host of gender pressures. And when old methods repeatedly fail, new and sometimes drastic measures are taken to restore white male privilege and vision. The extremes to which the films go in this period, I argue, reflect both the tremendous strains on, and the stubborn tenacity of, conventional representational systems. In chapter 6 such trends culminate in arguably America's favorite miscegenation film of the late twentieth century, *Guess Who's Coming to Dinner*. I probe the high stakes of this popularity by juxtaposing *Guess* with two other profoundly influential interracial texts of its day, the 1967 Supreme Court decision that put an end to laws prohibiting interracial marriage and Eldridge Cleaver's best-selling *Soul on Ice* (1968), a book that boldly diagnosed the effects of dominant miscegenation fantasies on the politics and experiences of everyday U.S. life. This triad throws into relief what the popular film could and could not do: it could embrace the transformation of the dominant racial order but only with forceful reassertions of the dominant sexual order; and it could renounce the miscegenation taboo only by updating and reasserting a series of classical Hollywood identities and forms that had long been sustained with it.

By the end of the book it is clear that American cinema has envisioned the very meaning, appearance, and limits of racial and gendered identities in perpetual relation. While the Biograph films openly display masculine failure and suffering, they can only do so against the backdrop of an extremely conservative racial order; and when that order is disturbed in the most popular silent miscegenation film, an emphatically white masculinity emphatically reasserts its authority and privilege. Conversely, Hollywood's codification of "race" through the Production Code utterly depends on the malleability of female bodies and identities. And as psychic and political battlefields shift in the late fifties and sixties, with new spaces opening up to black men—albeit in highly regulated ways—it is masculinity that is protected above all. Understanding this legacy, I hope, puts us in a better position to understand its continued, shifting forms and effects.

PART ONE

Exhuming the Silent Bodies

CHAPTER ONE

The "Agony" of Spectatorship at Biograph

A Backstory

The Birth of a Nation (D. W. Griffith, 1915) holds pride of place in cultural memory, and in film studies, as American cinema's primal fantasy of miscegenation. There is, however, a cinematic tradition behind that text that has yet to be fully considered, without which we cannot fully understand the racial, sexual, and cinematic significance of the epic film from 1915 and its formidable legacy. That tradition includes a host of short genre films from 1904 through 1911 that form a clear ancestry to *Birth*, but one that is not at all what its progeny would lead us to expect. For, especially in films directed by Griffith at Biograph, it includes flirtations with interracial desire in the pursuit of pleasures tied up with the subjection not only of white women, as is regularly the case in *Birth*'s fantasies of the black rapist, but also of men (white and not white) and the spectator.[1] Consequently, I approach the Biograph films with a dual purpose: to excavate an as of yet untold prehistory to American cinema's more "classic" renditions of race and gender as canonized in *Birth*; and to analyze this prehistory to develop a pretheory, if you will, that addresses the mutual constitution of difference and spectatorship in and prior to the "birth" of classical Hollywood cinema. In doing so, I propose that Griffith's Biograph films mark a significant transitional phase not only in the formation of dominant codes of film narration, as Tom Gunning has argued, but also in the cinematic formation of gender, race, and the spectator.[2]

Insofar as this chapter offers a new backstory to a series of film historical and film theoretical narratives, its impact is best understood in relation to the end point it seeks to reilluminate. For my purposes, that end point is most vividly distilled in the images of white women as tortured spectacles that appear throughout the most classic miscegenation films of the silent era—namely, *The Birth of a Nation*, *The Cheat* (Cecil B. DeMille, 1915), and *Broken Blossoms* (Griffith, 1919). For if a singularly charged image could be said to bind these films together, it would be the image of a white female body under assault at the hands of, or as a result of a relationship with, a man of color. Such images appear throughout these films, and each climaxes with a scene in which white female bodies that come into close contact with men of color are chased (*Birth, The Cheat*, and *Broken Blossoms*), bound and gagged (*Birth*), beaten and branded (*The Cheat*), and chased or beaten literally to death (*Birth, Broken Blossoms*; figs. 1.1–1.3).

As excessive as these images are, they are not altogether surprising in the context of turn-of-the century rhetoric in which "white men used their ownership of the body of the white female as a terrain on which to lynch the black male."[3] Nor are they discontinuous from those Griffith Biograph films that repeatedly stage and restage scenarios of white women under attack. Indeed, a textbook lesson in the development of continuity editing is readily outlined by charting Griffith's refinements of the scenario of white women and girls trapped and pursued—from his directorial debut in *The Adventures of Dollie* (1908) through films like *The Girls and Daddy* (1909), *The Lonely Villa* (1909), and *The Birth of a Nation*. A contemporary reviewer of *Birth* locates that film, and the pleasure it offers the viewer, precisely in this tradition: "Mr. Griffith has again shown himself a *master* in creating and prolonging suspense *to the agonizing point*. His favorite method of chasing pursued and pursuer through one room after another is still effective and always has the desired effect on the audience."[4]

This account of Griffith's "favorite method" of taking the spectator to "the agonizing point" underscores the need to place *Birth*'s fantasy of black men pursuing white women in the context of the ongoing development of the chase as it preoccupied Griffith's work. It can also invite us to recognize that despite the voluminous scholarship on Griffith and *Birth*, that context is as of yet incomplete. As the gender- and race-neutral nouns in the description of "pursued and pursuer" allow, that scenario frequently appears in Griffith's earlier films with significantly different castings than in the classic examples. In fact, subtending *Birth*'s images of white women chased, bound, and gagged at the hands of black men is an extensive repertoire of fantasies often similar in content and form (abductions, invasions, races to the rescue, and so forth) but radically different, and varied, in their casting of the roles involved. At Biograph, we also find images of white *men* chased, bound, and beaten—often at the hands of men of color, and even more often with *women* of various races coming to their rescue. Thus, the racial and sexual identities assigned to the positions of pursuer, pursued, and rescuer are considerably shuffled. And that shuffling, I propose, has significant consequences not only for the cultural fantasies of race and gender channeled through Griffith and Biograph but also for the history of difference as it is encoded in popular American cinema.

Fundamental to this and the following chapter in particular are a range of perceived challenges to dominant forms of power and privilege at the

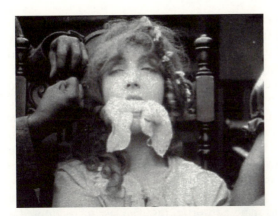

FIG. 1.1. Elsie Stoneman (Lillian Gish), bound and gagged at the hands of a black man in *The Birth of a Nation* (1915).

FIG. 1.2. Edith Hardy (Fanny Ward) branded with a hot iron by Haka Arakau (Sessue Hayakawa). *The Cheat* (1915).

FIG. 1.3. Lucy Burrows (Lillian Gish) being beaten by her father (Donald Crisp) after his discovery of her living with a Chinese merchant. *Broken Blossoms* (1919).

turn of the century, and the resulting turbulence in dominant conceptions of identity and difference. If we simply recall in combination some of the familiar markers of conflict in the period—increased racial violence and Jim Crow segregation in the South, increased migration of African Americans to urban spaces in the North, continued waves of immigration and accompanying nativism and xenophobia, exclusionary laws targeting Asians, the women's suffrage movement and cultural fears of the New Woman, the intensity and violence of labor struggles—we can begin to imagine the complexity of the context within which, as Gail Bederman has argued, "between 1880 and 1910 . . . [white] middle-class men were especially interested in manhood."[5] More precisely, as she summarizes, "Facing a variety of challenges to traditional ways of understanding male bodies, male identities, and male authority, middle-class men adopted a variety of strategies in order to remake manhood. Uncomfortable with the ways their history and culture were positioning them as men, they experimented with a host of cultural materials in order to synthesize a manhood more powerful, more to their liking" (16). This chapter considers early cinema, Biograph films especially, as a particularly rich site for such experimentation.

Like Bederman's study, mine will demonstrate how such gender projects perpetually drew upon and shaped various racial ones, in more and often less predictable ways. For with overt stagings of *racial* havoc through scenarios of miscegenation and interracial captivity come assorted displays of *gender* anxiety as well. At the same time, while Bederman finds "no evidence that most turn-of-the-century men ever lost confidence in the belief that people with male bodies naturally possessed both a man's identity and a man's right to wield power," the films under consideration in this and the next chapter suggest that such losses were, at the very least, vividly fantasized by popular filmmakers and their audiences (11). For prior to classical Hollywood's typical construction of white masculinity as a position of mastery often aligned with the camera itself, we find a proliferation of films that flaunt, and invite us to enjoy, white male insufficiency and suffering.[6] This in turn suggests that the familiar cinematic spectacle of tortured white female bodies so exemplified in the classic miscegenation silents is by no means a given in American cinema but is only achieved through a rearrangement of the far more vexed relations among gender, race, and cinematic pleasure that obtain in early cinema.

My analysis will consider how the Biograph films and their publicity materials racially and sexually code not only the roles of pursuer and pursued but also the experiences of the spectator. Such inquiry is of particular significance in this period of film history, since, as Tom Gunning has demonstrated, it marks a major transition in cinema's mode of address, one in which classical Hollywood discourse as we have come to know it is just emerging in embryonic forms. Whereas Gunning's study of Biograph films from 1908 to 1909 focuses on the development of cinematic narrative codes (e.g., the use of editing, compositional elements, acting, lighting, and camera movement to direct the viewer's understanding of narrative), I will argue that this period and the years immediately following it also mark an extremely important transition in the development of American cinema's representation of difference. In fact, several of the films Gunning selects to analyze key developments in narrative discourse—films like *The Adventures of Dollie, The Greaser's Gauntlet* (1908), *The Fatal Hour* (1908), *An Awful Moment* (1908), and *The Redman's View* (1909)—feature scenarios of interracial desire and captivity that significantly shape narrative content and propel precisely some of the developing filmic forms he identifies. Thus, following Gunning's isolation of "Griffith's Biograph films [as] rich contradictory objects" that reveal both "a founding moment of the later classical system, as well as an approach in some respects at odds to later practice," this chapter asks that we think through the "contradictory" nature of this phase of American cinema in terms of spectatorial positioning and the representation of racial and sexual difference.

The argument proceeds in three stages. First I consider the racial "switch" comedies (1903–8) that preceded Griffith's arrival at Biograph to establish the early interracial film tradition he entered into and its significant differences from the classical one with which he would become synonymous. Turning next to his short melodramas in which white women are trapped and pursued (1908–12), and then to his popular "Indian" films (1908–11), I argue that counter to the dominant modes of spectatorship and difference of later classical cinema, these Biograph genres invite spectators to identify variously with suffering white women and with white and nonwhite men in "feminized" conditions to produce the spectatorial "agony" often associated with Griffith's cinema. Finally, I read Griffith's popular Civil War shorts (1911–13) as a representational pivot that visibly displays how the erotics and politics detected at Biograph were fought against, and eventually overcome, by openly displacing white *male* agony onto white women. In part, then, this chapter could be seen as investigating a backstory to feminist diagnoses of classical cinema's displacement of male lack onto women, approaching early cinema with an eye to when and how those dominant maneuvers came into the filmic tradition.[7] At the same time, it insists upon the deep, and often unexpected, relations between such cinematic formulations of gender and those of race.

BLIND OLD WHITE MEN

Before evaluating the transitional period of Griffith's years at Biograph, it is instructive to consider the treatment of interracial desire that preceded it. In the tradition of the Edison-produced, Porter-directed *What Happened in the Tunnel* (1903), discussed in the introduction, Biograph produced a series of racial comedies that openly flirted with miscegenation.[8] While details vary from film to film, all are variations on the gag one titled *The Mis-Directed Kiss* (1904). In that film an old white man who is attempting to kiss the hand of a white woman accidentally kisses the hand of her black maid instead before looking at her through a magnifying glass to realize his mistake. Impaired white male vision causes similar scenarios in *A Kiss in the Dark* (1904) and *Under the Old Apple Tree* (1907), films that also manufacture white male blindness of one kind or another to set up the "unwanted" kiss or intimate touch of a black maid or mammy figure.[9] *Nellie, the Beautiful Housemaid* (Vitagraph, 1908) shifts the zone of confusion from vision proper to visual language, as three elderly white men who eagerly respond to an ad for a "brunette" maid named "Nellie White" discover upon her arrival that Miss White is black.[10]

A related set of films change the switch from women to babies, making the sexual nature of the racial joke less graphic, perhaps, but more explicit: we do not see interracial desire or sexual contact as such, but their potential outcome. This becomes evident in *How Charlie Lost the Heiress* (1903) when, at the moment Charlie has temporarily relieved a black woman from tending to twin black babies in a carriage, his fiancée happens by, sees the children, and flees in horror. In keeping with the tradition of the variously afflicted white men described earlier, Charlie faints. *Mixed Babies* (1908), a story written by Griffith upon his arrival at Biograph, subtly suggests the racial mixing its title could be read to imply through a story of separated and reunited black and white mothers and babies in a department store mix-up.[11] And in *The Valet's Wife* (1908), shot in the early months of Griffith's directorial career, after a white couple sends a nurse to an orphanage to procure them a baby, the camera reveals in a close-up that the baby delivered is black. Thus, entering a tradition that predates him, Griffith engages the theme from the earliest period of his career, playing with explicitly sexual and visual breakdowns of racial boundaries.

Although these films admit a circuit of interracial desire soon to be denied in mainstream American cinema, as suggested in the introductory discussion of *What Happened in the Tunnel* that admission is already partially mitigated by making black women the undesirable butt of the "joke."[12] Less predictable, however, is the repeated insistence on white male insufficiency, particularly failures of vision that lead to the breakdown of racial codes. The baby films take the kiss films a step further in this regard, imagining the kind of social and economic upheaval that could result from interracial desire. Social chaos is palpable in *Mixed Babies* as frantic mothers chase after the presumed culprit. And, as the title of *How Charlie Lost the Heiress* insists, not just any girl is lost but one with a fortune. That all of these films stage their interracial encounters with servants further underscores the social and economic hierarchies at risk. These films thus not only put white male authority and vision into question but also hint at the high social stakes involved in such (sexual) breaches of the racial order.[13]

Although distinctly unlike later dominant Hollywood renditions of white masculinity, the visual humor of these early switch films is of a piece with the pervasive cinematic mode of their time, as Gunning diagnoses it. In contradistinction to the classical cinema to follow, Gunning deems this one a "cinema of attractions," driven more by the display of spectacle than the elaboration of narrative (41). This exhibitionism is characterized by "cocky salutes and saucy winks shared with the camera by performers," a mode in which the camera is "a communal public audience with which the actor can share a joke" (263, 264). In this vein the switch films flaunt the spectacle of interracial sexual encounters to shock and amuse but also to invite the viewer to "share [the] joke," if not with the actor, certainly with the camera.

To articulate the racially and sexually coded disjuncture of vision at work in these films, also useful is Kaja Silverman's distinction between the look and the gaze.[14] While not a simple correlative to it, this distinction in the domain of the visual can be roughly compared to the more general feminist theoretical distinction between the penis and the phallus—that is, between the male organ and the cultural ideal of masculinity. With the visual inscriptions of race as well as gender at issue here, Silverman's distinction of the human look from cultural and theoretical abstractions of the gaze allows us to specify what the switch films continually insist upon: namely, the insufficiency of the white male look to the task of representing and enforcing a more abstract cultural gaze that sustains the dominant racial order. While that gaze defines race as a visual certainty, the switch films imagine potential breakdowns in the racial order as deriving from the failure of the white male look to *see* racial difference. And yet, these films simultaneously insist upon the self-evidence of that visibility to the films' own unimpaired spectators.[15] We can only laugh at the blind man's failures because "we know," because the camera and the cultural gaze it inscribes teach us, the visual-racial "truth" he fails to see. The switch films thus strip white male characters of symbolic authority in the visual field and hoard the pleasure of that fantasy (of authority/knowledge) for the camera and the spectator.

What makes these maneuvers of particular interest here is that they will be so dramatically reconfigured within the decade. Anxieties about the movement and demands of women and African Americans will not disappear within that interval (or even within the century), but by 1915 a remarkably different set of filmic strategies and tropes are in place, ones that still express those anxieties, but differently, containing and denying them all the more stridently. While such a change raises a host of questions, I will begin to address them by considering what this "transition" from the switch films to *Birth* consisted of—racially, sexually, and cinematically. Given the radical disjuncture in the switch films between the white man's diegetic look and the camera's gaze, such an undertaking in part begs us to ask when and how the more familiar conventions of white male look as gaze came to be systematically installed in the discursive system of American cinema.[16] While a teleological account might assume such a system emerged directly from embryonic predecessors, the filmic record reveals more circuitous representational paths—even in the Griffith films that most directly follow from the switch films to *Birth*.

To chart that course the following sections consider, first, Griffith's mapping of race and gender onto the chase and the ensuing whitening and feminization of the spectator; second, the generic preoccupation with (white) male suffering in the Indian films; and, third, the Civil War genre's radical displays of white male failure and its efforts to overcome that failure through a substitution of white women for white men. While I attempt to trace the mapping of difference on filmed bodies and implied spectators, it bears keeping in mind that standard forms of filmic discourse we typically analyze to determine how films address spectators in relation to difference (e.g., point-of-view shots, shot-reverse-shot constructions) are precisely the kinds of forms only just emerging in this period. This poses analytical challenges, but it also points again to the need to assess these films precisely in order to come to terms with the simultaneous development of cinematic codes and codes of difference. I will often consider publicity materials and reviews, as well as films, to expand the means with which to analyze how Biograph was mark(et)ing difference and soliciting spectators.

WATCHING GRIFFITH JUST LIKE A (WHITE) WOMAN

What the larger shift from the cinema of attractions to narrative cinema means for miscegenation films, in part, is a generic shift from comedy to melodrama. This in itself suggests an intensification of spectatorial pleasures in suffering.[17] Gunning addresses this indirectly in his chapter "From Obscene Films to High-Class Drama." There he sites the treatment of miscegenation in *The Heathen Chinee and the Sunday School Teachers* (1904), in which "female missionaries and Chinese men go to an opium den . . . lie on beds together and smoke opium until the place is raided by the police," all of which the film depicts as "subjects for an ungenteel laugh rather than moral condemnation" (157). Such lighthearted treatment is radically contrasted to the utterly tragic vision of *The Heart of an Outlaw* (1909), in which a white woman's affair with a Mexican prompts her husband to kill his wife and her lover and to accidentally injure, and later rape, his daughter.[18] Although miscegenation proves more catastrophic in this film than in most others, this is nonetheless the tonal direction the material will take in Griffith's cinema.[19]

Foreshadowing the classic miscegenation films to come, Griffith's Biograph films often cinematically intensify the spectator's experience of such melodramatic agonies through their use of white women as a synecdoche for the white family, white property, and white culture when these are represented as threatened by outside forces.[20] This rhetoric is echoed in Biograph's publicity for *The Tavern-Keeper's Daughter* (1908). Insisting upon the intruder's radical otherness and the "white whiteness" of his female victim, it describes how "one of those proletarian half breed Mexicans" pursues a white girl, "the fairest flower that e'er blossomed in the land of the golden sun," with "blue eyes, golden hair and sunny complexion [that] inflame him so as to make bold to kiss her."[21] After she rejects his advance, "The cruel, black nature of the brute now asserts itself, and barring the door, he seizes the helpless girl, who screams and struggles until her father, bursting in, engages the half-breed in a fierce conflict."[22] Hence, insofar as we are invited to identify with the "helpless girl" and her father in opposition to the "cruel, black" "proletarian half breed" Mexican through these marked descriptions, the publicity sheet already solicits the spectator's investments by coding the pursuer/pursued scenario in terms of race, gender, and class, as well as sexuality.[23]

Such deployments of difference have an extensive cinematic history throughout Griffith's work, beginning with *The Adventures of Dollie* (1908). Biograph publicized this film as "One of the most remarkable cases of child-stealing . . . the attempt to kidnap for revenge a pretty little girl by a Gypsy . . . [who] has come into the neighborhood [in] a band of those peripatetic Nomads of the Zingani type, whose ostensible occupation is selling baskets and reed ware, but their real motive is pillage."[24] Once again, Biograph pitches a racially charged abduction. Moreover, although the editing of *Dollie* is "primitive" in comparison to Griffith's later chases, it marks the first installment of what would be developed into his signature combination of narrative and spectacle: the potential threat to a white bourgeois family rendered through the scenario of an invasion halted at the last minute by a race to the rescue sequence assembled through parallel editing that alternates scenes of multiple locations, including the scene of the crime and the scene of the rescuer racing (on foot, on horseback, in a car, etc.) to save the victim. Assessing this "archetyp[al]" constellation of plot and editing in Griffith's Biograph shorts, Gunning notes its debt to various cinematic treatments of the chase, as well as the chase's considerable contribution to cinema's transition from spectacle to narrative. His description of *Dollie*'s use of the chase brings its propensity for narrative into focus: "The film creates a coherent geography as it follows Dollie in a circuit away from her home and back. *Dollie*'s editing creates a synthetic space by maintaining a line of action progressing continuously through a series of shots; Dollie's odyssey consists of thirteen shots spread over eleven different locations. The narrative logic of the film knits these separate views into a coherent continuous space" (66). While there are certainly other possible plots that could prompt this cinematic structure, it is evident that just as the chase is suited to the elaboration of narrative filmic forms—in particular here continuity editing, which joins a series of spaces to create the narrative unfolding of events—so stories of interracial abduction and captivity are suited to the chase and to Griffith's particular narrative and ideological preoccupations. Already in Biograph's publicity sheet the mapping of space and movement upon which the chase scenario depends is triggered by those "peripatetic Nomads of the Zingani type." And in the film itself the "coherent geography" that maps "Dollie in a circuit away from her home and back" is specifically facilitated by marking difference onto the distinct spaces and elements that unfold with each shot: the bourgeois home; the bourgeois garden; the gypsy camp; the gypsy traveler who invades the bourgeois space and abducts Dollie; the gypsy wagon that takes her away; and the barrel within it that first hides Dollie from her parents and then, falling into a stream, allows her to float back to the bourgeois garden and family. The viewer is explicitly guided to read these shots and locations as continuous not only by the spatial cues of editing (directional match cuts and the like) but also through the markers of difference that narratively relate these distinct elements to one another. In other words, Griffith's "inauguration" of continuity editing is explicitly propped upon signifiers of difference.[25]

While Griffith will also sometimes mark the intruder's difference as primarily one of class (usually also mixed with gender) in films where bourgeois white women and girls are trapped in houses fearing the impending entry of white working-class thieves (e.g., *The Lonely Villa*, *A Woman Scorned* [1911], and *Unseen Enemy* [1912]), there is never, at least in my experience, such a scenario that does not mark difference in some visible way. My point here, then, is not to pretend that all of Griffith's race-to-the-rescue scenarios are miscegenation scenarios but to interrogate some of the large number of them that are in order to better understand how forms of identity and difference fundamentally mark Griffith's protoclassical cinematic forms, and how those forms in turn give shape to cultural conceptions of difference.[26]

Further examples of the racialized chase are found in *The Fatal Hour* and *An Awful Moment,* both of which up the ante of suspense by binding their white female victims and positioning them as singular targets of guns rigged to shoot them. *An Awful Moment* continues in the tradition of *Dollie,* as the white woman is gagged and bound by the female half of a criminal "Gypsy couple."[27] In *The Fatal Hour* the villains are a pair of white slave traders, led by "Pong Lee, a Mephistophelian saffron-skinned varlet."[28] According to the publicity sheet, the men "seize the girl detective" who has caught their trail, "tak[e] her to the house, tie her to a post and arrange a large pistol on the face of a clock in such a way that when the hands point to twelve the gun is fired and the girl will receive the charge." Gunning discusses this film as marking an important developmental advance in parallel editing insofar as the film constructs the illusion of simultaneous time by alternating shots of different spatial locations. More important, as Gunning demonstrates in his shot-by-shot analysis of the police's ride to the rescue and the countdown of the clock hands within the image, "There is no possibility of rearranging any of these shots and getting a coherent narrative. . . . Each shot finds its place in an irreversible linear temporal logic" (99). As a result, he argues, the film "raises parallel editing to a melodramatic intensity through a new control over the portrayal of time" (95). While Gunning's analysis makes it clear that the cinematic apparatus is the ultimate agent of the victim's subjection, the concocted threat of white slavery nonetheless contributes to setting the scene: this particular "girl detective" is at risk of dying because she is onto the business of the "saffron-skinned varlet" and his partner; should she die, we know (from the folklore surrounding "white slavery") there will no doubt be an endless succession of white girls abducted and subjected by the racialized villains.

Although Gunning does not discuss this race to the rescue in terms of racial or sexual difference, his analysis of the spectatorial pleasure invited by *The Fatal Hour* is nonetheless extremely suggestive in this context. Indeed, it invites us to recognize a far less predictable or dominant form of cinematic pleasure to be had through Griffith's deployments of race, sex, and the chase. He considers how the race to the rescue "intensely involves the spectator through a pattern of delay" and argues that said pattern "flirts with its own dissolution by seeming to endlessly prolong the sequence, as if it were never going to reach a conclusion" (103). He continues: "Interrupting an action, delaying its resolution, yet creating a structure in which the outcome approaches inevitably, in which the flow

of time and narrative is unstoppable (the fatal hour draws near . . .)—
these are at the heart of Griffith's temporal and narrative logic" (104).
Thus elaborated are the cinematic components responsible for what
Gunning elsewhere calls, in language similar to Griffith's contemporary
critic, the "agonizing delay" of Griffith's race to the rescue (197). This
account suggests a clear parallel between the spectator's experience of
this cinematic delivery of shots and the girl detective's experience of
bondage and impending death: the editing of Griffith's race to the rescue,
here as elsewhere, similarly coerces the spectator to endure the unstoppable trajectory of narrative and editing over which we have no control.
Indeed, Gunning's description of the spectatorial experience of such a sequence equates it to the victim's position when he parenthetically invokes
what sounds like an intertitle description of the girl detective's fate to describe the spectator's. It is this spectatorial fate, positioned as the one
who must submit to the film's agonizing delivery of narrative and shots,
that invites us to identify with the experience of the victim facing the
threat of invasion at the hands of the "saffron," "Gypsy," or working-
class assailant.[29]

Clearly, then, the development of Griffith's "favorite method" of moving the spectator to "the agonizing point" entails a radical change in
spectatorship from the cinema of attractions as exemplified in the switch
films. Whereas there the spectator was invited to take pleasure in being in
the know, aligned with the gaze and authority of the camera, here spectatorial pleasure is organized around our having to submit to the machinations of the cinematic apparatus. As the resolution of our narrative desire is delayed and we are forced to endure the cutting back and forth
between locales, we are—like the onscreen victim facing a loaded rifle—
subjected to, rather than the subject of, the camera's shooting.

Moreover, insofar as the agony of spectatorship in Griffith's race to the
rescue is an agony of submission and vulnerability, it follows dominant
cultural logic when it equates that agony off screen with the agony embodied on screen by the white woman. In so doing, however, it simultaneously subverts such dominant logic by figuratively putting the viewer,
male or female, in her place. A contemporary review of *The Lonely
Villa*—a film in which Griffith again traps white women in the house at
the mercy of intruders breaking through door after door to reach them—
makes this equation quite explicit: "'Thank God, they're saved!' said a
woman behind us at the conclusion of [*The Lonely Villa*]. *Just like this
woman*, the entire audience were in a state of intense excitement as this
picture was being shown."[30] Inserting a gasping female viewer as the
bridge between the onscreen female captives and the film's "entire audience," the review clearly rhymes all such figures "in a state of intense excitement." Revising the formulation only slightly to mark the racial iden-

tity of such vulnerable "fair . . . flower[s]," as the same review calls the onscreen women, we could say that Griffith perpetually subjects his spectator "just like [a white] woman."

Examples of the white femininity of Griffith's agonizing subjects can literally be found all over the place, but one film is of particular interest here. In *The Girls and Daddy* (1909) we find the most obvious prototype of *The Birth of a Nation*, as a "low-down negro," whom the film codes as a mulatto, chases "two brave girls" through a series of rooms in their house.[31] The structure of the chase is by now predictable, but particularities of this text are quite instructive. After the sisters, home alone, have gone to bed, thieves come to rob them. First a white thief enters their room, contemplates robbing the money they have hidden under their pillow, but then has a change of heart and moves on. Having endured that near invasion, the spectator is treated to a second one. This time the girls are awakened by the sound of a breaking vase knocked over as a black(face) thief enters through a window downstairs. Although they slept through the white thief's visit to their room, this awakening to the black one fans anxiety both on and off screen as the girls panic, hug each other, fret, and flee. As the intruder enters the room on the left of the screen, the girls exit to the right, appearing in another shot behind a door they have passed through and barricaded. As they run upstairs toward the attic, the intruder breaks through their barricade and follows. In the attic the girls again block the door, and the intruder again breaks it down. Ultimately, while one sister attempts to hold the last door shut, the other flees to the roof and beckons the "good" white thief to come to her aid. He does, the girls' father returns, and the girls are reunited, briefly, with daddy. The father then steps to the extreme right edge of the screen, nearly out of the frame, and the girls kiss and hug repeatedly in the final shot.

This film is noteworthy not simply because it is about white girls trapped in the house and pursued by a black/mulatto intruder. Further, it emphasizes the extent to which the spectator's enjoyment of the chase is bound up with being positioned very much like the white female victims. For it is especially clear here that there is no other way for the viewer to identify than with the girls. The father is absent for most of the film, and unlike in later versions of this scenario, he is not shown to us through parallel editing. He simply shows up at the end to punctuate the girls' safety. Nor does the film solicit our identification with the thieves. At times the camera is clearly positioned on the girls' side of the barricaded doors, but it is never positioned with the intruder. Moreover, while the camera at one point oddly straddles the door frame, revealing both the artificiality of the set and the pursuer and pursued on either side of the door—a framing that might suggest the solicitation of the viewer's identification beyond the characters themselves and with the camera capturing the scenario—a close analysis of the circuits of desire established throughout the film again points to the alignment of the spectator with the girls.[32]

The film's invitation to identify with the girls is perhaps most visibly demonstrated through their mirroring throughout the film. From beginning to end the sisters are paired as a couple, and the libidinal charge between them is not only prominent but the primary one made available to us. The twinlike pair operates as a single unit as they greet their father in the living room, walk down the street arm in arm, greet others on the street, talk and giggle at the post office, return toward home arm in arm, again greet others on the street, help each other with coats and hats at home, tuck in their bed for the night, giggle and embrace, giggle and embrace, and giggle and embrace some more. In each of these sequences the girls are visually rhymed, and their identification with and desire for one another is evident, establishing in turn an obvious route for the spectator's desire and identification. In a kind of doubled circuit of narcissistic female identification, the viewer, as if mirroring the girls, who mirror one another, is insistently invited to identify and enjoy as one of them. *The Girls and Daddy* thus foregrounds the common tendency of Griffith's race to the rescue to position spectators so as to identify with white women on the verge of invasion. What is more, we should note here that, as we will see again in *The Birth of a Nation* when Flora giggles with delight as she and her sister hide from the black soldiers raiding their home, this representation is punctuated not only by fear and flight but also, as my description of the girls' giggles and hugs attempts to convey, considerable excitement and pleasure.

Although it transpires in a very different context, Carol Clover's account of a masochistically oriented form of film spectatorship is extremely useful here.[33] Analyzing scenarios of intruders pursuing (white) women in the slasher film, Clover argues that male viewers are invited to identify with the jeopardized women. Such cross-gender identification, she demonstrates, is reflected in part by the fact that the pursued functions at once as the victim and her own rescuer, a figure Clover dubs the "final girl." While Griffith's melodramas typically insert a male character in the rescuer position, the emphasis on the condition of the suffering woman and the rhyming of her "intense excitement" with the spectator's make her, I think, somewhat comparable to (a distant ancestor of?) the slasher film's final girl.

This is all the more vivid when the distinction between the victim and the hero is in fact considerably blurred, as in those Biograph films that connect the two via telephone during the attack. *The Lonely Villa* features a conversation edited between the space of the confined women and that of the absent head of the family such that he hears of their distress in real time but at a safe remove.[34] Similarly, in *An Unseen Enemy* two desperate sisters strangely trapped in a room with a gun pointing at them through a hole in the wall talk to their elder brother on the phone throughout the ordeal. Not only does he hear the sound of gunfire over the phone line, but it is *his* reaction shot to the noise that we see. Hence, paralleling the "unseen enemy" of the title, who taunts the girls with a gun poked through a hole in the wall, is the unseen (or at least disguised) *victim*, the white man who endures the trauma of the classic suffering (Gish) sisters over the phone, much as the spectator endures it through the technology of cinema.[35] Indeed, the marked invisibility of the enemy would seem to announce how little that position matters in a scenario that is rigged for the agonizing pleasures of its (on- and offscreen) victims.[36]

Thus far I have focused on early Griffith films that cast the chase with white women in the role of pursued—films that demonstrate already how even these scenarios, despite their predictable faces, can invite spectators to identify, less predictably, not with secure or impenetrable male figures but with giddy and hysterical female ones. The potential implications of such invitations become even more explicit in the Indian and Civil War genres where chase and captivity scenarios with quite different castings more explicitly display what these suffering white women might have to do with the men in the audience.

"As Kind-Hearted as a Woman and as Brave as a Lion"

Discussing the tremendous popularity of the "Indian film" from around 1908 to 1911, Eileen Bowser claims that it was so prolific as to constitute not simply a branch of the Western but a distinct genre.[37] She attributes its appeal to the combination of "beautiful landscapes and free movements of Westerns [*sic*] films plus elements of exoticism, nobility, and romance" (173). Often what made these films exotic was that the romance was interracial. As the phrase "squaw man" was sometimes used to indicate, such romances were commonly between white men and "native" women. A full-page *New York Times* human interest story from the period on real "squaw m[e]n" living with Sioux women in the West claimed that the phenomenon made several white men land rich (from the land entitled to Sioux and their children by the government) and allowed them to "enslave [women] in the same manner that the noble red man discourages the suffragette movement in his neck of the woods."[38] The backlash to contemporary feminism embedded in this journalistic account is sometimes visible in related fantasies from Biograph. However, as we will see, sexualized transgressions of racial boundaries in the Indian films also regularly facilitate the transgression of conventional gender identities.

Bowser suggests that the genre's erotic pleasures were organized around "the allure of nudity (of men only), which had the same respectability as the nakedness of indigenes in travel films from distant lands" (173). She cites a silent producer-director on women's reactions to a frequent actor in such films: "[Charles] Inslee made a striking appearance . . . and the ladies simply went gaga over him. Oh's and ah's came from them whenever he appeared . . . in one of his naked Indian hero roles, so naturally most of his pictures were on that order" (173). That such films provide "respectab[le]" means for viewers—female, as testified earlier, but possibly male as well—to enjoy naked male bodies is suggested further by the *Bulletin* description of *The Redman and the Child* (1908). Sandwiched between images of Inslee wearing nothing but a loincloth with his upper body flexed, it reads: "What a magnificent picture he strikes as he stands there, his tawny skin silhouetted against the sky, with muscles turgid and jaws set in grim determination."[39] But prior to this emphasis on the display of brawny, "tawny," "turgid" men comes the admiration that the "redman" is "as kind-hearted as a woman and as brave as a lion." And this double identity—brave yet kind, manly yet womanly—is repeatedly marked throughout the Biograph Indian films and their publicity material, considerably complicating the genre's fascination with the male body.

At one level this double identity parallels dual cultural discourses of Indians as noble and savage.[40] In light of later Hollywood's preoccupation with the latter construction, it is striking that that image is so often superseded in the early Indian films by images that presume, as one reviewer put it, "to do the Indian justice."[41] In a trade article titled "The Vogue of Western and Military Drama," this reviewer argues that "all of the more artistic Indian films exalt the Indian, depict the noble traits in his character and challenge for him and his views and manner of life the belated admiration of his white brother" (271). Drawing from the prevalence of such claims in the trade discourse that circulated around these films, Richard Abel has recently argued that while the films regularly offered the "openly racist, covertly masculinzed discourse" of earlier Western genres (e.g., fiction), "they also opened up anomalous social spaces where the regulations against certain kinds of border crossing (and cross identification) could be tactically, tactfully elided or eluded."[42] More specifically, Abel provocatively proposes that, for working-class immigrant viewers in particular, male and female alike, "the 'good' Indian (or Mexican) may well have been a . . . potent mirror image of cultural transformation, subjection, and assimilation (and managed social struggle)" (171). Here I want to focus, in the larger contexts set forth in this chapter, on the second of those three sets of images as they are articulated in Biograph films and related publicity materials. For while such scenarios are certainly not limited to miscegenation narratives, they regularly make complex relations between fantasies of race and gender more visible through assorted interracial pairs and triangles. Through their narratives of Indian sacrifice, torture, and bravery, especially noticeable are agonizing pleasures delivered to the spectator, variously, through implicit identifications with "red" men, with white men dressed up as such, and at times even with suffering white male bodies.[43]

One of the more detailed contemporary discussions of the genre suggests that the debate over the "accuracy" of Hollywood depictions of Indian character and culture that played out in the trades was in part concerned with distinctly racialized gender fantasies.[44] Critiquing an unnamed Indian film in 1909, a writer under the pseudonym "Wild West" complained, "To the trained eye, quite a few prominent defects stood out."[45] While the nature of West's "training" is at first unclear, his objections bring the underlying criteria into focus. First he complains about costume, specifically annoyed that the film's "little squaw" goes beltless, "for hardly ever do you see a squaw without a belt" (48). Although this comment may at first seem trivial, it becomes increasingly evident that the review's primary concerns about the inaccuracy of the Indian film all center around the "proper" presentation of gender roles—proper, that is, to "little squaws" and "brave chief[s]." Such investments are elaborated in the following account: "Indian maidens are known to be of a sedate and pensive character. But, of course, they are to be excused if they were the daughters of the brave chief, who displayed so much agony when being burned at the stake. That is another thing: no Indian . . . shows his agony when being tortured by an enemy. The bravest Indian is the one that stands the most punishment; but it may be like everything else: following in his white brothers' footsteps he has forgotten that" (48). As it specifies how "the bravest Indian" should be depicted, this passage speaks directly to what I would argue are the less "respectable" pleasures in male suffering offered up by the Indian films. The concern with the representational details of torture and especially, once again, "agony"— West's insistence not only that the films should get it right but that his "trained eye" knows precisely how much pain the Indian brave can endure—suggests that while these films may have invited viewers to "oh . . . and ah" at naked muscle men, such thrills were certainly not confined to normative female pleasure in phallic masculinity. Moreover, as the final sentence of the passage would have it, what this other kind of masculinity offers is seemingly lost to white men and diluted by whiteness generally, hence requiring vicarious enjoyment via the white man's native "brothers."

In the films themselves, the motif of Indian male suffering and sacrifice is often played out through narratives of interracial desire in which Indian men love white women and are rejected by them, and through ones in which white men take Indian women away from "braves" who remain loyal and stoic from a distance. Thus, for example, in *The Call of the Wild* (1908), "sad plight of the civilized redman," George Redfeather graduates from college with honors and is a star athlete but is rejected by the white girl with whom he falls in love.[46] Highlighting this as a story of insufficient masculinity, the *Bulletin* tells us that Redfeather is "crushed and disappointed, for he realizes the truth: 'Good enough as a hero, but not as a husband.'" The publicity further insists upon Redfeather's sacrifice at film's end, when he captures the girl "after a spirited chase and intend[s to] hold . . . her captive, but she appeals to him, calling to his mind the presence of the All Powerful Master above" (31). Thus, there is no race to the rescue in this chase per se, as Indian male self-sacrifice and submission to a higher power are called upon to "rescue" the white woman.

This kind of sacrifice is often characterized as "nobility," one of the elements in Bowser's triad of generic characteristics. The narrative that insists that "George" can never fully shed his "Redfeather" points to the ways in which this element too (like "exoticism" and "romance") is often bound up with questions of sexual, as well as racial, difference. At the same time, the rhetoric of nobility also clearly works to render "poetic" scenarios in which Indians get politically taken by whites and, all in the name of stoicism and noble sacrifice, submit without resistance. Such rhetoric fills the pages of Biograph's publicity for Indian films. Indeed, this colonial version of stoicism would seem to define *The Redman's View*, as characterized in that film's publicity. Attempting to distinguish it from the many others dealing with "the subject of the Redman's persecution," the *Bulletin* describes it as "a more beautiful depiction of trials of the early Indians" than the rest, particularly for the way "it shows how the poor redskin was made to trek from place to place. . . . [W]hite men appear and order the poor Indians to move. This they do with stoicism" (149). Such romanticized accounts of the history of whites displacing Native Americans make it evident that the transgressive gender fantasies we find in the genre are not uncontaminated by highly regressive racial ones. To the contrary, it seems, these films draw upon the latter and rework them in part to suit their alternative fantasies of masculinity.

The attribution of sacrifice and suffering to Indian *masculinity* in particular is especially vivid in *The Mended Lute* (1909). Here a love triangle pits against each other "good" and "evil" Indian men who desire the same woman. Although there is no interracial dimension to this film, it is relevant insofar as the two men (both unnamed) seem to embody, at least at the outset, the two poles of Indian temperament imagined throughout the genre: the evil one is savagely fierce (taking the woman against her will, threatening to brutally kill her and the other man), and the good one is tenderly brave (meeting his lover near a waterfall, enfolding her in his blanket). This rivalry climaxes in a race to the rescue (this time in canoes) in which the evil one pursues the lovers. Upon capturing them, he has them tied up together and pantomimes cutting up the chest of his rival. The film openly muses over these competing versions of masculinity as the two men, standing face-to-face and both with long dark braids and naked chests, visually mirror one another in the penultimate shot. The woman, with her back to them, is virtually incidental here, functioning primarily to facilitate this encounter between men. Suddenly, however, the evil one has a change of heart and cuts the ropes to set the lovers free. He then reenacts the pantomime, this time directing the knife toward his own chest. As the lovers exit the frame, their abductor, now turned soft, holds on to the ropes that bound them and wraps them loosely around his own wrists. The camera lingers for a moment on this image before concluding with a shot of the restored couple. Displaying both of these "naked Indian heroes" rope-bound, with knives poised to cut them, and staging the final and most symbolic wounds as self-inflicted, this film explicitly reconfigures Griffith's trademark captivity scenario with phallic masculinity as the sexual identity most radically, and overtly masochistically, in question.

Yet the preoccupation with male suffering is not confined to "tawny" male bodies; nor is it simply, as the story of George Redfeather might suggest, a preoccupation with stripping nonwhite men of phallic privilege in order to safeguard that privilege for white men. For films in which white men abduct, desire, seduce, and/or betray women of color feature those men at risk as well, and suffering at times more explicitly than the characteristically stoic Indian braves.

In *The Indian Runner's Romance* (1909), a white cowboy on horseback who has abducted an Indian's wife (in an attempt to rob their mine) is chased in a run to the rescue. At first it is the woman who is "brutally bound and thrown . . . across [the] horse," but her husband "with his knowledge of . . . trails . . . and a thrilling dash through the dangerous rapids . . . manages to overtake" the cowboy.[47] When he jumps onto his galloping horse, "a most exciting combat ensues—a bowie-knife conflict on the back of the horse, with the prostrate form of the squaw slung across its neck." But this victim is replaced by another as "on they gallop, the Indian fighting furiously, until at length the cowboy drops lifeless from the saddle." Thus, in a particularly racialized adaptation of Griffith's classic scenario, the white man is the villain and becomes the pursued, and the resolution is punctuated by his subdual at the hands of the Indian hero.

A white male body also vividly suffers in *A Romance of the Western Hills* (1910), a film that pairs a white college boy and a newly "civilized"

Indian girl. He lures her for a garden stroll, and then farther off screen for an unseen, but later revealed, sexual encounter. Later she sees him in the garden where he had courted her, now wooing a white woman. "Her simple faith betrayed," as the intertitle punctuates, she returns to the loyal brave she left behind in the mountains and prompts him to exact, as another intertitle describes, "retribution for the wrong." The brave confronts the white louse at the scene of his crimes, gestures threateningly with fingers extended like claws, and throttles him about the neck in one of the most graphic depictions of violence to a male body I have seen in a Biograph film. For not only does the Indian gesture madly in preparation for the assault, but during it the victim's body bends back severely in pain and submission. And whereas, for example, the beating of the gypsy in *The Adventures of Dollie* lasts briefly and in long shot, here a full shot proffers a clear view; our view is most closely aligned with that of the victim (we watch from behind him as he faces his attacker); and we watch his attack for several seconds—a duration that allows for the arrival of the betrayed woman, her plea to the Indian to stop, the arrival of the second (white) woman, her protestations, and an exchange in which the second woman is informed of the white man's betrayal of the first. Only after the white woman reacts with horror does the strangling assailant finally pull the bent body up from its compliant pose and let it fall to the ground. Adding sexual insult to racial injury, the white man is now rejected by his white girlfriend as well. Left alone in the frame, he stands and repeatedly fingers his neck, adjusting his collar and visually marking and remarking the assault. The film has one remaining shot, of the reunited Indian couple returned to the mountain, but this functions more as a tag, similar to that after the shot of the rope-bound brave in *The Mended Lute*. It attempts to provide normative closure after an extraordinary display of white male dissolution, but the intensity of the extended shot of the wrenched body arguably overshadows that attempt.

While such graphic images of white male suffering speak loudly in and of themselves, they also reverberate with, and extend the gender implications of, the agonizing spectatorial pleasures discussed previously in the context of Griffith's more familiar races to the rescue. One film suggestively ties the two discussions together, positing the ridicule and captivity of a white male spectator as the literal goal of a staged interracial drama. Made a couple of years into the boom of Indian films, *The Englishman and the Girl* (1910) uses the production of "Pocahontas" by a local drama club as the excuse to mock "an Englishman of extremely foppish demean" visiting America.[48] The *Bulletin* for the film takes considerable pleasure in ridiculing Arthur Wilberforce as a particularly unforceful specimen of Anglo-Saxon manhood: "He is a peculiar looking genius of cockney type, with a form of a lamp-post, and as graceful as a duck; in fact, he looked like the 'before' image of a Flesh Food advertisement. Over six feet tall, he is forced, when coming to a sitting posture, to make four folds instead of three of an ordinary human being."[49] After this visitor expresses his fear "that Indians are to be seen on the streets of the big cities in their primitive state . . . wild, ferocious, and shooting up things," the amateur thespians decide to playfully terrorize him. Dressed up in their Indian costumes, they perform an attack, "bind his hands and pretend to be about to despatch him, when Dorothy [in the role of Pocahontas] rushes in as the Indian maiden and saves him." As the film continues, the victim turns on his attackers and chases them; in the end he reunites with Dorothy, who "in the garb of an Indian maiden . . . stands regarding him admiringly, as if to say, 'Ain't he grand!' "

As a metastory about whites role-playing interracial drama, *The Englishman and the Girl* makes explicit several pervasive generic elements. With publicity that insists upon Wilberforce's wimpy character, and a climactic episode in which he is literally bound and humiliated, this film uniquely insists that such performances wherein white men imagine (themselves and other whites dressed up as) "Indians" enduring and inflicting various states of suffering are organized precisely to entertain the fears of, and conjure such agony in, a white male spectator.[50] At the same time, the film provides Wilberforce with a way out, a reversal in which "in an instant the tables are turned." This, too, is frequently a key element of these films. For while at times the Biograph Indian films and, as we will see shortly, the Biograph Civil War films end with such displays of threatened masculinity still exposed, they often provide escape routes via reversals of character and circumstance. In Wilberforce's case the reversal comes at the end, covering over to some extent his earlier emasculating display. The heading below the film's title on Biograph's publicity sheet asks, "And the Joke Was On . . . ?"—setting up the escape route whereby Wilberforce will "drive . . . the enemy to cover, . . . strut . . . back" to Dorothy's house, and bask in the phallic glow projected upon him by her newfound admiration.

This kind of restoration of masculinity can be detected elsewhere, with more and less elaborate deployments of plot and editing coming to the rescue. *The Greaser's Gauntlet* features two rescues: in the first, a white woman saves a Mexican man who secretly loves her as he dangles in a tree at the hands of a lynch mob; in the second, as a result of considerable plot convolutions, the same man saves the same woman. The *Bulletin*'s rhetoric of reversal here is similar to *The Englishman*'s, concluding in the penultimate sentence: "The tables are now turned and Mildred has a chance to thank him for his deliverance" (9). This double rescue plot not only restores gender roles within the film but foreshadows what we will come to see as a larger trend across Griffith's films in which scenarios of white women in distress come to take the place more systematically of what in the Indian films are often scenarios scripted so vividly for white men.[51]

This shift in the onscreen inscription of agony from white men to white women will become most explicit in the Civil War shorts, discussed in the next section, and in chapter 2 we will see the result of that transfer more fully realized in *The Birth of a Nation*. As an example of how this shift will play in the Indian film, I should note that by 1913—the year that also marks the end of the genre's cycle—the kind of imagery of male suffering displayed earlier will completely disappear in what, significantly, is Griffith's most remembered Indian film, *The Battle at Elderbush Gulch*.[52] Here all the Indians appear as violent savages, quintessentially depicted in the frequently reproduced image Biograph chose for its publicity in which an Indian raises a baby over his head before throwing it to the ground.[53] And the most intense agonies are endured by the film's white women. Indeed, Lillian Gish's performance as the desperate mother whose baby is missing during an Indian raid is of the kind that would later make her famous as the frantic victim-heroines of *Birth*, *Way Down East* (1920), and *Broken Blossoms* (perhaps explaining why this Indian film was rereleased on the heels of *Birth*'s success).[54] Trapped in a cabin surrounded by Indians, a hysterical Gish, shot repeatedly throughout the raid in close-ups and medium close-ups, carries the affective burden of the scene while the battle between men takes place at sizable distances from the viewer, at times shot in striking high-angle extreme long shots showing the surrounded cabin. In other words, by 1913 the representational schema of race, gender, and agony in Griffith's Indian films had gone the way of the classic miscegenation films to come.

Before leaving the earlier Indian films, however, we should remember that however transgressive their fantasies of *masculinity* might sometimes have been, such transgressions did not necessarily jeopardize the conservatism of their racial, and even their gender, politics. Indeed, the multiplicity of pleasures meted out in the genre suggest that it provided a very malleable framework that could at once allow for transgression and readily snap back to rigid racial and sexual conventions. Such malleability, stemming in part from the dual "brave yet kind" identities in circulation and the accompanying fantasy of the quick-to-change Indian temperament, would seem integral to the "success" of the genre, allowing the viewer to have his (or her) transgressions and keep them in check, too.[55]

BATTLING THE CIVIL WAR IN DRAG

As the Indian film came to a rather abrupt end in the early teens, the popularity of the Civil War genre swelled in 1911 and again in 1913.[56] While that popularity can in part be tied to the cultural interest in the fiftieth anniversary of the Civil War, a consideration of these chronologically overlapping genres reveals fantasmatic overlap as well. Specifically, although men keep their clothes on in these films (if not their uniforms), the preoccupation with masculinity stripped of phallic authority remains palpable. Bowser notes that whereas early Civil War films sided for the most part with the North, "producers soon discovered that the more romantic, noble, and heroic ideals to be found in the defeated South were attractive to both North and South"; as a result, the genre "shifted . . . to reflect a Southern point of view" (178).[57] Such descriptions of generic preoccupations with "loss and death, high nobility, and cowardice" echo the rhetoric of nobility tied to loss and defeat detected in the Indian films (177). And the Civil War films quickly demonstrate that such melodramatic wounds are again exceedingly male. Bowser cites *The Honor of His Family* (1910) and *The House with Closed Shutters* (1910), and to these I would add *In Old Kentucky* (1909), *In the Border States* (1910), *Swords and Hearts* (1911), and *The Battle* (1911); for *all* these films cohere around displays of Southern white male cowardice. Some of the men are just temporarily gun-shy, but others completely fail the Southern cause, their families, and the honor of both. And while these films do not treat miscegenation, they do stage their traumas around the same racial scene as *The Birth of a Nation*, the Civil War, but with white men, not white women, as the site of intense psychic and social breakdowns. In so doing, they form a kind of representational bridge, or pivot, between the Biograph genres discussed earlier and *Birth*, offering a unique glimpse at how agony goes from being a condition that can thoroughly engulf white men to one largely contained upon the bodies of white women.[58]

While the films discussed thus far usually put white male authority into question somewhat indirectly (through metaphors of vision, spectatorial positioning, and images of male pain), Griffith's early Civil War films relentlessly expose the gulf that lies between ordinary men and the phallic ideal. The most extreme example is the ironically titled *The Honor of His Family*. Henry Walthall, the actor who will play the rescuing Southern hero of *Birth*, also plays a young Confederate soldier; but his role here could not be more contrary to the later one. Whereas the "little Colonel" will lead the Ku Klux Klan's ride to rescue the white woman and white culture, in *The Honor of His Family* Walthall's character utterly fails all such charges and deserts his company in the midst of battle. This failure is underscored by his relationship to his father, the (big) Colonel of this film, who, as the *Bulletin* puts it, "was proud of the records of his ancestors" and whose "last behest [to his son] was, 'Go my boy, emulate the brave deeds of those who have gone before you. Be fearless, brave and fight, fight.'"[59] After the son has left for the front, the father proudly watches the battlefield smoke from his window; then, suddenly, the young man "bursts into the room and crouches nearly dead with fear." In order that the soldier not be hung for his cowardice, the father shoots him then and there. Hiding the corpse until dark, he then lays it out on the battlefield, arranging it with sword in hand so that he can lead officers to "discover" the evidence of a heroic death. This film, then, exposes not only a son's radical failure to measure up to the task set for him by his father and his culture but also the desperate lengths to which these paternal entities will go to keep the fiction of phallic "honor" in place. And by displaying the father's extraordinary fabrication, the camera belies the cover-up and further reveals the disjuncture between the power of its own gaze and the on-screen looks in the phallic charade. The father may deceive the officers, but we have a clear view of his macabre performance.

Whereas other Civil War films do not go as far as depicting fathers killing defeated sons, they play out similar moments of masculine failure with equally revealing treatments. *In Old Kentucky* also features Walt-hall as a Confederate soldier who runs home, in this case to hide in his mother's bed "while she lies alongside, armed with a pistol."[60] In an oddly regionalized version of white male cowardice, Walthall hides there from his own brother who is enlisted with the North. Describing the film's climax and conclusion, the *Biograph Bulletin* describes it as "the most impressive scene ever depicted in moving pictures. The mother folds her lost boy to her heart, and [her other son] with the Union flag thrown over his arm stretches forth his hand to his brother, who with the old tattered colors of the Confederacy held affectionately to his breast, receives the warm grasp, typifying the motto of Kentucky 'United we stand, divided we fall.'" It is telling that *Biograph* would praise as "the most impressive scene ever depicted" one in which broken masculinity returns to be enveloped in the safety of mother.[61] For while the story of divided brothers may "typify" the divided state of Kentucky (Griffith's own home state), it uses that division to juxtapose not only North and South but also two kinds of men—one "triumphant [and] promoted in rank" and the other "ragged and homeless for the 'Lost Cause.'" What would seem to distinguish this filmic scene from any other "ever depicted" is its open portrayal of the South's loss as a loss of masculinity, its intertwining of tattered flag and tattered manhood. Moreover, Biograph seems to bank on that image appealing to Northern and Southern viewers alike.

In keeping with the portrait of a mother in bed with a wounded son and her own pistol, these films often accompany imagery of wounded masculinity with that of phallic femininity. In *The Battle*, which the publicity sheet subtitles "An Influence That Makes the Hero," the credited influence is a hard-hearted woman.[62] The *Bulletin* claims that "this story tells of the transforming of a pusillanimous coward into a lion-hearted

FIG. 1.4. A confederate soldier (Charles West) is trapped in the house with his daughter (Gladys Egan), who rescues him. *In the Border States* (1910).

hero by the derision of the girl he loved" and continues to insist upon the depths of his "pusillanimous" character as "he, panic-stricken, rushes in [to the girl's home], trembling with fear, to hide."[63] In response to this unmanly performance, "she laughs in scorn at his cowardice and commands him to go back and fight." Thus, it is the woman's mocking laughter at the cowering boy, as well as her hitting and yelling, that prods him to fulfill his military duty. And although his humiliation comes early in the film, passes rather quickly, and is never referenced again, it is nevertheless the privileged scene and exchange in the publicity. Once again, Biograph saw fit to market a film on the strengths of its hero's weakness, combined in this case with the transformative effects of his girlfriend's tough love.

Other Civil War films in which women take up the slack left by men result directly in gender reversals of Griffith's classic scenario of pursuer chasing pursued. *In the Border States* traps a white *man* in the house, hidden there by his young daughter, who protects and effectively rescues him (fig. 1.4). The scene of father and daughter trapped in the house proceeds typically, with Northerners breaking first through the front door, then working on to the bedroom in which the father is hidden. It is only because the girl had earlier, bravely, taken pity on the same Union soldier who is about to kill her father that he leaves him unharmed. *The House with Closed Shutters* and *Swords and Hearts* take this kind of gender reversal much further, elaborating scenarios in which Southern white women literally take on the mantles of men who remain confined indoors. The considerable extent to which these films mix up (male) swords and (female) hearts makes them worth examining in close detail.

As suggested earlier, the larger transition marked by the Civil War films in the gendering of agony and spectatorship—from the inscription of suffering on male bodies in the Indian films to female ones in the classic miscegenation films—is most neatly articulated by the transformation Walthall undergoes at Griffith's direction from his role as the failed son in *The Honor of His Family* to the rescuing hero of *Birth*. In between these two radically opposed representations comes yet another Civil War role for Walthall, this time as the drunken and neurotic coward of *The House with Closed Shutters*. Like *The Honor of His Family,* this film goes to extremes to keep the myth of phallic masculinity in place. But this time it is not the failed son who is sacrificed to preserve that myth, but his sister.

When Walthall's character is asked by (none other than) Robert E. Lee to deliver a message to the front, he cannot perform. Instead, he gets drunk and stumbles home, to be taken care of by his mother and sister. When they discover the letter, his sister (Dorothy West) decides to deliver it herself (fig. 1.5). With her mother's help she cuts her hair (a gesture that echoes, with an explicitly sexual difference, her earlier "feminine" gesture of cutting a lock of hair to give to one of her war-bound suitors), dresses in her brother's uniform, and poses gallantly before the mirror as she adjusts his Confederate hat on her head (fig. 1.6). With her brother's sword on her hip, she mounts his horse and rides off. As she rides toward us, we see a pair of men approach from behind and begin to chase her. Earlier in the film we saw Walthall turn tail and run at the sight of oncoming riders, but his sister deftly loses them. Soon after, she delivers the letter and rides off again. Her success thus having supplanted her brother's failure, the film cuts back to a shot of Walthall in his bathrobe discovering Lee's letter gone from his pocket. Registering his mother's explanation that his sister has taken it, he panics, collapses back into his chair, and buries his head in his hands. We then return to his sister getting off his/her horse to cinch up the saddle. As she does so, an explosion goes off nearby, and the horse runs away. Suddenly, a battle erupts, and in a series of shots we see her, still in drag, behind a line of troops. She stands still for a moment, then yells, throws up her hands, pounds her fists, and runs boldly into the midst of the battlefield as shots fire across it. We soon see her purpose as she rushes to pick up a fallen Confederate flag. But just as she raises it over her head, she is hit from behind, arms and flag momentarily outstretched before she falls to the ground (fig. 1.7).

Despite such remarkable displays of female heroism, the publicity sheet for *The House with Closed Shutters* baldly announces the film's subject to be masculine failure. It opens: "What a contemptible type of

FIG. 1.5. The sister (Dorothy West) of a "drunk mad coward" (Henry Walthall) decides to do his duty. *The House with Closed Shutters* (1910).

FIG. 1.6. The sister, in her brother's uniform, cuts her hair to complete the disguise.

FIG. 1.7. The sister dies in her brother's place, trying to resurrect the Confederate flag.

human animal is the coward. He is totally devoid of all the elements that go to make up a man."[64] The film, too, relentlessly insists upon this crisis of manhood long after the sister's sacrifice. When the camera returns us to the family home, we first see the mother receive a letter. Repeating the titular irony of *The Honor of His Family*, the letter written to her daughter underscores the son's failure as it reports "his" death and honor: "Your brother, after nobly performing a perilous mission, was caught in the battle's maelstrom. . . . His death was an added honor to his family name." And like Walthall's murderous father in the earlier film, his mother here goes to extremes to maintain the fiction of her son's heroic masculinity: she vows to confine him in the house forever, pretending to the outside world that it was he who died and that his sister lives on in perpetual mourning. The son's cowardly fate, as memorialized in this film's title, is thus rendered a permanent one. As the years pass, the girl's aging suitors leave flowers on the doorstep while Walthall goes gray within. He peeks out of the shutters, and twice we see him throw them open in an attempt to reenter the world. On the first occasion his mother manages to throw a blanket over him just in time, but on the second, "twenty-five years afterward," the elderly suitors passing by are suddenly shocked by the sight of him, and this in turn gives him a fatal heart attack. The film here ends with the fiction of the brother's valor dramatically exposed.

In gestures that are quite remarkable to students of classical Hollywood cinema, and of *Birth* in particular, this film not only makes Walthall's failure explicit but displays it in the most visible of terms. While the spectacle of the white woman on the battlefield is extraordinary, that of the radically feminized and enfeebled white male lead is equally so, as "the drunk mad coward" perpetually drinks, cringes, and nervously flits about the house. Indeed, it is the excess of this spectacle of male lack that makes the overt masculinization of the woman not merely tolerable but necessary. Stepping into his uniform and the heroic image he cannot sustain, she takes on the role of masculinity he cannot bear to play. What is more, in her new role as the noble sufferer, the sister not only steps into his shoes at the level of narrative; in addition, I want to suggest, at the larger level of cinematic representation "she" takes on the role of embodying what is clearly defined as a "masculine" burden. The camera's depiction of her death on the battlefield would seem to insist upon this, as she does not just die in the likeness of her brother, but for him, taking on the risk and the pain from which he ultimately hides. Quite literally, then, the film thematizes what I suggest is a larger tendency at work in Griffith's films during this period in which the agony of male bodies and psyches is relocated onto female ones.

Made a year after *The House with Closed Shutters*, *Swords and Hearts* similarly features a Southern white woman assuming the uniform, horse, weapon, and duty of the Confederate soldier she loves.[65] Yet this film that also depicts her battling as a man while he remains safely indoors does not openly ridicule white male failure to the extent that the earlier film did because, I will argue, it is even more successful in transforming his failure into her suffering.

The masquerade sequence comes about because a Confederate soldier, Hugh Frazier, steals away from his post for a tryst with his society girl-friend. The poor girl who devotedly loves him, Jennie Baker (also played by Dorothy West), sees that he is about to be ambushed by a group of thieves who have spotted his horse unattended outside the rich girl's home. To divert the attackers, Jennie slips on his Confederate hat and cape and rides off on his horse. Reminding us of the typical Griffith home invasion, pursuer/pursued scenario that Jennie has averted, we see the "guerrillas" approach the front steps of the house, then point and ride off in Jennie's direction. A chase ensues. In keeping with West's earlier performance, Jennie handles the horse, the gun, and the villains with ease. It is not until she returns from battle, helped off her horse by the slave "Old Ben," that she nearly faints. After Ben returns her to her cabin, she stands alone, pallid and weak. Clutching her shawl about her shoulders in these shots, she finally pulls it down to touch, and reveal for us to see, a bleeding wound on her left shoulder. Jennie has not only taken on Hugh's military uniform and effectively rescued him from the thieves but also has literally taken his wound on her body. As we watch her pat the wound, a soft smile crosses her face. This image signals that the transaction has been completed, for the white woman takes the white man's wound and does so quite photogenically.

The success of this transfer is reiterated by the final sequence. Whereas Walthall's character was terminally castrated by his sister's performance of him, Hugh is simply off screen for the duration and reemerges, after the woman suffers in his place, a new man. Although the thieves have burned his plantation to the ground, the future remains bright thanks to Old Ben's loyal rescue of the family fortune and Hugh's efforts to rebuild the estate. In the final shot we see him tilling the soil and Jennie taking her place by his side. In other words, while in *The House with Closed Shutters* man and woman trade places to such an extent as to cause irreparable damage to both categories, in *Swords and Hearts* they do so only temporarily, and in the end masculinity, femininity, "the couple," and the dominant cultural functions of all three are securely restored.

Yet despite this restoration, I read these women in phallic drag as marking a shift in spectatorship precisely because we can still clearly see the maleness of the wounds they take on. That visibility would suggest that the pleasures to be had here stem in part from investments in these wounded manly women *and* the womanly men for whom they stand. Or, to recall the wide range of permutations considered in this chapter, we could say that the Biograph spectator is repeatedly solicited to take pleasure in and through those figures who are at once "as kind-hearted as a woman and as brave as a lion." As it turns out, this description ends up working to describe Griffith's classic suffering white women as much as his (ig)noble suffering men.

What is more, while spectacular images of women dressing up as men and men tragically failing draw our attention to questions of gender identity, a comparison of these Civil War films to the epic one to come foregrounds how differently they represent race as well. Whereas *Birth* will announce race as the central term of its representational battle, the Biograph films represent the Civil War as having virtually nothing to do with it. Their racial reticence becomes especially noticeable when we consider how the scenarios are recast in *Birth* such that the frail white subjects trapped in the house become women, the house-raiding "guerrillas" become black men, and white men triumph as the noble rescuing heroes. At Biograph, by comparison, the solidity of the racial order is ever present as dutiful black male slaves, in addition to white women, see white men through their phallic crises: these slaves close the shutters that hide the white man's wounds, rescue him from burning buildings, and safeguard his fortune to ensure his economic recovery.[66] Bracketing *Birth*'s reconstruction of identity and difference for the moment, the comparison encourages us to see that the openness with which the early Civil War films embrace white male lack is correlative to their refusal to cast black men as anything but loyal Uncle Toms.[67] Put another way, the genre's radical confessions about the fictional grounds of masculine authority are accompanied by complete silence about equally contested institutions of racial privilege.

SPECTATORIAL AGONY AT BIOGRAPH AND BEYOND

What *The Birth of a Nation* will make evident, among other things, is that once the racial order is disturbed—or, rather, once such disturbance is (again) openly registered—former admissions of gender chaos will be firmly put to rest. *Birth* does this not only by recasting the roles of victim, invader, and rescuer but also by establishing new visual and cinematic relations propped upon the new casting arrangement. While I will continue that reading in the next chapter, several points are crucial to recognize here. First, the racial and sexual fantasies at Biograph expose profoundly different fantasies subtending the image of the black rapist than the epic miscegenation film will lead us to imagine. Yet the Biograph fantasies of *male* agony are nonetheless also keyed to a series of racial fantasies. Indeed, it appears that the flexibility of Biograph's representations of gender is regularly facilitated in part by the rigidity of its representations of race. Just as Indian films ostensibly preoccupied with dominant racial fantasies of "noble" braves can tolerate quite transgressive gender fantasies of male suffering and insufficiency, so the Civil War films can temporarily allow quite radical confessions about gender so long as dominant racial ideology remains firmly in place. These findings combine to suggest that we must read such racial and sexual fantasies in relation to one another, not only in the specific contexts of Biograph and *Birth* but also in relation to the critical narratives we forge about difference and spectatorship in and across early and classical cinema.

In addition, the films considered here are notable for the varied forms of bodily and psychic subjection they offer and the considerable capacity of those forms for alteration, substitution, and reversal. This in turn suggests more mobile spectatorial pleasures than the rigidity of *Birth*'s classical schema will allow. This does not make these films inherently progressive, but it does suggest a filmic history of difference that begins with more variable modes of fantasizing identity. That variability would seem further enhanced by early exhibition formats in which viewers consume various combinations of such films within or across given screening periods, interrupted by assorted other films and entertainments; so, too, is the reduction of such varied pleasure further implied by the move to the more singular experience of the feature-length film. At the same time, this analysis invites us to refuse too simplistic a division between early "experiments" and classical conventions, demanding instead that we reevaluate precisely the singularity of the latter by reading them through the lens of ancestors they will sometimes attempt to bury.

CHAPTER TWO

The Mixed Birth of "Great White" Masculinity and the Classical Spectator

"THE BIG BURLY NEGRO ... BEFORE THE CAMERA'S EYES"

This chapter begins where the previous one left off, to argue that the inscriptions of white suffering and "agony" as variously male and female at Biograph coincide with a profound representational struggle in American cinema in this period in which the relation between two kinds of images—images of white men and white women being beaten, often at the hands of men of color—was being thrashed out quite elaborately. The majority of this chapter will interrogate this struggle as it played out in the most classic of silent miscegenation films, *The Birth of a Nation*, but it begins with kindred public controversies surrounding then heavyweight boxing champion of the world, Jack Johnson. While Johnson's international notoriety at the time arose from his having been the first black man to hold the heavyweight title, public interest in the mass cultural phenomenon that the figure of "Jack Johnson" became was clearly tied to, and tied together, his controversial beating and loving, respectively, of white men and white women. More specifically, popular, legal, and filmic constructions of Jack Johnson suggest, as we will find also to be the case in Hollywood cinema, that the repression of the image of a black man beating a white man has everything to do with the production of the image of a black man desiring a white woman.

Johnson held the heavyweight title from December 1908 to April 1915, beating a series of white champions and challengers in fights that received extraordinary attention for their pairing of black and white fighters. After Johnson's pummeling of Tommy Burns at the end of 1908, the white press rooted for former champion Jim Jeffries to return to the ring and take Johnson down. Enflamed over the "hopeless slaughter" of Burns by the "Ethiopian" "colossus," then sportswriter Jack London declared that "Jim Jeffries must now emerge from his alfalfa farm and remove that [golden] smile from [Jack] Johnson's face. Jeff, it's up to you. [The White Man must be rescued.]"[1] In his history of black and white reception of the phenomenon, Dan Streible confirms that as Johnson easily took down a stream of white challengers, "the white American public and press largely echoed London's cry."[2] What is more, Streible reports, the white press "largely ignor[ed Jeffries's] advancing age and . . . paunch" and instead "consistently represented [him] as a white ideal" in the face of his formidable black rival.[3] White reception of Johnson's successive victories over one "white hope" after another thus amply suggests that a black man's public beating of white men—specifically in 1908, 1909, 1910, and 1912—not only quickened the pervasive racism of the time but provoked the explicit, emphatic articulation of a desire for an as yet unseen specimen of "great white" masculinity.[4]

Having retired in 1904 precisely because he refused to risk losing his title to a black man, Jeffries finally responded to London's call almost two years after it was first issued in a fight scheduled for the nation's birthday.[5] The Johnson-Jeffries fight (1910) was more heavily anticipated, massively attended, and extensively reported than any before it. As one cultural historian recently retells it:

> The Johnson-Jeffries match was the event of the year. Twenty thousand men from across the nation . . . traveled to Reno . . . to watch. . . . Five hundred journalists [were] dispatched to . . . cover it. Every day during the week before the fight, they . . . wired between 100,000 and 150,000 words of reportage. . . . On the day of the fight, American men deserted their families' holiday picnics. All across America, they gathered in ballparks, theaters, and auditoriums to hear the wire services' round-by-round reports of the contest. Over thirty thousand men stood outside the *New York Times* offices straining to hear the results; ten thousand men gathered outside the *Atlanta Constitution*.[6]

Despite all the fanfare leading up to the Reno fight, the hopeful whites who cheered Jeffries on were again severely disappointed. The news of Johnson's victory prompted rioting in many cities; as Streible reports, "Some eighteen African Americans were killed and many more, of both races, wounded."[7]

A second wave of controversy erupted over the *filming* of the fight. Two of Johnson's earlier routs of white men had been captured on film, but the infectious anticipation of the Johnson-Jeffries fight spread to, and swelled, the cinematic field. An unprecedented number of officially sanctioned cameras (twelve) were trained on the main event, and others captured the fighters in training; new lenses were made for the occasion; and the "moving picture men" behind the cameras became a prominent part of the spectacle.[8] But Jeffries's defeat instantly sparked what would become a successful campaign to "prohibit the display of moving pictures of prize fights."[9] As one Johnson biographer summarizes them, supporters of such a prohibition "kept repeating the idea until it was a slogan: *The fight pictures will be worse than the fight!*"[10] Organized campaigns quickly led to local bans throughout the country and abroad, eventually finding success in Washington.[11] In 1912, reacting in particular to a fight between "a Caucasian brute and an African biped beast," as a representative from Georgia described Johnson and yet another failed white challenger, Congress passed "an act to prohibit the importation and the interstate transportation of films or other pictorial representations of prize fights."[12]

Legal scholarship as early as 1936 recognized that "the history and basis of the [Prize Fight Film] act . . . is peculiar, to say the least." The ensuing explanation of that peculiar history is worth quoting at length, both for its own racial rhetoric and for its emphasis on the role of the camera in the controversies surrounding Johnson. In his book, *Law of the Stage, Screen and Radio*, Roger Marchetti writes:

> At approximately the time the motion picture art was swinging into its tremendous growth . . . there was a "dark" menace in the world of sport. One Jack Johnson was banging on the gates of the house of the championship, then possessed by Jim Jeffries. It had been the custom in the past to make moving pictures of the fights from the ringside and to circulate them throughout the infant industry. Pictures of this fight between Jeffries and Johnson were made. *After Johnson, the big burly negro, had battered Jeffries before the camera's eyes, Congress immediately attempted to nullify the bad effect which such a graphic portrayal would create in the minds of those witnessing the film.* They immediately passed this act. . . . It represents only an emergency measure to meet a temporary occasion. . . . Many high-sounding and reasoning emotional defenses have been uttered by the courts in upholding the act, but the fact remains that had Jeffries won that fight, this statute would scarcely have been written.[13]

While this account overstates the immediacy of Congress's ban on fight films, ignoring the lag of two years between the Johnson-Jeffries fight and the passage of the bill in 1912, ample evidence nonetheless supports the claim that what provoked the congressional act was the image of a black man battering a white man "before the camera's eyes."

The most glaring evidence comes from the *Congressional Record*. Although attempts to ban fight films had begun as early as 1897 and had flared up again in anticipation of the Johnson-Jeffries fight, none succeeded until Johnson had handily beaten the most beloved white hope and was about to face yet another.[14] Only days before Johnson faced his first challenge to the title since Jeffries (in another fight scheduled for the national holiday), Representative Sims of Tennessee called forth a bill "to prevent the shipping . . . and . . . interstate commerce of moving-picture films of prize fights, especially the one between a negro and a white man to be held . . . on the 4th of July next."[15] Though a lack of quorum blocked Sims's attempted preemptive strike, another Johnson victory galvanized Congress by month's end. The intended isolation of *interracial* fight films was again announced on the House floor when Representative Roddenbery, who had introduced the bill, explained its purpose by way of his direct reference to "the recent ["repulsive"] prize fight . . . in New Mexico . . . between a Caucasian brute and an African biped beast."[16] More precisely, he continued, "This bill is designed to prevent the display to morbid-minded adults and susceptible youth all over the country of representations of such a disgusting exhibition."

At this point, one of Roddenbery's colleagues directly queried the interracial subtext of the bill under discussion, prompting a brief exchange on the matters of spectatorship and representation at issue:

REPRESENTATIVE SHARP (D-Ohio): I wish to ask the gentleman if he thinks it more indefensible for a white man and a black man to engage in a prize fight than for two white men to engage in such a conflict?

REPRESENTATIVE RODDENBERY (D-Georgia): The act as a matter of moral conduct is the same. It differs in degree. No man descended from the old Saxon race can look upon that kind of a contest without abhorrence and disgust.

REPRESENTATIVE SIMS (D-Tennessee): Mr. Speaker, the gentleman from Georgia has fully explained the bill. The object of it is to prevent demoralizing *pictures* from being exhibited all over the country–*pictures* which do not do any good, and might do much harm.[17]

Explicitly shifting the location of concern from "the act" of the interracial fight itself to those white ("old Saxon") men who would "look upon" it, Roddenbery clearly maintains that a fight between a white and a black man produces greater "abhorrence and disgust" than a fight between two white men. And lest this exchange dare to blur the distinction between films of fights and actual fights, Sims interrupts to redirect the discussion onto its properly filmic focus. Hence, no sooner have Sharp and Roddenbery identified the racial fantasy that is "indefensible" for white male spectators than Sims delimits and announces the "demoralizing" field of such fantasies to reside in "pictures . . . pictures which . . . might do much harm." Sims again insists on the cinematic specificity of the ban when he later corrects a colleague who "understand[s] that the bill does have to do with prize fights." Sims: "No; it has to do with *films; pictures* of prize fights" (9307, emphasis mine).

This testimony suggests that Congress explicitly registered the notion circulating throughout the wider culture that the cinematic rendering of a black man beating a white man was particularly dangerous, more so than any other form of representation of the same event—written accounts, wire reports amplified for public broadcast, cartoons, even photographs—none of which were censored. Following the riots sparked by the Johnson-Jeffries fight, many local agencies cited fear of further violence in defense of local bans prohibiting the exhibition of film footage of the fight. Despite such claims, however, cities that allowed the film did not suffer violent outbursts, which would explain why when Congress moved to pass the federal ban two years later, public violence was never once mentioned as a concern.[18] More persistent than the claim that Johnson fight films would spark racial violence was the sentiment that, as one Johnson historian quotes a Tennessee newspaper, "it would do white men no good to see a motion picture of a 'powerful negro knocking a white man about the ring.'"[19]

While this formulation seems to intuit something quite accurate vis-à-vis the various "old Saxon" male viewers at issue, the question of what exactly that "no good" consists has been surprisingly underexamined in discussions of Jack Johnson and the ban on prize fight films. The same historian who unearths such potent archival testimony as that just cited elsewhere generalizes the position into a "sentimental desire to spare the white race the humiliation of seeing its highly-esteemed champion knocked out in *vivid* repetition" (75, emphasis mine). In a similar allusion to filmic verisimilitude, Marchetti's 1936 explanation of the congressional ban on the cinematic image of "the big burly negro" and a "battered Jeffries" also centers on film's uniquely "graphic portrayal," more vivid, he implies elsewhere, than "vividly detailed" illustrations and radio broadcasts.[20] More recently, Streible explains the desire to censor the Johnson-Jeffries fight film as stemming from the fact that "it contained such an undeniable image of black power and white vincibility."[21] Implicitly yoking the earlier explanations, Streible's is the most compelling as it stresses that this "image of black power" was felt to be so threatening because of its "undeniable" presence. At a moment in cinematic history when no images of potent black masculinity had been seen, the combination of Johnson's highly cultivated image, his seemingly unconquerable success, and the documentary lure of the fight film footage formed a uniquely powerful image for black and white spectators alike.[22]

In their understandable focus on the overt racial rhetoric of the Johnson-Jeffries contest, assessments of the public consumption of these images have nonetheless typically elided the fundamental place of gender among the elements in contention.[23] There is an assumed interchangeability in Gilmore's language as cited here, for example, between "white men" and "the white race." Yet whether we focus on details like the sometimes (significantly) repressed culmination of London's rallying cry ("The White Man must be rescued") and attendant hopes that a great white specimen of manhood would arise to do the job, or on the pronounced attention paid to Johnson's sexuality—including his notorious relations with white women (wives and prostitutes among them) and mythologies about his oversized penis—it is multiply evident that sexual difference is, at the very least, deeply constitutive of the terms within which the "racial" battles pinned on Johnson's image were presented and imagined.[24] And, this chapter will further suggest, throughout the cinematic battles that took place around that image, gender identity was itself both on the line and profoundly shaped and reshaped through the color line in ways that demand further consideration. For not only were these racial images—images that were consumed (however differently) by whites and blacks, men and women—themselves relentlessly gendered, but it was their regendering, I will also argue, that made them ultimately tolerable to dominant white culture.

In addition, I suggest, the assumption that the significance of the cinematic specificity of the fight film ban resides in matters of verisimilitude has muted the complexities of spectatorial fantasy at issue. While the ban on actual prize fight footage might suggest concern about the sight of real black men (in the ring and in the streets) beating real white men, or about real white men retaliating, the ban's peculiar concern with the cinematic dissemination of such images—even after, as it turns out, they had been consumed with no evident signs of social unrest—obviously suggests instead a fear about the potential psychic effects of such images unleashed, as Marchetti put it relatively early on, "in the minds of" spectators.

Residue of such fears seems to linger in the fact that despite the enormous felt significance and photographic documentation of Johnson taking down a string of "white hopes," his photo-filled biographies contain surprisingly few images of him battering white men.[25] Reprinted there more frequently, however, are photographs of Johnson the dandy with (and without) white women.[26] This largely follows the historical fact that in the same period when Johnson's image with white men on screen was being censored, his "open preference for white women" off screen, as one writer describes it, was receiving considerable attention.[27] His relationships with white women not only were frequently remarked upon by the press but also led to a campaign against him by federal and Illinois state prosecutors that culminated in his conviction in 1913 for violating the Mann Act (aka the White Slave Act). Employing similar tactics as the law that censored the filmic image of Johnson beating white men, that act "forbade the interstate transportation of women for immoral purposes" and was used as an excuse to punish Johnson for his consensual relationships with white women—just months after his victory over yet another hopeful white man.[28] When, in October 1912, Johnson was arrested in Chicago on charges of violating the Mann Act, "effigies of the champion burned in white sections of the city," and "wherever [he] went [out on bail] he attracted angry mobs, which shouted 'Lynch him! Lynch the nigger.'"[29] Such sentiments spread throughout editorial pages of white southern newspapers and once again inspired national legislation aimed beyond the "temporary occasion" of Johnson himself.

The very congressman who had actively fought to suppress the "repulsive," "abhorrent" image of the "African biped beast" beating a white man in the summer of 1912 directed his legislative efforts, and the same adjectives, toward cultivating the image of the black rapist by year's end, conjuring yet another image of Johnson to do so.[30] Amid a larger wave of antimiscegenation legislation in which "a total of at least twenty-one bills were introduced between 1907 and 1921—two and one half times more than the anti-lynching bills," Roddenbery introduced a joint resolution that would amend the U. S. Constitution to deem "intermarriage between negroes or persons of color and Caucasians . . . forever prohibited."[31] To make his case for the proposed amendment, Roddenbery held up Johnson as the exemplary "fiendish" black male subject it would constrain. Speaking again on the floor of the House, he declared, "No brutality, no infamy, no degredation [sic] in all the years of southern slavery possessed such villainous character and such atrocious qualities as the provision of laws . . . which allow the marriage of the negro Jack Johnson to a woman of the Caucasian strain. [Applause.]"[32] Claiming that "no blacker incubus ever fixed its slimy claws upon the social body of this Republic than the embryonic cancer of negro marriage to white women," Roddenbery named Johnson (and only Johnson) no less than five times in this single diatribe, at one point restating the officially proposed language with him as its explicit subject (503–4). He urged his northern colleagues to join those from the "southern country" to secure "a constitutional amendment that will make it impossible forever hereafter for a brutal African prize-fighter to join to his name that of even a fallen American woman. [Applause.]" (503). While the proposed bill did not make it beyond the Judiciary Committee, others like it were passed in the House by wide margins before dying in the Senate, and still others did pass in states such as Virginia, Georgia, and California.[33]

Such legislation makes it increasingly evident that the controversies surrounding Jack Johnson's "villainous character" in the ring, on film, and in his own bedroom were intricately connected through wider discourses that feared, and fostered the threat of, black masculinity. Such connections were already detected in their day in black newspapers that repeatedly unmasked the "hypocrisy" of reformists who called for the censorship of films depicting a black boxer beating a white boxer, but who did nothing to fight the wave of lynching under way throughout the country.[34] One such newspaper painted this irony in quite explicit, and spectatorial, terms, accusing those who actively fought against the filmic image of a white man being beaten by a black man as being the very same who "would attend the lynching bee with their sweet innocent little children to witness the Negro being burned at the stake and gladly pay out money for slices of quivering flesh."[35] As evidence of this contradiction, the editor of the same newspaper (among others) mentioned the popularity of Thomas Dixon's play *The Clansman*, upon which *The Birth of a Nation* would be based.[36] In doing so the editor returns us explicitly not only to the nexus of the Johnson phenomenon and popular cinema but also to the nexus of images of white men and white women being beaten. Whereas dominant white culture denounces the Johnson fight films, he contends, it celebrates *The Clansman*, "which depicts a Negro raping a white woman . . . glorif[ying] it from the pulpits as the noblest work of their hand-made God."[37] This juxtaposition invites us to recognize that in popular representation, as in historical practice, dominant American culture moves from the fantasy of white men being beaten by black men to the fantasy of black men being beaten by white men by way of the (persistent) intermediate fantasy of black men beating white women.[38]

While the second and third permutations in that sequence and their cinematic codification will be vividly displayed in *The Birth of a Nation*, the feverish production and consumption of Jack Johnson beating white men on film begs us to pay closer attention to the complicated stakes of the first. The pleasures evidently taken in such images, for white spectators in particular, raise significant questions about the conjoined history of film spectatorship and difference in their own right, and further reverberate with that history as it unfolds from Biograph to *Birth*.

Although the Johnson story is often told, as I have done thus far, to emphasize the regulation of the image of the black man beating the white man, to do only this is to ignore the significant appeal that such images did in fact have for white viewers before they were censored. Of the Johnson-Jeffries fight film Streible writes, "Black spectators saw [it] as a signifier of racial equality, but in numbers they remained only a small percentage of the total audience for the film. Despite the opposition by so many white segregationists and progressives, most fight film customers were white. Many of the film's largest crowds were exclusively so."[39] And these white audiences, though racially segregated, otherwise varied considerably; the Johnson-Jeffries fight film not only ran in local theaters throughout the country but also enjoyed special screenings for audiences as dissimilar as National Guard troops, on the one hand, and party guests of at least one rich white couple, on the other. It was this predominantly white-consumed film of a white man being beaten by a black man, Streible further documents, that "became as widely discussed as any single [film] production prior to *Birth of a Nation*." Bracketing for the moment the question of why and what it means that this remarkable fact has been previously missed by histories and theories of American film and film spectatorship, we must ask what white fascination with such images meant, both for the cultural moment in question and for the early history of American film culture. What do we make, for example, of the two-year lag between a "battered Jeffries before the camera's eyes" in 1910 and the lack of serious congressional support for the fight film ban until the next "big 'race fight' approached in 1912"?[40] Or, perhaps all the more significantly, of the tremendous cinematic anticipation of the Johnson-Jeffries beating in Reno, despite Johnson's known advantage and the preexisting filmic record of him handily beating two previous white opponents? Although the Gaumont cameras trained on the Johnson-Burns fight in 1908 were stopped by police in the fourteenth round "to prevent any further humiliation or bloodshed," Johnson's continual "battering" of the white champion as he lost the title had already been recorded. London, for one, even accused Johnson of manipulating his cinematic image: "He cuffed and smiled and cuffed, and in the clinches whirled his opponent around so as to be able to assume beatific and angelic facial expressions for the cinematograph machines."[41]

Querying white reception of such footage, Streible finds evidence that the Reno fight film was exhibited to some whites as "an opportunity to rally for Jeffries' return."[42] The film's promoter accompanied screenings with London-like narration, hype for a "Jeffries-Johnson grudge match," and footage of Jeffries's earlier victories. Similar logics might explain white consumption of the Johnson-Ketchel films, since audiences had also known going in that they were paying to see a film in which a white man is badly beaten and loses. With that 1909 fight, instead of a steady beating as the main event of a ninety-minute film, as had been the case in the Johnson-Burns fight, "the champion merely 'toyed' with the challenger for most of the fight," only to then excite spectators with "a stunning climax to the fight and film."[43] As Streible describes it, "Ketchel swung a roundhouse through an opening to Johnson's head. Retreating from the punch, the champion fell to the mat—perhaps knocked down, perhaps having slipped. The crowd of white men rose to cheer the underdog white hope's feat. But before any celebration could take hold, a deliberate Johnson lunged across the ring, smashing Ketchel squarely in the mouth and immediately rendering him unconscious. Johnson leaned casually on the ropes, hand on hip, as the referee counted out his victim."[44] Well before the Johnson-Jeffries fight film sparked local and national bans on Johnson's image, this film of him "toying" with a white man sold well, "along with the widely reprinted still photos of Johnson standing over a bloodied, unconscious white hope." Indeed, it was with these very images that "the myth of Johnson . . . grew as replays of his knockout artistry spread."[45]

In the face of the "historically unprecedented image[s] of black power" these widely consumed films presented to white viewers, and the "antidote to . . . pervasive negative stereotypes" they offered to black ones, Streible asks the pivotal question, "Why would the ruling race permit and even promote a cinematic negation of its own ideology?"[46] Reposing the question from the side of consumption, we can also ask, What pleasures might white viewers take in these images? Streible's reception research leads him to three answers: genuine boxing fans could appreciate Johnson's performance regardless of race; whites who "envisioned Johnson as a monster . . . came to see him put on display at his most ferocious"; and, presumably for the same crowd, the footage offered a foretaste of a "seemingly inevitable bout with Jeffries," and "Ketchel's alleged knockdown of the champion gave a glimmer of hope that the 'Ethiopian colossus' [as London had called him] could be vanquished."[47]

While Streible documents evidence for each of these explanations, contemporaneous filmic entertainments of white male agony at Biograph invite us to consider in addition a messier possibility that the white press no doubt would not be eager to confirm: that white fascination could be captivated not only by the image of the black male "monster" but also by that of his white male victim. For the fact remains that *any* pleasures taken in watching the black champion beat Burns, Ketchel, and/or Jeffries clearly required watching the repeated blows and falls of "bloodied" and sometimes "unconscious white hope[s]." Indeed, in the serial context of Johnson's deft performances—in the round-by-round bouts within each of these major fights, and with the stream of knockouts from one heavily anticipated event to the next—it becomes increasingly curious not only that white fans but also white cameras would so fully invest their faith in a paunchy retiree. On the one hand, as I suggested earlier, such investments bespeak the extremity of desires for a triumphal display of "great white" manhood. On the other hand, I am now suggesting, in light of the known dearth of actual white champions, and the ample record of what such failures could look like on film, the fact that dominant white culture would effectively set itself up so elaborately (with an unprecedented number of cameras, etc.) when there was such a good chance of Jeffries's *defeat* would seem to speak to something significantly less than a wholesale aversion to filmic images of white men being beaten.

Certainly, as previous scholarship on Johnson and my own readings here variously demonstrate, loud evidence exists to the contrary. My purpose in raising the possibility of something like a white masochistic pleasure in watching Johnson and his battered opponents is therefore not to deny the force of the historic efforts that would deny it but rather to reconsider what prompted those denials to be so virulent. The fact that filmic images of a black man beating white men were, arguably, solicited (by promoters, fans, "picture men," etc.), and in fact lingered on the national retina for a palpable moment before they were repressed, suggests that they were perhaps intolerable precisely because they so resonated with white viewers in a period when white male dominance was widely imagined to be at risk. No doubt white viewing pleasures in such beatings could themselves vary. Turn-of-the-century white men already perceiving their social privileges to be at risk, and patriarchally-identified white women for that matter, might take comfort in at least having their fears "vividly" registered—perhaps in an enabling projection of white male vulnerability onto the localized bodies of the boxers on screen and/or, perhaps more likely in light of the continual reopening and failure of the position of the "white hope," in a more purely agonized identificatory lament; white women might also be desirous of, or identify with, Jack Johnson, possibly enjoying attendant fantasies of challenging, even re-voking, white male power; finally, white male and female viewers alike, like viewers of the multiple agonies staged at Biograph, might well enjoy such racially and socially inflected beatings as the occasion for more un-abashedly sexual and psychic masochistic thrills.

As the delineation of such possible pleasures and their implications might well lead us to predict, they were not permitted to last openly. Moreover, and with striking synchronicity, not only does the peak period of the popularity of images of Johnson beating white men (1908–10) co-incide with that of the popularity of Indian films that subject white men and assorted melodramas that figuratively bind and gag their male and female spectators in fictional cinema (1908–11); so also does the period of Johnson's decline and public reconfiguration as an abductor and abuser of white women (1912–15) temporally coincide with, and script a parallel representational substitution of white women for white men as, the path that moves Griffith's fictional cinema from early rescue attempts of white men detected in the Civil War shorts (1910–11) to their full, tri-umphant restoration in *The Birth of a Nation* (1915).[48] For, as I have said, it was precisely in that transitional period, just months after another white hope's failure in July 1912, that governmental bodies explicitly in-vestigated, prosecuted, and sentenced Johnson on bogus charges of ab-ducting white women. And despite his flight from bail and the country, his image would not recover. Instead, with further cinematic timing, his loss of the title in April 1915, just months after *Birth*'s premiere, would be filmically memorialized through yet another interracial beating fan-tasy. For even though the fight film ban was still in effect, promoters fought doggedly to get the film of his downfall shown, and "lacking cin-ematographic proof of the events in Havana, newspapers seized upon the final frame and made it into an icon. The shot of the giant Willard strid-ing away from the vanquished Johnson, prostrate on the mat, was widely reproduced and became . . . 'a standard wall decoration' in sports bars for many years."[49]

Reverberations of the representational battles waged through the filmic images of Jack Johnson are tremendous, and tremendously long-lived, in American fiction film. There, too, the repeated fantasy of white womanhood being threatened by men of color works to cover over, and elaborately overcome, fantasies of the violation of white manhood. And although the images of miscegenation at issue in silent American cinema are more explicitly the product of fiction and fantasy, they clearly share a range of desires, anxieties, and representational politics with these non-fiction films and their contentious reception. For, as I will argue through an extended reading of *Birth*'s elaborate cinematic efforts to distinguish white masculinity from white femininity, and from black masculinity, not unlike the way in which images of Johnson inspired hopes of a great, idealized form of white masculinity—of "pure manhood," as Rodden-bery would hope for it—so Hollywood's most celebrated miscegenation fantasy battled perceived racial and sexual threats to white American manhood by producing new cinematic forms of "great white" masculinity and spectatorship.[50]

MISCEGENATED CLASSICS

The period I am proposing to have been pivotal for the filmic (re)config-uration of what has become a normative scheme for representing racial and sexual identity—be it through the representational dramas sur-rounding Jack Johnson or melodramas produced at Biograph—also co-incides with the pivotal years, most broadly construed, of the develop-ment of classical Hollywood cinema.[51] We have long had evidence that such projects were related, most obviously in *Birth*'s dual delivery of much-celebrated forms of cinematic narration and much-disputed dis-plays of a decidedly phallic white supremacy. What the fictional and non-fictional pretexts here exposed help us to reconsider is what it means, and how it was, that such a pair—unnatural though it was—was "born" to-gether, and that this tricky twin birth was itself so anxiously marked as the product of miscegenation fantasy.[52]

Vivid, feature-length fantasies of miscegenation burst onto the screen of American fiction cinema quite spectacularly in 1915 with *The Birth of a Nation* and *The Cheat* (Cecil B. DeMille) and lingered there for several years, as evidenced by *Broken Blossoms* (Griffith) in 1919.[53] While none of these go so far as to depict interracial sex, in its place are so many im-ages of white women under siege. For, as I suggested in chapter 1, these films are bound together by graphic images of white female bodies being beaten by, or as a result of relationships with, men of color, and these images repeatedly function as privileged sites of male exchange, racial violence, erotic investment, and spectatorial interest. In addition to Flora's suicidal leap to escape Gus, *The Birth of a Nation* punctuates the Klan's climactic ride to the rescue with close-ups of a nearly unconscious Elsie Stoneman (Lillian Gish) bound and gagged for her refusal to submit to a mulatto, Silas Lynch (George Siegmann) (see fig. 1.1). Kindred images in *The Cheat* feature a white socialite dragged by the hair and held against her will as "a Burmese Ivory King" burns his brand of ownership into her (ivory) flesh (see fig. 1.2). And in *Broken Blossoms* Griffith again directs Lillian Gish in the role of tortured victim, this time one who hides frantically in a closet from her father upon his discovery of her stay with "the yellow man," only to be forcibly wrenched out of it and beaten to death (see fig. 1.3).[54] The repetition, intensity, and context of these images underscore the degree to which the white female body under siege becomes a primary representational site for playing out these films' highest racial, sexual, and spectatorial stakes.[55]

Such filmic representations are clearly embedded in a larger web of cultural discourses, the most obvious being the rhetoric of lynching that preceded them and the cinematic traditions of shooting white woman as spectacle that would follow. Presaging by nearly a century Angela Davis's critique of "the myth of the black rapist," Ida B. Wells identified the sexual politics of lynching in terms easily extendable to Hollywood's classic miscegenation fantasies.[56] Discussing black feminist writings from the late nineteenth century, Hazel Carby cites Wells when she explains that, once "black disenfranchisement and Jim Crow segregation had been achieved . . . the annihilation of a black political presence was shielded behind a 'screen of defending the honor of [white] women.'"[57]

Critics have shown how this logic was projected onto the cinematic screen in *The Birth of a Nation*, *The Cheat*, and *Broken Blossoms* to contain threats to white male hegemony posed not only by men of color but also by white women.[58] Such readings have been variously situated in historical contexts that make these doubly high stakes for white male privilege readily apparent: the extreme xenophobia and racism of a period marked by a recent surge of immigration, labor unrest, racial violence, Jim Crow laws, and exclusionary laws, on the one hand; and the revival of the suffrage movement and the emergence of the image of the New (White) Woman, on the other. The miscegenation fantasies of *Birth* and *The Cheat*, especially, directly transpose their anxieties regarding the political and economic threats posed by men of color into images of those men as sexual threats to white women, displacements that in turn prompt virulent punishment of the former and dramatic containment of the latter through their victimization and rescue. These classic miscegenation fantasies thus neatly fend off two kinds of "others" of white patriarchy—racial and sexual—with a single set of narrative and cinematic devices.

But the classic silent miscegenation films do more than reiterate the rhetoric of lynching at the movies; they unleash and elaborate it in particularly cinematic ways. As Robert Lang writes in regard to *Birth*: "The film's obsession with miscegenation is the key to its structure and meaning as a melodrama."[59] Put otherwise, this obsession scripts the film's content and further gives rise to its historically lauded cinematic form. The plot develops from four escalating scenarios of black men pursuing white women: the "guerilla" soldiers' raid on the Camerons' home in Piedmont; Gus's pursuit of Flora; the black soldiers' surrounding of the Cameron family in "the little cabin"; and Silas Lynch's attempted forced marriage to Elsie Stoneman.[60] These scenarios in turn generate much of the film's most famous editing and mise-en-scène: most notably, Gus chasing Flora through the woods, prompting her suicidal leap to escape him, and the Klan's epic ride to rescue Elsie and the Cameron family in the final sequence. What is more, as the organizing principle that gives the film its overarching structural unity (the rape-revenge plot) and generates discrete and linked causal chains of narrative action elaborated through cinematic continuity devices, the film's primary miscegenation fantasy is clearly the narrative kernel out of which emerges its innumerable demonstrations of classical cinematic form.[61]

With significant echoes of the film's own rhetoric, the specter of miscegenation haunted virtually every aspect of *Birth*'s production and reception as well—from the segregation of the cast on the set and off (as well as of theater audiences) to heated public exchanges following the film's release.[62] On at least two occasions Griffith responded to his film's critics by calling them "people who believe in the intermarriage of the races."[63] One such accusation came in response to an editorial that condemned the film for "pander[ing] to depraved tastes and . . . foment[ing] race antipathy": "To present the members of the [black] race as [white] women-chasers and foul fiends is a cruel distortion of history. Bad things occurred, but what man will say that the outrages of black on white equalled in number the outrages of white on black? Which race even to the present day has the better right to complain of the unfairness and brutality of the other?"[64] Griffith's published response to this critique cites "an organized attack of letter writers, publicity seekers, and fanatics against our work," a campaign he conjures in deeply conspiratorial tones: "We have traced this attack to its source, and know the reasons for it."[65] After first withholding them, he eventually names names and accuses the "fanatics" of being themselves parties to miscegenation:

The attack of the organized opponents to this picture is centered upon that feature of it which they deem might become an influence against the intermarriage of blacks and whites. The organizing opponents are white leaders of the National Association for the Advancement of the Colored People, including Oswald Garrison Villard and J. E. Spingarn, who hold official positions in this prointermarriage organization.

May I inquire if you desire to espouse the cause of a society which openly boasts in its official organ, *The Crisis,* that it has been able to throttle "anti-intermarriage legislation" in over ten states? Do you know what this society means by "anti-intermarriage legislation"? It means that they successfully opposed bills which were framed to prohibit the marriage of Negroes to whites.

Do you know that in their official organ, *The Crisis,* for March 1915, they brand 238 members of the Sixty-third Congress as "Negro baiters" because these Representatives voted to prohibit the marriage of Negroes to whites in the District of Columbia? (169)

Here Griffith repeats a primary rhetorical gesture from his film: to fend off a critique of his racial/racist vision, he figures the critics themselves as miscegenating aggressors, in this case ones conspiring to "throttle" legal attempts to secure the dominant racial order.[66] This extrafilmic discourse thus echoes the film's own structuring paradox, obsessively conjuring the very desire it ostensibly seeks to eradicate.

Birth inadvertently announces this structural dependence when, in an intertitle, it names interracial desire, in a clear adulteration of the film's own title, "the weakness that . . . blight[s] a nation." While the film's actual title is never overtly stated within the diegesis, this shadow title sets it up to be read as the overcoming of such miscegenetic "weakness." At the same time, the textual play between this "blight" and its opposing "Birth" forever joins the two, virtually announcing that the film and the pure white "nation" it attempts to produce both fundamentally depend upon the fantasy of miscegenation. And the film itself of course bears this out, as its purifying project requires the possibility of such contaminating encounters and uses the conjured threat of the black rapist to justify white men terrorizing, and as some accounts of the original version have it, expressly castrating and eradicating, black men.[67]

We should go no further, however, without recognizing that while *Birth* repeatedly fantasizes miscegenation through scenarios in which black men pursue white women, its compulsive fantasy of the black rapist is itself the product of a profound historical and textual relocation of interracial desire, a relocation that is in fact marked by the film itself. For the "blight" of the intertitle in question punctuates an encounter between Austin Stoneman (Ralph Lewis), the white Northern congressman, and Lydia (Mary Alden), his mulatto housekeeper, and the "weakness" is here clearly legible as the white man's own.[68] At one level, as Michael Rogin has argued in his tour de force reading of *Birth*, the film thus projects sexual economies characteristic of the racial and domestic arrangements that obtained in the South onto the North.[69] What is more, by Rogin's formulation, with its preferred fantasy of miscegenation the film systematically "displaces sexuality from white men to women to blacks in order, by the subjugation and disempowerment of blacks, to re-empower white men" (213). This combined set of reversals and substitutions, I would add, will arguably become the most profound and consequential of the many unearthed in this book, because with it the historical legacy of sexual exploitation sanctioned under slavery is replaced with the Jim Crow era fantasy of the black rapist, a substitution that will forever mark the meaning and memory of interracial desire in the popular American imagination.[70]

While *Birth* is of course by no means alone in scripting such a profound revision of interracial sexual history (as is evidenced most obviously by the history of lynching and its rhetoric), the particular contributions of such a phenomenally popular and influential film are formidable indeed—not only for popular film history, I would argue, but also for the cultural production and dissemination of racial fantasy, memory, and myth more generally. Particularly striking are the ways the film's recasting functions at once to deny white male pleasures, privileges, and abuses under slavery *and* simultaneously to allow for the vivid, albeit significantly disguised, rehearsal of intense anxiety about black male claims to power, even as it also works to obliterate such claims. For while *Birth*, like *The Cheat* and *Broken Blossoms*, insists that the extreme vulnerability of white *femininity* is what is at stake, it becomes equally clear that it is the frailty of white *masculinity*, and its claims to authority and privilege, that these fantasies worry over most and work most vigilantly to protect. Even though the Southern-identified film projects and contains white male "weakness" by figuring it as a blight that issues from the North, a reading of the text as a whole quickly verifies that such conditions, generally conceived, are not regionally bound. Rather, in the face of the palpable susceptibility of white men in both the North and the South, *Birth* systematically displaces its fears about the breakdown of white patriarchy through its increasingly elaborate scenarios of the assault of white women.

This displacement is most obvious when one considers the means through which Griffith rescues, in one and the same gesture, Elsie Stoneman, white culture, and white patriarchal privilege. As Rogin points out, Griffith himself gestured toward the condensation of multiple categories into the singular body of a white woman when he described his inspirational reading of Thomas Dixon's *The Clansman* and his visions of bringing it to the screen: "Now I could see a chance to do this ride-to-the-rescue on a grand scale. Instead of saving one little Nell of the Plains, this ride would be to save the nation."[71] This recollection confesses several things. Insofar as the fantasy of miscegenation serves as the device by which "one little Nell" becomes a synecdoche for the nation, it draws attention to the ways in which the "birth" of that psychic and ideological fiction is mapped through boundaries of racial and sexual difference. And those boundaries, as the previous chapter reminds us, are drawn on (and off) screen through a particular set of cinematic forms—the chase, women trapped in the house, the race to the rescue, and so forth—with a long history of their own. While that chapter confronted how such projects had earlier come together in ways that were by no means originally or seamlessly "classical," I will now consider how *Birth* realized its more classical vision only with the continued substitution of white women for white men, and the concomitant reconfiguration of black and white masculinity and the spectator.

White Men Suffer at War, White Women Suffer at Home

That *Birth* employs white women to suffer on behalf of white men would explain why a contemporary review takes issue with the fact that the film's avenging white male hero—the only son of three to survive the Civil War, who then goes on to lead the Klan's climactic ride to rescue white woman, and in effect all of white culture, from the hands of black men—comes out of it all a bit too unscathed: "He might at times have shown a little trace of the grime and the hardship of soldiering. It seemed somewhat improbable that a soldier could look so trim and spick and span after what 'the little Colonel' passed through."[72] Recognizing that what has transpired in *Birth* should have taken a remarkable toll on this white male body and soul, the observation is all the more pertinent in light of prior incarnations of the "little Colonel" in actor Henry Walthall's Biograph roles as Southern soldiers with war wounds openly displayed. Indeed, despite this significant transformation of white masculinity, *Birth* looks like an elaborate collage of the short films explored in chapter 1. In addition to shared Civil War vignettes and motifs (soldiers going off to war, women left behind, etc.), here again Griffith's stock cinematic methods of articulating racial and sexual difference through chases, captivity scenarios, and various forms of bondage are assembled to fantasize the fragility of white male power. However, in *Birth*, unlike the Biograph films, the psychic traces of the "grime and hardship" of such fantasies are not nearly as visible. The remarkable transformation of Walthall's performance in particular, from infirm masculinity (as quintessentially exemplified in *The House with Closed Shutters*) to the "trim and spick and span" heroism of *Birth*, begs us to consider what exactly the little Colonel has "passed through" to enable this resurrection.

Although rarely as severe or permanent as in the Biograph films, images of white male suffering are clearly visible in *Birth*. Yet the differences are significant. The fragile and flawed white men unable to support phallic demands are not the young ones, as in the earlier Civil War films, but the older patriarchs—Dr. Cameron (Spottiswoode Aitken) of the Southern family and Austin Stoneman of the Northern one. Cameron is visibly ill throughout the film, and in the hysteria of the finale we find "the master in chains paraded before his former slaves." And Stoneman's "weakness" is marked on his own deficient body from the outset. In the film's first properly diegetic image, we see his daughter, Elsie, adjust his obvious wig, and the film later calls attention again to this wig, as well as to his cane, clubfoot, and pronounced limp.[73] These physical imperfections clearly foreshadow his sexual and political flaws to come.

In the context of this less than masterful portrait of white male fathers, the condition and fate of white male sons are all the more critical, for it is at their feet that the burden of restoring patriarchy is laid. Here the contrast with Griffith's Biograph versions of the Civil War is most pronounced, as the young men of *Birth* do not flee from the hardships of battle but heroically embrace them. Within the flash of a single intertitle, the film skips over the early years of the war, bypassing the South's initial military hope and occasional victories, moving instantly from the troops' departure for Bull Run to "Two and a half years later"; the film thus quickly turns its focus in part 1 to war's "bitter, useless, sacrifice."[74] Here the men of *Birth* die noble and heroic deaths, never hesitating to sacrifice themselves for the cause.[75] This is largely possible because the war's psychic toll is most visibly played out on the surface of female bodies. While men are composed in tragic postures of death on a few striking occasions, it is women who more often, and more increasingly, endure the most excessive symptoms of grief, anger, hysteria, and even shell shock.

The better part of the film's first half is split between scenes of battle and scenes on the home front, which also, if differently, linger over the losses of war.[76] Following an exchange of letters that ties the little Colonel, Ben Cameron, "in the field" to his now "big" little sister Flora (Mae Marsh) at home, the most trying times begin.[77] Significantly, the turn to violence and loss begins not with Ben's or his brothers' experience on the battlefield but with that of his mother and sisters when an "irregular force of [mostly black] guerillas" led by a "scalawag white captain" raid Piedmont and the Camerons' home. Setting up the first of four race-to-rescue-white-women-from-black-men scenarios, the film here encloses Flora, her older sister, Margaret (Miriam Cooper), and their mother

(Josephine Crowell) deeper and deeper within the house as they flee behind one door after another, finally hiding from their pursuers in a stairwell to the cellar. Thus replaying Griffith's by now well rehearsed editing of the hide-and-seek arrangement, the film invites us to worry over the fate of the girls as the black soldiers (one with partially exposed arms and chest) penetrate the house, door by door, room by room. While we are here quickly primed in the grammar that will recur in increasingly dramatic scenarios to come, we are let off the hook relatively quickly in this first case. Nevertheless, the girls' potential danger is strikingly marked by Flora's seemingly hysterical reaction in the stairwell. As Griffith cuts back and forth from the girls to the intruders, we twice see her visibly giggling, presumably overwhelmed with an excitement that, however sexually ambiguous, clearly demonstrates her being psychically, if not quite physically, overtaken.

The Piedmont raid is particularly significant for the racial and sexual politics it cinematically orchestrates through the fantasy of black men nearly overtaking white women, and for its relation to the war sequences that immediately follow it. Whereas the myth of the black rapist was historically conjured after the war to constrain black men when slavery had ceased to do so, *Birth* retroactively inserts the myth to affectively punctuate and historically revise the war's beginning as well. In so doing, the relation of the Piedmont raid to the extensive battle footage that follows sets up what will become the film's preferred gendering of white suffering and loss. Firing the war's first onscreen shot, as it were, at these white women, and thus unleashing Flora and Margaret's horror and hysteria, the film emotionally sets the tone for, and in some respects safeguards us from, the male suffering to come. Whereas the medium close-ups of Margaret's fright and Flora's giggles invite us here, as elsewhere, to relish their psychic violation in intimate detail, the film will go on to show the horror of battle—with a few important exceptions—mostly at a considerable distance, in the epic dimensions of long shots and extreme long shots.[78]

The stage affectively set with this first attack on white womanhood, the film moves into its extended contemplation of "war's sad page." Alternating between the spaces of battle and domesticity, it takes us through a series of losses as they occur on the front and are then emotionally registered at home. The film continually orchestrates the weeping and prostration of women who, like an emoting Greek chorus, act out the escalation of trauma and loss. This tendency is emphasized cinematically in the scene of *Birth*'s famous pan that travels from a medium close-up of a mother and her children huddled together in despair on a hillside to a high-angle, extreme long shot of Sherman's march driving through the valley down below them. As if the pan alone could be misunderstood,

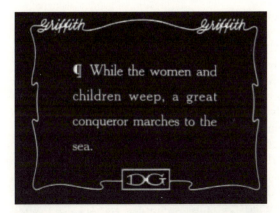

FIG. 2.1. "While the women and children weep. . . ." *The Birth of a Nation* (1915).

FIG. 2.2. The epic pan that lands on Sherman's march at a distance.

FIG. 2.3. Images of maternal suffering bookend the distant image of the march.

an intertitle prepares us for it: "While the women and children weep, a great conqueror marches to the sea" (fig. 2.1). Moving continuously from the weeping maternal image to the distant march, the film carefully binds them together. It then cuts back to a medium close-up of the family, back again to the distant march (fig. 2.2), and finally again to the family (fig. 2.3). At one level this maternal suffering that visually bookends Sherman's march tells the story of families devastated by war; but at another it dramatically demonstrates the film's ongoing method for registering grief and loss, on the agonized bodies of women and children.[79]

Dramatic exceptions to this general rule include a close-up of worn soldiers' hands preparing to eat "parched corn their only rations" and a medium shot of a heap of dead male bodies wounded and contorted in a highly stylized, almost Mannerist, composition (figs. 2.4–2.5). In both of these unforgettable shots, as in a few other medium and long shots of dead soldiers on the field, white male suffering is visibly rendered on white male bodies. But the differences between these images and those of women suffering at home are substantial. The shot of faceless hands struggling to survive moves beyond the specificity and psychic pain of individual men and renders instead a portrait of the heroic, anonymous suffering of Man and/as the South. Similarly, the images of already dead bodies, though gruesome and tragic, shift to a moment beyond actual suffering and weakness, and memorialize instead the monumental losses of the war as an epic whole. We do not see men who still breathe and move amid the dead; instead, Griffith focuses on final breaths—the Cameron and Stoneman brothers dying in each other's arms—and the shocking carcasses left behind. Hence, even when wounded male bodies are literally close to view, such images keep the psychic experience of battle at a considerable distance.

Indeed, the most psychically present face we see during the battlefield sequences is that of the (here nicknamed) little Colonel at his most phallic, charging forth wildly as he "leads the final desperate assault against the Union command." Visually foreshadowing the Klan's climactic ride, Ben's charge is shot with a camera that swiftly tracks backward as he runs fiercely forward (fig. 2.6). His assault may be "desperate" and doomed, but he is represented with all the movement and purpose of a conquering hero. And, in now typical fashion, as Ben and his company charge and face Union fire, the film cuts back to a tableau of the Cameron home, where mother and children strike a frozen, painterly pose of mourning as a disheveled Dr. Cameron prays (fig. 2.7).

This gendered distribution of psychic labor continues to war's end and beyond. After news of the death of the second Cameron son and the wounding of the third reaches the family home, our experience of battle ends much as it began with a return to the Cameron women. But now the

FIG. 2.4. Heroic images of white masculinity: "parched corn their only rations."

FIG. 2.5. A stylized composition (bathed in red) of dead men on the battlefield.

FIG. 2.6. Ben Cameron (Henry Walthall), "the little Colonel," charges on the battlefield.

devastation escalates with a new set of emotional performances. Adding to the weeping and shock of earlier scenes, the news of her brothers' fate intensifies Flora's grief, transforming it first to rage and then to apparent catatonia. After an intertitle announces, "War, the breeder of hate," Mae Marsh performs as much in an outburst of angry gestures—throwing down the letter that has conveyed the grim news, clenching her fists, and grabbing her sister by the shoulders. But these sentiments fade as she lands in an almost hypnotic trance, staring blankly into the distance and slightly wobbling, numbly (fig. 2.8), until her sister comforts her. Having brought these tortured reactions to this frenzied climax, the film pauses to openly designate their role in the larger drama, naming them in a title that announces simply: "The woman's part" (fig. 2.9).

If the first half of *Birth* alternates between the spaces of war and home to register and deflect male loss through female mourning, the second half thoroughly sloughs off any vestiges of white male trauma once and for all, repositing it entirely onto white women and black men. I will turn to the relation between black and white men momentarily, but one last consideration of the relation between white men and women is in order here. For the cinematic form of that relation is most vivid in a scene well into the second half, when the men have returned from war. The scene in question opens with the intertitle: "Bitter memories will not allow the poor bruised heart of the South to forget." That injured Southern "heart" is then embodied in the image of a wistful Margaret Cameron sitting alone in the garden, gazing downward as she fingers (and "bruise[s]") a rose that also falls to pieces. Like us, Phil Stoneman (Elmer Clifton) catches Margaret in this private moment. After spotting her from a distance, he approaches and moves to touch her from across a fence. Margaret pulls away and exits the frame, further isolating herself in a thicker part of the garden, now in a frame by herself. She stares off into the distance and crushes another flower tightly in her grip. Her face changes from the melancholic expressions of the earlier shot to a mesmerized, wide-eyed stare that recalls Flora's earlier trancelike performance (fig. 2.10). The image fades to black, and an iris shot marks a flashback of Margaret's brother Wade (Maxfield Stanley) as we have seen him earlier in the battle footage, dead in another soldier's arms (fig. 2.11).[80] When the flashback ends, the image fades in to Margaret, who still stares widely as if transfixed by the vision (fig. 2.12).

The intertitle's narration of this sequence would have us read it as marking the "bitter memories" of lingering regional resentment that still separate (Southern) Margaret and (Northern) Phil.[81] But, particularly striking in the context of this chapter, the flashback delivered as Margaret's cinematically inserts into her memory an image she cannot have seen. She does not recall her brother at home as they once were together,

FIG. 2.7. The female Camerons, posed in mourning back at home.

FIG. 2.8. Little Sister (Mae Marsh) numb with grief.

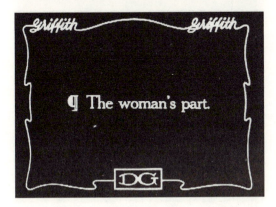

FIG. 2.9. The film expressly names the gendered distribution of representational labor.

FIG. 2.10. A woman, Margaret Cameron (Miriam Cooper), is transfixed by war memories.

FIG. 2.11. The battlefield flashback that haunts Margaret (not Phil or Ben).

FIG. 2.12. A return to Margaret seals the memory as hers.

or even in some imagined battlefield scenario, but lying there exactly as only we and other soldiers have seen him. And even though the additional shot of the younger Cameron and Stoneman brothers dying in each other's arms earlier invited us to imagine precisely such male union at the moment of suffering and death, ironically the surviving veterans, Phil and Ben, are free of such haunted memories. In the scene prior to this one, Ben charms Elsie with a dove, and here Phil attempts to woo Margaret, grinning about in the foliage, seemingly oblivious to the visions that torment her instead. Hence, the men we saw endure lengthy, bloody (red-tinted) battle now appear psychically "spick and span," while a woman bears the most visible and debilitating traces of the psychic "grime and hardship of soldiering."[82]

This systematic gendering of affect during and well after the Civil War allows us to understand with hindsight the tremendous representational consequences of, in effect, beginning that war with the guerilla raid on Piedmont. For even before the film fully unleashes its obsessions with black rapists, it has deployed the classic miscegenation fantasy so as to script "victim" as quintessentially white and female in a way that is particularly suited to the task of soothing and overcoming white male wounds, be they in the form of war trauma or anxieties about Reconstruction. Indeed, pulling back from the frame of *Birth* alone to the wider text of Griffith's corpus as it extends back to Biograph, we can already see how the fantasy of the black rapist offers an "ideal" solution to what in the Biograph Civil War films repeatedly appears as a *gender* crisis for white masculinity. Henry Walthall no longer weeps, binges, or hides because an ever more elaborate representational scheme moves ever more fluidly (through the juxtaposition of scenes, the varied distances of the camera, flashbacks, etc.) to register the most devastating effects of his travails upon the bodies and psyches of his mother, sisters, and wife-to-be.

These representations of war in part 1 directly pave the way for those of Reconstruction in part 2. And, we can see already that (what has come to be) the conventionality of *Birth*'s repeated spectacles of suffering white women should not blind us to their multiple functions and effects. For these images testify that very early in the classical canon such imagery was bound up with racial and national politics, as well as sexual and cinematic ones, and in more complex and contradictory ways than we have formerly recognized.[83] As we have seen, *Birth*'s images of tortured white women serve not only as the excuse to lynch black men and the means to contain white women but also as the vehicle to express white male suffering and loss. What is more, insofar as the viewer is invited to look not just *at* the white woman bound and bruised but at times *as* that woman, we might describe her as functioning like a racialized version of horror cinema's "final girl" as theorized by Carol Clover: soliciting a cross-gender identification, the white woman under siege allows the white male viewer to fantasize a kind of "race horror" that is psychically and even sexually explicit, but representationally tolerable through the substitution of her body in place of one like his own.[84] As my analysis suggests, this happens at times through compositions and juxtapositions of shots and scenes that channel the onscreen affect of loss through white women. As we will see later in this chapter, it is also encouraged by the film's increasingly elaborate choreography of space and time through editing. At its most intense such editing induces a kind of spectatorial captivity not unlike those bound and transfixed states endured by the film's virginal victims, even as it also offers us cinematic forms of escape perpetually denied them.

TOO MANY MEN

Increasingly in *Birth*'s second half, women no longer suffer part of the time in alternation with white men or as occasional psychic substitutes for them but are so repeatedly the target of black men that suffering becomes their primary function. Whereas Flora managed to keep the home fires burning with faith and spunk while Ben was away, and gives him a hero's welcome upon his return, soon after she is spectacularly sacrificed to justify and advance the film's white supremacist vision. The hysterical force with which the fantasy of the black rapist is unleashed in part 2 is so excessive that any lingering traces of white male loss from part 1 are entirely eclipsed by, and relentlessly worked over through, portraits of white women in agony at the hands of black men.

Birth reveals the political motivation behind this fantasy by endlessly equating black male desire for white women with black male desire for social and political power. This equation is literally written on a sign we see repeatedly at black political meetings and at the polling place in the election that will bring a black majority to the South Carolina legislature: it demands "Equality" in large letters, defining that in smaller print as "Equal Rights, Equal Politics, Equal Marriage." This platform becomes law when the black majority takes office. The two pieces of legislation the new lawmakers pass include a mandate that "all whites must salute negro officers on the streets" and another that legalizes "the intermarriage of blacks and whites." Having planted this pair of seeds, the imagined double agenda of power over white men and white women, the film immediately grows and intertwines them. Just after the scene of new black legislators celebrating the passage of the intermarriage bill, an ominous intertitle declares: "The grim reaping begins." Next we see, in this order: Gus (Walter Long) spying on Flora and Elsie from behind a tree before they are approached by Silas Lynch; Ben angered first at Lynch's greeting of Elsie and Flora, and then at Gus's insubordination on the street; and in the immediately following scene a brooding Ben "in agony of soul over the degradation and ruin of his people" until he is inspired with his originary vision of the Klan. The act of defiance toward Ben (not white womanhood) that immediately follows the newly sanctioned act of interracial voyeurism, and immediately precedes the birth of the Klan (and Gus's pursuit of Flora in the woods soon to come), implicitly reveals that the film's vision of the black rapist is in fact utterly bound up with the perceived threat to white masculinity. In its wake Flora will once again suffer for Ben, this time taking the fatal brunt of the black man's demand for equal treatment.

As successful as this gender substitution is at safeguarding white masculinity from immediate psychic and ideological risk, however, it brings with it a new set of representational complications. For while *Birth*'s triangular miscegenation plot dramatically cleaves white manliness from white womanliness, and offers up white women as the sacrificial victims of (imagined) black aggression, it also produces a formidable male rival. Indeed, by going out of its way to establish the threat that black men pose to white women, the film continually emphasizes the potential potency of black masculinity. This typically results in an emphasis on black male sexuality, as in the images of half-naked black male bodies penetrating the Cameron home, for example, or of Silas Lynch rubbing his widespread thighs as he savors Elsie's panic following his "proposal of marriage." Despite its dual "utility" in fighting racial and sexual battles, the film's primary miscegenation fantasy thus carries with it a significant representational dilemma, the production of too many men.

Amid *Birth*'s more than two-and-a-half-hour buildup to the crescendo of its most fully developed miscegenation scenario (when Lynch holds Elsie captive with intentions of a "forced marriage"), one extremely brief and almost forgettable scene stands out in this context. Not unlike the way the scene of Ben's altercation with Gus on the street is tucked between Gus's spying on Elsie and the conception of the Klan that will ostensibly punish black men for their crimes against white women, sandwiched exactly between Flora's suicide and the retaliatory murder of Gus is a scene that oddly confesses who the film fears to be the real victim at issue in these atrocities. Most unexpectedly, the scene of the search for Gus not only figures white men in literal postures of violation but further meditates on the precariousness of white male claims to phallic privilege.

All this transpires, ostensibly, in the search for Gus. He hides because Flora has just leapt to her death from a cliff in order to escape his (slow) approach. The Klan immediately mobilizes to capture and punish him. It eventually does so, but the film takes the manhunt as an opportunity, however unconsciously, to reflect on the representational stakes in question. Two moments during the hunt for Gus are of particular note. The most obvious is when, following a row between (uncredited) black men and a white blacksmith (Wallace Reid) looking for Gus at a saloon, the black men take the upper hand and assault the white man. While the camera has drawn our attention to this white blacksmith's physical prowess earlier in the sequence (we have seen him carry a heavy iron anvil in one shot, and display his muscular torso and flexed muscles in others), and while he initially dominates his (nine!) opponents in the bar brawl, the tables turn when one of the black men draws a gun. Upon exiting the saloon the blacksmith is first shot from behind; the gun is then passed to Gus, who quickly shoots at him again, this time aiming roughly in the direction of his crotch. In these pointed, albeit brief, allusions to anal rape and castration of a white man by a black man—the same black man who has just nearly raped (we are asked to believe), and thus prompted the death of, a white girl; and upon whom vengeance will soon be brutally wreaked—the film flashes upon the screen a momentary admission of whose violation and subordination is in fact of deepest concern in the surrounding instances. Indeed, the scene would seem to momentarily belie the film's obsessive interest in fantasies of white women being raped and black men being castrated as projected reversals of, and punishment for, the film's fear of white male submission. And if ever there were a "safe" moment to slip in the psychic truth, this would be it: with the image of Flora's dead body still lingering on our retinas and Gus's soon to (gruesomely) replace it, this fleeting moment in between quickly fades in spectatorial memory.

At the same time, an earlier moment in the sequence suggests perhaps an even greater, though less explicit, horror that itself must be replaced (according to the dominant logic of the film) before we think about it too much. Shortly after the blacksmith has entered the bar (or "ginmill," as an intertitle calls it), he questions its proprietor, a white actor in blackface identified as "'white-arm' Joe" (Elmo Lincoln). When the smith turns away, Joe pulls him back in a gesture the smith reads as provocation. What ensues, at the level of narrative, is an altercation between Joe and the smith that leads to the eruption of the barroom brawl mentioned earlier. Of particular interest is the visual articulation of the tension between Joe and the smith. Their initial conversation transpires in a full shot in which the standing smith fills the height of the frame, flanked by a group of black men in the background on the left and Joe, who rises from a chair on the right to a slightly shorter height. Once Joe grabs the smith, the film cuts to a closer view of the two, who now face each other in a medium shot, their upper torsos filling the frame (fig. 2.13). Both men wear sleeveless shirts that fully expose their arms and partially expose their chests. The smith's shirt is bright white against his pale body, and Joe's is dark against his somewhat darker body. They lock eyes. The smith faces us almost frontally, with clenched fists that bulge the veins in his tightly flexed arms. Joe faces him such that the side of his body faces us, revealing his bare arm and a glimpse of his plump and hairy upper body. The screen momentarily goes black, then fades in to a medium close-up of the smith alone, still staring intently, still solidly stiff. He slowly raises his right hand and slowly begins to form a fist, a gesture that accentuates his well-developed and well-defined muscles (fig. 2.14). A cut to Gus hiding beneath the bar shows him peering up at the smith and furrowing his brow. Returning to the medium close-up of the smith, we see him fully clench his fist and slowly pull it down. Answering these imposing shots, the film cuts back to another side view of Joe, who continues to stare back in anger and begins to shake his head and speak. This shot brings us in for our closest view of Joe's large, flabby "white-arm"—an arm clearly not blacked up like the actor's face—and his chubby, hairy body (fig. 2.15).

I recount these images in detail for their striking visual fascination with the bodies of these two men. In the midst of a film which elsewhere insists that the danger of the black male body lies in the threat it poses to white women, this extended, and narratively unnecessary, meditation on the juxtaposed images of ostensibly black and white male bodies not only foregrounds the power play between black and white men at issue but momentarily digresses from the revenge plot just set in motion to visually linger over the difference, and sameness, of these two bodies. Indeed, inserted precisely between Flora's death and Gus's murder (and likely castration), this scene would seem to acknowledge that what is in fact at issue is the degree to which these two male bodies can be equated and/or differentiated.[85] The signs of differentiation are obvious. Despite their ironically reversed names, the juxtaposition of "white-arm" Joe and the blacksmith perpetually emphasizes the whiteness of one and the blackness of the other. In addition to the contrast of light and dark clothing and skin, the film adds the illuminating effect of the fade-in to further brighten the pale white male body. And it clearly extends its connotations of white and black to the shape and texture of these bodies, emphasizing the smith's taut and muscular form in contrast to Joe's round and undefined corpulence.

Yet the obvious efforts to differentiate these two male bodies must also be read in relation to their visible similarities. Their potential sameness is implicit not only in the racial ambiguity of a black man who goes by the nickname of "white-arm" and who (in visible contrast to some of the other black actors in the bar) is played by a white actor, but also in the comparable markings of gender and class. Certainly the literal and figura-

FIG. 2.13. Two male bodies compared.

FIG. 2.14

FIG. 2.15

tive elevations of the smith work to unsettle the comparison, but the shots that face them off against each other, repeatedly juxtaposing their similarly clad bodies, nonetheless invite us to see them as two somewhat comparable types of working-class men. Unexpectedly, then, and potentially catastrophically for the film's vision of black and white power relations, the implication seems to be that these men are not different enough.[86]

The problem visualized at the gin mill, in other words, comes down to this: having created and extensively flaunted the cinematic image of a hypersexed black male, how now can the film distinguish between white and black masculinity so as to defend one claim to phallic privilege over another? As my descriptions of Joe and the smith indicate, some predictable solutions are already at work in this scene. Like Western culture generally, *Birth* defines the black male body as, in effect, all body, and elevates the white male one to some more refined state beyond that.[87] Joe is short, hairy, and fat; the smith is tall, smooth, and rigid. The long, slow displays of the smith's well-veined arm rising and falling figure his as a posture of phallic potency as compared with Joe's obvious flaccidity. And the distinction of penis from phallus here will turn out to be far more than a jargon-ready reading of the sequence, as the film will increasingly conjure it to enforce a differentiation between these two kinds of men. One will be endlessly equated with carnality and bodily limitation; the other will be endlessly lifted up to a comparatively omnipotent mode of authority and symbolic abstraction.

Birth's efforts to firmly fix black masculinity in the body are seemingly inexhaustible. Amid the many scenes of blacks working in the fields, dancing, lusting after white women, and so forth, the scene of the newly elected legislature stands out for its relentless reduction of black men to states of physicality at precisely the moment when they have technically acceded to a position of symbolic power. In this scene titled "The riot in the Master's Hall," Griffith features the black legislators in one outrageously inappropriate bodily display after another. While at the front of the room leaders of the House attempt to conduct business in an orderly fashion, the camera cuts between several slovenly members at their desks on the House floor. One eats with his mouth open, another sneaks a drink from a flask, a third takes off his boots in a close-up to rest and wiggle his naked feet on his desk, and a fourth gnaws and waves about a large joint of meat while addressing his colleagues.[88] When a flamboyantly dressed gentlemen complains of the smell of the exposed feet, the whole legislative process is sullied by this carnal display: "The speaker rules that all members must wear shoes." Following the passage of a second bill, the one that requires whites to salute black officers, the overarching chaos soon to climax with the intermarriage bill is further marked by a long shot that captures the roomful of black leaders moving carelessly about the room, several in gaudy striped and checkered jackets. This group portrait of disorderly conduct is then contrasted to "the help-less white minority" that looks upon it. Positioned as if seated among them, the camera shoots from behind their white-haired heads as they sit quietly in neat rows bearing witness. This scene thus not only refuses the serious possibility of black power by insisting on the embodied limits of black masculinity but also gestures toward the representational alterna-tive that the film will increasingly articulate for white masculinity.

A Gaze among Looks

The foregoing attempts to differentiate black and white masculinity are compounded by many others in the film that assert two very different kinds of male vision. To understand these it is again useful to invoke Kaja Silverman's distinction of the look from the gaze. Whereas the gaze refers to an abstracted, authoritative form of vision beyond any individual human eye, she suggests, the look can be understood as that compara-tively impotent form of human vision.[89] Like feminist theory's distinction of penis from phallus, this one also seeks to disentangle a bodily attribute or function from a cultural or symbolic position of privilege that is often claimed with recourse to, but in fact has no natural relation to, its bio-logical correlate. While it is not uncommon for dominant culture to de-fine black masculinity around the penis, over and against phallic depic-tions of white masculinity, *Birth* goes further; it inscribes the distinction in visual, and particularly cinematic, terms. The difference between these two types of men, the film systematically insists, is that although black men can (voraciously) look at the white woman, they can never assume the position of phallic mastery that visually possesses her, and indeed all it surveys.

The authority of white male vision is established early on in *Birth* in a way that not only exemplifies classical feminist models of the male (look posing as) gaze but further demonstrates the racial and economic sup-ports upon which such claims to visual mastery depend. Indeed, during the Northern Stoneman boys' visit to the Southern Camerons, when the film paints its nostalgic image of the status quo before the war, it cine-matically articulates an elaborate visual regime that simultaneously posi-tions the variously marked bodies on screen, and the film's own specta-tor, to form an intricate, interlocked structure of racial, sexual, and economic relations.[90]

The sequence consists of roughly three segments, each worthy of some thick description to fully demonstrate the visual regime in question. In the first we see Ben Cameron and his "little sister" Flora, and then Phil

Stoneman and Margaret Cameron, walk "over the plantation to the cotton fields." We then have an intimate glimpse of Phil and Margaret in a private moment, tucked between a picket fence in the foreground and the Camerons' plantation home in the background, and nestled on all sides by the canopy of an old oak and warm, dappled light. The romance continues in the next shot, but the camera pulls back a sizable distance to place the lovers in a pastoral river landscape, strolling among pines and a pair of cows. The shot fades in from black with an iris that continues to encircle the image, further marking it as emphatically picturesque. The iris closes in on the image, and an intertitle nominates the landscape and narrates their journey, "By Way of Love Valley." Following another encircled view of the lovers in the valley, the second segment begins.

The romantic melody from the previous shots continues without interruption, but this time when the light fades in from darkness we see slaves working in sun-drenched cotton fields. Our first view is a long shot filled entirely with cotton plants, out of which emerge two slaves bending and picking in the middle ground. More than a dozen hunched-over bodies are barely visible in the extreme background (fig. 2.16). A high-angle medium shot brings us up and over for a closer view of the two men in the foreground, and our inspection culminates in an extreme close-up of black arms and hands picking white cotton. The camera then pulls back to its original long shot, but now Ben strolls through the image, his dark top hat and tails sharply popping him out from the cotton into which the slaves now almost disappear. He is joined by his sister Flora, and then by Phil and Margaret. A medium shot moves in to capture the three young white adults in the foreground, slaves working all the while in the background. Phil, also in top hat and tails, gestures to Margaret over a small book, and Ben gazes upon a cotton flower (fig. 2.17). The camera offers us an extreme close-up of the flower, as Ben slowly twirls it for us to enjoy along with him (fig. 2.18). As he passes it on to Phil, he sees, and takes in exchange, the small book. As Ben focuses intently upon what he sees in it, we see his lips move, "Who is it?", and Phil mouths in response, "My sister." Ben is openly smitten, tips his hat as if to introduce himself to the girl in the little picture, and exits the frame to be alone with his newfound object of desire. A second medium shot now frames Ben virtually alone (save young Flora playing behind him), isolating him in a patch of tall corn, again with slaves working in the background. Ben continues to look off screen left to Phil and Margaret, beaming with glee and waving the picture book proudly (fig. 2.19). Spelling out what has already become evident, a title interjects: "He finds the ideal of his dreams in the picture of Elsie Stoneman, his friend's sister, whom he has never seen." We return to Ben standing amid the corn, now daring to take a good long look at the photograph as Flora exits the frame. Finally, after the long pe-

FIG. 2.16. The visual economy of the plantation begins. Black bodies merge with the landscape.

FIG. 2.17. White families take in the scenery.

FIG. 2.18. Ben and the spectator enjoy a cotton flower in close-up.

FIG. 2.19. Ben steps aside to enjoy the picture just acquired from Phil.

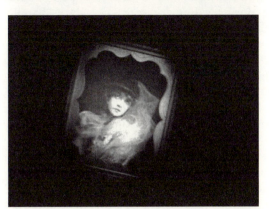

FIG. 2.20. In another point-of-view shot, Ben's first view of Elsie.

FIG. 2.21. Ben enjoys the image of the white woman.

riod of buildup and withholding, the film allows us, too, to see the portrait of Elsie in another shot aligned with Ben's point of view, a position again confirmed by another shot of him gazing at the photograph (figs. 2.20–2.21). Ben then lovingly closes the picture book and tucks it in his breast pocket, where it will effectively remain until we see him pull it out (from the breast pocket of his uniform) during the war. Throughout these shots of Ben and his introduction to Elsie via the photograph, and the subsequent ones that finish out the scene, we can almost always see, if we look for them, the bodies of slaves working at the edges of the frame. The visitors' departure from the cotton fields is marked by shots in which they travel out of the frame, leaving as if undisturbed the shot of black labor with which the scene began.

In the third segment of the plantation stroll the white party moves through the slave quarters during a dinner break. The slaves happily greet the master and his guests and spontaneously perform for their entertainment (fig. 2.22). As black men dance and clap, the white visitors watch, bemused. When they have had their fill, they move along, leaving the scene of smiling, bowing slaves, much as they left the scene of laborers bending in the fields.

This sequence relentlessly demonstrates not only that black labor forms the economic structure that makes white romance and sexuality possible (it is because slaves pick cotton in the background that white youth have the leisure time to flirt and meander in the foreground), but that those dynamics give rise to a very particular and intertwined cinematic grammar of racial and sexual difference. Here, before the "agony" of war and Reconstruction, an undisturbed state of white male authority is cinematically represented as a gaze that is both racially and sexually authoritative. The white man's visual mastery is flaunted not only in the master's leisurely surveillance of the plantation and in the exchange between men that transpires there of a white woman's image but also in the visual mapping of this racial-sexual economy for the spectator. Our look is grafted on to Ben's at key moments in this narrative, and well before and after black bodies entertain white spectators within the diegesis, they function as a kind of cinematic wallpaper (reduced to arms, backs, and legs that blend into the scenery of the "beautiful" cotton) to situate the film's spectator within the "romantic" mise-en-scène of white plantation life.[91]

As the pastoral vision of the plantation ruptures, *Birth* repeatedly registers black male challenges to white male authority as challenges to this visual regime. This occurs in the form of increasingly voracious black male looks, met in turn by increasingly omnipotent forms of white male vision. In the legislature scene, for example, whereas the "helpless white minority" is nonetheless represented by a shot from behind the white

FIG. 2.22. White spectators enjoy the spectacle of black
slaves performing for the master.

male heads that survey the action staged before them, marking their vision as an activity of minds more than eyes, black male looking is accentuated at the moment the intermarriage bill passes in highly sexualized
looks at white women. Just before the intertitle that announces the new
law, the laughter of white women in the gallery draws the eyes of black
legislators toward them in a shot in which three black men turn their
heads at the same moment, and two others look on in the background, all
five looking in the direction of the white women in a single shot. Another
shot reveals the women's nervous response to these looks, and a title then
announces the passage of the intermarriage bill. Once interracial desire is
legally sanctioned, sober black stares turn visibly into sexualized, smiling
ones, and the men leap up in celebration. This labored interarticulation
of black men's laws and black men's looks at once transposes black political power into a sexualized threat and condenses both of these in the
figure of the black male look unleashed.

Even when white women are not the alleged focal point, the textual
join between black power and black looks is vividly apparent. When Silas
Lynch and Austin Stoneman approach the door to a black political meeting (a gathering marked by the disorderly display of bodies and gestures
that sets the stage for the legislature scene to come), Lynch's knock at the
door is met by a black man's eye peering out through a peephole. The
white of this eye surrounded by dark skin is already visible in the initial
shot (a close-up of Lynch as he knocks at the door), but a second one
nonetheless moves in to an extreme close-up that magnifies the eye
and targets it with a bright shaft of light, pulling it out of the darkness

(fig. 2.23). Above and beyond the conspiratorial tone these shots set for the meeting within, this detailed focus on a black man's eye again figures the new black political threat (Lynch and Stoneman will move within to rally for support from the new black voters) as a menacing black male look. Once again, however, any rivalry this look might pose to white male claims to the gaze is quelled almost as quickly as it is registered by literally reducing it to a flat, isolated body part. If Ben and the "white minority" are all brains and authoritative vision, this soon-to-be black voter is pure eyeball.

Without detailing the full catalog, it is fair to say that such embodied black male looks stare and peep throughout the second half of the film. We have already encountered Gus peering at Elsie and Flora from a distance, a voyeurism marked by his framing through the limbs of a tree, and Silas Lynch similarly spies Elsie during one of her trysts with Ben. Moreover, in both of these sequences, as in many other shots of Lynch looking at Elsie throughout the film, the black male voyeurs are encircled in a framing iris that draws attention to their looks as spectacles in and of themselves (figs. 2.24–2.25). Whereas the classical mode of editing white men looking at white women typically works to align our look with the diegetic male look (as with our/Ben's view of Elsie's photograph), here black male looks are visually set off not only through the iris but also through their direction. Lynch often watches Elsie in setups that have him looking off screen in a direction sharply perpendicular to that of our look at him. In short, we do not look *with* these black men looking so much as we watch them watching. Unlike the classic white male voyeur, this black peeper exposed is represented not as the source of the film's vision but as one of its objects.

Doubling up its defense of white masculine claims to the gaze, *Birth* juxtaposes these images of embodied black male looks with increasingly abstracted representations of white male vision. Yoking the present discussion of racial differentiations of masculinity to the earlier discussion of sexual differentiations of whiteness (white women suffering for white men), we could say: as vulnerable whiteness becomes quintessentially mapped onto female bodies in *Birth*, white masculinity is increasingly freed up to become ever more disembodied, represented in various forms of abstraction. This is nowhere so evident as in the visual rhetoric of the Klan that renders white masculinity as something well beyond ordinary corporeality.[92] No viewer of *Birth* is soon to forget the phallic aura of white-robed and white-masked Klansmen riding swiftly on white-robed and white-masked horses, moving ever forward with the speed and direction of rushing horses and cameras, and ever upward with tall, pointed hoods and swordlike spindles rising out of their white caps (figs. 2.26–2.27). In addition to such overt imagery, the discourse surrounding

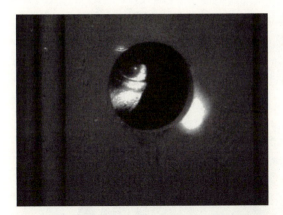

FIG. 2.23. Black looks threaten black power: a black man's eye, peeking out from a political gathering.

FIG. 2.24. Gus (Walter Long) watches white girls from a distance.

FIG. 2.25. Silas Lynch (George Seigmann) spies on Ben and Elsie.

FIG. 2.26. Hooded Klansmen ride to the rescue.
FIG. 2.27. Ben beneath the hood.

the Klan further connotes its members in phallic, gazelike terms—
removed, omniscient, seeing but not seen.

The most striking representation in this regard comes not in the Klan's
final ride but in its moment of origin. Central to the narrative chain that
will lead from black power to black sexuality to white vengeance to
white power restored, the Klan's primal scene follows just after those of
the new black legislature and its threatening effects (Gus's foreshadowing
glance at Flora and Elsie and the subsequent altercation with Ben). "In
agony of soul" over the new social order of Reconstruction, Ben seeks
solace atop a hill overlooking a river valley. This time, however, Walt-

hall's agonized performance is explicitly staged to produce forms of white male power that will solve both his and the film's primary dilemmas. As he rings his hands in despair, two white children play at the water's edge below him. With eyes cast downward in contemplation, he catches sight of them as they cover themselves in a large white sheet. When a group of younger black children happen by, they first laugh at the anonymous white mound that begins to move, but then are frightened by it. We see this little drama unfold through a series of shots that stitch Ben watching intently from above to the children's encounter (fig. 2.28). Once the black children have run off in fear, a title flashes: "The inspiration" (fig. 2.29). Ben rises to his feet and holds his arms out in triumph, now fully registering the vision (fig. 2.30). In this final shot, as throughout this scene, Ben's elevated distance from the encounter, indeed from the rest of the world, is marked by his perched vantage above the river that recedes into the horizon behind him and seems to open up in the direction of offscreen space onto which his inspirational gaze and gestures are now cast. Indeed, while the Klan is here born through what appears to be an originary drama of racial and sexual difference, its discursive origin clearly resides not in the spectacle itself but in the godly vision of the man who sees it.[93] From the start, then, the "Invisible Empire," as the film dubs the Klan, is represented as sprouting from a gaze of divine proportions.[94]

Birth's infamous grand finale elaborately weaves together the various representational maneuvers I have outlined here. In its extensive crosscutting it swiftly and strategically moves among four major spheres of action: Lynch's proposal to, and captivity of, Elsie; the Cameron family's attempt to flee black soldiers set to arrest "master" Cameron and attack his daughter; a growing black mob in the streets; and the Klansmen who ride in droves on horseback to eventually quell each of these threats. Through the articulation of more than four hundred shots, the film bombards us with by-now-familiar representations of white woman as suffering object of black male desire, black masculinity as fatally embodied, and white masculinity as triumphant, phallic ideal. As viewers of *Birth* intuitively know, it is through the calculated deployment of these three representations that the sequence attempts to lure us once and for all. Will the Klan arrive in time to save the (progressively) defiant, hysterical, unconscious, gagged, and bound Elsie from the lustful machinations of a drunken and overpowering Silas Lynch? Will that same Klan also arrive in time to save the prostrate white family in the little cabin (where white fathers ultimately hold guns to their daughters' heads in case they do not) before black soldiers break through the ultimate threshold of the cabin's innermost door?[95] And will the rescuers, finally, curb the violent mob in the streets before it grows beyond containment? These are the narrative

FIG. 2.29

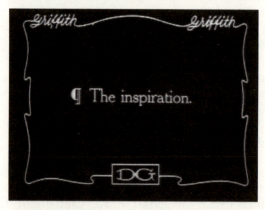

FIG. 2.30

questions perpetually dangled before us. While the film repeatedly answers at key moments with the "Yes!" sounded by shots of organizing Klansmen (immediately following Elsie's hysterical recognition of
Lynch's sexual intentions, for example), the intensity of the spectator's
"ride" is clearly calibrated by the intensity of so many fantasies to the
contrary: the breakdown of the Camerons' escape wagon, an unconscious Elsie in one room of Lynch's house while her father unknowingly
encourages her captor in the adjacent one (see fig. 1.1), an anonymous
white man tarred and feathered in the street, and so forth. It is, of course,
the combination of the film's ability to string us along to imagine the possibility of such violations with its absolute assertion of white, phallic sal-
vation that makes the finale so ideologically overwhelming. Griffith had
toyed with such cinematic effects in the Biograph films, but here he compounds and extends them all the more relentlessly.

Significantly, however, in the representational distance from Biograph
to *Birth*, yet another sphere of action emerges, and with it appears a new
cast of onscreen stand-ins that signals the means by which the filmic spectator so beset is nonetheless extended the lifelines, or sight lines, of *Birth's*
burgeoning cinematic classicism. For in the midst of the crosscutting
among the four major spheres of action, when all the dangers have been
unleashed and the risks have become most acute, a new position is suddenly inscribed in the literal form of anonymous white spectators witnessing the action within the film. After Elsie's father has left Lynch's
house and she has been tied up after an escape attempt, we see the first
close-up of her bound and gagged head with a black man's fists raised
next to it; immediately following this shot an intertitle states, "While
helpless whites look on" (fig. 2.31). We then see a series of shots of
unidentified white men and women transfixed at their windows (figs.
2.32–2.34). Although easily forgotten in the context of the monumental
dramas that drive the final half hour of the film, the placement and conditions of these "helpless whites" are of particular interest here for the
ways they clearly rhyme, and differentiate, Elsie's and our own.

Arguably, the immediate effect of the intertitle that directly follows the
close-up of Elsie bound and gagged by black hands is to inadvertently announce for whom this spectacular threat is being staged, and to textually
channel the affect of the racial-sexual violation signified in that condensed image onto the experience of the so-named "helpless white" spectators. Indeed, the fragmentary "While" of the title and its placement
after the shot of Elsie's spectacular captivity, but before we have any
knowledge of the diegetic spectators to come, conjoin to allow the momentary inference that *she* is the object of this nominated look (not the
rioters we have yet to see), and that we, *Birth's* own spectators, are the
"helpless whites" looking on (not the new, anonymous characters we

FIG. 2.31. The film calls out a vulnerable position of whiteness as (gendered) spectatorship.

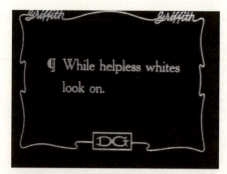

FIG. 2.32

FIG. 2.33

FIG. 2.34

have also yet to see). And the horrified poses of the white witnesses soon displayed do more than just articulate and racialize the agonies of spectatorship; they also articulate a sexual differentiation of variously crippling and restorative states of white looking, and a modulating arc of spectatorial transformation that roughly parallels the one offered by the film itself.

Although male and female spectators on screen are designated "helpless" by the intertitle, and by association to the hysterical Elsie silently screaming before a window just moments before they desperately look out of theirs, the gendered distribution of representational labor detected elsewhere in the film continues here to mark white vision. Twice, following the first close-up of Elsie bound and gagged, and again after her rescue amid the celebratory "Parade of the Clansmen," we see the onscreen spectators in a series of shots, one for each of the four distinct families shown within their respective homes. While the families appear (variously) rich, poor, and in between, in each the men stand or sit closest to, and typically crane their necks and eyes to see out of, the visual frames heavily marked by draperies and windowpanes, whereas women and children more often stare inward in frozen poses of fear and fatigue. Although some women are allowed to rejoice along with the men after the rescue, the overwhelming condition of white female impotence contrasted to the resilience of white male vision—however momentarily helpless the second may be—is vividly evoked through two figures: an amputated old man whose wooden stump below the knee is prominent when we see him prior to the rescue, but disappears from view when he stands eagerly at the window in the moment of celebration; and a female invalid displayed in the foreground of the last shot of both series, lying prostrate in her sickbed with eyes glazed over and rolled up from her first appearance to her and the other onscreen spectators' very last.

Although this gendering of vision among the diegetic white spectators buffers some of them from the extreme vulnerability demanded of others, the means of negotiating such risks for the filmic spectator are not reducible to such gendered divisions. Despite our structural kinship to the "helpless white" witnesses trapped at their windows, that very phrase, and the more omniscient modes of cinematic vision to which we are in fact privileged, rhyme us also with those earlier "helpless white" heads in the legislature scene whose vision, albeit then in the minority, was nonetheless marked by the capacity to transcend the embodied limits of its black counterpart. Indeed, the relative omniscience of what and how we see in the finale, granted an understanding of all the multiple events unfolding over time in many locations—including the regularly repeated promise of shots of the omnipotent Klan ever multiplying, ever approaching—far exceeds the spatial and temporal confines of any onscreen, embodied looks.[96] Hence, the actual presence and articulation of a position of "helpless white" spectators does two things at once: it reminds us for whom this suffering is imagined, the white spectator the film seeks to construct; but it also points up by contrast the visual authority held out for that spectator—the unique cinematic means by which he is offered the promise of a delivery not unlike, although sometimes even in excess of, Ben's most triumphant vision that leads him to overcome his "agony" and "degradation."

In short, I am suggesting, the sudden appearance of the "helpless white" spectators in the finale marks both our proximity to Elsie's condition and our distance from it. Like her and them, we are always at the mercy of the film's well-planned chaos; but even more protective than the windows they hide behind are the illusions of masterful vision the film perpetually holds out for us. Those illusions are most vividly manifested in the finale's tour de force demonstration of classical editing, camera placement, and the like, that positions us to see, with a fullness and detail well beyond the rescues at Biograph, virtually all that we think there is to see.[97] That we teeter in *Birth* between the captivity of the race to the rescue and the omniscience of classical cinema reminds us, in part, that the latter is as precarious as the former.[98]

What is more, insofar as this coupling of spectatorial agony and mastery is arguably a structuring paradox of classical cinematic discourse itself, what *Birth* does, in effect, is capitalize on both poles of the opposition in its feverish attempt to produce the "great white" subjects it desires on and off screen.[99] By coding the agonized pole vulnerable/feminine and the masterful one omniscient/phallic, the film can offer up the pleasures of, and solicit our investments in, each without risking onscreen damage to its most privileged bodies. And we are invited—regardless of sex or race, and even if we refuse or resist—to oscillate between these modes, but always on a path that promises and finally delivers the stabilizing cinematic structures of classical order and omniscience, and further codes that renewed order phallic and white.[100] Put otherwise, the classical turn from Biograph to *Birth* lies not in a complete repudiation of the agonized pleasures that once taunted so many but in a more textually and ideologically rigid restructuring of the agonized cast and an accompanying expansion of the cinematic means whereby the spectator's own vulnerability—most optimally if he is male and white—can be deeply indulged and ultimately denied.

If any doubt remained after the editing of the final rescues, the film's final minutes go out of their way not only to restore Ben's look to the gazelike potency it once enjoyed in the cotton fields but also to further graft that look to our own. In so doing, the film both implicates the spectator's "ideal vantage point"—as Kristin Thompson has described the position offered the classical spectator—with Ben's and/as the Klan's and in turn implicates classical cinematic form and the mode of spectatorial vision it solicits as coproducers, and arguably here in part as products, of the film's phallic, white supremacist visions.[101]

Following the cheers of the anonymous diegetic spectators, the film ends with two more celebrations of phallic white vision restored: first when the Klan's silent looks and drawn guns send black voters running scared on election day, and finally—most elaborately—with the double honeymoon "at the sea's edge." The second is depicted first with a shot of Phil and Margaret looking out at a seascape projected beyond them (fig. 2.35); we then see Ben and Elsie perched on a cliff, also overlooking the ocean (fig. 2.36). A lofty intertitle proclaims: "Dare we dream of a golden day when the bestial War shall rule no more. But instead—the gentle Prince in the Hall of Brotherly Love in the City of Peace." A pair of highly allegorical shots follows in illustration: the first, tinted "War" red, shows a mass of dead and writhing bodies presided over by a "bestial" human figure astride a large animal; the second replicates that general composition but washes it in a golden tint, replaces the decaying mass with happy toga-clad revelers, and superimposes over them a reigning Christlike "Prince." This shot then alternates with that of Ben and Elsie gazing out onto the sea, such that this image of the "City of Peace" effectively becomes the object of their vision. That relation is cemented in the film's final image as they look out onto a fairy-tale castle superimposed over the ocean (fig. 2.37). While these allegorical shots would seem to turn emphatically "beyond" the national politics that have been of the utmost concern throughout the film, an orchestral version of "The Star-Spangled Banner" triumphantly asserts the new white nation onto which Elsie and Ben presumably look, and the film closes with the intertitle "Liberty and union, one and inseparable, now and forever!"

Read in the context of the chapter at hand, these remarkable final moments would seem to answer all that has gone before them not only by restoring Ben's masterful vision but also by anchoring it to, and producing from it, a new white order divinely envisioned by him, the film, and its spectator. Elsie sits by Ben's side, swathed in a cascading veil reminiscent of the costume she wore in the portrait that originally drew Ben's gaze to her, and ours to his. Ben has now acquired the very feminine image he once coveted in miniature replica, and his pleasure in that spectacle (which he also gazes upon here) is overlaid with the pleasure of a gaze that surveys his newly whitened "City of Peace." Hence, in this shot that effectively superimposes and extends Ben's and the spectator's greatest visual achievements—contemplation of the white woman's image, the epic pan from the cliff, and the originary vision of the Klan from the hilltop—the film thoroughly weds and finally insists upon its preferred

FIG. 2.35. White order, and white vision, restored.

FIG. 2.36

FIG. 2.37

visual regimes of racial, sexual, and now explicitly national identity.[102] Indeed, this reading would suggest that the new subject/spectator that has been birthed, looking out with Elsie and Ben into that distant space that signifies the newly segregated future, has been cinematically constituted precisely through those layered visual regimes. Situated now to rest finally with Ben's lofty vantage point that organizes those overlaid visions, *Birth*'s spectator is clearly invited to own and invest in this view of an imagined "golden day" as his own, even as that view—dependent as it is on special effects like rear projection, split frames, and mythic imagery—ironically reveals its profound cinematic debts.

PART TWO

Color Coding Identity and Desire

"The Un-doable Stories," the "Usual Answers," and Other "Epidermic Drama[s]": Coming to Terms with the Production Code

THE CODE, POPULAR MEMORY, AND THE CINEMATICS OF RACIAL FORMATION

While fantasies of interracial desire are vivid in silent American cinema, we could miss them altogether in the classical period if we failed to take into account their systematic repression. Once we begin to do so, however, nothing gives greater testimony to their imagined cultural power than the express prohibition against them for the better part of Hollywood's "golden age."[1] From 1930 to 1956 the Production Code's sixth regulation on matters of "sex" boldly declared: "Miscegenation (sex relationship between the white and black races) is forbidden."[2] While the Code deemed that adultery "must not be explicitly treated or justified, or presented attractively," that rape "should never be more than suggested," and that "in general, passion should be treated in such a manner as not to stimulate the lower and baser emotions," only miscegenation and "sex perversion"—read, the unspeakable, homosexuality—received the absolute stamp of "forbidden."[3]

Yet despite the ring of certainty to this decree, the censors at the Production Code Administration (PCA) who enforced it did so ambiguously and at times with glaring contradiction. As we will see, they invoked it not only to suppress some "sex relationship[s]" between "white and black" but also at times to deny relations between whites and Asians. The inherent opacity of such applications in turn demands an extensive interpretive project of its own. While the next chapter focuses on two films that received particularly extraordinary PCA attention regarding "miscegenation," the current one attempts a more wide-reaching history of the clause's origins and effects. In so doing, it considers the Production Code's significant role in codifying the meaning, visibility, and invisibility of "race," as well as sex, in American cinema.

One of the obvious difficulties of assessing the impact of the Code's miscegenation clause is that its literal purpose was to excise its subject from American cinema—and by extension from any filmic projection of

America itself. That this excision was enormously successful is reflected not only in the films produced in the thirties, forties, and into the fifties but also in the surprising silences on Hollywood's miscegenation ban in film scholarship. It has been noted occasionally in studies of race and censorship, but comments typically are brief and often do not appear at all in places one might expect to find them.[4] Such silence might lead us to imagine that the subject in fact disappears in the classical period. What this assumption ignores is precisely what the current chapter calls to our attention.

The significant presence of "miscegenation" in this period of American film culture is detectable in several ways. First, it was a subject the Code directed studios to avoid and the PCA censors to detect as they reviewed, revised, rejected, and approved the vast majority of commercial American films.[5] To understand the impact of what Ella Shohat thus designates a "significant structuring absence," we must seriously examine the role of the miscegenation clause within the elaborate filter of industry self-censorship through which all of classical Hollywood cinema passed.[6] Second, as critics have also noted, while some interracial fantasies were filtered out entirely, others persisted—if not in "America," in jungles, beaches, opium dens, and the like of faraway or ambiguous locations.[7] Finally, subtending such literal traces of miscegenation as it was explicitly prohibited and implicitly allowed, I will argue, is an even more unspoken filmic discourse enacted in part through the miscegenation clause that profoundly shapes how classical Hollywood spectators were directed to see and not see "race." For within the written and filmic negotiations of "sex relationship[s] between the white and black races" are significant negotiations of how the very meaning of those identities would be defined in and through the filmic image. In short, as will become increasingly apparent, a correlate to the invisibility of black life generally, and of sexual relations between blacks and whites in particular, is the production of race, and especially blackness, as utterly visible.[8] But producing racial visibility is by no means an easy or simple matter, as various subjects are made to appear more and less raced than others to meet a range of historical, ideological, and fantasmatic demands.

Although such demands were rarely announced by the agencies that created and enforced the Code, psychological models of censorship prove fruitful in assessing it as a product, and formative mechanism, of cultural fantasy. Just as Freud invokes "censorship" as a mechanism of repression through which the individual psyche can push down, and thus tolerate, unconscious desires that would provoke profound anxiety if allowed to surface into consciousness, so the miscegenation clause can be read as a mechanism of cultural repression that seeks to repudiate fantasies that, if represented freely, could destabilize the culture's ordinary functioning.[9]

While strict adherence to this analogy would overlook the distinctly conscious nature of film censorship (unlike the psyche, which does not publicize guidelines of what must remain unconscious!), this chapter and the next consider the precise forms that censorship takes in part to resist the quick assumption that we *already* know what exactly is being repressed and why.

My analysis will suggest that Hollywood's miscegenation ban sought to push down two related, but significantly different, kinds of knowledge. The first we might think of as the repression of actual, historical relations, an impulse to deny, or at least dramatically revise, narratives that point to the decidedly miscegenated America of the past (and any subsequent present), in particular the sexual "story" of white men and black women sanctioned under slavery. Indeed, one of the most obvious yet remarkable feats of popular American miscegenation fantasies of the late nineteenth and twentieth centuries, cinematically canonized with *The Birth of a Nation*, has been the wholesale disavowal of the substantial history of white men sexually desiring, exploiting, and assaulting black women, and the substitution in its place of the myth of the black rapist. That much of this historical information was decidedly knowable, and decidedly disavowed, in the era of the Production Code is suggested by the opening paragraphs of a doctoral dissertation titled "Miscegenation in the Ante-Bellum South," completed at the University of Chicago just three years into the Code's enforcement. Soon after the author prefaces his findings with the caution that "any picture of the situation must be incomplete [and] conclusions must remain tentative," he nonetheless proposes two decisive conclusions: "Of only [this] can we be reasonably certain; miscegenation was a normal consequence of human beings living and working together at common tasks," and "the mulatto was in most cases, it seems certain, the descendant of the white man and the Negro woman."[10] The Production Code and its influence will attest that the only certainties on the subject visible to a history student at a premiere, northern, research institution in the mid-1930s were precisely the ones Hollywood deemed intolerable for the dominant American imagination.

Ella Shohat and Robert Stam suggest what made these particular facts intolerable. The miscegenation clause, they write, took part in a "broader exclusion of Africans, Asians, and Native Americans from participation in social institutions" and, more specifically, imposed "blanket censorship of sexual violence and brutality, thus foreclosing any portrayal of racial and sexual violence toward African-Americans and implicitly wiping the memory of rape, castration, and lynching from the American record."[11] The erasure of these crimes against black women and men, the accompanying exculpation of white men and women who committed and encouraged them, as well as the foreclosure of any recognition of such histories, are undoubtedly tremendous effects of what might otherwise appear as one small component of an elaborate censorship apparatus.[12] Also significant, certainly, is the refusal of any joyous screen fantasies of interracial desire, be they tied to real histories or liberatory imaginings.[13]

Any extended analysis of Hollywood's miscegenation ban thus needs to consider which particular narratives and interracial combinations it blocked from the field of representation and how, and what returned or appeared instead. In addition, I suggest, we need to recognize how the attempted disavowal of "sex relationship[s] between the white and black races" as they actually occurred and were imagined in American history also attempts to deny the profound political, psychological, and epistemological fallout of any account of interracial sex. For as fierce as the Code's attempt to repress interracial history is its insistence on the existence of the singular, distinct categories of "the white and black races"— categories upon which multiple structures of American social hierarchy depend, and which any hint of interracial sex quickly threatens to dissolve. For perhaps the most radical knowledge miscegenation always threatens to portend is not simply that racial "lines" have been sexually transgressed, and thus might disappear, but that the original categories they were assumed to delimit were only, necessarily, imagined.

Lest it be thought such an invocation of "race" as a fictive category overly privileges recent theoretical concerns at the expense of the historical material in question, a letter written to the PCA in 1937 quickly demonstrates how real the psychic and political investments in such categories and their demarcation were. Complaining about how "dreadfully disappointed and displeased" he was to see "the mixture of negroes with white persons" in the film *Artists and Models*, a mixture that seems to have consisted of black and white dancers in a musical number, a newspaper editor from Louisiana rants for nine paragraphs against "the practice of mixing the races in pictures," threatening that the southern "reaction will be very hurtful to the picture industry."[14] What the letter builds to and climaxes with, however, is the language of differentiation:

> I realize, of course, that there is no protest or resentment in some part of the country, where *the color lines are not drawn*. I have no complaint to make about what other sections of the country think about the social equality matter. That's their business. But in the South *there is a color line, and it always will be drawn*, and when negroes and white persons act together there will always be a bad reaction.
>
> . . . I am a loyal picture show enthusiast. The folks here engaged in the business are my close friends. I have an idea that they, too, feel just as I do about sending to the South pictures in which negroes and whites play in the same pictures, with *no distinction drawn* as to the races.[15]

However extreme such a response to interracial *dancing* might seem, even by the standards of the PCA, it nonetheless spells out what is perpetually at issue in the application and negotiation of the miscegenation clause.[16] For that clause plays a fundamental role not merely in drawing "lines" of racial distinction but in cinematically painting, if you will, an entire filmic-racial schema that suggests new implications for old metaphors of "color."

Recent scholarship on race has increasingly recognized that "miscegenation" commonly appears precisely as a textual trope through which to fortify and contest the meaning of "race" and particular "racial" identities; the PCA's enforcement of Hollywood's extended ban provides a critical window into the cinematic history of such "racial formations."[17] As a literal mediator between dominant cinema and the larger culture, and between the written word and the visual image, this censorial work allows unique glimpses of the racial work the filmic medium was marshaled to do as it negotiated racial terms in the wider culture and helped to shape popular conceptions of racial meaning through the particular demands and practices of classical cinema.

To establish a broader context out of which this censorship emerged, and some of the dominant racial formations with which it engaged, this chapter will first consider some cultural practices producing "race" beyond cinema. It will then offer a history of the miscegenation clause itself. Informed by these contexts, I turn to the writings that transpired between the studios and the PCA censors on film projects containing a range of forms of interracial and cross-cultural desire. Reading selectively from more than one hundred relevant PCA files reviewed for this study, I attempt to decipher the most telling texts and subtexts I find there to discern what was, and was not, identified as miscegenetic material and what these writings can teach us. My readings interrogate how the regular policing of "miscegenation" not only produced "the white and black races" in very particular ways, but with contradictions, preoccupations, and sanctions that suggest a uniquely filmic mapping of "race" as largely an optical range we might appropriately call "color." At the same time, and despite the apparent expanse of that range, I will argue that the language of the miscegenation clause and the censors' uneven application of it worked to reduce articulated notions of race to the binary of "black" and "white" and to define those ostensible identities in increasingly visual terms.

DELIRIUMS OF BLOOD, MATH, AND THE VISIBLE

Conceptions of race as something the eye can see are by no means unique to the twentieth century. By Robyn Wiegman's account, European thinkers had "beg[u]n in earnest to define race as a visible economy in the sixteenth century," and "[b]y the late seventeenth century," in keeping with the widespread rise in the authority of vision and observation, "color had become the primary organizing principle around which the natural historian classified human differences."[18] While Wiegman further traces the nineteenth-century turn to biology whereby race became "more than skin deep," "an inherent and incontrovertible difference of which skin was only the most visible indication," she nonetheless maintains that in the United States there is "a less emphatic break, a more troubled confusion" between these racial regimes (30, 31, 34). Here I will pursue this twentieth-century confusion, but earlier traces of formidably visual racial regimes are certainly evident in the United States as well. Adrienne Davis locates legal recourse to what she coins "the scopic rule," for example, as early as 1806.[19] Insofar as the law authorized judges to determine racial identity (in part) by their own surveillance of bodies in the courtroom, "national racial taxonomy took differences of phenotype and reified them into bases for legal and social discrimination and violence" (709). At the end of the nineteenth and into the twentieth centuries, the rise of photography and cinema, and their dissemination of visual representations and viewing positions, thus clearly interact with visual histories of racial meaning that predate and extend beyond such "new" visual technologies.

Appropriate, then, is Wiegman's reminder that "the history of the visible that undergirds . . . fashionings of race is not, as our assurance in the visible may often lead us to believe, always the same" (24). As we attempt to make sense of some of that history as it is recorded in various Hollywood texts, Wiegman's articulation of the complex interactions in play at any racial "sighting" will be especially useful. She writes:

> We must take seriously the notion of race as a fiction—as a profound ordering of difference instantiated at the sight of the body—in order to jettison the security of the visible as an obvious and unacculturated phenomenon. For what the eye sees, and how we understand that seeing in relation to physical embodiment and philosophical and linguistic assumptions, necessitates a broader inquiry into the articulation of race, one that takes the visual moment as itself a complicated and historically contingent production. (24)

Locating cinema within a wider range of such productions makes the unique contours of cinematic racial formations all the more apparent. The long view of the history of "race"—a history that has conceived of it variously as derived from religious and mythic texts, biology, genetics, and so forth—quickly exposes its instability and perpetual *re*formation.[20] Zeroing in on the period out of which cinema and, eventually, the miscegenation clause emerged, multiple signs indicate that U.S. racial discourse was at a particularly unstable point. Primary among the reasons for this are the end of slavery and the pronounced influx of immigrants. While the former marked the end of long-standing modes of defining and asserting race through laws keyed to property, the latter gave way to a felt proliferation of cultural differences, as evidenced by the period's expanding xenophobia. Resulting demands for new means of defining "white" versus "black," and for managing additional categories beyond that binary, are particularly evident at the turn of the century in the widespread growth of state laws prohibiting interracial marriage and in the perpetual revision of racial categories in the federal census. Both sets of texts register the pervasive addition of various terms differentiating Asians from whites, as antimiscegenation statutes in the West especially were added or amended to prohibit intermarriage between whites and, for example, "Japanese or Chinese" (e.g., Nebraska, 1913) or "Corean, Malayan or Mongolian race[s]" (e.g., South Dakota, 1913).[21] The census reflects a kind of frenzied climax of the discourse of black and white "blood," especially as it had been articulated in a language of mathematical fractions that Werner Sollors has aptly characterized, in an analysis of kindred texts, "the calculus of color."[22] A brief consideration of how such mathematical rhetoric once functioned begins to suggest why it lost its hold by the early part of the twentieth century, and what discursive demands that followed.

Sollors reads the mathematics that permeated "classification schemes of racial names [in the] eighteenth- and early nineteenth-century" as an outgrowth of Enlightenment faith in empiricism, dovetailing here with racializing pseudoscience. His most remarkable example comes from a man no less invested in the volatile boundary between black and white than the "Enlightenment mathematician" and slave-owning and slave-fathering Thomas Jefferson. In its attempt to calculate the "blood" of the offspring of a series of racial "crosses," Jefferson's equation quickly reveals the excess of the cultural "obsession" with racial math:

> Let the third crossing be of q [quadroon] and C [a "pure white"], their offspring will be $q/2 + C/2 = a/8 + A/8 + B/4 + C/2$, call this e (eighth), who having less than $1/4$ of a, or of pure negro blood, to wit $1/8$ only, is no longer a mulatto, so that a third cross clears the blood.
>
> ... Let h [half blood] and e cohabit, their issue will be $h/2 + e/2 = a/4 + A/4 + a/16 + A/16 + B/8 + c/4 = 5a/16 + 5A/16 + B/8 + c/4$, wherein $5/16a$ makes still a mulatto.[23]

This excerpt is itself only a small fraction of the original, which finds "algebraical notation . . . the most convenient and intelligible" method for calculating such "crosses," "compounds," and "fractional mixtures" (113). Sollors's analysis of such formulations recognizes both their attempt to assert "an ultimate racial boundary that would support the notion of racial difference" and the simultaneous tendency to retreat into a realm of rhetorical absurdity: "In their differing quests for cutoff points and dividing lines, they may indeed take mathematics to the point of delirium" (115, 114, 119). I would venture to add that such calculations precisely risk exposing the arbitrariness of their racial signifiers. When reading equations like "$h/2 + q/2 = a/4 + A/4 + a/16 + A/16 + B/8 + c/14 = 5a/16 + 5A/16 + B/8 + c/4$," it becomes increasingly difficult to conceive of how, or even remember that, such figures refer to actual racial subjects, human beings.

While Sollors detects the critical recognition of such "delirium" in some nineteenth- and twentieth-century literary texts, especially by African American authors, a federal census report from 1918 suggests that even some in the mainstream business of racial math had come to recognize its shortcomings by the early decades of the twentieth century. Fulfilling the obligation of the report, a summary titled *Negro Population 1790–1915*, its authors attempt to relay the methods and logic of prior census practices, and in so doing confirm that after the Civil War the discourse of "blood" dominated for several decades.[24] For example, "the term mulatto [was] defined in 1870 to include 'quadroons, octoroons, and all persons having any perceptible trace of African blood'"; and "in 1890 the term 'black' was defined to include all persons 'having three-fourths or more "black blood,"' other persons with any proportion of 'black' blood being classified as 'mulattoes,' 'quadroons,' or 'octoroons'" (207). While the emergence and shifting placement of the original quotation marks already suggest some interesting flux in the texts of 1870 and 1890, most interesting in our context are the footnotes that soon follow from 1918.

The first of these notes that "regarding the classification of the Negro population of mixed blood in 1890 . . . the following statement is made in the report of the Eleventh Census: 'These figures are of little value. Indeed, as an indication of the extent to which the races have mingled, they are misleading.'"[25] The 1918 authors do not yet comment on why or how the figures mislead, but as the summary continues they are at pains to report and explain increasingly baroque calculations of blood "fractions" from 1890.[26] After this difficulty is first expressed in the body of the text, the uncertainty of the math is worked over in an extended footnote that torturously carries the double burden of explaining the fractional logic and admitting its delusions.[27] It begins with a dizzying demonstration of how "fine gradations of admixture" of white and black blood "may be simply illustrated." I quote here only a portion: "If, for example, six individuals, in which the proportions of Negro blood are respectively precisely one-sixteenth, one-eighth, two-eighths, four-eighths, six-eighths, and eight-eighths, be presumed to intermarry, the number of possible different proportions in their children are 14; and if the group be presumed to be segregated for several generations, the possible different proportions in their great-grandchildren would be represented by approximately 70 fractions having 128 as a denominator and numbers ranging between 17 to 100 as numerators."[28] After concluding, assuming "complete segregation," that the variation in "differences in the proportion of Negro blood would tend to become less from generation to generation"—a conclusion that surely wants to make some racially purifying "black" sense of all these calculations—the same footnote nonetheless finally lands on this critical conclusion: "In the mulatto population of the United States as a whole the number of proportions of intermixture is exceedingly great, and *there is no reason to suppose that these proportions are concentrated in any considerable degree upon such simple fractions as one-eighth, or one-quarter, or one-half.* In the Negro population at the present time, *it is not mathematically improbable that any given union of mulatto* with either a black or a mulatto, *will in its offspring represent a unique proportion of admixture of white blood.*"[29]

Ultimately, this 1918 negotiation of a racial logic still imaginable a few decades prior is remarkable not only because it must acknowledge the fallacies of the fractional formulations it is charged to report but also because that acknowledgment would seem to arise *not* out of some moral or political higher ground but rather out of the exhaustion of the mathematical paradigm. For even this text, which shows traces of still wanting to calculate miscegenation away, or at least to gradually calculate whiteness out of the "Negro Population" (e.g., the comfortable assumption of "complete segregation," the theorizing of future "admixture" only between all categories other than white, etc.), can no longer retain faith in the "accura[cy]" of "simple fractions."[30] It must also admit the mathematical probability that in children of "any given union of mulatto," some "unique proportion of admixture of white blood," however small, will always remain. Well before the myth of racial "blood" is debunked, in other words, the ultimate "cut off points and dividing lines" once imagined through racial math now seem only belied by it.

I emphasize this historical breakdown of the calculus of color and blood to establish something of the particular, critical state of dominant racial formation it indicates just prior to the moment the miscegenation clause was about to appear in Hollywood. Indeed, it will become increasingly meaningful as we chart the alternatives to blood and math provided by popular cinema that the language of "blood" so central to census definitions of "color and race" from 1870 to 1920 gradually disappears from the summary reports of the census of 1930 and beyond.[31] Moreover, and perhaps most significant for the inquiry at hand, those reports indicate that the dissipation of faith in the mathematics of (invisible) blood is followed by an equally remarkable faith in the visibility of race that appears to take its place by midcentury.[32] Because Hollywood's production of such faith in the very same decades will be among our primary concerns in this and the subsequent chapter, its evident usurpation of blood math in the census is of particular note.

The role of observation in racial counting is not explicitly explained until the summary report of the 1950 census, but the 1960 report notes that "in previous censuses the racial classification was made for the most part by the enumerator on the basis of observation."[33] And the 1918 report notes the difficulties (in the previous century) of perceiving properties of "blood": "The perceptibility of a trace of Negro or of white blood probably does not correspond uniformly to the physiological proportion of Negro and white blood in the individuals enumerated. Moreover, perceptibility is dependent upon the ability of the enumerator to perceive, and this ability varies from enumerator to enumerator."[34] This manifest doubt in 1918 about the "perceptibility" of race, in keeping with the same text's doubt about the inadequacies of racial math, is followed in census reports for 1920, 1930, and 1940 by continual revisions and additions of racial names, until the 1950 report directly disassociates itself from recently debunked biological models of race.[35] Instead, it virtually announces that term's social construction: "The concept of race as it has been used by the Bureau of the Census is derived from that which is commonly accepted by the general public. It does not, therefore, reflect clearcut definitions of biological stock, and several categories obviously refer to nationalities."[36] Immediately following this open critique of one racial paradigm that "lacks scientific precision," however, it describes the current method of assessing race as one "not based on a reply to questions asked by the enumerator but rather . . . obtained by observation." That observation was assumed to be the *primary* method of ascertaining racial identity is confirmed by the additional note that the observing "enumerators were instructed to ask a question *when they were in doubt*" (35, emphasis mine). Even as this formulation thus admits the possibility of "doubt," the fact that it nonetheless maintains observation as the primary method indicates if not an absolute faith in the visibility of "race," at least a profound, structuring desire for it to be readily apparent to the unguided eye.[37]

After looking at such explicit negotiations of racial taxonomy, "perceptivty," methodology, and so forth, paradigms of racial formation at the cinema appear far muddier. Even at the PCA, a relatively retentive organization that systematically deliberates and records its interpretive judgments, relations between processes of "racial naming and scopic norms of bodily framing," as Lauren Berlant has coined them in another context, are not nearly as evident. Rather, the PCA's files of correspondence with the studios confront the archivist as a monumental pile of fragments that occasionally reveal their racial logics through evocative pronouncements, but more commonly code "race" and "color" in partial, unpronounced ways.[38] Nonetheless, the extracinematic practices considered here help to prompt significant questions about the forms and effects of racial formation in the cinema and its censorship. The distance between the trepidation about calculations of "blood" in 1918 and the practical faith in the racial legibility of bodies to the naked eye in 1950 helps us to ask, What makes a culture, in a century marked by intense waves of racial and ethnic immigration and migration, mixing and contestation, form and sustain the belief that "race" is something we know when we see? My work here will suggest that we have much to learn in this regard from cinema, a medium that profoundly contributes to the ascension of the visual as a dominant location and guarantee of racial meaning in the twentieth century.[39]

Before moving to precise enactments of that work as it unfolds in the interpretations and implications of Hollywood's miscegenation clause, however, my argument calls for historical evidence to demonstrate that the clause being interpreted by a select set of individuals was itself very much a *cultural* production.

A Short History of Cultural Repression

The miscegenation clause of the 1934 Production Code predates that text by several years. While local calls to censor filmic treatment of miscegenation date back to the controversial reception of *The Birth of a Nation* (following the less memorable censorship of *The Heart of an Outlaw* in 1909), the industry's first attempt to do so systematically came in 1927 when the Motion Picture Producers and Distributors of America (MPPDA) adopted its list of Don'ts and Be Carefuls.[40] Specifically, the sixth "don't" of eleven of "those things [that] shall not appear in pictures . . . irrespective of the manner in which they are treated," targeted "Miscegenation (sex relationships between the white and black races)."[41] Variations of this clause were later inherited by the more elaborate Production Code of 1930, and again by what was long understood as the more enforceable Production Code of 1934, from which it would not be fully lifted until 1956.[42] I have found no definitive source for the first clause from 1927, but tracing what we do know of this censorial lineage offers some crucial evidence.

In an attempt to stave off growing public criticism of his failure to radically reform the motion picture industry since his appointment as "Moses of the Movies" (as the *Nation* dubbed him) in 1922, MPPDA

president Will Hays expanded his New York operation in 1926 by opening an office in Hollywood that would attempt to run interference with
the studios.[43] To be able to flag potentially controversial subject matter
on their behalf (so as to avoid costly cutting due to local censorship),
the director of this new Studio Relations Committee (SRC), Jason Joy,
consulted with numerous state and municipal censor boards "to
find . . . what sort of thing they objected to and why."[44] The fruits of this
labor were so considerable that it turned into a "formal study," submitted to the MPPDA, which reported what the censor boards tended to
cut, as well as "the criticisms, objections and suggestions of . . . public-
relations groups" (63). On the basis of this report, studio representatives
resolved to adhere to guidelines set forth as the Don'ts and Be Carefuls.
While this list had no effective mechanism of enforcement, it nonetheless
specified "miscegenation" as one of the agreed-upon don'ts.

The miscegenation clause was new in 1927, but this type of industry
list of unacceptable screen material was not. In 1921 the producers, then
organized as the National Association of the Motion Picture Industry,
had adopted the Thirteen Points in an effort to appease calls for government censorship. The Thirteen Points consisted of a list that similarly attempted to discourage commonly censored material. Yet while that list
covered much the same ground as the Don'ts and Be Carefuls—with
clauses on sex, nudity, drugs, and crime, for example—it did not contain
any mention of miscegenation. This suggests that the miscegenation
clause was drafted as a result of Joy's research, a deduction further sup-
ported by the fact that censor boards commonly did object to scenes suggesting interracial sexual contact. Such objections are documented from
censor boards in southern states like Virginia but also in northern ones
like Ohio and Pennsylvania.[45] And since, according to Raymond Moley,
such boards were only in agreement on "less than ten percent" of all that
they considered objectionable, it follows that the specific subjects that
made it into the Don'ts and Be Carefuls were gleaned from those on
which they tended to agree (63). Thus, although a singular moment of
origin has yet to be found, and is likely impossible to find if the clause issues from a dispersion of sources, the evidence suggests that the miscegenation clause of 1927 emerged from shared concerns of censorship
boards throughout the country.

In slightly modified form, that clause was incorporated into the more
elaborate Production Codes of 1930 and 1934. Like the industry's earlier
attempts to establish self-regulatory guidelines, the creation of the Code
was largely a public relations move. Far better for the producers to censor themselves than be censored from without, and far better to appear
to share pervasive public concerns with "decency" and "morality" than
not. The Code thus adopted by the MPPDA in 1930 contained two dis-

tinct sections. One, though more extensive, is akin to the Don'ts and Be Carefuls, listing guidelines for, and prohibitions against, specific subject matter.[46] As written in most reprints of the 1930 Code, the miscegenation clause here retains the language from 1927, modified only by narrowing the "sex relationships" to a singular form and putting what was simply a noun with a parenthetical elaboration into a complete sentence containing the entire prohibition: "Miscegenation (sex relationship between the white and black races) is forbidden."[47] The pamphlet form of the Code published in 1930 did not include the parenthetical definition but merely stated: "Miscegenation is forbidden."[48] While it is not certain whether this reflected official language, or whether it was simply a shortened form used for the pamphlet (which seems more likely), it is clear that the earlier parenthetical definition was eventually incorporated into the official language of the Production Code of 1934.[49] Thus, the clause that would shape the face of American cinema for two more decades to come strictly pronounced: "Miscegenation (sex relationship between the white and black races) is forbidden."

Although we do not know who or what was determining this exact language, we can rule out one significant source. A former PCA censor who eventually replaced Joe Breen as its director, Geoffrey Shurlock, recollects with persuasive certainty that the clause was inserted into the Code by the Hays Office and was never part of that portion which derived from the "Catholic movie code" drafted by Daniel Lord and Martin Quigley: "To Quigley's credit . . . he was absolutely infuriated all the time that I knew him with the original Code where it said that we could not treat a picture dealing with miscegenation. He thought it was outrageous and un-Christian. He was right, of course. But I could see why Will Hays and his staff put it in."[50] Corroborated by Lord and Quigley's original document, Shurlock's testimony dismisses the possibility that the miscegenation clause reflected the particular interests of the powerful constituency of Catholics instrumental in forming the Code.[51] And while Shurlock does not elaborate his understanding of Hays's inclusion of miscegenation in particular, he suggests it when he explains that "Hays and his staff in New York had to deal specifically with the complaints from the public. They collated their complaints and shook them up in a bag and took out the ones that seemed the most important and put them down as the specifics."[52] While envisioning a rather arbitrary selection process, this account nevertheless suggests miscegenation was, or was at least presumed to have been, among the "most important" of "public" concerns. And there is evidence that such concerns reached the Hays Office, like the local censor boards before it, from various corners of the nation.[53] Such a broad cultural ancestry is confirmed further by the widespread expansion of antimiscegenation marriage statutes in the decades just prior to the Code, a fact adduced by the PCA at least once in explanation of its own ban.[54] However, although a secondary account of that explanation (referring to an original PCA judgment not itself in the file) located such laws as being "in the South," they had in fact been enacted of late in more than a dozen nonsouthern states, especially in the West.[55]

Threats by organized religious groups to boycott "indecent" movies provoked the MPPDA to fortify the Production Code in 1934.[56] In addition to such general pressures, we could map an economic account of the rise and fall of the miscegenation clause in particular. The reformist backlash against the studios' peddling of "salacious subject matter" to boost declining attendance in the late twenties and early thirties, as well as vivid memories of the outcries against *The Birth of a Nation*, likely played a role in getting miscegenation into the Code and keeping it there.[57] Similar profit logic could explain why it was one of the first Code prohibitions to be softened, when it (along with the ban on alcohol) was moved under the heading of "Special Subjects" to be "treated within the careful limits of good taste" by 1955, before it was removed altogether in 1956: an industry facing poor returns during its postwar decline wanted more titillating subject matter to entice viewers back into the theater.[58] While the industry preferred to paint the lifting of the ban as a socially conscious revision, the sensational boom of "new 'miscegenation films'" in the late 1950s clearly reflected, as one critic noted, a deft "balance between liberal principles and shrewd business sense."[59]

The history of the miscegenation clause thus supports Richard Randall's assertion that "it would be a mistake" to dismiss the particular details of specific film censorship guidelines as the anomalous result of a few noisy citizens.[60] He argues instead, and this history repeatedly demonstrates, that these guidelines "reflected . . . the range of concerns and values held by a large part of the nation." As such, we should no longer overlook the miscegenation ban as an insignificant, anomalous, or peculiarly "southern" chapter in film history. To pinpoint what exactly it attempted to keep in check, as well as what it endorsed and elaborated, I turn now to the everyday interpretive practices of the PCA.

"Reasonable Interpretation"

The parenthetical inclusion of a definition in the miscegenation clause can be read simultaneously as an attempt to avoid interpretive confusion and as an inadvertent announcement of its likelihood. While other subjects deemed unrepresentable in the Don'ts and Be Carefuls and both Production Codes include such ambiguous categories as "sex perversion," "white slavery," and "sex hygiene," none are comparably defined. Moreover, scrutiny of the SRC's and the PCA's actual interpretations of the miscegenation clause verifies that the potential for confusion marked in the very language of the mandate continues in the censors' efforts to enforce it—so much so that the facts quickly undermine PCA director Joe Breen's official position that "the provisions of the Code are reasonable and, consequently, require only reasonable interpretation."[61]

Rather, my study confirms Lea Jacobs's argument that industry "self-regulation," as she often calls it, was not a simple process of prohibition but "a constructive force, in the sense that it helped shape film form and narrative."[62] As she explains, "Self-regulation was an integrated part of film production under the studio system. Industry censors were in a position to request revisions in scripts and, in consultation with writers, directors, and producers, to effect changes of narrative."[63] The censors' formative powers, as we will see, are detectable in their written responses to proposed treatments and scripts, and in their ongoing negotiations with studios as projects evolved over the details of everything from dialogue to costume to camera placement. And, further in keeping with Jacobs's findings, the process was by no means entirely stable. For while certain named and unnamed scenarios served as informal precedents, correspondence in the files (which include some MPPDA and SRC documents predating the PCA) reveals that the meaning of "miscegenation" was not clear to begin with and was continually modified as censors attempted to accommodate angry studio heads, litigious exhibitors, and potential audiences. Despite how *un*reasonable they could be, such shifting interpretations of "sex relationship between the white and black races" played a significant role in defining each of those terms in classical Hollywood cinema.

Typically, the meaning of "sex relationship" was the least contentious component of the clause. Although marriage occasionally surfaces in the files as a potential mitigating factor, generally "miscegenation" was never confined to, or legitimated by, marriage.[64] Judging from the PCA's warnings, a "sex relationship" extended to any number of forms of sex or romance in and out of marriage, as well as to far more ambiguous encounters; from what Hays once nebulously describes (as I will consider later) as "social relationships" to what in another case is targeted sheerly as an erotic look: "We recommend care with this action of a native ogling a white woman."[65] As these two examples attest, the exchanges most openly policed were those between black men and white women.[66] This already leads us to the repeatedly confirmed conclusion that what a miscegenetic "sex relationship" consists of depends largely upon the identities of those between whom it obtains. Indeed, it is there that the greatest amount of unreason surfaces, as the censors' definitions of "black" and "white," and the methods by which they are ascertained, are rarely self-evident and at times wildly arbitrary. Unreasonable and unconscious though such methods may be, their analysis leads to some of the most revealing findings about the function and effects of this portion of the Code.

In light of the diversity of immigrants and the multiplicity of racial and ethnic targets of the pervasive xenophobia that marked the United States in the decades out of which the Code emerged, one of the most striking features of the miscegenation clause is the narrowness and binarity of language that names only "the white and black races." This narrowness is all the more apparent when compared with contemporaneous productions of racial names elsewhere. For example, as already noted, while the Hollywood censors at least once invoked (privately) "southern" inter-marriage law as the miscegenation clause's precedent, the resurgence of new and revised antimiscegenation legislation throughout the country into the 1920s was in fact systematically expanding the black-white binary, widely adding "Mongolians" (among other Asian names) in the age of "yellow peril" that also produced federal exclusionary laws targeting Chinese, and in fewer cases including "Indian" in attempts to negotiate definitions of white versus nonwhite.[67] The changes that racial names underwent in the census in this period reflect even more variation and range. In 1920 census categories for "color or race, nativity, and parentage" (significantly shortened in tables and headers to simply "color or race") include "White," "Negro," "Indian," "Chinese," "Japanese," "Filipino," "Hindu," "Korean," "Hawaiian," "Part Hawaiian," and "Other Races" for the continent, Alaska, and Hawaii; plus "Chamorro," "Polynesian," "Mixed," and "Mulatto" for additional U.S. territories.[68] While such a list is at once questionable and expansive in its attempt to designate a wide range of "racial," national, cultural, and even religious differences, it nonetheless already noticeably delimits (what it imagines as) the "Negro" range from prior censuses, which had included the category of "mulattoes" for the continental United States.[69] By 1920, in keeping with the racial fantasies Hollywood will perpetuate, that category and "mixed" become possibilities recognized only in the "outlying possessions" (11). And by 1930, the year Hollywood's miscegenation clause would be imported from the Don'ts and Be Carefuls into the Code itself, the census categories have again significantly changed: all "mixed" and "mulatto" categories disappear, and Mexicans appear in significant numbers that make them the third-largest group after "White" and "Negro" and before "Indian." Hence, although the census and state antimiscegenation statutes in this period, like the Code, are invoking racial categories and territories to deny the existence of mixture or undecidability, they nonetheless name and seek to identify (for whatever purposes) a range of "race and color" that is considerably more diverse than the Code's "white and black."

We know that Hollywood films were not quite as reductive as this censorial language, and that films before and after the Code featured interracial and intercultural relations, most always between whites and nonwhites, especially Asians, Native Americans, and Mexicans. Even though Dolores Del Rio vehicles like *Wonder Bar* (1934), *I Live for Love* (1935), and *In Caliente* (1935), as well as the trade reviews of them, clearly marked the Mexican actress as "a Latin stage star" paired with white men, no mention is made of such differences in the PCA files on these films.[70] Nor do the censors object to romantic and marital relations between whites and Native Americans in films like *Whoopee* (1930), *Behold My Wife!* (1935), *Ramona* (1935), and *The Last of the Mohicans* (1936). To the contrary, in a 1936 telegram from the PCA in Hollywood to Hays in New York, a list announcing "WHAT LOOKS LIKE OUTSTANDING PICTURES OF EXCEPTIONAL MERIT" to be released later that year includes both *The Last of the Mohicans* and *Ramona*.[71] The PCA's praise of these films, the former based on James Fenimore Cooper's *Leatherstocking Tales* and the latter on Helen Hunt Jackson's novel *Ramona*, is typical of its esteem for films derived from highbrow literature.[72] The cultural status and tradition of such literary texts, as well as the larger cultural and racial conventions in which they partake, would seem in turn to help explain their acceptability as filmic material. For while the censors find no fault with it, the synopsis of *The Last of the Mohicans* in the PCA file explicitly mentions "the love of Uncas, a Mohican Indian[,] of Cora Munro," a white woman, and goes on to reiterate that "Uncas loves Cora devotedly."[73] Synopses in the *Ramona* file similarly identify love between whites and Indians in relation to no less than three different couples but never register concern about any of them.[74]

While tolerance for such pairings seems in keeping with the Code's specified target of "white and black," a curious history of deviation from that alleged target in the late twenties and early thirties seriously complicates assumptions about what those terms refer to and the PCA's adherence to the apparent letter of its law: stories of liaisons between Asians and whites were regularly rejected in the late twenties and early thirties on the grounds that they violated the miscegenation clauses of the Don'ts and Be Carefuls and both Production Codes. Thus, for example, a synopsis of the play *Congai* drafted by the Hays Office, probably in 1929, describes it as "deal[ing] with the relations of a half-caste woman of Indo-China with French officers," and goes on to say that she "is the mistress of many white men."[75] Immediately following this description the synopsis concludes: "'Congai,' in other words, deals directly with miscegenation—with sexual relations between yellows and whites . . . one of the eleven themes the producers . . . agreed to avoid." Pointing to the eleven Don'ts of 1927, this invocation clearly brings the status of the delimiting parenthetical definition ("between the white and black races") into question. Moreover, as various studios show interest in *Congai* from

1929 through 1932, the PCA continues to identify miscegenation as part of its "very dangerous material."[76]

One obvious explanation for the seemingly unreasonable application of a clause prohibiting "sex relationship[s] between the white and black races" to scripts depicting relationships between "yellows and whites," is that, as I noted earlier, the 1930 pamphlet form of the Code did not include the parenthetical definition. Certainly the mandate that "miscegenation is forbidden" opens up a much wider territory of fantasies and identities. However, there are at least two reasons to doubt the "official" status of the more ambiguous clause from the pamphlet. First, it seems probable that the abbreviated form reflects a format designed for public relations, not official reference. Second, the account of a PCA "inside[r]" from 1937 suggests that there was in practice an explicit disjuncture between the printed definition of the full miscegenation clause and the PCA's working definition of it.[77] In her explanation of the "*modus operandi* of the Motion Picture Production Code," Olga Martin gives an explicit gloss on the regular interpretation of the miscegenation clause: "The Code specifically prohibits miscegenation in its regulation which reads, 'Miscegenation (sex relationship between the white and black races) is forbidden.' The dictionary defines miscegenation as, 'A mixture of races, especially amalgamation of the black and white races.' The Production Code Administration, in interpreting this regulation for application to stories, has regarded miscegenetic unions to be any sex relationship between the white and black races, or in most cases sex union between the white and yellow races."[78] Martin's account thus confirms a contradiction between the clause's actual language and the censors' applications of it. Indeed, her articulation of the PCA's interpretive practice is noteworthy in that it triply insists upon the "white and black" definition (quoting the Code's language, bolstering that with a "dictionary" definition, and then asserting the PCA's adherence to it), only then to amend it with a contrary alternative: "or in most cases [of] white and yellow." While the "or" admits an interpretation beyond the designated terms, Martin's lack of concern for the apparent contradiction reflects the ongoing status of that contradiction throughout the PCA files.

The expanded working definition Martin offers is strikingly verified in an interoffice exchange regarding a series of film projects that were repeatedly submitted for approval, and repeatedly rejected, in the late twenties and early thirties. An exasperated letter from Jason Joy to Will Hays in 1932 refers to *Congai,* as well as to another script treating desire between Asians and whites, *Shanghai Gesture,* and to the highly controversial *Lulu Belle,* a story that originally featured an affair between a black woman and a white man. This letter not only lumps together stories of black-white and white-Asian desire but further reveals the perpetual interest in such stories at the studios, and their perpetual dread at the PCA. Joy writes:

DEAR GENERAL [HAYS]:

This is only one of several attempts this week to revive interest in *the undoable stories*. Paramount indicated interest in CONGAI and LULU BELLE, and Charlie Sullivan, who is now at RKO, broached the subject of SHANGHAI GESTURE. Our *usual answers were given* in all of these cases and I doubt very much if we will be pressed concerning any of them with the possible exception of CONGAI. If you haven't already seen the letter sent to Mr. Schulberg on this subject you may want to dig it out of the files. We didn't mince any words about it. *Apparently these four four [sic] stories are like cats with nine lives or like Hamlet's father, whose ghost wouldn't be laid.*

Sincerely yours,[79]

While Joy actually names only three "un-doable" titles in this letter, his miscounting them as four (coincidentally doubled by the typo) speaks to his inundated sense of their prevalence and persistence. The censors' assessments of each of these particular projects reveal that all three are based on plays containing such "bawdy" subjects as illegitimacy, prostitution, murder, and drug use—subjects treated such that, as one PCA synopsis deliciously put it, they are "at times . . . unusually attractive and at other times wretchedly sordid."[80] Yet while these projects share a variety of sordid credentials, "miscegenation" is the subject they all hold in common, and one that typically leads off, or climactically ends, any given list of objections in the PCA's correspondence, suggesting that it was precisely the thing that made them "un-doable." While brothels could be transformed into dance halls, and murder paid for through punishment and retribution, the censors seem to have had a harder time imagining how to remove forms of desire from a plot without removing the plot itself.[81] This dilemma would at least partially explain the repeated rejections, resubmissions, and a growing repertoire of "usual answers." Most significantly at the moment, the fact that Joy here lumps together the "white and black" and the "white and yellow" as a singularly haunting ghost suggests that they coexist in some shared conceptual space.

At a time when anti-Asian sentiments were being expressed in part through the expansion of definitions of "miscegenation" in state law, the confusion surrounding the applicability of that term to screen fantasies about Asians and whites in part reflects a wider cultural uncertainty about its referent.[82] And how the Hollywood censors dealt with that uncertainty in turn illuminates the cultural stakes of the fierce negotiations of such racial terms at the time. An exchange from 1939 that demands that the PCA reflect on the history of its own application of the clause sheds considerable light in this regard.

Following ten years of interest in the story (registered in letters from five different studios, major and minor alike), yet another proposal of *Shanghai Gesture* is made. Attempting to head off the PCA's objections at the pass, a producer hoping to make the film under Fritz Lang's direction explicitly, and convincingly, makes a case against the miscegenation clause's relevance. The argument rests largely on a series of claims about the history of the clause itself:

> The point of Poppy consorting with an oriental we think, does not violate the code—Poppy is not a white girl—as is found out at the end—She is an Eurasian. Another moral point is brought out—it is not right to intermingle the races—
>
> May I point out several pictures where this identical theme was used—
> "Madame Butterfly"
> Made twice into a picture—Pinkerton never married Cho Cho San. They had an illicit affair and a child was born of it.
> "Thunder in the East"
> John Loder—portrays an ENGLISH NAVAL OFFICER that has an illicit affair with the wife (Merle Oberon) of a Japanese Official (Charles Boyer). This picture passed the censorship in England.
> *When the play "The Shanghai Gesture" was originally banned the code at that time had a point*
> *—Miscegenation is not permitted—Since then it has been deleted to include only relations between Blacks and Whites.*[83]

While objection by the PCA over other issues continues in this very thick file, and this particular production (like many) never got off the ground, "miscegenation" drops from the discussion after receipt of this letter. The PCA's copy of it is marked in pencil with a check at the beginning of the paragraph italicized here and with double vertical lines at the indented clause on miscegenation below that, suggesting that it was the historical reading of the Code's language that won the censors over. And it is true, as we have seen, that at least one pamphlet version was as minimal as the language cited in the letter. Thus, the confusion regarding Asian and whites could, once again, be read as in part stemming from a confusion of documents.

However, if we turn to the PCA's own file on the version of *Madame Butterfly* cited in this appeal, as the PCA staff members reading it likely would have, we see that when the question of "miscegenation" is raised there in 1932, the PCA specifically dismisses it on the grounds that "broadly speaking the miscegenation under the Code usually presupposed whites and negroes."[84] This qualified definition is composed by a Hays Office staffer in New York after consulting with Joy, whose telegram had advised her more unequivocally: "THE INTERPRETATION OF MISCEGENATION UNDER THE CODE HAS ALWAYS BEEN GUIDED BY THE SECOND DICTIONARY DEF-

INITION WHICH SPECIFIES WHITES AND NEGROES ONLY."[85] While the PCA's invocation of the miscegenation clause before and after this assertion shows it to be untrue—in ten years of correspondence prior to International's appeal evident in the files of *Congai* and *Shanghai Gesture*—it is nonetheless extremely significant. For, in light of all the exchanges regarding Asian and whites cited here, it appears that even though the copies of the Code in public circulation did not always say so, and even if the PCA itself did not always practice it, the PCA at some point adopted the position, as expressed in Joy's telegram, that the ban on miscegenation "ha[d] always been [a question of] whites and Negroes."

My reading, in other words, of the confusion surrounding the applicability of the miscegenation clause to Asians and whites is that it cannot be readily untangled to reveal a logical or "reasonable interpretation." Rather, it (1) points up the considerable uncertainty in the PCA's interpretation of the miscegenation clause, despite its language of presumed certainty; and (2) bespeaks the PCA's ultimate preference (beginning in the early to middle thirties) for the notion that "miscegenation" had always already been a question of desire between blacks and whites. By reading the documented contradiction in this way, I am attempting both to make sense of the facts as presented in the archival record and to read their inconsistency. It is clear that the PCA's ultimate stand, as expressed here by Joy, parallels Hollywood's complicity in general with the reduction of questions of "race" in the United States to issues of "black" and "white." Moreover, Joy's formulation needs to be recognized as a kind of active rewriting of the PCA's own recent history, one that "forgets" the rejection of projects such as *Shanghai Gesture* and *Congai*.

This revision, intentional or not, suggests the need to consider the implications of the miscegenation clause both for Hollywood representations of "black" and "white" and for forms of interracial desire that *were* permitted. The remainder of this chapter will begin to do so by focusing on the meanings that circulated in the regular policing of "the white and black races," and then shifting to locations where desire between white and "brown" was openly indulged.

BLACK AND WHITE LIMITS

> Through the simple expedient of demonizing and reifying the range of color on a palette, American Africanism makes it possible to say and not say, to inscribe and erase, to escape and engage, to act out and act on, to historicize and render timeless.
>
> —Toni Morrison[86]

Classical Hollywood's regular adherence to the miscegenation clause functioned perhaps above all else to perpetuate the fiction that "the white and black races" are self-evident categories. Even though the PCA takes its job as an interpretive body extremely seriously, regularly producing voluminous close readings (of a peculiar sort) of synopses, scripts, and preview prints, in all the correspondence I have read no one ever thinks to pose directly questions like "Who is 'black'?" or "Who is 'white'?"[87] Indeed, because the clause works extraordinarily effectively to prevent studios from even proposing what they imagine the clause to prohibit, and because when questionable cases do arise, "white and black" are the least negotiable terms, the number of instances in the files when their meaning is even implicitly discussed is relatively small. This particular silence makes it all the more difficult to ferret out the working definitions, and visual assumptions, of these racial names. Before tackling their more illusive qualities, however, let us first clarify what is most certain about "the white and black races" at the PCA.

The files reflect that even the slightest intimations of sexual desire between "white" and "black" *Americans* always alarmed the PCA and were consistently rejected without hesitation. In an advisory telegram to his Hollywood staff in 1928, prompted by controversy surrounding a film entitled *The Love Mart* (1927), Will Hays articulates what would become a virtual corollary to the miscegenation clause from the late 1920s through the 1940s: "Inadvisable always to show white women in scenes with negroes where there is any inference of miscegenation or social relationship."[88] While reflecting the PCA's hypersensitivity to any and all combinations of black men and white women, the severity of this interdiction could also be read as a response to *The Love Mart*'s explicit address of the permeability of racial categories. For the film turns on the accusation that a "white" southern belle is in fact part "black." Even though that accusation is eventually proven false, the narrative nonetheless imagines the possible breakdown of social hierarchies that miscegenation can threaten, jettisoning the woman from privilege to slavery before the lie is exposed. While such stakes become far less explicit as such narratives are increasingly discouraged, the PCA's ongoing sensitivity to "any inference" of the kind described not only testifies to the predictable fact that the particular combination of black men and white women continued well after *The Birth of a Nation* to be American cinema's favorite miscegenetic nightmare but also suggests that the "white and black races" at issue were the very categories that a dominant white culture required to keep its dominance intact.

Given that, it is not surprising that just as *Birth* had worked not only to project the myth of the black rapist but also to repress the fact of the white one, so the PCA also explicitly objected to depictions of white men chasing black women. Breen makes this clear in response to a proposed reissue of a silent version of *Uncle Tom's Cabin* in 1939.[89] He writes: "Today we had the pleasure of reviewing your picture UNCLE TOM'S CABIN, and regret to inform you that, in its present form, it does not comply with the provisions of the Production Code. . . There is a serious problem of miscegenation, both as to Casey, the older woman, and as to Liza, toward whom Legree is making overtures of an obviously sexual nature."[90] Like Hays's advice on *The Love Mart*, this ruling further demonstrates the PCA's interpretive bottom line: the possibility, much less the actual depiction, of sexual contact between "white" and "black" in the United States, especially during slavery, marked a kind of absolute limit that could not be crossed. Residue of this tradition is detectable even after the clause is removed from the Code. Although many films in the late fifties begin exploring interracial romances in American contexts, the only such case with a recorded PCA objection is one that imagines interracial sex under slavery. A memo documenting a meeting with Warner Bros. regarding *Band of Angels* (1957) reports that the script "in its present form was an unacceptable treatment of illicit sex," but that "it was agreed that the element of illicit sex would be removed and in its place would be substituted a desire on the part of the leads for each other, but *because of the fact that they are master and slave . . .* they would refrain from indulging in sexual intercourse until they are married."[91] How exactly the PCA imagines marriage to mitigate the sexual exploits of slavery is not made clear here, but anxiety about depicting slavery's sexual economy is. And insofar as that economy produced the interracial combination that had been most historically prominent, and remained ready to undermine dominant racial categories and hierarchies that would deny it and its many offspring, we could well read fantasies that recalled such encounters—the sins of white fathers that could still return to haunt their white and not-as-white sons—as the real "Hamlet's father" that beset those charged to enforce the Code's miscegenation clause.

The other salient feature of "the white and black races" as they appear in the writings of the PCA is the stubborn binarity with which they are regularly invoked. Parroting the structure of the clause in question, these writings almost always invoked pairs of one with what the censors deem to be synonymous with the other—for example, "white women in scenes with Negroes," "white man living with native girl," "white woman living with the native aborigine."[92] The effects of this routine fact merit some consideration.

The rhetorical power of the black-white binary has been suggestively theorized by Werner Sollors in his work on interracial literature. Commenting on a turn-of-the-century postcard featuring a black and a white cat dancing together (in bathing suits, at the beach, with other cat "bathers" about cabanas in the background) under the small caption "Mixed Bathing" and on a children's book featuring a wedding between black- and white-furred bunnies from 1958, he writes: "'Black' and 'white' could serve as such forceful agents that they have had the power to eclipse, or racialize, what they referred to; and the metaphoric significance of color could be more important than the ostensibly represented subject" (17). Although Sollors is here theorizing the power of these terms in cases where he deems the subject is *not* ostensibly racial, a claim he himself later complicates, his larger insight proves valuable even when the content in question clearly *is*. For the terms "black and white" have accrued the power not only "to eclipse, or racialize," I would argue, but to radically reduce whatever they refer to such that the potential meanings and complexities of the subjects so modified—all the cultural, historical, political, economic, and psychological meanings that can circulate when we talk about "race"—become absurdly reduced to something as dualistic and flat as the most simplistic juxtaposition of dark and light.

Sollors's own assertions about the role of the visual in black-white rhetoric are also provocative here. He acknowledges that racial and gender coding of the cats give the postcard its potential interracial connotation, but then argues that it is the heading ("Mixed Bathing") that clinches it. Having imagined other possible headings ("'Cats by the Seaside,' 'The New Beach Apparel,' 'Family Vacation,' or 'Summer,'"), he claims, "In each case . . . it would be the title, a *text*, that would give the central theme to the image: the image would seem to be 'about' different things, dependent on the heading it received" (17). Although I have more difficulty imagining titles connoting public space and family, or even leisure and fashion, to be race-free at the turn of the century, I would certainly grant that writing can inflect such readings of images. Nonetheless, I would insist more forcefully on the power of contexts, at this and other historical moments, that could well induce interracial readings of images of such decidedly gendered and sexualized, as well as color-coded, anthropomorphic figures. Indeed, in this case and that of the bunny book attacked by some as integrationist in the late fifties, the facts that the figures are heterocouples (holding hands and frolicking on the beach, courting and wedding), and the male figures are coded "black" and the female ones "white," make it hard to imagine how some audiences, primed to read and reject such images on so many fronts, would *not* read them as interracial. The obvious but important point for my argument is that to assume that writing has the power to mean more, or to control meaning more authoritatively, than visual language not only prematurely invests faith in the word but also ignores the potential discursive power of the visual in racial representation.

Instead, I suggest, we need to consider further the relations that can obtain between visual and linguistic racial codings. This of course returns us with yet another purpose to the PCA and the SRC and their peculiar job of reading for, and writing out, potential filmic representations of miscegenation. As they do so, what are the regular assumptions about both linguistic and visual forms of "white" and "black"?

Although whiteness itself typically surfaces as an assumed subject, not a nominated object, in the writings that pass between the studios and the censors, it gets direct attention on a few interesting occasions. A file from the SRC on a film produced before Breen's more exacting oversight of the Code demonstrates that the meaning of whiteness was by no means fixed or unquestioned in mainstream Hollywood of the early thirties. In Jason Joy's review of the script for *Aloha*, a small South Sea island film from 1931 that features a doomed marriage between Jimmy, a white American, and "Ilanu, a half-caste native girl," he warns about a series of "dangerous" details that might provoke local censorship. Among them is the remark of "the little Japanese boy . . . when he sees the negro at the gate: 'Aw! He don't belong with us white people—his dad' a street sweeper.'"[93] Joy suggests that "as a matter of public policy this statement be omitted." Whatever the original intent, this suggestion effectively mutes humor that might jog thought about, or even critical pleasure in, the social and economic meanings of whiteness and its felt detachment from "racial" identity.

At the same time, while such an example suggests that the censors' work functions to safeguard dominant discourses of race (and class), the same file reflects a more ambiguous schema of color that the SRC and even its more regulating successor *do* tolerate. In documentation of material included in the film, but deleted by at least two local censor boards, we read of a telling exchange that did not appear in Joy's letter of objections. Kidding his friend Jimmy about the island's "brown skin native" women, Steve cracks, "The longer you're here the lighter they get. Look, that one's nearly white now."[94] While the PCA will be much less comfortable with such an overt announcement of slippage, linguistic or otherwise, between "brown" and "white" in the South Seas, it will nonetheless confirm what is unusually announced in the cited dialogue: the definition and redefinition of whiteness is very precisely keyed to the desires of white men.

In part this example manifests one of the primary powers of whiteness, as theorized by Richard Dyer. Recognizing "white as a skin colour" to be "internally variable and unclear at the edges," Dyer proposes perhaps the most astute definition of whiteness as a cultural identity when he writes that it is "a matter of ascription—white people are who white people say are white."[95] The dual insight is that the meaning of "white" (or "black," for that matter) is produced through processes of ascribing racial names, and that whiteness in particular maintains its distinction through alignment with the position of discursive power in that very process. As Dyer also puts it, "Whites are those who have such knowledge, but are themselves less readily the object of it" (20). Hence, insofar as Steve commands the knowledge and the names of "brown" and "white," whiteness is still very much intact. Just as "the little Japanese boy" is not permitted to redefine "white people," so Jimmy's "half-caste native girl," we can be quite sure, is not making jokes about the browning of Steve and Jimmy's desire.

The implications of such readings extend productively to the larger processes of racial ascription filtered through the SRC and the PCA. Not only does the power of whiteness accrue to the censors who call the shots about who is and is not white, but their negotiations of race and color contribute to the endowment of whiteness with precisely that power of knowing and not being known, naming and not being named, seeing and not being seen. This is in part analogous to the fortification of whiteness through the judges of courtrooms past who were granted the power to determine racial identity by their own sight.[96] What is more, as the apparatus of Hollywood eventually disseminates such sights, judgments, and discursive positions to national and international spectators, that particularly "white" imprint so literalized by the censors' power of ascription marks popular ways of seeing and naming as well.

Some aspects of the PCA's production of whiteness are very much in line with those already familiar from other cultural practices. Like census takers instructed to mark the race only of those who are not white, so too do PCA censors using forms eventually used to streamline the review process assume whiteness to be the unmarked, invisible norm, listing under the heading "Portrayal of 'Races' or Nationals" most anything but "White" or "Caucasian" (e.g., "Negro," "Mulatto," "Mexican," "Irish").[97] Similarly, "white" is only named when it comes in close proximity to its imagined other, as in the kinds of binary pairs previously cited (e.g., "white women . . . with Negroes," "white man . . . with native girl"). Insofar as white men and women who cross the PCA's desk are otherwise treated as "just" men and women, and others are necessarily racially marked, one could say, again invoking Dyer, that "other people are raced, [white people] are just people" (1). In regard to one of the rejected "un-doables" the world itself is figured as if white, and judging, when a staffer reports, "The whole world seemed to think it was entirely without the pale."[98]

If whiteness typically inheres in the position that knows and names, blackness is invariably assumed as the site of racial content.[99] Similarly, whereas whiteness is cautiously regulated as that territory people are privileged to be included within or are excluded from, by opposition and in regular Hollywood practice blackness is treated as if its meaning were more fixed, the last thing in need of definition.[100] Such assumptions are explained in part by the function of blackness in relation to, and at the service of, whiteness. As Toni Morrison suggests in her reading of the American literary tradition, blackness must be "enslaved," "repulsive," "helpless," "history-less," "damned," "a blind accident of evolution," so that whiteness can figure itself as "free," "desirable," destined, and so forth (52). Hollywood cinema, which has traditionally excised blackness perhaps even more forcibly than has American literature, has staged this oppositional drama with perhaps even more pronounced enactments of the distances between its two poles. That is, just as the miscegenation clause explicitly refuses black-white encounters of the most intimate, proximate, kind, so does Hollywood cinema regularly project blackness to spatial and temporal extremes—in jungles and outbuildings, at the edges of the picture frame and civilization. Such figurative remoteness is evident at the PCA in the regular interchangeability of the terms "black," "native," and "native aborigine."

Significantly, however, although this chain of associations that links "black" to "native" at times does so by way of "Africa" and other "primitive" signifiers, thus implying recourse to an ancestrally organized racial paradigm, close scrutiny of the PCA files reveals that its working definitions of "black" do not in fact strictly follow from that paradigm.[101] That is, when push comes to shove and definitional boundaries need marking or clarification, early and late indicators suggest that it is not blood or ancestry that the censors rely upon to make final calls but precise negotiations of word and image—negotiations that seem uniquely informed by, and formative of, the discursive properties of Hollywood cinema.

The primacy of the black-white opposition at the PCA, and its ultimate detachment there from biology or ancestry, are particularly evident in two cases involving efforts to put to rest lurking uncertainty about the race of female characters paired with white men. In each the PCA defines the women's whiteness as their lack of blackness. Reporting on a meeting with MGM about *Never the Twain Shall Meet*, one staffer writes, "I told them that I felt that the story was all right from the point of view of miscegenation because the father of the girl is white and . . . [t]he mother was a Polynesian queen and *Polynesians are not black*."[102] Similarly, after years of dismissively rejecting *White Cargo*, the censors finally tolerate this former Broadway hit when its African "native siren" who seduces white men is revealed to be "white" (a curious complication I will attend to shortly); and the way they repeatedly define her whiteness in correspondence to MGM is, singularly, by her lack of "negro."[103] They worry about the timing, not the method, of "the trick of holding back to the end of the picture the fact that Tondelayo is *not a negress*," and hence insist the studio "remove any flavor whatever of miscegenation, and . . . establish from the very beginning that Tondelayo has *no negro blood* in her *at all.*"[104] Such negative definitions of whiteness—never defining what it is, but only what it is not—not only perpetuate what Dyer diagnoses as that term's perpetual cultural status as an absence (an absence of "race," an absence of marking, etc.) but also, in the latter case especially, stand in lieu of what would likely be a more problematic recourse to ancestry. For it is only in the final review form prior to the PCA's certificate of approval that that agency acknowledges in writing, and in passing, the following explanation of Tondelayo's whiteness: "Roberts can't refuse to wed them for he reveals she is a white woman. (Orphan of Arab-Egyptian parents)."[105] That the film circumvents miscegenation to the PCA's satisfaction by transforming Tondelayo, seemingly in name only, from "black" to "white" by making her an "Arab-Egyptian" seems remarkable in at once no longer being a story about "miscegenation," yet at the same time clearly still being one.[106] In part, by sanctioning a white Englishman's relationship with a woman of potentially African descent, this "liberal" (by PCA standards) reading from 1942 again returns us to the national subtext haunting the miscegenation clause—a touch of African is tolerable, in other words, so long as it is not African American and is paired with a white man from England and not Mississippi (or Indiana or California, for that matter). In addition, the particular way in which this "trick" of transforming Tondelayo from black to white is pulled off also points to other modes of racial formation at work.

The complications of translating Tondelayo's "not" blackness from paper to screen are already curiously hinted at in the PCA's own writings about her, especially in their explicit retraction of their original emphasis on asserting her lack of "negro blood." Pleased with a revised script, their last words on the matter are: "We strongly urge that there be *no actual discussion of the alleged negro blood* in Tondeleyo [*sic*]. This, we believe, could be handled *largely by inference*, up to the point where you clear the matter up and indicate that she is white."[107] While the letter does not specify what methods of "inference" might be employed, the film that was ultimately made featured the by then well-recognized (as white and European) Heddy Lamarr in a coat of dark body paint, slinking about the jungle with a visible and voiced appetite as much for bangles as for the white plantation overseers she seduces to acquire them for her. Thus, "native" blackness is ultimately conveyed through Tondelayo's image, supplemented by her speech and that of the men who discuss her dangerous sexual presence. Indeed, the nominal absence and eventual disavowal of her being "black" by no means fully contains the visual "inference." Although *White Cargo* remains a rather exceptional case, and one that would not be acceptable as an openly American fantasy for some time, the fact that the PCA can stretch its still strict regulations in this way demonstrates the considerable flexibility of such racializing processes. Whether or not the PCA avoided discussion of racial "blood" out of an awareness of its increasingly objectionable status, it effectively avoided the imagined fixity and substance that such language attempted to evoke.[108] Instead, *White Cargo* conjures ambiguous mixtures of word and image suited to more mobile, indefinite fantasies: the film can both indulge in the titillations of a racialized sexual difference and regulate such transgressions with the logocentric fantasy of words that trump appearance.

This recorded impulse to silence "blood" and conjure blackness through "inference" indicates a more common, if unconscious, practice of racial formation through the image. That practice is already apparent in the attempt to assert the "not black[ness]" of the female lead in *Never the Twain Shall Meet*. What my ellipsis in the first citation from that file momentarily withheld was the coupling of the binary logic that defines the questionable Polynesian mother as "not black" to a strikingly visual one: "The story was all right from the point of view of miscegenation because the father of the girl is white and he is the only one shown in the picture."[109] Such a formulation would seem to announce the inadequacy of ancestry and the necessity of the visual in Hollywood's racial scheme. Not satisfied to define the child's race simply after "the condition of the mother," as the legal tradition of slavery typically did, nor even after the more decisively white line of the father, it supplements both with the privileged status of what, or who, is "in the picture."

These local articulations, I suggest, speak to one of the most enduring assumptions of the racial productions at the PCA, and in Hollywood representations more generally. And once again, such long-term effects of decades of racial-film practice under the Code are vivid even after the miscegenation ban has been lifted. For just as the PCA's hypersensitivity to exploitative interracial sex under slavery comes out most openly in its review of *Band of Angels*, so too does its unspoken faith in the visibility of black and white "in the picture" itself come out most strikingly in its reading of an interracial scenario from *Night of the Quarter Moon* (1959) a few years later.

The revealing remarks are occasioned by a scene that oddly mirrors the racial operations of the PCA. In the courtroom climax of an annulment case against a woman on the charge that she concealed her "black" identity from her husband before their marriage, *Night of the Quarter Moon* stages its racial, legal, and dramatic resolution in the exposure of the woman's body to the judge. Her defense attorney rips her dress partially away from her to establish that her fiancé, having frequently skinny-dipped with her during their courtship in Mexico, "couldn't help but

FIG. 3.1. Hollywood's faith in the visibility of race, on display in *Night of the Quarter Moon* (1959). Publicity still. Courtesy of Academy of Motion Picture Arts and Sciences.

know that those parts of [her] body normally covered by a bathing suit were the same color as the rest" (fig. 3.1). While I will return to this extraordinary scene in another chapter, its relevance for the moment can be confined to the PCA's assessment of it. Although that assessment is consistent with multiple warnings about the "exposure" of the female body (warnings that reflect a near obsession at the PCA in the fifties), the crucial point is the racial logic it accepts: "The business of a woman being allowed to expose her intimate parts in the presence of a judge and other principals, in order to prove the color of her skin is the same all over, is in our judgment an unacceptable portrayal of our Courts of Law. . . . any judge in maintaining the dignity of the Court would in a situation of this kind appoint a female doctor to make this examination privately and report her findings. Further, it goes without saying that any undue exposure of Ginny's person would in itself constitute a Code violation."[110] Most astounding here is that such an extended meditation on what makes this scene objectionable is utterly blind to its most objectionable premise, the "logic" that assumes that because Ginny is part "Negro," her skin will not show a tan line but will appear "the same all over." This premise raises no questions from the PCA, I suggest, because it is fully in keeping with that organization's habitual faith in the visibility of race. That faith is revealed at an extreme here (even without the further complication that Ginny is portrayed by a known white actress), as the film imagines not only that the sight of skin will verify instantly a "Negro" identity, but also that that identity is fixed upon that surface in some absolute, unmodulated fashion. Putting it in terms (invited by the film) whose weight will become all the more apparent as we consider the status of skin color in the South Seas, black is defined quite explicitly as *not* a tan. Rather, the PCA censors have no trouble imagining it as a permanent visible state unaffected even by the sun. More revealing testimony as to their wholesale investment in the fiction that race, or at least blackness, is transparently visible is hard to imagine.

As this kind of visual rhetoric becomes apparent through the daily writings of the PCA, so does the significance of the fact that it is embedded in the language of the miscegenation clause itself: while we have seen PCA documents discuss "Negroes," "native[s]," "native aborigine[s]," "Arab-Egyptian[s]," "French," "half-caste[s]," "Eurasian[s]," "English," "Polynesian[s]," and so forth, the clause reduces such categories to "the white and black races." This not only defines race as a chromatic, visual difference but in so doing attempts to render multiple and often unstable conceptions of identity (regional, national, ethnic, etc.) into a singular, rigidly binarized, and easily legible distinction. Hence, while the PCA's own interpretations of the miscegenation clause indicate that its terms were never simple or straightforward, those visual names function to make such complex matters of difference *appear* to be so. That the censorial practices that sought to write racial instability out of the image had as much effect on the filmic envisioning of "race" as on its written and spoken articulation behind the scenes becomes increasingly apparent as we turn to the filmic treatment of desires that, if not "white and black," were nonetheless undeniably marked by more questionable exposures to the sun.

From the South to the South Seas: "A Brown Jill for Every [White] Jack"

Thus far it appears that in negotiating questions of racial difference, the PCA censors were commonly operating as much, if not more, within discourses of color as within those of race conceived in biological or ancestral terms. The stakes of such practice become all the more intriguing when we consider that the very same agency that sought to block fantasies that would blur the distinction between the "white and black races" also simultaneously sanctioned the routine productions of an entire genre in which white men openly desired, married, and often procreated with what some scripts temporarily articulated as "brown" women in distant, unspecified island locales. Such fantasies could be tolerated, could even seek to titillate and amuse, I will argue, because the South Sea Island film effectively tamed formerly haunting miscegenation fantasies through a series of entwined substitutions: (1) it displaced the historical and political realities of the American past and present onto virtually atemporal and aspatial scenes of exotic-erotic utopia; (2) it transposed ostensible "nightmares" of free men of color abusing white women, and disavowed histories of white men abusing enslaved black women, with daydreams of white men being pleasured and served by women ambiguously "colored" and decidedly pliant; and (3) it replaced increasingly fraught questions of "race" with a visible, but largely unspoken, discourse of "color." While this last substitution will provide a critical conclusion to this chapter and a segue to the next, the work it achieves is best understood after a consideration of the first two.

While seemingly innocuous island romance pictures like *Aloha* (1931), *Jungle Princess* (1936), *Paradise Isle* (1937), *Her Jungle Love* (1938), and *Aloma of the South Seas* (1941) might seem the furthest thing from the epic imagery and ideology of *The Birth of a Nation*, the lines connecting the two have already been partially traced. Thomas Cripps and James Nesteby have suggested that the movement can be read in two stages: first in the shift from racial fantasies set in the South to ones set in the jungles of Africa, and from there to the more racially and politically benign tropics of the South Seas.[111]

A more direct path from the South to the South Seas, and one that highlights fantasies of miscegenation as the critical link between them, is charted by none other than D. W. Griffith.[112] Griffith made two South Sea Island films, *The Love Flower* and *The Idol Dancer*, both released in 1920, five years after *The Birth of a Nation* and a year after *Broken Blossoms*.[113] Analysis of *The Idol Dancer* invites a comparison to those texts not only for the recycling of Griffith's trademark scenario of light-skinned women trapped in a house on the verge of assault by dark intruders and its obligatory race to the rescue, but also for the explosion of racial and sexual relations configured through these and other filmic structures. Moreover, with the historical and political weight of American locations and relations lifted in the transportation to a virtually mythical place, it seems that most anything goes.[114] In a gesture that at once radically distances the film's multiple interracial fantasies from things American and yet simultaneously announces that very projection, an early intertitle establishes the location: "On Rainbow Beach, Romance Island under the Southern Cross." Not so incidentally, the landscape here is marked by palm trees, coconut, and the "odor of Magnolia bloom." The full significance of the romances that will occur in this *other* "Southern" location during the years of the Code is illuminated by an assessment of the racial and erotic substitutions that so manifestly unfold in this initiate voyage to the South Seas.

With the historical and political safety of this spatial relocation, *The Idol Dancer* not only repeats *The Birth of a Nation*'s primary miscegenation fantasy of the black rapist but goes further to represent some of the things *Birth* worked most forcefully to repress. Not the least of these is the sheer range of "racial" identities and desires depicted. Whereas *Birth* divided the world into white and black, and vilified mulattoes precisely because they blur the line between them, "Rainbow Beach" (although of course shot in black and white) is populated by a much wider spectrum of lights and darks. We do find extreme racialized poles, marked by white missionaries from New England, on one end, and a "black" chief and tribe, on the other. Both groups are portrayed by white actors, but the latter's blackness is conjured through intertitles as well as dark body paint, fright wigs, "savage" scraps of clothing, and an assortment of skull and bone accessories. But the woman who falls most clearly in the middle of these black and white extremes—aptly named "The White Almond Flower"—far from being vilified, is the favorite object of desire for men of all shades. Her whiteness inheres primarily in the pale skin of the actress who plays her (Clarine Seymour) and in her relation to her adopted, and depicted, white father; her "almond[ness]," reading that as the signifier of her not-so-white parts, is filmically marked once by an intertitle ("the blood of vivacious France, inscrutable Java and languorous Samoa mingles in her veins") and perpetually through her visual representation.[115] She wears, alternately, a grass skirt and palm-frond tube top ensemble, and a floral sarong, and until her last-minute Christian conversion, she worships a pagan idol and is prone to primitive, and explicitly tinted, dancing: "The mystic visions of her people move through the exotic coloring of her dance." In addition to White Almond Flower's clearly "interstitial" racial position, to borrow a phrase from Rhona Berenstein, other characters are coded either more or less white or black than she, indicating further fracturing of the optical-racial spectrum.[116] These include not only a white outlaw who fraternizes with blacks—à la *Birth*'s Austin Stoneman—earning him the name "Blackbirder," but a "native" man with an emphasized fondness for Western apparel, and a host of island women who wear "native" attire, but whose long, flowing hair and absence of body paint clearly position them as "less black" than the chief's dark, fright-wigged companion. This relatively wide optical range on Rainbow Beach both compromises the dominant cultural binary and provides the opportunity for an even greater number of permutations of interracial desire, many of which are imagined in the course of the film.

Most strikingly, the film not only replicates familiar images of more and less white women pursued by more and less black men but explicitly implicates white men as investors in that fantasy, as well as in interracial fantasies all their own—something Griffith could never do back on the plantation.[117] Blackbirder, the white outlaw, encourages the black chief to pursue White Almond Flower and also joins him in ogling her in a shot reminiscent of so many black looks at white women from *Birth*. But unlike that film, it is not only the white man who conspires with blacks who desires the woman with "exotic coloring." This film's main plot follows the triangle of two "whiter" white men openly competing for her affection. What is more, these same white men are visibly marked by a variety of afflictions: one, the Beachcomber (Richard Barthelmess), falls in and out of consciousness due to his habitual consumption of gin; the other, the missionary's visiting nephew whom the film dubs "an invalid," coughs excessively, spends a good portion of the film sick in bed, and does not survive the race to the rescue.

While it is not surprising, ideologically speaking, to find more images of *black* savagery and sexuality with Griffith's travel to the South Seas, it is surprising to find *white* men so openly indulging in the "rainbow" romances that flourish there, and to see their infirmities so visible long before and even during the climactic scene in which the (white and black) "savages" are put to rest. Most remarkably, insofar as *Birth* can be read as already having projected white male sexuality onto black men and as having projected white male vulnerability onto white women, *The Idol Dancer* comes increasingly to look like not just a simple relocation of American miscegenation fantasies but a kind of reversal that allows for the return of much that was formerly repressed.[118] With its images of the white rapist as well as the black one, and the insufficient white male figures who are by turns drunk, sick, trapped in the house with the women, and dead, this film knows and shows, far more flagrantly than *Birth* ever did, that popular American fantasies of interracial desire and assault are largely propelled by anxieties about *white* male sexuality, not black, and about white *male* insufficiency and vulnerability, not female.

To be sure, many things change as we leap forward to the increasingly classical Hollywood of the thirties and forties. There, as we have seen, images of black men "ogling" white women in any location will be especially policed. Nonetheless, while it is true that not *all* white men on South Sea Islands in the classical period will be marked by infirmity, many will appear variously lost, blind, sick, and/or otherwise in need of excessive pampering.[119] What is more, with the advent of sound and color, the women they desire will become noticeably infantilized, often speaking with "native" accents that sound a lot like baby talk, and always bronzed, be it through casting or other forms of filmic artifice.[120] Indeed, typically removing black masculinity as any kind of threat whatsoever, and pairing white men with passive women of color, the South Sea Island films will reinforce and eroticize white male privilege through their tropical scenarios of master and servant, voyeur and spectacle. This new configuration of interracial desire and power, seemingly far beyond the boundaries of any social institutions (much less American ones), will allow for not only interracial romance but also cohabitation, marriage, and babies.

The genre's third displacement, transforming race into color, returns us one last time to the censors at the PCA. Insofar as the South Sea Islands are increasingly invoked as a kind of utopic stage for certain straight white male fantasies wherein women of color willingly pleasure and serve, the question becomes not simply, how could the Code censors tolerate one set of interracial fantasies so similar to another set which they simultaneously sought to block? Additionally, we need to ask, what happens to filmic definitions of "race" in the course of their doing so? More specifically, what happens to how Hollywood as a cultural institution helps to shape and define our very notion of what racial difference is and how we filmically read it?

Much of what I have said and still want to say is invited by a marvelous trade review of *Her Jungle Love*, starring Dorothy Lamour, in 1938. I cite a large portion of it to offer a taste of a genre readers may not have the good fortune, or bad luck, of being very familiar with, and to tease out further what is at stake in its visualization of desire and difference. The review proclaims:

> This is a *pictorial wish fulfillment for about eight of every 10 males, picture-goers and other kind*, [sic]. . . . It is set in an isolated South Pacific isle. Cocanuts [sic] drop from the trees and the passion fruit glows red. There are some nice friendly animals. A gorgeous swimming lagoon. A cozy cave. A coral strand. *And a girl, all togged out in a seductive sarong and a fine tan. It all adds up to the ultimate illusion, with Technicolor to make it more luscious.* . . .
>
> "Her Jungle Love" is *epidermic drama*—skin deep. The story will not matter a great deal, as to detail and plot, although it is *precisely the kind to cater to the dream wish, not to be scanned too carefully as to geography, geology or zoology.*
>
> Dorothy Lamour comes upon them, scantily saronged, with her companion ape and lion cub. She is white but believes herself native. . . .
>
> *The color camera emphasizes her appeal and the setting is particularly becoming to her talents.*[121]

This review not only posits a theory of the forms of spectatorship and sexual fantasy that drive the film ("pictorial wish fulfillment for about eight of every 10 males"—a theory that knew even then that the dominant model does not apply to *all* male viewers), but goes further to see the visual pleasures on display as decidedly generic. The gradual crescendo of the catalog of elements, "Cocanuts . . . passion fruit . . . swimming lagoon. . . . And a girl," makes it abundantly clear that the film maps a particularly classic male fantasy through a particularly generic scene. Indeed, it is because the generic mise-en-scène so thoroughly sets the stage for the mise-en-scène of desire in question, our Freudian reviewer leads us to understand, that narrative and plot "will not matter a great deal." It all unfolds on an "isolated" and significantly unspecified "South Pacific isle" conjured merely as the setting in which this "dream wish" can be most pleasingly fulfilled.

So what exactly *is* this wish? While the reviewer's description of the film as "epidermic drama" claims to mark its superficiality, the epithet also seems appropriate in locating one of the genre's primary erogenous zones. Recall that the climax of the generic catalog was not just "a girl," but one "all togged out in a seductive sarong and a fine tan." This review would seem to be saying, and the viewer of this or any other Lamour South Sea Island film can readily attest to this, that the particular "talents" and "appeal" so nicely emphasized by "the color camera" and the setting inhere precisely *in* the sarong and the tan.[122] Or, as another reviewer of another such film put it, "They are packing the place to watch Dorothy Lamour tame tigers and errant explorers, clothed in nothing more than *a swell coat of suntan and a calico shift*."[123] Even if it does not openly depend on racial difference, this fantasy of scantily clad bodies, bronzed by tropical suns or, if need be, by makeup, lighting, and eventually Technicolor, is at the very least thoroughly invested in a series of particulars that are systematically attached to bodies with color.

Trade reviewers were on to much of this with the release of *Mutiny on the Bounty* in 1935. *Variety* went so far as to question, and partially answer, how the film could have passed the test of the Code's miscegenation clause: "Delicate romancing amidst picturesque scenes in Tahiti by the English sailors is handled with finesse by the script, and the boys must have worn out plenty of kid gloves in slipping this part of the story in with diplomacy. Polynesians are considered members of the white race by many experts, but whether they are so held by the majority of lay men is questionable. [The] girl friends are *very much Poly in appearance*. But it's all done so neatly that kicks won't be numerous."[124]

Striking here is the marking of, and distance between, racial names and scopic norms. Although one PCA insider suggests there is no objectionable racial difference between "Polynesians" and "whites" (because the former are neither "black" nor "yellow"), more interesting at present is the way in which this reviewer *sees* a form of difference ("very much Poly in appearance") despite whatever racial name he, the PCA, or ordinary viewers might give it.[125] (The mental image to recall here, of course, is "a girl, all togged out in a seductive sarong and a fine tan"). Indeed, regardless of what the PCA does or does not think it is doing, contemporary reviews of South Sea Island films read their romances between white men and "tanned" women on a continuum with other interracial film fare, even if on a decidedly less "serious" end of the spectrum.[126]

Here, I think, is where we come to see what the censorship and production of South Sea Island films has to teach us about Hollywood's contribution to the cultural production of racial names and scopic norms. Throughout their interpretations of the miscegenation clause, the PCA censors perpetually define race in both fields: the determination of what is "white" and what is "black," of what is "yellow," "brown," and "red" for that matter—all terms one is likely to read in the PCA files— has to do both with how we apply these names to various bodies on screen and with how we see and conceive of the identities thus fashioned. What is more, in the case of the South Sea Island film in particular, the PCA censors tolerate the visibility of desire between white men and women "very much Poly in appearance," so long as that appearance is not overtly, racially, named. What I mean by this, and its potential implications, becomes clearer with a look at some of the censors' most precise negotiations of such words and images.

A synopsis of the *Mutiny on the Bounty* script quickly endorsed by the PCA describes how the mutineers "select native wives" in Tahiti, one in particular "falling in love with the beautiful daughter of one of the chiefs[,] marrying her [and i]n time . . . hav[ing] a child" by her.[127] Breen not only accepts the state of these affairs but compliments L. B. Mayer on the "general strength and beauty of the story."[128] Yet despite his "great interest and admiration," he warns Mayer of objectionable content, including violence, the ship's "bawdy atmosphere," and "most dangerous . . . of course, the nudity of the native men and women Tahitians and the relationship between them and the crew of the Bounty."[129] Breen is highly cautious in particular about the representation of the sexual relationship between Christian (eventually played by Clark Gable) and his "native" wife, Maimiti (eventually played by "Movita," an actress the studio packaged as an authentic South Sea Islander but who, *Variety* claimed, was "really a Mexican girl . . . from the South Main Street cabarets").[130] In all such correspondence in this genre, Breen consistently pitches his warnings in terms of nudity and "explicit" sexual behavior, never invoking race or miscegenation. At the same time, and this is the telling detail, he makes a point of deleting dialogue that draws attention to the colorization, if you will, of the island fantasy. With *Mutiny* he calls for the revision of the line "Wot would a brown gal *do for that*," and of a speech by Captain Bligh about "a brown Jill for every Jack."[131] The unstated principle would thus seem to be that it is perfectly acceptable to *film* fantasies of "a brown Jill for every [white] Jack," as long as one does not *name* them as such.[132]

Similar deletions of the words "brown" and "red" are recommended by the SRC in 1930 regarding the script of *Aloha,* discussed earlier in this chapter in connection with the PCA's regulation of its jokes about whiteness and lightness. In that film Jimmy similarly marries and procreates with Ilanu before she throws herself into a volcano at film's end. And again, as in the PCA files on *Mutiny on the Bounty* and all other South Sea Island films I have read, there is no written concern regarding miscegenation. However, SRC director Jason Joy flagged as "dangerous" "from the standpoint of censorship" dialogue that included the line: "I can think of so many things with a red hot hula baby like that."[133] He also advises that they "leave off the underscored phrase or use a different expression" for "it was your island you wanted—*and your brown lover.*"[134] These directions to avoid naming "brown" and "red" come precisely at the moments when such colors are used to modify the objects of white male desire.

Similarly, in another genre, the Hays Office objects to the color coding of the title, but not the premise, of a script in which a white man marries a Native American woman. In that case, also indicative of the larger trend, the objectionable title that announces the "color" of the white man's lover, *Red Woman,* is swiftly replaced by a colorless one, *Behold My Wife!* This example succinctly condenses the trend: a form of desire understood as interracial is sanctioned and/as visible, so long as it trades in its racial announcement for a language that speaks instead in the classical terms of (proprietary) masculine vision and feminine specularity.[135]

What I am proposing here, then, is not simply that the PCA and the studios partook of a kind of winking and nodding, conscious or unconscious, about the acceptability of unspoken interracial fantasies. Additionally, what made this possible, and what in part results from it, is a way of constructing difference that in effect replaces previously conventional but increasingly strained discourses of "race"—ones that negotiated the relation of racial names to scopic norms through mechanisms of math, family trees, and the like—to one that rests more and more heavily on the image, an image commonly produced and perceived on the surface of female bodies.

While the next chapter will continue to examine the unique cinematic possibilities and limits of such a paradigm, we have already begun to see some of its potential effects. Like so many of their racial practices, the PCA censors' attempts to erase "brown" and "red" from filmic speech and writing are by no means absolute, as evidenced by their tolerance of the joke from *Aloha* that figures "brown skin native" women lightening, even whitening, albeit under the desirous looks of white men. Most important, although they certainly do not make what was formerly announced disappear, the censors' repeated impulses to mute the various

"colors" of white male desire clearly attempt to leave the image unmarked in a certain sense.[136] As a result, the *images* of "a brown Jill for
every Jack" are more easily consumable by certain (on- and offscreen)
subjects because the spectator is asked to read the "brown" of bodies not
as signifiers of "race" per se—there are, after all, only "the white and
black races" in the language of the Code—but, in effect, as pure cinematic color, "a fine tan . . . with Technicolor to make it more lus-
cious."[137] This at once serves and elides the racial and colonial politics of
the sexual fantasies in question, and further extends the visual and erotic
reach of Hollywood's overall racial map, where the only colors we are
regularly asked to see *and* name, and thereby to know and fantasize in
much more rigid and regulated ways, are black and white (and sometimes yellow).

CHAPTER FOUR

Picturizing Race:
On Visibility, Racial Knowledge, and
Cinematic Belief

THE PROBLEM WITH PEOLA

Implicit already in the last chapter is that Hollywood cinema has con-
tributed to the cultural production and dissemination not only of particular racial fictions—the wide array of types and stereotypes—but of an
entire racial epistemology, a system of knowledge that deems "race" to
be a visible fact. This chapter expands that argument to consider the
work of dominant cinematic structures of gender and belief, especially at
moments when racial meanings are far in excess of, and can even contradict, the bodily markings we do or do not see. Such inquiry is invited by
two extraordinary cases, both involving tremendously popular films, at
the beginning and near the end of the enforcement of the Production
Code's miscegenation clause: the 1934 version of *Imitation of Life* and
Pinky, from 1949. Because their most troubling "black" female subjects
at times appear to be "white," and because the potential histories and
fantasies surrounding this apparent contradiction received such radically
different treatment at the PCA, together these films suggest an extended
narrative about Hollywood's ongoing construction of racial visibility and
spectatorial belief. For close analysis of them and their PCA files will reveal a gradual shift in the location of racial meaning from invisible discourses of "blood" and ancestry to visual discourses anchored increasingly by the properties of classical cinema itself. Such claims will invite us
to reconsider the dominant cultural assumption that racial difference is in
fact visible as, in part, an elaborate cinematic production.

When Universal submitted a script of *Imitation of Life* for approval
under the Production Code in March 1934, the PCA initially rejected it
on the grounds that it violated the miscegenation clause. What is strikingly odd about this original ruling, however, is that the objectionable element was not any visible or even expressed "sex relationship between
the white and black races," as prohibited by the Code. Indeed, like Fannie Hurst's best-selling novel on which the script was based, the film
melodrama was far more concerned with relationships among black and

white women than with any heterosexual ones.[1] Nevertheless, in a letter to Universal supporting PCA director Joe Breen's nebulous interpretation of miscegenation, Will Hays, Breen's boss, expressed the PCA's "considerable worry" on the subject and urged the studio to drop the project lest it "develop into a case very near the borderline."[2]

The borderline Hays specifies refers to the PCA's divided obligations to the studios, on the one hand, and "to Society," on the other. The extensive PCA file of correspondence on *Imitation of Life,* however, reveals that the censors' concern was in fact tied to a range of more profound borderlines—in particular, those marking differences of race, color, blood, and skin. As we will see, the character Peola, the light-skinned daughter of the black maid Delilah, not only confounded the PCA's ability to discern racial identity but perpetually threatened to unmask "race" as itself an imitation through and through, a cultural fiction in which we are asked to believe that has no natural life of its own. Moreover, *Imitation of Life*'s perceived danger "to Society," I will suggest, was that it threatened to expose cinema's unique contribution to dominant constructions of race. That contribution is inadvertently suggested in Breen's (multiple) rejection letters when he deems that "no *picturization* of miscegenation is permitted" and identifies *Imitation* as "the type of story, which, if *picturized,* will necessarily have to be rejected."[3] Hays echoes this formulation when he pleads, "In a case like this, of course, it would be hoped that *the picture not be made.*"[4] What this contemporary movie jargon brings to the surface is that the PCA's "considerable worry" in this case was keyed to yet another borderline, that between the visibility and invisibility of racial identity.

The PCA's heightened anxiety is apparent throughout this unusually voluminous file. Zealously zeroing in on what he interpreted as miscegenetic material in his first year as director of the PCA, Breen penned a strident rejection of the script only two days after it was sent to him. While this letter was typed up, but never sent—perhaps because he sensed the sticky questions his reading would prompt—it nonetheless reflects the alarmist tone Breen and others would subsequently take in numerous letters, memos, reported meetings, and phone calls. Referring to what he calls the script's "main theme . . . founded upon the results of sex association between the white and black race (miscegenation)," he warns that "it not only violates the Production Code but is very dangerous from the standpoint both of industry and public policy."[5] Monitoring the situation from New York, Hays voiced his concern in a single-sentence letter: "Dear Joe: I note your worry about the possible miscegenation angle in the Universal proposed picture *The Imitation of Life* and know you will watch this carefully."[6] Continuing in this vein, letters and memos are riddled with the PCA's "grave . . . concern" over the script's "very dangerous," "extremely dangerous subject."[7] After four months of deliberation and negotiation with Universal, and at least three revisions of the script, Breen rejected yet another draft, writing: "We still feel that this story is a *definitely dangerous* one. It is our conviction that any picture which raises and elaborates such an *inflammable racial question* as that raised by this picture, [*sic*] is fraught with *grave danger* to the industry."[8]

Despite such continual red flags, however, the cause of the PCA's concern is in fact difficult to pinpoint. Two specific elements of the proposed script are at times discussed as potential violations of the miscegenation clause, but neither fully accounts for the extent of the recorded apprehension. One is a scene (which did not occur in the novel) of a misinterpreted encounter between a black man and a white woman. Yet this, which the PCA refers to as "the lynching scene" because of the man's near lynching as a result, poses no interpretive confusion for the censors and is ultimately dropped by the studio.[9] The other distinct element, which is more extensively debated, is the story of Peola. Recounting a meeting between the PCA and the studio, one memo notes, "It was our contention that this part of the plot—the action of the negro girl appearing as white—has a definite connection with the problem of miscegenation."[10] This connection is made again when a producer tries to appease the PCA with a suggested revision that would "avoid the inference that the leading character was a descendant of a white ancestor."[11] Like other PCA descriptions of the script, "which deals with the problem that follows as the *result* of miscegenation," this conversation suggests that it was not any actual depiction but the assumption that interracial sex had to have happened (fictionally) as the unmentioned backstory of the film's narrative, that initially made it, in Breen's eyes, a Code violation.[12] We do not have a copy of the originally proposed (and rejected) script, but none of the extant versions of *Imitation of Life* (the 1933 novel, the 1934 film, and the 1959 film) ever specifies if, when, or by whom any interracial sex took place. In all these texts our only knowledge about Peola's ancestry comes in the form of images of her dark-skinned mother and brief, vague references to her light-skinned black father.[13] In short, the PCA reads Peola's light skin and her eventual passing as signifiers of "miscegenation." By conflating miscegenation and passing in this way, the censors attempt to extend the Code's ban on sex and desire across black and white racial boundaries to prohibit identification across them as well.

While complex, controversial interpretations of "miscegenation" are thus indirectly suggested by various staff members at various moments, the PCA remains ambiguous about them, and the "inflammable racial question" is never precisely posed. One in-house note reports having "advised the studio that in our opinion it ["Hurst's novel dealing with a partly colored girl who wants to pass as white"] violates the Code clause covering miscegenation *in spirit, if not in fact.*"[14] A range of equally opaque formulations are given. In an early letter on the subject Breen writes that "while there is said to be *no active portrayal* of miscegenation, of course, yet *the suggestion is omnipresent.*"[15] And an internal staff memo similarly reports, "The script is based wholly on the *suggested* intermingling of blacks and whites and, *although it has no actual case in point*, the entire plot evolves on miscegenation."[16]

Although Breen never offers or exacts elaborations of such tenuous distinctions, he inadvertently admits his own uncertainty on the subject when he assigns a staff member to look it up. The staffer's research for precedents does not end the confusion, but it does suggest how we might interpret it. The "MEMORANDUM FOR MR. BREEN re—MISCEGENATION" reports, "I am sorry to say that there is very little in the files on the subject of miscegenation—certainly nothing that is a specific example of our present problem."[17] The closing paragraph repeats this sentiment but also tries to account for it: "I am afraid there is very little here of assistance to us, but I should say the reason for that is, that the subject has always been taboo, and that there has been no opportunity to collect evidence referring to it." This assessment of precedents "in the files" is only partly accurate.[18] More important, the tautological invocation of taboo (it "has always been taboo" and therefore there is "no . . . evidence referring to it") is indicative not only of the depth of the PCA's uncertainty (despite language and posturing that would suggest otherwise) but further of its participation in Hollywood's ongoing desire to remake interracial sex, a historical fact, as always already having been a taboo. That is, the claims of absence work precisely, even if unintentionally, as a means to forget the historical evidence—in American history and in the files of the PCA—and consequently to attempt to forget the considerable challenges that evidence poses. In that light, it makes a certain kind of sense that the PCA would never specify the "inflammable racial question[s]," because to do so would invite precisely the kinds of eruptions a ban on miscegenation would seemingly want to keep at bay.

Such details invite us to recognize already the extent to which the PCA's "considerable worry" and confusion are coded in fantasmatic terms. Because there is "no actual case in point," at stake is not historical or even fictive practice (what people or characters do) but cultural and spectatorial belief. The language even suggests that the manifold objections fear "miscegenation" not only as something in the present that might imply an unspecified fictional past, or as something reaching far back in cultural memory (it "has always been taboo"), but as something that threatens to encroach upon the future as well. The potential danger of a plot that "evolves on" miscegenation (not "revolves" around, as we would expect to hear it) would seem to lie in the damage the subject has brought or could bring. While the future of filmic characters is partially at issue, as we will see, the evolution of belief in cultural fictions of race haunts this file most pervasively.[19]

The psychic dimension of racial ideology at issue in the *Imitation* file is implicitly revealed by the PCA's initial conflation of interracial desire and cross-racial identification. Even if the story in question lacks a sexual transgression of "the color line," it imagines psychic and social ones in Peola's desire to be, and her ability to be seen as, white. The PCA's confusion thus serves as a reminder that Hollywood investments in fantasies of miscegenation are so dear precisely because those fantasies have everything to do with how subjects—characters on screen like Peola, as well as spectators in the theater—believe in and identify in relation to the designated "white and black races." And while cross-racial identification might appear less prurient, less "bawdy" as Breen might write it, than interracial sex, it clearly poses an equally if not more radical threat to systems of racial difference than "sex relationships" might indicate. Whereas the latter can result in "mixed" bodies and communities that can destabilize social hierarchies based on ostensibly clear and visible racial distinctions, the former threatens to destabilize those hierarchies in the domains of identity and belief.

Despite the theoretical logics we might apply to the PCA's extension of the miscegenation clause to passing, however, it nonetheless raised objections at the studio, and even at the Hays Office.[20] At a certain point, when debate on the project in Hollywood had been going on for some time, Breen wrote to New York for "counsel" from several men in the Hays Office there. They replied, "It is the opinion of us all that picturization of this subject matter would be fraught with the gravest danger." They disagreed, however, as to what exactly the ostensible subject is: "It is not, as we see it, a problem of miscegenation—that is, the act of miscegenation has occurred so remotely in the ancestry of the characters that it need not concern us. The girl's father and mother are both negroes though the father had white blood which gives the girl the appearance of a white person."[21] By distinguishing miscegenation from what actually occurs in the script, the reading from New York attempts to clear up the confusion in Hollywood between interracial desire and cross-racial identification. In addition, however, it again suggests that identification is the more fraught issue: "The big problem," they write, "is . . . the subject matter of the proposed picture as a whole." So big, in fact, that after the New York staff argues that miscegenation per se is *not* an issue in this case, they nonetheless urge Breen "to persuade the company to abandon its plans for production." While they provide no further explanation of "the big problem," one is suggested by their strained description of Peola's racial identity: "The girl's father and mother are both negroes though the father had white blood which gives the girl the appearance of a white person." Choosing to apply the "one-drop rule" in its traditionally unilateral direction, they here define the (absent) father with "white blood" as "negro." "The big problem" that nonetheless continues to surface does so with regard to the daughter's "appearance."

As the PCA struggles with Peola throughout its correspondence on the project, it becomes increasingly clear that far in excess of the question of her "remote . . . ancestry" is the immediate problem she poses for systems of marking and securing racial difference. In addition to the description from New York just cited, Peola is characterized throughout the PCA's memos and letters as, variously

the white child of a colored mother [with] negro blood in her veins

the negro girl appearing as white

the half-white, half-black girl

the white skinned negro girl

[one of] the two negroes

a girl with some negro blood who is confronted with the temptation to pass herself off as white

a partly colored girl

the girl [with] the appearance of a white person

the daughter of the colored woman [who] can pass for white

[the] mulatto offspring

pretending to be white when black

a part negro girl who is tempted to pass as white

a light colored negro girl who desires to go white[22]

The first thing to be noted about this remarkable catalog is that no two items in it are alike. Three of them, three with significantly different connotations, even appear in a single memo: "the half-white, half-black girl," "the white skinned negro girl," and one of "the two negroes." While such continual attempts to name Peola's racial identity suggest the PCA's desire to pin it down, the impossibility of ever doing so is indicated by the fact that none of these descriptions adheres, but each is displaced by yet another attempt—so much so that the PCA's own inability to clearly identify, delimit, and secure racial difference on and through Peola begins to reveal the "inflammable racial question," or questions, that *Imitation of Life* poses. And if the perpetual (failed) attempts to describe her beg the question as to the very meaning of "race" itself, the inflammable answer that the PCA's own readings of *Imitation of Life* threaten to invite, even if against the grain of that text, is that "race" is not fixed or verifiable but perpetually and unreliably "evolves" through language.

The PCA's ever-changing racial names for Peola expose the discursive construction of race in their deployment of four separate, and sometimes seemingly contradictory, categories. Whereas "black," "white," and "colored" operate through a discourse of color, which is often, but not always, tied to "skin," "negro" works through a separate discourse of race (in the traditional/archaic anthropological sense) that is sometimes, but not always, tied to "blood." In attempting to describe Peola, the PCA variously combines such signifiers of color, skin, race, and blood, and as a result often marks her doubly (as in "the *negro* girl appearing as *white*"), and even triply (as in "the *white* child of a *colored* mother [with] *negro* blood").[23] Peola prompts such multiple markings, in effect, precisely because she confounds the notion that these categories are continuous, that they exist in any natural or seamless relation. The "danger" of her story, then, especially as written at the PCA, is that it calls attention to the disjunctures between "race," "color," "blood," and "skin." Peola threatens to rupture the constellation of discourses that work to construct the fiction that "race" is a natural category, especially the one that imagines bodily wrappings (and the metaphors grafted to them) to be tied to interior essences.

That the relation between color and race was very much at the heart of the question of "miscegenation" in the PCA's treatment of *Imitation of Life* is implicit in a memo, cited earlier, recording an early meeting with Universal. In it the PCA expresses its position that "the action of the negro girl appearing as white . . . has a definite connection with the problem of miscegenation," a position that again doubly marks Peola as "negro" and "white" and ties that conflicted identity to miscegenation. Additionally, a producer attempts to appease the censors' objection by proposing that the film could "definitely establish that [Peola's] white skin was due to a rare but scientific fact that such a child might come of a line of definitely negro strain."[24] That such an explanation is never again mentioned in the files is not at all surprising. Not only would it fail to allay the censors' greatest fears regarding identification and desire (she could still pass, and viewers could still *imagine* that miscegenation had taken place "in spirit, if not in fact"), but it would also explicitly draw attention to the disjuncture not only between race and color but further between these and "blood," or ancestry, as well. Attempting to keep in place a system of racial difference that depends on the elision of these disjunctures, the PCA opts instead to ultimately insist on making Peola essentially "black." Thus, we see in its late correspondence on her that she is no longer described as "the white child" "with some negro blood" but increasingly becomes "a negro," "pretending to be white, when black." Foreshadowing the discourse of the film to come, this last description would seem to redefine "black" as not simply a color but an essential identity.

The problems Peola's identity posed to the censors who attempted to classify her in writing already point to the even more complicated stakes that would arise in "picturiz[ing]" her. While the PCA's written accounts could counterbalance her exterior "whiteness" by reimposing an interior "blackness"—doubly marking her, in effect, as looking white but being black—that strategy would not suffice on film. In Hollywood's system of racial difference, a system fully invested in a visual discourse of race, how could the image of a "negro girl appearing as white" be safely projected?

Universal attempted to do so in part by casting Fredi Washington, an African American actress, in the role of Peola and, as rumor had it, by having her wear makeup to darken her light complexion.[25] Whether founded in truth or fiction, the mere circulation of such a rumor attests to an understanding that Hollywood cinema had its own demands and devices for constructing race.[26] As the following analysis of the film that ultimately got made will demonstrate, that cinema would pull heavily from its own bag of tricks to insist upon Peola's being *and* looking "black."

"That's It! . . . A Great Big Picture of Delilah, Looking Like That"

While the PCA file fails to document what exactly moved the censors to finally approve *Imitation of Life*, another kind of answer presents itself in the film that eventually emerged.[27] Hollywood's cinematic solution to the inflammable image of Peola, I propose, came in the unequivocal image of her mother, Delilah. That solution is worked out in the 1934 film through an overwhelming preoccupation with the production and reproduction of Delilah's image. The hyperspectacle that "Aunt Delilah" (read Aunt Jemima) almost instantly becomes in her first appearance, and is eventually memorialized as in her final incarnation as a giant flashing neon sign, is elaborated throughout the film in significant contrast both to her daughter, Peola, and to her white mistress, Bea Pullman. Indeed, the film is devoted, perhaps above all else, to distinguishing these images of black and white femininity. That project lingers in the differing significance the film would come to have in the careers of its two female leads. For Claudette Colbert, winner of an Academy Award that year for her performance in *It Happened One Night*, the film served as a star vehicle in which her character's transformation from widow to CEO facilitates a kind of coming out as erotic spectacle; from struggling to survive in modest working girl outfits to elegantly roaming about her urban mansion in elaborate designer gowns (figs. 4.1–4.2).[28] For Louise Beavers the same film would signal a future career playing, as Beavers herself described it, "likeable Negro maids—plump and happy and quick to laugh" (fig. 4.3).[29] While that

FIG. 4.1. Bea Pulman (Claudette Colbert), from modest working girl . . .

FIG. 4.2. . . . to glamorous CEO.

FIG. 4.3. Delilah (Louise Beavers), sustaining the white woman and her erotic image.

"mammy" character had been well established in Hurst's novel, the film directed by John Stahl not only brought it to the screen but thoroughly worked it over through the apparatus of cinema.

I want ultimately to consider the film's implicit construction of Delilah's image as a solution to the potential *racial* crisis detected in the PCA's anxieties regarding her "white skinned negro" daughter, but we need first to consider the film's explicit presentation of Delilah from the outset as the solution to a *gender* crisis. For here again we find that an attempt to resolve deeply troubling ruptures in one system of difference is facilitated by the overt manipulation of another. And, in the case of *Imitation of Life*, the interaction operates in both directions: the presentation of a dutiful black servant as the answer to a single white mother's unspoken prayers not only leans on an entrenched racial tradition to put down the film's anxieties about working (white) women but in the process also finds a highly gendered means to overcome "the big problem" posed by Peola to the filmic security of racial identity.

The opening scene emphatically announces the manifest gender problem that the rest of the film will take upon itself to correct: Bea Pullman, the young mother who carries on her dead husband's business selling syrup door-to-door, is having trouble fulfilling her role as "woman." Hurst's novel contextualizes such trouble by first chronicling Bea's misery in a dismal marriage and by playing androgynous name games that allow her to pass as her husband Benjamin for some time after his death by delivering merchandise incognito and using his business card, inscribed simply "B. Pullman."[30] The film skips over such potentially feminist contexts and begins instead with the husband long since dead, immediately privileging the "dilemma" of a working woman without a man.

Following the credits and an intertitle that situates us in a residential area of Atlantic City in 1919, we first see a shot of a rubber duck floating in a bathtub and hear an offscreen conversation between a small child and her mother. The child voices her desire, "I want my quack quack," and the mother begins a series of refusals. At first the mother simply defers the child's request ("Not now, wait 'til mother finishes your bath"), but by the end of the scene the weight of the demand and the refusal have grown dramatically. When the mother talks of having to get the child "dressed and fed and down to the day nursery," the baby declares her disapproval: "Don't want to go to the day nursery, want to stay home with mommy!" Baby Jessie repeats this incantation several times and by the end lodges it in our ears in the form of a song: "I love you and you love me, and I don't want to go to day nursery." While the child's emphatic protest to day care makes the point impossible to miss, the film further insists on Bea's domestic failure in a series of shots in which she struggles to juggle at once the crying baby in the bath upstairs, a ringing phone and subsequent conversation with a client downstairs, and pots boiling over on the stove. The same scene ultimately comes to Bea's rescue, however, with the surprise delivery of a black maid. While diegetically Delilah has come to the "wrong" address, confusing Bea's address on Aster Street with an advertised job on Aster Avenue, the film has clearly sent her here on a mission to attend to the (gender) chaos so insistently established for us in the film's opening minutes.

The film marshals considerable cinematic energy to insist upon the destiny of Delilah's arrival. We first briefly see her framed through the rectangle of a screen door at the back of Bea's kitchen (fig. 4.4). But her official introduction comes in her second shot. As Bea responds to the ringing doorbell, poking her head around the banister at the bottom of the stairs and moving swiftly through the hall and kitchen toward the back door, the camera pans quickly to follow her brisk movement (fig. 4.5). The force of these movements, Bea's and the camera's, continues across a cut to the next shot that first returns to Delilah in a medium shot behind the screen door but quickly moves in to capture her in close-up as she smiles to warmly greet the white woman (figs. 4.6A–4.6B). This camera movement anticipates the narrative and visual trajectories to come, finding Delilah—particularly a magnified image of her dark, round, and smiling face—as that which settles Bea's chaotic struggles about the house.[31] This problem-solution pattern is continued in the same scene as Delilah fixes breakfast without being asked, convinces Bea to give her the job that wasn't advertised, and delightedly accepts it without pay.[32] The pattern climaxes visually in the final shots of this opening scene. When Bea returns upstairs to find that a fully dressed Jessie has fallen back into the tub, she drops her head in utter dismay; the white mother's bewilderment upstairs is answered by a high-angle shot from the top of the staircase, looking down through the banister rails to find the dutiful black servant smiling warmly upward. With this shot, staged for our eyes only, we know without doubt that this heaven-sent lowly angel is here to set things right.[33]

In the course of the film it becomes clear that Delilah's magical delivery both helps Bea with the tasks of motherhood and helps her become a "proper" woman. Even though Delilah enables Bea to pursue a demanding career, Delilah's presence, and eventual death, also works to eventually restore Bea to the feminine roles of mother and potential wife. This is evident in the final scene when, following Delilah's funeral, Bea and a now grown Jessie are brought together to reminisce about the first time Bea met Delilah. The film ends with the same words with which it began, "I want my quack quack, I want my quack quack," but now delivered by Bea, not Jessie, as she walks in the moonlight with her arm around her daughter. As Bea has just given up the man she loves for the sake of her

FIG. 4.4. Delilah's arrival: a cinematic solution to the white woman's many problems.

FIG. 4.5

FIG. 4.6A

FIG. 4.6B

child (who is also in love with him), this wistful (re)incantation points at once to her grand attempt to finally satisfy the child's desire and the deferral of her own in the process.[34] In a fitting memorial to the woman who perpetually mothered both Jessie *and* Bea, this scene thus signals Bea's full transformation into a "properly" sacrificial woman.[35]

While both supplementing and restoring Bea as a mother, Delilah also functions as the backbone of her economic success, supplying not only the secret recipe for the pancakes that Bea sells first in a small restaurant and then boxed for national distribution but also the labor upon which her escalating profits depend. Bea openly announces this division of labor when she first shares her idea to open the pancake shop: "Delilah, we're going into business. . . . You're going to make pancakes and I'm going to sell them." When we see Bea in the restaurant she is typically standing behind the counter, sometimes exchanging money with customers and creditors and sometimes just standing. When we once see her flip a cake on the griddle, it is an act of charity that in turn leads to the expansion of her small business into a major corporation. Feeding a penniless man off the street during a heavy rainstorm that keeps away the paying clientele, Bea is graced with his two words of advice that will make her fortune: "Box it!" Thus, Bea's labor is directed toward capitalistic expansion, while it is Delilah who not only makes the product for sale, without compensation, but insists upon being Bea's "cook" at home as well. The radical economic disparity in this arrangement is only flaunted more boldly by the fact that it is more than five years into "their" business before Bea finally offers Delilah a percentage of the soaring profits, and even then only a meager 20 percent. After Bea explains that this means Delilah can own her own car and home, Delilah responds in (unbearable) terror: "My own house? You gonna send me away Miss Bea? . . . How am I gonna take care of you and Miss Jessie if I ain't here? . . . I's your cook and I want to stay your cook."

Most pertinent to the argument at hand, Delilah's excruciating internalization of the role of faithful servant is accompanied by an incessant projection of that role in visual form. Just as her fixed social position facilitates Bea's seemingly limitless economic mobility, so, too, does the inscription of Delilah's/Beavers's image in a stubbornly static and permanent form facilitate the classical inscription of Bea/Colbert as a white woman in the visual domain. Indeed, even when Bea falls short of her feminine functions as mother and (potential) wife, her image as a classically eroticized object of male desire is firmly established, bolstered in part by contrast to Delilah's dark, heavyset "mammy" image. Reminiscent of her first appearance in the film, Delilah is perpetually captured and frozen in a wide-eyed, open-mouthed caricature that becomes the face on the pancake label that makes her white mistress's fortune. Moreover, in the course of the film that image is perpetually magnified and frozen, plastered on the surfaces of windows and logos, mass-produced on an assembly-line production of pancake boxes, and ultimately rendered a giant, permanent cutout surrounded in neon (figs. 4.7–4.10). The sign's only movement is from lights that flash "Aunt Delilah" (the name and image) on and off, and gradually flip her pancakes out of the pan and back again. It is this image of Delilah that remains after her death, visible in the distance from the rooftop garden where Bea and Jessie nostalgically stroll in their final display of evening wear (figs. 4.11–4.14). In other words, as if to further animate that final, revised image of white woman as "proper" mother/daughter and erotic spectacle, the film pulls out all the cinematic stops to blow up, flatten, and immobilize the image of black woman.

The film's obsessive compulsion to immobilize Delilah as image is even more elaborately articulated in an early scene in which she and Bea prepare the empty space that will become the restaurant. As Bea begins to tell a sign maker what she wants him to paint for her storefront, she is suddenly inspired by the sight of Delilah. The extraordinary production of this originary sign—one that will be replicated endlessly throughout the film—and Bea's and the camera's tremendous investments in it make its details worthy of close consideration.

In her first moments as the new occupant of the space she has rented for her pancake business, Bea Pullman announces the consequences of this venture for Delilah. Eagerly placing the order for the sign she wants to have custom-made, she describes: "I tell you what I want. I want a *great big sign*, with lots—" Her speech suddenly halts as her eyes fix on Delilah passing before them. A reverse medium shot reveals Delilah's movement through the room, and Bea's offscreen voice calls out to her, "Delilah?" Delilah turns around in response, clearly confused: "Ma'am?" (fig. 4.15). Bea then commands simply: "Smile." Another medium shot shows Delilah's continued confusion. With hand and facial gestures Bea prods her, "Smile, you know, smile." Still confused, Delilah pulls her head back slightly and smiles gently (fig. 4.16). Still unsatisfied, Bea now directs her emphatically, and ungrammatically, "Oh no! Great big one!" As if in full recognition of the request, Delilah laughs and complies, "Oh, yessum!" and her laughter now opens into an exaggerated open-mouthed smile with eyebrows lifted (fig. 4.17). Pointing with excitement, Bea continues to perfect the image: "That's it! Now, now turn to the right. Hold it." Seconding Bea's confirmation, the camera cuts to Delilah's frozen expression in a close-up, then instantly moves in for, and noticeably lingers on, an even tighter frame of her smiling face (fig. 4.18). With this last shot the image not only expands, but the angles of Delilah's posture and the camera shift, her face and eyes finally cast upward, her round cheeks

FIG. 4.7. The mass production and distribution of the image of "Aunt Delilah."

FIG. 4.8

FIG. 4.9

FIG. 4.10

FIG. 4.11. White women
stroll in evening gowns
while "Aunt Delilah"
flashes in the background.

FIG. 4.12

FIG. 4.13

FIG. 4.14

FIG. 4.15 Bea directs Delilah to become "the great big sign."

FIG. 4.16

FIG. 4.17

FIG. 4.18

shining in the light from above. Because Delilah remains perfectly still as the camera methodically zeros in on this pose, the effect is one of simultaneously discovering this image, fixing it, and pulling it into sharp focus. While the camera lingers here, Bea's voice affirms again from off screen: "That's it. That's what I want! A great big picture of Delilah looking like that, and underneath, 'Aunt Delilah's Homemade Pancakes.'" When we are finally released from the oppressive stasis of Delilah's oppressive image, we return to Bea, still talking, still gesturing, her movement accentuated by a short cape that flutters over her active arms and body.

With a remarkable explicitness that seems nonetheless unconscious of much of what it reveals, this scene openly displays the film's dominant visual logic.[36] For just as Bea trains Delilah to become the image of the "great big sign" in her mind's eye, so the film perpetually orchestrates cinematic elaborations of this "great big picture of Delilah looking like that." Although the film here posits Bea as the director molding the image, the sequence's cinematic echo of Delilah's introductory shots (framing her at a distance, reframing her more tightly, closing in quickly to fix the servant's smile) allows us to consider the larger cinematic apparatus calling each and every shot.

The subsequent mass production of Delilah as "Aunt Delilah"—the logo on signs, boxes, the neon billboard, and so forth—quickly exceeds the original scenario such that Delilah is not simply the (carefully directed) model for this endless stream of visual representations; the frozen mammy portrait of those two-dimensional images in turn becomes the model on which future representations of the "real" Delilah are based. Immediately after the scene in which Bea coaxes Delilah to become the sign for the shop window, the camera opens on the resulting painted image of her, frozen as the smiling cook who flips pancakes (fig. 4.19). Redoubling the effect, the camera tracks up the shop window to reveal the living Delilah behind the glass, donning the very apron and chef's hat of the sign, and making pancakes not only for us to see but also on display for the passersby who stroll the boardwalk (fig. 4.20). Taking this process of "life" imitating representation yet further, the camera moves inside the shop with a cut to a side view of Delilah behind the griddle and the window; boardwalk flaneurs frame her on the left, and another advertisement image of "Aunt Delilah" hangs on the wall just behind her at right (fig. 4.21). In short, set up as a live boardwalk attraction, and literally surrounded by the multiple markers that visually define her as the mammy icon, Delilah's actual appearance here reads as an animated version of the visual caricature she has become. My point, to be clear, is not merely that the image of "Aunt Delilah" is a caricature but that Delilah herself is incessantly identified and defined through that image.

While Bea's original vision/projection of Delilah as logo visually in-

FIG. 4.19. The "great big
sign" . . .

FIG. 4.20. . . . comes to life.

FIG. 4.21

scribed the women's respective positions of dominance and submission, and the pleasure taken in that relation by Bea and (so the film imagines) Delilah, the final versions with apron, spatula, and perpetual smile clarify that the pleasure these signs imagine resides in the master's fantasy of servitude.[37] And even though the caption on the storefront window reads "Aunt Delilah's Pancake Shop," the film continues to display Bea as the true beneficiary of the entire arrangement. Despite the sign's obvious deceit, it is increasingly apparent that Bea's "success"—at work, at home, and before the camera—clearly depends on the immortalization of Delilah's mammy image. That image allows Bea to function as both scheming capitalist *and* erotic spectacle, the latter identity explicitly softening the potential ideological distress provoked by the former. She can play male roles at home and on the job, so long as she is visually displayed like a female star. And the film's conjuring of that image in contrast to Delilah's casts Bea's gender transgressions in a racialized light that sees her as a "properly" masterful white mistress rather than an improperly masterful woman.

TWO HUNDRED POUNDS OF BLACK MOTHER

The effects of the film's hyperproduction of the black woman's image are not limited to negotiating the demands of the white one. Returning to the "big problem" detected at the PCA, it is clear that the film provides its own (big) solutions there as well. Even though Peola does temporarily pass, the manner in which we see her do so works forcefully to contain the potential threat her body poses. While Peola explicitly states her problem as "look[ing] white and be[ing] black," the film manages to never quite allow us to see her as the former and always represents her so as to convince us firmly of the latter. It does so through an ongoing association of her whiteness with deceit, but it redoubles and finally guarantees that narrative through the image by answering her misrepresentations of whiteness with ongoing presentations of her mother as the embodiment of a purportedly authentic and transparent blackness.

The film quickly taps the intelligence it grants a young Peola as a capacity for inappropriate longings and deception. Upon overhearing the young girls quiz each other for a geography test, Bea remarks to Delilah that "Peola's smarter than Jessie." Delilah's unbelievable reply: "Yessum. We all starts out that way. We don't get dumb 'til later on." But very soon, the only alternative to stupidity the film has to offer Peola is deviance. When the girls return home from school, Peola runs through the house crying, "I'm not black, I'm not black, I won't be black." Distraught over Jessie's accusations to the contrary ("She called me black, Jessie called me that!"), Peola weeps in her mother's arms while Delilah comforts her and urges her "to learn to take it." While even Bea recognizes something "mean" and "cruel" in the treatment Peola faces, Delilah practices only passive acceptance: "It ain't [Jessie's] fault, Miss Bea. It ain't your'n and it ain't mine. I don't know exactly where the blame lies." In the face of this kind of comfort, Peola chooses active defiance and begins at some point to pass for white at school.

Despite the "cruel" consequences that await Peola if she is to live "honestly," the film construes her as one who inappropriately defies the "truth" of her racial identity. Indeed, with the minor exception of the scene just cited, the film excludes any real consideration of the conditions that lead her to pass but instead jumps to scenes that catch her in the act, figuring her not as a victim of social injustice but as (always having been) a misbehaving liar. Her mother, by contrast, repeatedly exposes Peola's secret, arriving at her school and later her workplace to publicly identify her as a black subject ("There's my baby!") and temporarily end her deceptive transgressions. When Peola later disowns her mother in an effort to escape such markings and assume a permanent white identity, her deception is compounded by the cruelty of this act. Delilah openly suffers at this rejection, weeping and begging, "It's too much to ask of me. I ain't got the spiritual strength to bear it. I can't hang on no cross. I ain't got the strength. You can't ask me to unborn my own child." Proving once again that Delilah has a privileged relation to truth, her words are soon borne out by her sudden ill health and death.

The narrative motif of Delilah as the black truth haunting Peola's white lies finds its strongest support, however, in the image. We see this already in the scene, discussed earlier, in which young Peola repudiates the "black" label Jessie projects onto her. Despite Peola's insistent refusals ("I'm not black! I'm not black! I won't be black! . . . I won't, I won't, I won't be black!"), and despite the contrast between the dark and light skin of Louise Beavers and the young (uncredited) actress playing Peola, the film forestalls the kind of rupturing of the meaning of race that Peola's utterance might invite by visually recontaining her, and her contestable racial identity, in her mother's large, dark body. As the scene culminates with Delilah's blind acceptance of the racial order ("I don't know exactly where the blame lies"), it also culminates with a variation on the now familiar close-up so carefully orchestrated in the shop (window sign) scenes just before this one. As Delilah delivers her lines, she fills the frame in a medium close-up—still wearing her chef's hat—cradling Peola like a baby in an embrace that virtually engulfs the child (fig. 4.22). Although we can at first see the small portion of Peola's face that is not buried in her mother's chest, after the camera twice cuts away to Jessie and Bea on the other side of the room it finally returns to Delilah in a tight, lingering close-up that literally excises Peola from the frame (fig. 4.23). As Delilah

FIGS. 4.22–4.23. The problematic image of Peola's body disappears within the by now well-rehearsed image of Delilah.

delivers the scene's final lines, the visual correlate to her verbal acceptance of the racial order is clear: Peola's questionable image is now supplanted by a somewhat quizzical, but nonetheless resigned, variation on the pancake logo's theme before the fade to complete blackness.

At this moment when the repeatedly accused "black" mother ("You! You! It's 'cause you're black! You make me black!") copes with her child's anger and pain, this sorrowful version of the pancake logo simultaneously redefines the young actress's small, light-skinned body through the magnification of Beaver's large, dark one and offers up the most intense visual expression of mother and daughter's emotional struggle. While the degradation of the mammy image could be said to amplify the degradation Peola resists, this image nonetheless also contains Peola's dilemma as yet another of the mammy's (dark) burdens. In so doing, I suggest, the sequence not only "allude[s] to the laws governing slavery, by which the child 'followed the condition' of the mother," as Valerie Smith rightly reminds us, but cinematically updates that tradition (49).[38] Whereas the "very very light" black father is never seen, it is the black mother's visible blackness that repeatedly enforces Peola's "true" racial identity—in this scene and a related one we will consider shortly, twice more when Delilah arrives at the scenes of Peola's passing, and finally at Delilah's funeral, where the pointedly "black" spectacle beckons Peola to publicly confess and accept her mother.[39] The "truth" of Delilah's visible blackness, and the blackness it holds out for her child, is further guaranteed in such scenes by the affective saturation of the black maternal image.

The melodramatic plot line that takes Delilah's life as the price for Peola's transgressions might call into question whether Peola's "big problem" is in fact finally solved. But, as the mass production of Delilah's image on shop windows and pancake boxes nationwide quickly reminds us, that image persists. And it is that permanent image, I am arguing, the one the film so carefully manufactures well before and long after Delilah's death, that tames Peola's potentially volatile one. For the compounded effect of the many inscriptions of "Aunt Delilah" that insistently eclipse those of Peola is to define "black woman" ultimately as that image, an image that the film, like Bea's and the camera's initial discoveries of it ("That's it!"), posits as an immediately recognizable and transparent signifier of blackness. The film announces the transparent meaning of Delilah's appearance in the opening sequence, not long after the camera itself has rushed in to recognize, and fetishize, her face. When baby Jessie first sees Delilah, she points to her and calls out: "Horsey!" While this declaration partially admits that the baby does not yet understand racial difference, it insists that that difference, however inaccurately named, is self-evident even to the untrained eye. This is, presumably, why the women laugh at the baby's outrageous mistake and why Bea does not correct her. As Peola later verifies ("She called me black, Jessie called me that!"), Jessie will soon enough learn the "accurate" name of the difference she "naturally" sees.

Although my own reading of the cinematic production of Delilah's image diverges markedly from hers, Lauren Berlant's formulation of the problem posed by the mulatta subject points sharply to what I am claiming to be the particular solutions Hollywood provides in its various treatments of Peola.[40] Berlant writes:

> The mulatta figure . . . gives the lie to the dominant code of juridical representation by repressing the "evidence" the law would seek—a parent, usually a mother—to determine whether the light-skinned body claimed a fraudulent relation to the privileges of whiteness. By occupying the gap between official codes of racial naming and scopic norms of bodily framing conventional to the law and to general cultural practices, the American mulatta's textual and juridical representation after 1865 always designates her as a national subject, the paradigm problem citizen.[41]

What I have tried to articulate here is not only how cinema operates as a cultural practice through which such "scopic norms" *become* "conventional," but further that the gap Berlant identifies between those norms and racial names is precisely where Hollywood steps in to provide the missing evidence—evidence that is in this case primarily (though multiply) visual, and that seeks to "prove" the certainty of racial identity by projecting Delilah's blackness in no uncertain terms. By projecting a racial image ("Aunt Delilah" . . . "looking like that") and a racial name ("black") in virtual, if not always literal, simultaneity, the film effectively welds them together *as if* they were one and the same, as if neither were a signifier but (together) a single signified delivered up for our immediate understanding.[42] The track-ins, cut-ins, and interminable close-ups of Delilah's "great big" black body and face perpetually offer up an image that makes "obvious" her racial identity.[43] The familiarity of the Aunt Jemima image by 1934 only further works to produce the effect I am describing.[44] Just as Bea "recognizes" Delilah's image in the moment in which she in fact projects it ("That's it!"), so the film's spectator is repeatedly invited to recognize it: "Oh yes, I know who that is, *that's*. . . ." Complete the ellipses as you wish: "Aunt Delilah," "Aunt Jemima," "the pancake mammy"—in effect, "the (image of) black woman I know so well." And it is precisely that certain visibility ascribed to Delilah's blackness, I am suggesting, that works throughout the film to counterbalance Peola's potentially troubling image.

This is the case even in what might otherwise be the most visually vexed sequences in the film, those in which the adult "light-skinned black body" declares, and demands recognition of, its whiteness.[45] One such sequence begins with Peola standing before a mirror. With her mother off screen at left, she gazes at her reflection at right and declares, "I want to be white, like I look. Look at me! Am I not white? Isn't that a white girl there?" At this critical moment, with Peola herself demanding the evidence, the film gives it up. No sooner has this speech begun than the camera moves to reframe it. With a few minor adjustments it moves first to include Delilah and then to excise the mirror. Peola still looks in its direction, but what we see is not her critical look at herself but mother and daughter in a rhymed set of postures, wherein the stance of the larger, substantially darker mother's body nonetheless mimes her daughter's, as do, roughly, the lines and shapes of their dresses and hair.

While visible differences between the women remain in this scene, they are considerably narrowed in the one that follows later that evening. When Delilah finds a still distraught Peola lying on her bed in a dimly lit room, the film answers the daughter's critical questions with a maternal speech encouraging her to accept her God-given blackness ("He made you black honey, don't be telling Him His business. . . . Accept it honey"), and with further visual efforts to assimilate Peola increasingly toward Delilah. The low lighting darkens her skin considerably from the earlier scene, and the remaining distance between the women's bodily images is gradually closed, first by Peola covering her face with her hands as Delilah turns her own more into view, and then by a maternal embrace reminiscent of the earlier one (figs. 4.24–4.26). This time, Peola's face and skin are immediately hidden behind and within her mother's.

Similar strategies intervene when Peola returns home after her mother has discovered, and interrupted, her passing. Determined to live as a white woman, Peola seeks to cut all ties between them: "You mustn't see me, or own me, or claim me or anything. I mean, even if you pass me on the street, you'll have to pass me by." Peola's wish to be a white woman is further reflected in her continual interactions with Bea throughout this scene. Her speech addresses Delilah, but her glances continually focus on and react to Bea. Nevertheless, despite the multiple paths tying Peola to Bea, the scene transpires not in the elegant upper stories of Bea's home but in Delilah's modest basement quarters; and Delilah, like this setting, insists that Peola and the viewer recognize their natural relation: "I can't give up my baby. I bore you, I nursed you. I loved you. I loved you more than you can guess. You can't ask your mammy to do this. . . . I'm your mammy! I ain't no white mother! . . . You can't ask me to unborn my own child." The camera again rhymes mother and daughter despite their dissimilar looks, visually tying them in a face-to-face composition for the better part of the scene. What is more, the camera refuses us any chance to similarly compare Peola and Bea within a single shot. While they, too,

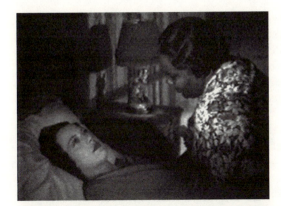

FIG. 4.24. Struggling with her appearance, Peola (Fredi Washington) again disappears into Delilah.

FIG. 4.25

FIG. 4.26

are visually rhymed across shots (their similarly tilted hats especially showing that Peola's aesthetic is modeled after Bea's), in the only one that contains them both Peola has her back to us as we see Bea. Thus, while the camera draws together the righteous and transgressive "black" women, we are never given a comparable shot that would allow us to study the visual difference/sameness of the "real" and "imitation" "white" ones.

In so many ways, then, the film cinematically restricts the representation of Peola's pale appearance, perpetually burying her in representations of her dark mother and, when necessary, removing her from the frame altogether. Indeed, although Peola's story provides the film's melodramatic core, she herself is excised from the diegetic scene—not once but three times. In the first, her mother implores her to go to a college "down South," a gesture Peola clearly reads as a demand for racial training ("A Negro school?"). While her departure from that course signals her deviant return to whiteness (and her second pronounced disappearance in the film, after she disowns her mother), she thoroughly renounces that desire before film's end. In her return to her mother's (now dead) body at Delilah's funeral, she not only publicly names their relation ("Mother! Mother! Please forgive me!) but does so with an excess of emotion and spectacle (openly crying out from the crowd, weeping, throwing herself at the casket) that matches the force of her mother's earlier melodramatic performance at the daughter's severing of ties. The shots that follow in which we momentarily see the adult Peola alongside Bea and Jessie now seem sanctioned by her spectacular reclamation of her "true" matrilineal identity.

Making that Peola's final appearance, however, the film takes no such risk of displaying her with the white women back at their rooftop garden but instead simply informs us through their conversation that she has agreed to return to her ("Negro") education. With Peola safely confined to an unseen black space beyond the frame, the spectator is again, and finally, prevented from having the kind of visual-epistemological crisis that the sight of her might otherwise provoke. Instead, the image of her dark, caricatured mother as mammy flashes in the distance (see fig. 4.11). Long after the film has finished, the image of "black woman" that is sure to be impressed on our retinas is that giant icon of Aunt Delilah/Jemima ("plump and happy and quick to laugh") blinking in perpetuity.

As cartoonish as Delilah's image is, the film dares to pass it off as the "life" that provides the contrast to Colbert's "imitation." While the white career woman leaves her child in day care and later sends her to boarding school, Delilah is painted as the authentic black mother par excellence; as Bea describes her on the day they first meet, "Just two hundred pounds of mother fighting to keep her baby."[46] Defining her precisely as that "two hundred pounds" of maternal blackness, that "big mountain," as Bea also describes her, the film incessantly figures Delilah as that corporeal image. And it is that unequivocal image of the black maternal body that not only distinguishes Delilah from Bea, black femininity from white, and supplants Peola's confounding appearance, but cinematically insists on the join between "black" and "Negro," color and race. More simply put, the filmic inscriptions of Delilah relocate the meaning of race (which again in Hollywood discourse effectively means blackness) in and through the bodily image: whereas the PCA's writings on Peola drew upon discourses of the invisible (blood and ancestry) to shore up the meaning of "black," the film deploys an array of cinematic devices to forcibly shift the locus of racial identity to the domain of the visible—the color, size, shape, and comportment of the maternal body. In so doing, so many blinking images of the black mammy epitomize *Imitation of Life*'s filmic solution to Peola's troubling image, one that insists that "race" is instantaneously visible, an essence guaranteed by an image.

COMMON KNOWLEDGE AND AN UNCOMMON CONFESSION

The overt *fabrication* of the alleged visibility of blackness in *Imitation of Life,* and of Hollywood's racial images generally, in turn demands consideration of how that cinema has nonetheless worked to make spectators believe in such visual fantasies.[47] While I will pursue this first as a practical matter at the PCA and a theoretical one of continued importance, this chapter will culminate with a reading of *Pinky* that proposes a further cinematic shift of the locus of racial meaning: from the production of bodily surfaces to the unfolding of racial subjects in and through cinematic space. This second shift will demonstrate even more dramatically classical cinema's powers to solicit our faith in fictions of the visibility of race, even when we know we cannot see it.

At times the miscegenation clause led censors and studios to squarely deliberate how viewers might read race on actual bodies and on bodies disguised through conventions of racial masquerade. An exchange dating back to the miscegenation clause of the Don'ts and Be Carefuls indicates that "the white and black races" could be stretched to refer to pairs of white actors, one in blackface and one not. A memo concerning *Lulu Belle* reports the Studio Relations Committee's having had a meeting with Fox in which the "precise point" of concern was "whether they can escape the implications of miscegenation if the romance occurs between a white person and another white person made up to represent a negro."[48] While it becomes moot in this particular case with the multiple revisions *Lulu Belle* undergoes before finally making it to the screen in

1948, in others the interpretive question remains as to whether "the implications of miscegenation" are confined to scenarios mixing black and white actors in black and white roles, or include whites "made up to represent" an interracial couple.[49] By posing the potential problem in this fashion, the censors reveal in this early example that what is at stake is not a fear merely of mixing "actual" black and white bodies on screen (as had been in part the case with Griffith's refusal to cast black male actors opposite white female ones) but of imagined mixing.[50]

Additional PCA assumptions about spectatorial belief are revealed in 1935, when Universal worries about the risks of casting Paul Robeson and a white actress in blackface with the stage persona of "Aunt Jemima" as a married couple in *Show Boat*. After consulting Hays on the matter, Breen responds to Universal in a letter I quote nearly in full to capture its detail and repetition:

> DEAR HARRY:
>
> With regard to your letter . . . in which you discuss the casting problem you have with Paul Robeson and Aunt Jemima: It is our judgment that *there can be no serious objection* to our casting Robeson, the negro, to play the part he played on the stage, and, at the same time, to cast the white woman, Aunt Jemima, for the part of Robeson's wife. *I think you should be extremely careful, however not to indicate any physical contact* between the white woman and the negro man *for the reason that many people know Aunt Jemima is a white woman and might be repulsed by the sight of her being fondled by a man who is a negro.*
>
> To answer your specific question: *I see no objection* to your casting Robeson for the one part, and Aunt Jemima for the other part, despite the fact that Robeson is a negro and Aunt Jemima is a white woman—*but I do urge the utmost caution and care* in shooting any scenes between them where they are playing the part of man and wife.
> Cordially yours,[51]

The fact that the studio itself is worried here, even before the PCA, suggests that despite the public's acceptance of so many racial and ethnic masquerades over the years, this is one that might not go over.[52] That the studio fears as much reflects that the myth of the black rapist is certainly, once again, in the air.[53] And, despite the PCA's ultimate approval of the pairing, its warning, indeed Breen's repetitive double warning (which is utterly uncharacteristic of his usually economic style in these letters), signals the PCA's shared concern. Even so, Breen's concern focuses on how audiences might read the image: Would they know the actress to "really" be white, and/or would they accept the fiction that she is black and thus not read her pairing with Robeson as miscegenation? Despite the evident anxieties, which the studio's ultimate casting of a black actress in the role could be read to share, the fact that Breen was nonetheless willing to put the PCA's official faith in spectatorial belief in the proposed fiction (that Robeson and Aunt Jemima would make a "black" couple), is indicative, I would argue, of the PCA's standard position that the meanings of "black" and "white" are ultimately defined through the visual terms set within the frame.[54]

In light of that tradition, there are several things that make *Pinky* an especially intriguing text with which to consider issues of racial visibility and cinematic belief. The first of these is that the film not only includes but is entirely centered around the problems posed by the paradoxical figure Valerie Smith has called "the light-skinned black body." Smith's discussion of this body in literature, and the forms of knowledge and belief it portends and denies, is especially suggestive for considering the implications of its appearance at the movies. Such a body, she writes, "def[ies] the binarisms upon which constructions of racial identity depend. [Not only because it] testif[ies] to the illicit or exploitative sexual relations between black women and white men or to the historically unspeakable relations between white women and black men[, but also because i]t indicates *a contradiction between appearance and 'essential' racial identity within a system of racial distinctions based upon differences presumed to be visible*" (45, emphasis mine).

This last contradiction—of an ostensibly "black" body that isn't visibly "black"—not only threatens to rupture the assumptions of a visually grounded epistemology of race but poses a particularly pointed problem for a cinematic institution that upholds it through images. Whereas *Imitation of Life* attempted to overcome that contradiction by replacing images of Peola with those of Delilah, *Pinky* confronts it through a complex series of inscriptions that direct us when to see the white actress who plays Pinky as white, when to see her as black pretending to be white, and when to forget she is white at all and see her as "really" black.[55] The complicated twists of spectatorial belief at work here are compounded by the equally dramatic acrobatics of racial knowledge enacted around this film at the PCA.

Fifteen years after the interpretive confusion sparked by *Imitation of Life*, the PCA not only approved a script about a light-skinned black woman's identity crisis but went so far as to encourage the studio to come clean about her mixed racial heritage. Initially, when Twentieth Century-Fox asked the PCA to review "Quality," the story on which *Pinky* would be based, the PCA cited negative southern reactions to "President Truman's Civil Rights Program" and warned of related retaliation (especially in the form of local censorship) from those who "might accuse the industry of lining up with" it; nonetheless, the PCA also then decided "to leave the matter entirely up to the studio as to whether they . . . wish to proceed."[56] The studio did proceed, and a year later, in response to a script sent for review, it received the following impassioned plea from the PCA's "house Southerner," Francis Harmon: "I have not read the book on which this script was based. However, to be true to life in the South, it seems to me that Pinky should be shown to be the daughter of one of [the white plantation mistress] 'Miss Em's' male relatives. I know case after case where just such situations arose. . . . There is a constant conflict in Southern life and thought around this point: that Southern white people condone or tolerate 'social equality' on the level of vice while shouting to high heaven their opposition to 'social equality' on the level of virtue."[57] To substantiate his claims, Harmon provides historical evidence and personal testimony. He describes a "Governor of Mississippi, about the beginning of the century," and "one of my best friends, a key man in the Mississippi legislature in the 1920's," as examples of white men widely known to have kept "colored mistress[es]," despite, in the latter case, having "lost no opportunity to pass high-sounding resolutions condemning social equality [and] maintaining the statutory ban against intermarriage." As if this indictment were not explicit enough, Harmon goes a step further, providing two and one half pages of rewritten dialogue that would revise the script to expressly reveal Pinky's father to be Miss Em's brother in the film's courtroom climax.[58] Seemingly as surprised as I to find such a suggestion coming from the PCA, Darryl Zanuck responded personally with "a great deal of interest" but nonetheless declined the budding author's revisions. Claiming to be more concerned with "the larger good" of race relations than with the "considerable" profits to be had by "injecting the illicit miscegenation angle," Zanuck rejected Harmon's suggestions by saying, in so many words, we want to advance into progressive territory with this film, "but not as far as you . . . suggest."[59]

This unparalleled exchange raises several critical questions. Most obviously, Why did the PCA so dramatically change course from its initial reading of Peola in 1934 to its reading of Pinky in 1949? And what made Twentieth Century-Fox decline such a salacious invitation? Clearly, the answers are tied to changing national consciousness about race in the eras of the New Deal, World War II, and the war's domestic aftermath. Although the PCA would not remove the miscegenation clause until the fifties, it was asked to do so as early as 1942 on the grounds that it was anathema to contemporary efforts toward racial reform.[60] What is revealed in the case of *Pinky*, in particular, is that such conflicted changes in part entailed shifting thresholds of racial knowledge and belief: Harmon, for example, wanted the white South's historic contradiction to be openly avowed; Zanuck wanted to play a part in the nation's racial progress, but he feared audiences, white and black, could not tolerate that much of the truth.[61] Further reflecting and negotiating such conflicted impulses is the film that ultimately emerged.

The very fact that the vexed identity of a light-skinned black subject was not simply confined to a subplot, as Peola had been, but entirely structured the second-best-selling film of 1949 clearly indicates widespread fascination with the issues she raises.[62] At the same time, the film suggests that extended contemplation was only permissible with additional means to handle the knowledge Pinky's paradoxical body threatens to evoke. Among them were the following: unlike Harmon's fantasy about her parents, Pinky's love affair would not indict white men; she would ultimately forsake her white lover in the final reel; and, as the studio stressed in the closing line of a decisive letter to Breen, "of course, . . . the actress who will play the part of Pinky w[ould] in fact be a white girl."[63] Because this last condition would seem to beg as many questions as it allegedly answers, and because all three were elaborately intertwined, we must closely consider the film itself to understand what exactly it signals for the shifting status of racial knowledge and belief.[64]

Reduced to its fundamental elements, the ultimate project of this film, as I read it, is to make Pinky, and the viewer, see and accept her light-skinned body as being inescapably black. While she begins the film adamant in her desire to live, work, and love in a white world, by the end she has embraced not only her black "Granny," who literally enfolds Pinky in her large, dark maternal body, but her social, psychic, and geographic "roots" as well. In the final scenes she decides not to return to the North and marry Tom but to remain on the former plantation where she was raised to found a school of nursing for black women. The radical essentialism of this segregationist narrative ("Stay on the plantation and take care of your own") is, however, not as simple as it might at first seem.[65] The film does not pretend that there is a seamless connection from the outside to the inside of racial identity (from skin to blood); it goes a step further to insist that even if one's skin does not reflect it, one's racial identity is inescapable on the inside. It is this further essentialist turn that allows Pinky to be visually "white," to be played by Jeanne Crain, and yet at the same time to become "colored" in the course of the film, before our very eyes, even though her bodily image does not change. This transformation unfolds as a kind of tour de force demonstration of the power of cinema not only to fabricate racial fictions but also to compel us to believe in them, even when we can see that they are untrue.

Implicit already is that the sight of a "light-skinned black body" can provoke a striking case of divided belief about the meaning and location of racial identity. In the case of *Pinky*'s spectator it might be summed up as: "I know she looks white (she is after all a white actress, Jeanne Crain), but all the same she is black." While this formulation speaks to the ideological nature of this divided belief, less apparent is how the film can make us read a body that looks "white" as "black."[66] A quick recollection of Freudian and film theoretical paradigms of divided belief proves useful on this question.

Freud's case of divided belief also marks a potential epistemological crisis prompted by the sight of another's body, as it is the little boy's discovery of the female genitals that threatens to radically destabilize what he knows about identity and privilege.[67] The analogy is by no means exact, but it is nonetheless productive: if the potentially castrating knowledge for Freud's little boy is that the girl's lack of a penis means he could lose his, and the social power linked to it, so we can imagine white spectators who see Pinky similarly at risk by the thought that white skin does not guarantee racial privilege. And, although this film is most concerned with safeguarding the meaning of "race" for the sake of whiteness, certainly Pinky's body could evoke radical knowledge for black spectators as well.[68] Most central at the moment, and particularly relevant in the first case, is Freud's insight into how the destabilizing new sight is managed so that the boy can disavow it. Applying his vocabulary to my reading of *Imitation of Life*, we could say that the visibility of the mother's dark-skinned body is obsessively reproduced as a fetish that stands in to facilitate the disavowal of the daughter's light-skinned one—effecting "a displacement of value," as Freud describes the fetish, not from one part of the body to another, but from one entire body to another.[69]

In ways that are further suggestive to our analysis of seeing Pinky, Christian Metz famously articulates the unique condition of classical film spectatorship as itself one of divided belief ("I know very well it's just a movie, but all the same it's so real"). Metz ties this condition to the equally divided character of the cinematic signifier, a signifier marked at once by an "unaccustomed perceptual wealth" of sound and image, "but at the same time stamped with unreality to an unusual degree" in a medium that is nothing but light and shadow.[70] Despite this apparent opposition, however, Metz suggests that it is precisely this combination of perceptual plenitude from without and the spectator's imaginary investments from within, both heavily buttressed by a host of cinematic conventions, that makes cinema such a compelling inducement of fantasy— that makes possible "a certain degree of *belief* in the reality of an imaginary world" (118, original emphasis).

My reading of *Pinky* draws from Freud and Metz, and feminist interventions with both, to argue that film can prompt us to believe in the "true" blackness of a body that looks white precisely by conjuring the perceptual plenitude of cinematic sound and image on, around, and ostensibly beneath the malleable cinematic surface of the female body. For while in Pinky's case a pale body is again taken into a dark maternal one to mark its blackness, that second body is not enough. Instead, I want to suggest, this film orchestrates a more elaborate method by which to assert Pinky's racial identity, a method that makes cinematic space and the unfolding of subjects within it the new guarantee, the new fetish if you will, of racial difference. To understand how this works, and its larger implications for the cinematic production of racial knowledge, we need to consider the manifold ways in which the film makes Pinky "black," how it also makes her "white," and how it manages that divided belief to temporarily resolve the "contradiction between appearance and 'essen[ce].'"

How We See Pinky (Exacting Race through Space)

While Jeanne Crain's skin may not be "colored," Pinky is culturally and cinematically inscribed as such throughout the film. The opening shots allow us to read her as a white woman walking down a country road but then swiftly move her into settings and compositions that reframe her to be read ultimately as a black subject. This transition is already anticipated in the effect of the first three shots through a dramatic tightening and darkening of space, and consequently of the subject placed within it. The opening shot widely pans a light, open landscape with a train passing in the distance and then moves to a space bound by trees, a few buildings, and a fence. The fence motif continues through a dissolve to the second shot, a long shot featuring another fence that spans the entire screen in a more densely wooded landscape. Here we see a woman walking along the border marked by the fence, first at a considerable distance, then slowly coming closer to us until we see her just behind the fence in a medium shot (fig. 4.27). By now her image is clear: she is a young, modern, seemingly white woman, carrying a suitcase and dressed in a dark suit and light blouse. In the background dogs and black men on horseback pass by her. In the third shot she has traveled beyond the fence, suggesting her transition from one space to another, and is now caught by the camera from above, positioned within an ever darker space, now literally thick with moss-draped trees and other vegetation. She walks into a crossroads, passing black children and men with heavy loads on their backs. She continues to move toward us, and the camera moves in to fix her tightly within this space (fig. 4.28). She suddenly pauses from her walk across the frame and looks back into the deep center of the shot, where we see with her the almost unreal facade of a white-columned mansion in the distance. That image makes it now absolutely clear that she has arrived in the black quarters of a former plantation, as her distance from, and relation to, the master's house is marked by the extreme depth of the shot as well as another fence that bars her from it.[71]

FIG. 4.27. *Pinky* (1949) begins with the arrival of a
white-looking woman
(Jeanne Crain) in a rural
landscape . . .

FIG. 4.28. . . . where she
is quickly redefined
through her placement
in increasingly dark,
enveloping spaces.

FIG. 4.29. Pinky's transformation from white to black
culminates in the reunion
with her grandmother
(Ethel Waters). Even so,
here the light face is not
entirely hidden by the dark
maternal body, signaling
a complex divided belief
about Pinky's racial
identity.

The camera pulls in tighter and follows her from behind now as she continues along the dirt path, passing more black children and entering a small encampment. Visibly familiar with her surroundings, the young woman steps onto the porch of a small, rustic cabin. An older, heavy, and dark-skinned woman (Ethel Waters) greets her and proceeds to hang laundry on her line until she turns, blinks, drops the laundry, and stares with recognition. "Pinky, Pinky child?" she asks. And Pinky confirms, "Yes, Granny, it's me." With Pinky thus interpellated as the granddaughter of the black woman, her relocation from "white" to "black" is official; but their relation is sealed in the image. The women move toward each other, and Pinky buries herself, weeping, in her granny's outstretched arms (fig. 4.29). Yet in this film the light face is not entirely hidden by the dark maternal body, the first of many signs that the latter is not enough to settle our divided knowledge.

Despite Pinky's various urges to flee this place and the identity it holds out for her, the forces detected in the opening sequence nonetheless continue to work on her, and us, throughout the film. This is manifested in part in an ongoing discourse of "truth" and "pretense." Pinky is repeatedly lectured by her granny, whom others call "Aunt Dicey," and by Dicey's white mistress, Miss Em (Ethel Barrymore), about the inescapability of her "colored," "Negro" identity. Suspicious of Pinky's desire to pass, Miss Em lectures her: "Nobody deserves respect as long as she pretends to be what she isn't . . . just prove you're addicted to the truth like you pretend." Aunt Dicey makes similar speeches with dialect for greater "authentic" effect: "You know I never told you pretend you is what you ain't." These personalized sentiments accrue the force of law when, after Miss Em has died and a legal battle ensues over her will, Pinky reads (with us) her identity writ large in the posting outside the courthouse: "Jeffers and Melba Wooley vs. Pinky Johnson, colored."

Such inscriptions persist and culminate in Pinky's ultimate identification with them. Having resisted others' attempts to identify her throughout the film, and having made plans to return to the North on several occasions, she gradually submits and finally internalizes the endless speeches she has endured. Late in the film, trying to make Tom (William Lundigen) understand why she chooses to stay on and fight for her right to the property willed to her by Miss Em, she explains, "If I should back out now, I'd be letting Miss Em down. I can't do that, letting myself down . . . my . . . my people." Tom bristles at this identification, refusing it with a matrimonial renaming that makes her all-white as it makes her all his: "They're not your people, Pat, not really. There'll be no Pinky Johnson after we're married. You'll be Mrs. Thomas Adams for the rest of your life." Doubtful about both the "Pat" and the "Mrs. Thomas Adams" he thrusts upon her, Pinky replies, "Tom, you can change your name, but I wonder if you can really change what you are, inside." Any such wondering is entirely put to rest by the end of the film, when she refuses Tom once and for all: "How can I be myself [if I live a white life in Denver]. . . . I'm a Negro. I can't forget it and I can't deny it. I can't *pretend* to be anything else, I don't *want* to be anything else." Thus, by the end she not only emphatically adopts Dicey and Miss Em's rhetoric about the "sin" of pretending but takes the cultural imperative ("I'm a Negro. . . . I can't pretend to be anything else") a step further by claiming it as her own desire ("I don't want to be anything else").

Despite the persistence, and eventual triumph, of these designations of Pinky as "a Negro," the always visible fact remains that she does not look "colored."[72] Indeed, the fact that her blackness is so often reiterated through speech and writing serves as a reminder that that identity is precisely *not* guaranteed by her image. For while light and shadow often play dramatically across Pinky/Jeanne Crain's face, thematizing her (in)visibility, that face never entirely loses its "white" appearance. Without question, the white identity of the actress—a model and former Miss Long Beach before her film career began in 1943—is among the elements most responsible for the viewer's divided belief about Pinky's racial identity.[73] At the same time, there are other elements in the film to make us speculate as to the possible origins of Pinky's white appearance. These elements need to be considered in part to understand that side of the film's divided belief ("I know she's white"), and also so that when we eventually return to its insistence on her blackness ("but all the same . . ."), we do so with a clear understanding of the fraught racial context within which that identity is ultimately asserted.

Unlike Harmon's suggested revision, the film never offers an explanation of Pinky's ancestry. On the contrary, we are denied any knowledge of her parents whatsoever, not even whether Dicey is her maternal or paternal grandmother. One could argue that the repression of her parents and the confused familial relation of her granny/Aunt Dicey work both to refuse us any knowledge about the possibility of miscegenation and to leave us the spectatorial freedom to imagine it for ourselves.[74] For while I would not go so far as to say that "the suggestion is omnipresent," this film's refusal to specify is accompanied by a series of subtextual details that can easily be read as traces of Pinky's "white" heritage.

Aside from Pinky's love for and embraces with Tom (which in fact play out, in his eyes, as if she were "Pat," the white woman he first thinks her to be and later wants her to remain), the most explicit treatment of miscegenation is Pinky's near rape by two white men. What is more, the scene unfolds in such a way as to suggest what might have happened to Pinky's mother. As Pinky walks alone one night, again in a thickly wooded, mossy space, a pair of drunken white men suddenly approach in an open convertible and begin to harass her. When she tries to dismiss them, they follow her, training the car's spotlights to search across her body. The metaphoric rape of the lights shining through the dress she nervously clutches takes a literal turn when the men run her off the road, trap her, and begin to fondle her. Pinky manages to break away, and the camera follows with a cut to her running in fear through the trees with the spotlights searching after her. When she suddenly stumbles, we can see that she has landed in a graveyard. The image is relatively brief, but the prominent headstones eerily lit from behind are unmistakable. Taking Pinky through this cemetery as she attempts to flee her attackers, the scene would thus seem to announce, however subtly, that Pinky's assault by white rapists signifies the past as well as the present. Whether or not this is her mother's story precisely, the ghosts of that black graveyard quietly attest that this is the story of Pinky's ancestry.[75]

Such a reading of the film's unspoken knowledge of Pinky's white ancestry is further discernible from her otherwise unbelievable relationship with Miss Em. While Pinky's initial return to Dicey is prompted by her confusion at Tom's proposal of marriage, she stays on, at Dicey's request, to nurse Miss Em's failing heart. She begins this job with doubt and bitterness, loath to serve the master who has taken Dicey's life in servitude. In the first several scenes depicting nurse and patient, the film waivers between presenting Pinky's pride as legitimate self-respect and selfish indignation. In part, the latter depiction speaks to the film's ongoing sentimentality for a system of servitude that masks its power relations as family ties. Or, as Dicey puts it in response to Pinky's complaint that Miss Em "means to put me in my place," "Pinky child, when folks is real friends, there ain't no such thing as place."[76] Denying the structuring significance of "place" with an irony that will grow as the film's investments therein become increasingly apparent, that ideology of sentiment is the most obvious explanation for Pinky's radical change of heart toward Miss Em, as she suddenly warms to the old woman in the brief span of two scenes. After softening to Miss Em's crotchety wit in one, Pinky discovers her passed out on the floor in the next and rushes to her in a panic, calling her name and clutching her desperately. This is the response not of a professional nurse but of "real friends" and family. Although Pinky visibly catches herself in this flood of pathos, pulling back to attend professionally to the patient's pulse, the scene signals a decisive turn in their relationship. During the brief recovery that follows, Pinky's bitterness disappears, and Miss Em writes a will that bequeaths (we will learn at her death) her home and property to Pinky. This bequest nominates Pinky as the white woman's literal benefactor, as she would be if she were in fact "family," and more figuratively marks that Miss Em has become a kind of second grandmother to Pinky. Adding a whole new reading of the miscegenetic union that produced Pinky, the virtual couple that the two Ethels (Barrymore and Waters) have clearly become over their long years together as master and (loving) servant is oddly formalized when Pinky becomes Miss Em's heir.[77]

Traces of Pinky's mixed roots—be they literal of the sort suggested by Harmon and the graveyard, or figurative as symbolized by the inheritance—continue to hover over the film's final scenes. A particularly striking example comes in what is in effect a delayed response to earlier point-of-view shots (the first from the opening sequence and the second from a later scene) that position Pinky near Dicey's cabin staring at the plantation mansion in the distance (fig. 4.30). Immediately after Miss Em dies, Pinky exits the master('s) bedroom to walk out onto its second-story balcony. The camera does not follow her point of view, however, but instead cuts to a virtual reverse shot that resembles the perspective of her earlier views of the master's house (fig. 4.31). We look in long shot roughly from the place she originally did to see her now within that picture. Seeing her from that distant vantage point, we cannot make out Pinky's face, but she clearly stands out from the dingy facade by the brightness of her nursing whites. In a strange twist of fate, Pinky is now the "white" occupant of the house that she once contemptuously described (while gazing at it from Dicey's cabin) as "slave built, slave run, and run down ever since."

Pinky's occupancy of the estate in fact goes on to explicitly mimic Miss Em's. Upon learning of her inheritance, described in the will as "an expression of my genuine regard for [Pinky] and my confidence in the use to which she will put this property," and again after the judge upholds it, Pinky struggles to interpret the intent: "What did you mean, Miss Em? Tell me." In the final scene, the mansion now bustling with black nursing students inside and black children playing outside, we see that she ultimately interprets her benefactor's last wishes in such a way as to be true to her race (as Miss Em had urged her to), and to carry on the tradition of Miss Em's own former boarding school. The sign in the film's final shot reads: "Miss Em's Clinic and Nursery School." In the end, then, Pinky not only is the white woman's heir but literally carries on her legacy as headmistress, albeit with the significant difference of filling the plantation house with an all-black student body.

Which returns us, quite emphatically, to the other side of the film's divided belief. Despite the blatant rhyming of Pinky and Miss Em in the final scene, that same scene desperately wants us to see Pinky as fully and finally accepting her position as a black subject. Now, immediately following her declared desire to be black ("I'm a Negro. . . . I don't want to be anything else"), we first see her moving through the estate turned clinic, populated with dark-skinned black students. Also there is Dr.

FIG. 4.30. Pinky, dramatically located and relocated as a racial subject.

FIG. 4.31

FIG. 4.32

Canady, the black doctor who originally proposed the idea of the nursing school and earlier told Pinky he had "never been North" despite the temptation because "I felt my job was here." Clearly, then, the "use to which she [has] put" her inheritance is a project of racial "uplift," a signal not merely of the end of her disavowal of being "colored" but of her wholehearted embrace of it. The final shot of the film cinematically cements Pinky "in [her] place" once and for all. Having emerged from the new clinic/school, she walks to ring the school bell in the yard. Standing next to the school's sign and ringing the bell, she is fixed from above in a high-angle shot. She looks down at first and then lifts her head. Light and shadow play across her face, continuing to signify the inessentiality of her skin, but as she beams upward, almost beatifically, it is clear that Pinky now embraces her position from within (fig. 4.32).

In light of the fact that Pinky's/Jeanne Crain's skin does not guarantee her racial identity, and, as we have seen, that even narrative subtexts and implied backstories fail to do so, the question becomes, How does the film make Pinky "black"? For while it openly admits that "race" and "color" are disjunctive, can even flaunt that in its title, it has other means to make Pinky "colored." Well beyond the spoken and written inscriptions discussed previously (e.g., "Pinky Johnson, colored"—the legal inscription that in fact fails to matter in court), the film racially locates her in and through the unfolding of cinematic space. Pinky's blackness is cinematically asserted from without her, as begun already in the opening sequence, and as the film proceeds, that process becomes increasingly elaborate, finally inserting blackness firmly within her as well.[78]

The first five scenes are dedicated not only to making us see Pinky as "a Negro" but also to making her identify as such herself. Soon after returning to her grandmother's arms and cabin, she finds herself in her childhood room, framed by a window in the foreground and by a series of receding door frames in the background. This spatial insistence on a "deep" reentry into blackness is echoed in the dialogue: Pinky regrets having been sent away and sobs on the bed of her black childhood as Dicey shames her for "denying yourself like Peter denied the good lord Jesus."

The second and third scenes stand out for their elaborate articulation of the relation between Pinky's cinematic placement and her racial subjectivity. The fade-out on her sobbing in shame is followed by a fade-in that finds her, now tucked in that bed, talking in her sleep in the middle of the night. We see her call out "Tom" and then hear a breathier inner voice call "Tom" again, and finally scream it, waking herself in a terrified start.[79] Framed in a close-up, she sits up instantly, disoriented. As soon as she awakes, the sound track comes alive with a pulsing chorus of insects. The camera slowly pulls back, and a train whistle sounds. Still reorienting herself, Pinky rises and looks out the window, where we see a dark, crowded image filled with moss-draped trees, a fence, and train smoke. Like the train that brought her here in the opening sequence, and the train in which she first passed for white as a child (as she recounts to Dicey during their reunion scene), this train again marks the border between her white life with Tom in the North and her black life here with Dicey. She slams the window shut, but the schism that haunts her persists at scene's end, marked on her face by lighting that puts her half in the dark and half in the light. Nevertheless, the thick atmospheric envelope that still surrounds her—the cicadas, the darkness, the blankets, the close-up, and so forth—already suggests that the film's orchestration of space has considerable power to relocate her, psychically as well as physically.

That process continues with increasing force and effect. The very next morning, after Dicey has gone to check on Miss Em in the big house, Pinky slowly walks toward it, moving between trees that again serve to play light and shadow upon her face (fig. 4.33). Another distant train whistle triggers her breathy inner voice to again speak her white desire. It whispers a telegram to Tom promising her immanent return, repeating, "I love you . . . love you . . . love you. . . ." But this daydreaming inner voice falls suddenly silent when a wrought iron fence stops her in her tracks (fig. 4.34); here again, the film spatially maps the racial limits confining her identity and desire. Pinky then sees a small black girl who also stands at the fence, gazing through it to the unattainable other side in an image that echoes not only the one of Pinky we have just seen but also a painful memory voiced elsewhere from her own childhood (fig. 4.35). That black fence and the rhyming of the child's position before it to the grown woman's forcibly relocate Pinky's subjectivity from the inner "white" voice just subdued to a "black" body she clearly recognizes, and identifies with, as an earlier version of her self.

Pinky's blackness is again identified from without in the fourth scene in which she visits a neighbor to retrieve money he has pocketed from her grandmother over the years. When he asks her who she is, she tells him "Patricia Johnson," a name he quickly revises: "Pinky!?! Well what do you know." His jealous girlfriend, who pulls a knife on Pinky and causes a scene, later identifies her to the police as "nothing but a low-down colored gal." For the first time, Pinky herself explicitly accepts that identity: "Yes, it's true, I'm colored." Her doing so amid this scene of "money and a man" in the black part of town (as one of the cops recalls it during the trial) has immediate institutional effect, as the police take it as cause to arrest her without charges.

After Pinky is released by the judge, we find her once again in the dark and heavy space that surrounds Dicey's cabin, and her identity is again spatially constituted in the scene of her near rape. When the white men

FIG. 4.33. Tension between
Pinky's inner voice, speaking her white desire, and
the play of light and
shadow upon her image.

FIG. 4.34. Pinky's inner
"white" voice is suddenly
brought to a halt by the
fence that marks her dis-
tance from the big house.

FIG. 4.35. The film makes
Pinky recognize herself in
the image of a black child
positioned just as she has
been.

first see her from their car, assuming her to be white, one of them calls, "Excuse me, ma'am, you must be a stranger 'round here. We can't let no girl walk through this here nigger section." Pinky corrects their misreading, a reading based on skin, with an affirmation of her proper location: "I live in this section." When they react, she again insists, "I said I live here, now just leave me alone." Although she manages to escape their clutches, it is the men's knowledge that she "live[s] here" that instantly turns the encounter from sexual harassment of a woman they assume to be white to sexual assault of one they now "know" to be black.

While Pinky's spatial profiling by police and white rapists points to dominant racial practices well beyond the field of cinematic representation, the film exposes its own unique investments in the equation between where you live and who you are as a racial subject when Tom later visits her at Dicey's cabin. Having fled Boston after his proposal, afraid of what might become of her racial secret, and now suddenly surprised by his visit and his inquiries ("What are you doing, charity work?"), Pinky again attempts to explain herself with the statement "I live here." Unlike the local white men who grasped it instantly, however, Tom is slow to understand the racial identity implied by such an utterance. The way in which she spells it out for him, and for us, not only reaffirms the degree to which Pinky's blackness is generated through her placement in a particular space but further demonstrates cinema's ability to construct from that spatial relation an ensuing psychic identity.

When Tom does not understand the significance of "I live here," assuming it at first to mean she is poor, Pinky gradually reveals it by taking him on a narrated tour of her grandmother's cabin. Stepping up onto the porch, she asks, "Don't you know who lives in this kind of house?" She then walks toward the front door and beckons him to follow. As they stand at the threshold, she begins an oddly dissociated tour, mapping the identities that inhabit the cabin through a narration of the space and objects within it. In a slow, purposeful voice she recites:

> There's an old colored woman who can't read or write, a washer woman people around here call Aunt Dicey. There's the basket she carries her clothes in. There's the ironing board she uses. And those are the heavy irons she heats on that old wood stove. Year in and year out she's washed and ironed, and carried the clean clothes to people's back doors, through rain and cold and the heat of summer. She saved her money and lived on the scraps white people gave her. Why? For me. So she could send me off to school. So I could learn to be a nurse. So her granddaughter would be spared the kind of life she's had to live.

Having meandered about the room as Pinky narrates the story, Tom suddenly responds to the final revelation: "Granddaughter?" Pinky reaffirms the relation: "Yes, her granddaughter, me. Now you understand." He replies, "Pat . . ." She interrupts, "My name is Pinky."

Nearly mimicking the process by which the film has worked to construct Pinky as Dicey's "colored" granddaughter, this scene demonstrates that Pinky has internalized not only that identity but also the film's very means of constituting it. Racial identity is conjured by directing the viewer to interpret sets, props, atmosphere, and narrative, out of which emerge a position within which the racial subject can be seen. What becomes uniquely visible here is that this cinematic process produces not only a black subject situated deeply within the narrated space but also a white one guided to see her as if from a point beyond or outside it.[80] Like the film itself, Pinky must construct racial identity in this way because her bodily image alone does not tell Tom, or us, who she is. While her voice-off narration might seem to invite a visual miming by the camera that would reveal the basket, ironing board, and so on, as she describes them, the images of the objects do not match up simultaneously with her naming of them (fig. 4.36). Like Pinky's own body, the visual signifiers are insufficient in and of themselves to reveal the meaning of the story; they require Pinky's orchestration of the elements into a larger, imagined, scene. It is only after she does so that she can reemerge in the story, verbally and visually, so that we, and Tom, see her anew. Only then do first-person pronouns emerge in the third-person account, joining the "granddaughter" of the story to an "I" and a "me." As this new identity is revealed, Tom moves slightly such that he is brightly lit and she is entirely covered in an even darker shadow (figs. 4.37A–4.37B). Now that the scene has been set and the viewing guided, Tom, like the film's spectator before him, sees the formerly white "Pat" as the now "colored" Pinky.

In keeping with the perpetual division of belief that marks the film, this scene can be read as one that clearly knows, at some level, the process it so overtly enacts and yet remains deeply invested in the identities thus constructed. For despite the fabricated quality of cinematic signifiers here and elsewhere in the film—noticeable plays of light and shadow, phony-looking exteriors, and the like—the film not only insists that Pinky, Tom, and the spectator recognize her irrefutable blackness but posits quite a different explanation for its source in its ongoing discourse of essence that emanates from within. Upholding Dicey's dictum that you can't "pretend you is what you ain't," this logic argues that the appearance of the bodily image doesn't matter, because the inside will shine through. This lesson is made explicit by the former school teacher when she tests her visitors' judgment by asking them to assess a piece of her jewelry. Whereas her superficial cousin Wooley mistakes the broach for a "real antique," Pinky recognizes it to be a "rather clever imitation." Like the subject who passes, the didactic lesson goes, junk jewelry will be recog-

FIG. 4.36. As Pinky narrates for Tom (William Lundigan) a story of the black woman's cabin, visual signifiers do not immediately match up with verbal ones.

FIG. 4.37A. At first Tom does not recognize Pinky's relation to this place.

FIG. 4.37B. Only after she fully conjures the scene does he see her, now in full shadow, as a black subject defined by this black place.

nized by those in the know, despite its deceptive surface. But the parable does not explain *how* the viewer knows or does not know. Painting Em's cousin Wooley as a greedy fool and Pinky as a subject fated for an authentic life, the film again returns to a faith in essence as the determining factor.

What my larger reading of the film's own methods suggests instead is that that faith in essences from within is itself the fiction posited to mask the cinematic conjuring of "essence" from without. For it is the arrangement of cinematic elements, and not any innate vision or knowledge on the part of the viewer, that directs us to see Pinky—as first white (walking down the country road), then black (weeping on the black maternal body, deep inside Dicey's cabin, etc.), then black pretending to be white (kissing Tom when he first visits her), then white on the outside struggling to be black on the inside (indignantly confronting "you Whites" in and out of the courtroom), and finally black through and through ("I don't want to be anything else" and the all-black uplift project on the plantation).

The ultimate force of this process is perhaps most evident when it finally seems, in fact, to make us recognize Pinky's as a black body. This happens late in the film, after she has decided to stay and fight for her legal inheritance and "my people," when the camera discovers her earning her keep at Dicey's washboard. The scene opens with a close-up of arms working in soapy water overlaid with the voice of a black woman singing (fig. 4.38A). As the camera pulls back, we realize that the voice and image, once again, do not match up: the arms are revealed to be Pinky's and the voice emanates from Dicey seated on the porch nearby (fig. 4.38B). But initially, the superimposition of Waters's voice and Crain's partially obscured body momentarily invites us to read them as a unified whole, announcing that the white voice that formerly haunted Pinky has been silenced and supplanted. Not only does she now reside fully within the space of the black washerwoman she described to Tom— doing the laundry outside, wearing a kerchief and apron—but an "authentic" black voice in turn has been cinematically inscribed as if residing within her as well. When Tom arrives unexpectedly, Pinky manages to rearrange herself, nervously pulling off the kerchief and tugging at her clothes. Yet, although she has not yet decided to make Tom accept it, in the eyes and ears of the spectator she has already been transformed. We may have once known her to be white/Jeanne Crain, but through "this kind of house," her washboard, her kerchief, and the voice of her "old colored" grandmother, she is now black from the inside out *and* from the outside in.

While *Pinky*, not unlike *Imitation of Life*, thus clearly threatens to destabilize conventional conceptions of racial identity, it too marks Hol-

FIG. 4.38A. Ethel Waters's offscreen singing voice invites us to read this close-up of hands at a washboard as belonging to a "black" body.
FIG. 4.38B. When the camera pulls back, we see Pinky fully inhabiting the place of the black washerwoman.

lywood's unique abilities to manage such crises. For while it allows extended looks that can see that skin color is no guarantee, it goes a step further, in effect, returning us to a discourse of interiority, or "essence," as the source of racial identity. No mere throwback to nineteenth-century discourses of blood, however, *Pinky* overlays those with a properly cinematic addition. Indeed, while it would be narratively convenient to invoke "black blood" in the many speeches about pretense and true identity, the film does not. It need not, as I hope to have shown, because it is working within a different epistemological framework, one that induces Pinky and the spectator to believe in the "truth" of her invisible blackness through a series of insistent cinematic emplacements. The extended process required to achieve this belief, even temporarily, testifies to the difficulty of erasing the paradox of the light-skinned black body. But ultimately, I would argue, the film's segregationist project succeeded at the most entrenched level, that of psychic belief, insofar as it made Pinky ultimately internalize the film's desire for racial essentialism and made white audiences of the second-highest-grossing film of the year believe they had seen and understood what racism was "really" like.[81]

Although admittedly limited in significant ways by the two exceptional cases here examined, this chapter's readings nonetheless further suggest a larger historical analysis not only of the PCA's dramatically revised approach to miscegenation and passing from 1934 to 1949 but also of classical Hollywood cinema's contributions to the construction of racial difference. Namely, by 1949 the PCA could go so far as to confess the legacy of miscegenation it had so staunchly worked to repress—even if studio heads were not yet ready to do so openly—in part because the cinematic means to overcome its ideological fallout were powerfully in place. For if *Imitation of Life* marks an epistemological shift from "blood" to the bodily image, with *Pinky* we witness a further shift to a method of defining race that is less bound by the props of "real" bodily attributes and takes even greater advantage of the attributes of cinema itself and its dual propensity for fiction and spectatorial belief. Indeed, whereas racial epistemologies organized around discourses of blood and skin were only becoming increasingly vulnerable to dilution (through growing resistance to segregation, scientific research, etc.), cinema could counter the evident "facts" with the fabrications of fantasy, and with the medium's particular knack for wedding fantasy to the impression of encounters with "real" phenomena (skin, voice, space, etc.). Thus, these films suggest, as a site for constructing racial knowledge classical cinema was ideally suited to conjuring belief, albeit at times divided, in visible and even invisible fantasies of race.

PART THREE

Rebirthing a Nation?

Out of the Plantation and into the Suburbs: Sensational Extremes in the Late 1950s

RACE FILMS THAT ARE "ALL THINGS TO ALL MEN"

After nearly thirty years of regulated repression, interracial romance erupted in Hollywood in markedly sensational terms. In the summer of 1957, just months before southern resistance to integration crystallized on television screens with images of the crisis at Little Rock's Central High School, on the big screen the lifting of the Production Code's segregationist miscegenation clause was signaled by the highly publicized release of *Island in the Sun*.[1] Noting only *some* of the excesses of a film that paired a black man and a white woman, a black woman and a white man, and an assortment of more ambiguous couples, *Life* magazine declared it "a lush Technicolor romance with so many interracial subplots that telling white from black becomes a guessing game."[2] And while this film is usually remembered, when remembered at all, as the first of the era to transgress the miscegenation taboo, it was part of a much larger wave of films featuring a variety of mixed couples. These included whites and Native Americans in films like *Broken Arrow* (1950), *The Far Horizons* (1955), *The Vanishing American* (1955), *The Searchers* (1956), *Mohawk* (1956), and *Run of the Arrow* (1957); whites and Asians in *Love Is a Many-Splendored Thing* (1955), *The King and I* (1956), *Sayonara* (1957), *China Gate* (1957), and *The World of Suzie Wong* (1960); whites and Mexicans in *The White Orchid* (1954) and *Touch of Evil* (1958); and further combinations in *Bhowani Junction* (1956), *South Pacific* (1958), *West Side Story* (1961), *Mutiny on the Bounty* (1962), and others. Emerging within this field while also expanding it, *Island in the Sun* had tremendous box office success in the United States and abroad—despite early fears of widespread banning in the South—and was partly responsible for the cycle of black-white "miscegenation films," as some called them, that followed it.[3] That cycle included *Band of Angels* (1957), *Kings Go Forth* (1958), *Tamango* (1957), *Night of the Quarter Moon* (1959; rereleased as *The Flesh and the Flame* [1961]), *Imitation of Life* (1959), and *The World, the Flesh, and the Devil* (1959). As the familiarity and relative obscurity of these titles might suggest, they collectively span most every range of high and low. Some are lavish productions that shimmer and shout; some are bargain Bs that sputter and clank. Several were box office giants, several remain popular and/or critical favorites, and several others faded quickly or never got off the ground.[4] Despite such differences, the sheer volume of such films attests to the popularity of the trend. Add to that the simultaneous burst of solicited and unsolicited publicity around actual and imagined interracial star romances—by the likes of Harry Belafonte, Sammy Davis Jr., Kim Novak, Dorothy Dandridge, Eartha Kitt, and others—and the unprecedented visibility of interracial couples seems to have been hard *not* to see by anyone looking in Hollywood's direction.

Since viewers were in fact looking elsewhere more than ever before in this period, namely, at their televisions, this spectacular display of interracial couples can be read in part as an attempt to reattract their attention. But, at a historical moment when the word "miscegenation" was regularly linked to violent national debates over integration, this gimmick stands out as a particularly vexed one, far more overdetermined than wide screens and 3-D glasses, or even teenage angst and adultery.[5] This excess is quickly suggested by a brief sampling of plot sketches.[6] *Band of Angels* resurrects Clark Gable as a Southern gentleman facing the Civil War, but this time one who confesses a brutal slave-trading past and openly takes up with his light-skinned slaves; *Kings Go Forth* pits GIs Frank Sinatra and Tony Curtis in a rivalry over a French-raised, biracial American (Natalie Wood), resolving the triangle in a battle with Nazis that kills the womanizing Curtis and forces the amputation of humble Sinatra's right arm; *Night of the Quarter Moon* pairs a white, American POW with a "quadroon" from Mexico; and in *The World, the Flesh, and the Devil*, Harry Belafonte is again involved with a white woman—as he had been in *Island in the Sun*, and in real life and press coverage since his second marriage, also in 1957—but this time the couple only tentatively comes together after the rest of the world has been destroyed by nuclear war. These stories are delivered through an equally sensational range of cinematic forms: from convoluted plot twists to remarkably bad dialogue; from swollen musical scores to garish Technicolor landscapes; from tired racial mythologies to exhausted sexual archaisms. As a result, in addition to their shared thematics, these films are further connected by what we might call, inspired by Thomas Cripps, their "tortured . . . manneris[m]."[7] What is more, I propose, the critical interest of these tortured texts lies precisely *in* the brash and desperate terms with which they speak of and to urgent social questions of their historical moment.

Nothing so quickly demonstrates the odd mixture of profound social conflict and summer-blockbuster superficiality that marked these films as a sampling of the published words that circulated around them. Hollywood's new exploration of interracial romance was touted by the industry, trade journals, and occasionally the white and black popular presses as a welcome, bold, even enlightened sign of changing times; for others it fulfilled the deepest nightmare of segregation; and yet others derided it as a pathetically inadequate and exploitative response to any and all such social dilemmas. Hence, whereas *Life* judged *Island in the Sun* "the worst of the summer's 'adult' films . . . pretend[ing] to be something it isn't, a hard look at racial tensions," the *Hollywood Reporter* deemed this "daringly conceived tapestry" to be "sensational" but worthy of lofty moral discourse all the same: "It is a commentary that the breaking of God's commandments seems less sensational than the abrogation of man's taboos. [*Island*] is certain to be the most talked about picture of the year, the most controversial in many a year. If the frank treatment of miscegenation makes it unwelcome in the South, this same boldness may well be compensated by returns from overseas."[8] Just weeks later, however, *Band of Angels*, and implicitly its Hollywood-style southern kind, was thoroughly mocked: "Every so often in this gumbo (thick with pathos, miscegenation and all the romantic clichés known to Hollywood), somebody forces out a speech on the meaning of freedom."[9] Even so, by year's end the *New York Times* soberly weighed in, noting that "motion picture exploration of the previously taboo field of miscegenation and its peripheral areas seems to be progressing cautiously."[10]

Such schizoid responses continued as the cycle wore on, albeit with evidence of growing disappointment. In the spring of 1959 a reviewer from *Cue* lamented, "At best, miscegenation is a difficult enough movie theme when handled intelligently. It is embarrassing when badly done, and meaningless in any social sense when the story is phonied up and the direction slapped in with a shovel to widen its so-called 'exploitation' appeal."[11] Yet despite such criticism, at least two black newspapers, the *Chicago Defender* and the *Pittsburgh Courier*, continued to invite their readers to await the next specimen in good faith. The very film so derided by *Cue*, above, for example, was held up by the *Defender* as a potential Oscar contender and celebrated as "one of the most spectacular . . . of the . . . interracial releases . . . a frank and daring treatment of an unconventional subject."[12]

The incongruities and contradictions that riddle such responses, not unlike divergent opinions about interracial marriage at the time, make it extremely difficult to neatly characterize how these films were received, even by particular kinds of audiences.[13] Film marketing indicates that white and nonwhite viewers were clearly targeted, albeit at times with significantly different appeals, and audience reactions were undoubtedly marked by differences of class and sex, as well as race and region.[14] But the capacity for "the new 'miscegenation films'" to be "all things to all men," as a writer in *Commentary* put it in 1957, was evidently even more complex.[15] In its original context the description signified a kind of crossover exploitation factor that would "attract the Negro and Asian audiences, but, at the same time, . . . not alienate the South." Hence the writer begins his essay with the story of segregationist picketers in Charlotte, North Carolina, who, upon being told by exiting viewers that *Island in the Sun* was " 'in fact . . . a pro-segregation picture,' went in to see [it] and picketed no more."[16] Such an effect is understandable when we recall that the film's ending forces a final wedge between the characters played by Harry Belafonte and Joan Fontaine, and that even the film's middle never allows more physical contact between them than some intense leaning that could well be mistaken for a kind of erotcized contempt (figs. 5.1–5.2).[17] This might explain why, "despite . . . pre-release hubbub," by mid-July 1957 *Island* was "outgrossing such top films as 'The King and I' in such unlikely cities as Lexington, Louisville, Oklahoma City and Charleston, W. Va.," and "prompt[ing] the producers to set dates in Texas, Virginia and Florida, too."[18] Perpetually complicating one set of indicators with another, however, bookings were not without protest and censorship, in the North and the South.[19] Although the film was reportedly able to appease some segregationists in Charlotte, "more than 100 members of the U.S. Ku Klux Klan" and a White Citizens Council picketed it in Jacksonville, Florida, in late August, keeping on enough pressure a month later to prompt a meeting there of the Motion Picture Association of America.[20]

In short, not only were there no signs of consensus about these films, individually or collectively, but they seem to have been simultaneously rejected and consumed, hated and (occasionally) loved, by segregationists and integrationists alike, black reviewers and white ones, the South and the rest of the world. The reception evidence thus quickly shatters any assumption that these films had singular, or even predictably split, ideological effects and suggests instead that they seized with contradictions and incoherencies not unlike those that marked national racial sentiment at the time. Such documented confusion, combined with the tortured mannerism of the films themselves, only further begs us to reconsider how they could appeal "to all men."

The proposition that they might have is especially intriguing for the way it inadvertently joins these films' highly uneven racial politics to their equally convulsive preoccupations with gender and sexuality. For while their publicity and reception materials loudly announce race as the term most radically in question, the films themselves also regularly display serious, sometimes deranging, doubts about contemporary states of masculinity and femininity—terms we know also to have been, if not making daily headlines, under serious and sometimes open scrutiny at the time.

FIG. 5.1. When a white woman (Joan Fontaine) and a black man (Harry Belafonte) enjoy their first interracial romance in a Hollywood film, *Island in the Sun* (1957), they nonetheless keep their distance.

FIG. 5.2

FIG. 5.3. The failures of the white man's "odd look" are announced immediately.

As the urgency of the civil rights movement became increasingly evident with the events in Little Rock, for example, a less visible but intensely felt protohistory of the modern women's movement was surfacing as well. For also in 1957, inspired by testimony from other college-educated white women like herself, Betty Friedan began composing what would become *The Feminine Mystique*. First produced as a series of magazine articles in the late fifties, and eventually selling three million copies after its publication as a book in 1963, Friedan's work would make widely public a certain white, middle-class female voice dissatisfied with the stifling constraints of the era's housewife ideal.[21] And, as Steven Cohan has reminded us, this period was also marked by widespread "bewilderment about the proper masculine role."[22] So much so "that in 1958 *Look* published a series analyzing what it named 'The Decline of the American Male,'" announcing a masculinity crisis of national importance: "'Scientists worry that in the years since the end of World War II, [the American male] has changed radically and dangerously; that he is no longer the masculine, strong-minded man who pioneered the continent and built America's greatness.'"[23] Pressing beyond common explanations of such anxieties like those offered by *Look* (domination by women, overwork, "conform[ity] to the values of the crowd"), Cohan traces "the unease with which" conceptions of masculinity as a set of gender practices, and as a set of sexual ones, came together in this period: "For while the fifties marks the historical conjuncture when the hetero-homosexual binarism governing the way our culture now interprets gender distinctions and maintains sexual conformity achieved its hegemonic standing, this era also records, especially in predominantly middle-class entertainment such as the movies, how gender and sexuality did not easily or securely meld together as the coordinates of a normative masculinity committed to heterosexuality and applicable to all men everywhere" (xv).

Insecurities about the very meaning and (im)mutability of "male" and "female" were so acute in fifties interracial films, this chapter will demonstrate, that only by paying close attention to how those films negotiate *both* the overt racial struggles *and* the palpable gender anxieties of the postwar era can we begin to discern how and why miscegenation fantasies vividly pursued and denied in earlier periods returned, and were revised, with such a vengeance. Indeed, the multiple points of intersection between these identity territories will suggest that the meanings taken from these films depend not only on which of multiple racial threads are seized in a given text but also on how those are repeatedly woven in highly gendered ways.

The most ordinary, but arguably the most structuring, gender rhetoric of popular liberal interracial discourse in the fifties is articulated with particular clarity on the eve of the decade in testimony gathered by

Ebony on the subject of famous mixed marriages. A writer from the *Oklahoma Black Dispatch* claimed that the ideal "in human relationships and marriage" would only be achieved "when we can think in terms of women and men and not in terms of colors."[24] As is still often the case, even when the dominant terms of racial difference (or "colors") are openly resisted, those of sexual difference are tenacious, figured as the baseline "ideal" of all human relations. And here this ideal is posited on the heels of a telling "racial" lament: "When we set the white woman out aside from the Oriental, the Indian and the Asiatic, we are agreeing in the concept the white man offers that his mate is something different from other women in the world." Thus worried about the relative worth, for men, of the women typically claimed by them, this writer implicitly envisions racial equality as all women having equal value for all men.

While the Hollywood texts to come are less eager to permanently expand the access of all men, they nonetheless share a tendency to reduce all women to the value they hold for them. Thus, for example, throughout press copy on interracial star marriages, brides, regardless of race, are figured repeatedly as dutiful wives and mothers. When Belafonte writes his own story for *Ebony*, "Why I Married Julie," he insists upon a shared passion for ideas, the arts, and political activism. Usually, however, reporters and photographers were more interested that his white wife, a professional modern dancer, "has given up her own work and stays home and cooks 'crazy, exotic, things' to please Harry's gourmet tastes. They expect their first baby in December."[25] In the case of Eartha Kitt, a black woman whose professional success and passionate appetite for (frequently white) male companionship were well known long before her feline purr, announcements of her engagement to a "white real estate investor" seemed as eager to settle her down into proprietary conventions of matrimony as to query the racial implications of her choice.[26] When a British tabloid reports the engagement in a story on interracial celebrity couples (a story that concocts almost as many of them as it reports), it concludes of this internationally successful soloist: "For the Southern sharecropper's daughter the breakdown of the social barriers means a good marriage."[27] After the story proper ends, the last word on interracial romance, set apart in a different typeface, comes in the form of the alleged testimony of an "obedient" woman:

QUOTE . . . from Nancy Kwan (the screen Suzie Wong): "Chinese women have sex appeal because they are considerate and obedient. As Confucius say [*sic*]: 'What good sex appeal if girl spit in eye [*sic*], for goodness' sake.'"

Whether interracial screen discourse served as a convenient contemporary occasion to appeal to "all men" by the publicized submission of all women, or whether the reliable strictures of patriarchy were the most reliable means (for journalists, photographers, and the stars themselves) to navigate the rocky racial terrain charted by such unions is at times a difficult, and at other times a painfully easy, call to make.

As we turn to the films directly, several less publicized trends become strikingly clear. Predictably, the men whose interests are most at stake are white, and appearances of men of color regularly function in relation thereto. Less predictably, many of the white men around whom these interracial plots circulate bear the incriminating scars of the master at the end of his rule. In *Band of Angels*, for example, the former slave trader's guilt returns even before Hamish Bond (Clark Gable) speaks it in the form of excessive drinking and a tormented soul, and a late speech sharply captures the film's reluctant recognition that his end is near. As he watches his slaves express their joy at the freedom soon to come, the voice of Gable/Butler/Bond intones, "If we could live another hundred years, we'd probably see white justice for the blacks. We'd know by then that men don't make history, but are shaped by history, history takes its time." Imagining the possibility of racial justice in "another hundred years" from the fictional date of 1865 at the moment of the film's release in the summer of 1957, his words eerily refuse contemporary demands for racial justice even as they indirectly acknowledge them; privileging white agency over black ("white justice for the blacks"), denying agency altogether as if to deny white guilt ("men don't make history, but are shaped by [it]"), and denying the possibility of immediate action in a call for that brand of patience so fiercely rejected by the civil rights movement ("history takes its time").[28] What is more, the film goes to great lengths to legitimate the white man's sins in excessively gendered ways. It is exposed in the last reel that his most loyal male slave (Sidney Poitier) owes his very life to Bond for having taken a wound to save him as a child in the slave trade and possibly, it is strongly hinted, for being his actual father as well. And we are positioned to hear the white man's guilty words through the onscreen ears of faithful slave mistresses, so that we might love and forgive their master as they have been scripted to do throughout the film. His current mistress even chooses slavery over freedom in order to remain by his side! Even so, these sensational appeals cannot deny, but desperately try to cope with, the undeniable fact that the master's time is up.[29]

As a white man of privilege showing obvious signs of social and psychic strain at the heart of a late fifties interracial romance film, Hamish Bond is not alone. In *Bhowani Junction* the British Colonel Savage (Stewart Granger) appears just prior to India's decolonization, and his nominated savagery is momentarily exposed when he responds to the peaceful resistance of Indian protesters by commanding his men to defile them with buckets of urine and feces. As *The Searchers* begins, Ethan Edwards (John Wayne) still proudly wears his Confederate coat three years after the Civil War has ended, but in the course of the film's epic quest he infamously loses his cowboy grip. Marlene Dietrich's enigmatic eulogy at the end of *Touch of Evil*, delivered in the role of an aging gypsy at the passing of her sporadic but longtime white male companion, could be said to speak to the ambiguously shared lot of these formerly central white men. As the bloated, corrupt, and emotionally broken Detective Quinlan (Orson Welles) floats away in putrid waters off screen, Dietrich/Tana remembers, "He was some kind of man." The line's past tense, the Dietrichesque performance, and the garbage dump setting make the memorial decidedly uncertain. Could a man this decayed by alcohol and loss ever have been an idealized "some kind of man"? Or was his kind always far in excess, or far short, of any such ideal? Although *Touch of Evil* is more fixated than other interracial films from the period on the late stages of decay of such a no-longer-classical male subject, it nonetheless makes all the more apparent their shared preoccupation with white men whose former states of privilege and idealization are now openly questioned in the exposure of profound weaknesses—social, psychic, and corporeal.[30]

Even films that don't foreground white men's social and institutional losses display pronounced concern for their mental health. Well before Chuck Nelson (John Drew Barrymore) falls in love with his "quadroon" wife in *Night of the Quarter Moon,* he suffers from debilitating trauma as a former prisoner of war in Korea. Another white man under obvious strain, Major Lloyd Gruver (Marlon Brando), is introduced at the opening of *Sayonara* as an exhausted and somewhat troubled pilot, also in the Korean War, whose doctor declares, "You've had it. You're through flying for a while," and sends him to Japan for a rest cure by special orders from the general. Although Gruver must confront a host of gender troubles when his white fiancée surprises him there, he finally gets his vim and vigor back through his romance with a Japanese showgirl. In *Kings Go Forth* Sinatra plays yet another victim of war whose losses are best offset by his love of a woman of color. Sam Loggins's psychic wounds are clearly established even before he loses an arm fighting Nazis, but that loss finally renders all his others strikingly visible with multiple shots of an empty sleeve pressed crisply flat against his body. Loggins is unique among the white male subjects of trauma and loss in these films for his lack of ever having had a permanent position of social privilege. "Born poor and not handsome," his suffering in ordinariness nonetheless could be said to epitomize what the other characters most fear losing or have already lost.

What is both new in this chapter and ties it back to earlier ones is that the late fifties interracial films repeatedly represent their concerns about the social instability and psychic frailty of their formerly dominant subjects in terms that are strikingly visual, and find various forms of correction through elaborate interracial maneuvers. Tapping into a long cinematic history of miscegenation fantasies that facilitate shifting definitions and relations among masculinity, femininity, whiteness, blackness, etc., these films map their interracial terrain in ways that at once anxiously imagine the loss of privileges formerly assumed by the classical white male subject, and navigate that terrain as a means to negotiate his best chances for survival. That such maneuvers regularly take place in and through the field of vision is quickly demonstrated by the large population of white men in this chapter who show clear signs of failed, failing, and assaulted vision: Chuck Nelson's vision blurs through distorted camera techniques at the moment of his mental breakdown; an archaeologist's command of patriarchal and colonial gazes is put into question in *The White Orchid* by an uninvited female photographer and natives who surround them in a Mexican jungle; and in *Touch of Evil* the field of vision is so unreliable for all male subjects (who are actually, nearly, and figuratively blinded by darkness, acid, and textual alignment with feminized forms of visual impairment and vulnerability, respectively) that the climactic battle between men is staged as an elaborate challenge, in the dark, to authoritatively hear and capture another's voice.[31] This ailing visual register, and the white men associated with it, are routinely worried over, and tended to, through these films' interracial scenarios.[32]

While these scenarios variously work to forestall the outright death of the white male gaze, their excesses nonetheless signal its health and hegemony to be seriously at risk. Indeed, it is in the face of such risk that some of the most drastic interracial measures are taken to keep former subjects of privilege alive and consequentially looking. This becomes evident in the recurrent articulation of three distinct, albeit at times overlapping, tropes: (1) women of color who are imagined to be far more classically "feminine" than white women and hence provide unique means to restore the white men they love; (2) white women who tend only to exacerbate crises of white masculinity with emergent identities of their own, and who are thus supplanted or refashioned on the kinder, gentler, and more classically spectacular models ascribed to their sexual rivals of color; and (3) less frequently, but pronouncedly, potent men of color whose vision and virility are temporarily unleashed to refortify ailing masculine forms. Fifties interracial films are by no means reducible to these tropes (as evidenced by examples within and beyond the films discussed in this chapter), nor do they always neatly "succeed" in restoring conventional structures of power. Rather, I propose, their considerable repetition across a wide range of films and the ways they anxiously register and respond to imminent social change merit close attention in our attempts to further historicize the cinematic forms and identities here in question.[33] The following sections thus interrogate each of these tropes in some depth. After first introducing all three as intertwined in *Island in the Sun* (long regarded as the exemplar of its lot), in subsequent sections devoted to each one I analyze examples in which they are pressed into particularly dramatic, and revealing, service.

"A VERY ODD LOOK"

Although publicity and reception materials posit interracial desire as *Island in the Sun*'s central subject, that is not in fact the case. The couples formed by David Boyeur (Belafonte) and Mavis Norman (Fontaine) and by Margot Seaton (Dorothy Dandridge) and Denis Archer (John Justin) are peripheral to the film's protagonist, Maxwell Fleury (James Mason), and even that character's discovery of his own black ancestry is not the film's central plot. The proliferation of interracial subplots is essential to its vision, but at its center is a murder plot that derives from Maxwell's paranoid sense of having lost hold of the cultural privileges he expects: the native population of his Caribbean island is on the verge of self-governance; the plantation he has inherited is literally rotting away (plagued by dampness and worms that "eat right through the furniture"); and he fears that neither his father nor his wife is granting him the phallic recognition he deserves. What binds Maxwell's prominent maladies together, then, is a profound inability to sustain the authoritative command and coherence of a classically white and male subject. Groping desperately for respect vis-à-vis father, (a dead but favored) brother, wife, other men (white and black), and eventually the entire community (when he decides to run for political office), Maxwell is repeatedly reduced instead to headaches, emotional outbursts, visible perspiration, and uncontrolled acts of violence. It is in this context that his whiteness is tainted with "the tarbrush," as his imagined rival will fatefully call it, when his father's "colored" ancestry is suddenly revealed in the local newspaper. With that revelation an already consuming paranoia that initially led Maxwell to imagine his wife, Sylvia (Patricia Owens), in a nonexistent affair, and to sexually assault her as punishment, swells entirely out of control when he murders the man he assumes to be her lover.[34] Particularly intriguing here is that Maxwell Fleury's neuroses (amplified by James Mason's classically neurotic performance) provide the structuring, affective core of a film riddled with interracial plots and subplots, and the latter can clearly be read as functioning in the service of the former. For those plots not only serve as the film's indirect explanation for what makes Maxwell come unglued, I will argue, but also chart the film's best (if tenuous) hope for restoring white masculinity more generally—if not yet the suicidal and soon-to-be imprisoned Maxwell we last see.

Significantly, the jealous obsession that sets the murder plot in motion is precipitated by Maxwell's misreading of visual evidence. In his first scene he spies another man's gold-tipped cigarette butt in his ashtray and mistakenly deduces that his wife's denial of any visitors covers an affair.[35] His paranoid (visual) state, which will lead to his undoing, is remarked upon soon after his anxious eyeing of the cigarette when his sister Jocelyn (Joan Collins) declares, "You have a very odd look." Her diagnosis is confirmed, in this scene and others, by Maxwell's repeated failure to conform to Hollywood's classical visual scripting of masculinity, especially in relation to women and mirrors.

In the scene that prompts Jocelyn's telling remark, she has just returned from the beach and is adjusting herself before a mirror at the back of a shot while a disturbed Maxwell faces us with his back to her, looking off screen in the direction that Sylvia has just exited the shot, and the room, after rebuffing his kiss (fig. 5.3). With Maxwell clearly not in sexual command of his wife, his additional failure to share our voyeuristic look at steamy young Collins in the role of his sister—doubly displayed here in her skimpy beach cover-up and in the mirror—further underscores the point in visual terms. He is not much better off when he follows Sylvia upstairs. Although he watches her prepare for a party at her vanity, he is also caught within the visual frame of its mirror, and we watch the two of them in the reflected image, a visual space that she (again) exits before he does. In the third such scene, toward the very end of the film, Sylvia is again at her vanity mirror when Maxwell suicidally contemplates his own image in the mirror of the adjoining bathroom (Figs. 5.4–5.5). He finally breaks that mirror with the butt of his gun instead of shooting himself, a gesture that reads simultaneously as one of cowardice (he cannot actually bear killing himself) and aggression against precisely that image that signifies his own failure to occupy the classical cinematic position of male mastery (figs. 5.6–5.7).

Just before the film introduces Maxwell and his "odd look" festering at his decaying estate, Belfontaine, it begins by introducing a larger, colonial power struggle at stake, and this struggle, too, is represented as a contest over claims of ownership, authorship, and a commanding gaze. The credit sequence opens with a map of a small island surrounded by a much larger ocean, followed by a related series of aerial shots that invite us to survey the landscape at an all-seeing, disembodied distance (fig. 5.8). The film gradually cuts in to reveal a coastal town, a beach, and finally black men and women working in boats and fields (figs. 5.9–5.10). In short, the spectator is invited to occupy a conventionally white cinematic point of view, much like the one established in *The Birth of a Na-*

FIG. 5.4. A suicidal Maxwell (James Mason) desperately shatters the mirror image that reflects his growing distance from the privileges he expects.

FIG. 5.5

FIG. 5.6

FIG. 5.7

FIG. 5.8. The opening shots of *Island in the Sun* offer the spectator familiar viewing pleasures of surveying the landscape and black bodies who labor in it.

FIG. 5.9

FIG. 5.10

FIG. 5.11. The image of an initially anonymous black man also taking in the view signals looming questions about traditional orders of race, masculinity, and vision.

tion, as outsider looking in, from above, enjoying the display of black laboring bodies on a continuum with the display of attractive scenery.[36] And yet, as soon as this visual tour begins, Belafonte's voice also begins singing the film's title song, complicating the tropes just described with a competing set of authorial claims. With the first shot of the island from above, in the Caribbean tones and rhythms his voice was already famous for, Belafonte sings: "This is my island in the sun, where my people have toiled since time begun. I may sail on many a sea, but her shores will always be home to me."[37] As the footage unfolds, his lyrics at times echo it (we see men with nets and women cutting cane as he describes them), but they also assert a notion of black ownership accrued from black labor: "Oh island in the sun, willed to me by my father's hand." Curiously, the camera once spots Belafonte walking in the landscape, but with his back to us in a way that neither confirms nor denies the source of this black voice (fig. 5.11).

The questions of textual and political authority implicitly raised in the credit sequence are curiously redoubled in the first diegetic scene to follow. With the title song ended, we return to the image of the island from above and again move from it to the beach to the townspeople; but now an unidentified British male voice-over describes the island in the explicit language of tourism ("Towering mountains, white gold beaches, coconut palms and hot tropical sun . . ."). As if the credit sequence left matters too ambiguous, this one is visually repetitive, but with the clear purpose of asserting a colonial authority: "Originally a French island, its laborers were brought in slave ships from the gold coast of Africa four and a half centuries ago. And now it is a British crown colony." The image concurs with a shot of the Union Jack flying outside an official residence. When we move inside, the former voice-of-God narration is given a body, that of the British governor introducing his domain to a visiting journalist. When the visitor asks about a new constitutional proposal for self-governance by native residents, the governor defers, but the question hangs in the air.

This is the context, then, in which the film introduces Maxwell and his paranoid vision at Belfontaine in the following scene. And in the party scene immediately following that one it begins to formulate its interracial remedies for many maladies. For while there is a good deal of (what appears to be) white-on-white sexual attention at the governor's house that evening, with two sets of male eyes vying for the company of Jocelyn Fleury (whose racial identity will later come into question), by its end all necessary introductions have been made for the two primary interracial romances that soon develop—one between a proud black union leader, David Boyeur, and a dissatisfied white socialite, Mavis Norman, and the other between the governor's aide, Denis Archer, and a drugstore clerk–cum–aspiring stenographer, Margot Seaton. To consider the particular problems and benefits that accrue to these very different interracial pairs, we should consider each in turn.

Whereas, as we will see, the women of color on the fictional island of Santa Marta are (for white men) loyal, hardworking, and overflowing with friendly sexuality, the white women of at least two generations are variously suspected and guilty of cheating on their husbands, spending time and money wastefully, and desiring ambiguously and without fulfillment. This kind of behavior torments Sylvia Fleury's paranoid husband and markedly impairs, even as it seems to underwrite, David Boyeur's attraction to Mavis Norman. It is Mavis, in fact, who delivers the film's most bitter lines of contempt for white femininity, scripted as self-loathing in her first intimate conversation with David. At the film's second big party, she questions the meaning of her life as an idle, affluent, unmarried woman: "Does it make any difference, having an *aim* in life? . . . not just floating about—tea at five, dinner at eight, Tuesdays at the hairdressers?" As she continues to berate herself and women like her, she shifts the terms to impute the increasing disdain of her remarks to David: "You think I'm rather useless, don't you? Parasitic. That all women of my kind are. Oh it's true. That we don't know *anything*." Despite initial softenings between them, that Mavis has correctly surmised the labor activist's critique is implied in part by the space that will continue to separate them. Certainly, in a film that denies them a single kiss, much less a future, their mutual discomfort has multiple causes and effects. One set of these, however, is the persistent exposure of the white woman's multiple flaws. For while the white men on the island show little sign of enlightenment, Mavis is singled out to enact some of the most pernicious forms of white condescension and assumed privilege.[38]

Despite the fact that *Island in the Sun* clearly offers, indeed cashes in on, the titillating new possibilities of an onscreen affair between a white woman and a black man, it leaves us hard-pressed to understand what it is that ever attracts David to Mavis, or Mavis to David. More to the point, almost as soon as the spectator is invited to imagine the possibility of the formerly prohibited voyeuristic pleasures they represent (of watching a black man kiss a white woman? of watching a white woman kiss a black man? of watching the still recent phenomenon of a sexy black male star kiss anyone?), their dead-end affair works more as a means for the film to discredit them both. With strange echoes of the pairing of white women and black men in *Birth*, their relationship is a vehicle, at once, to tolerate but also compromise a black man's political activism, and to voice but also ridicule a white woman's doubts about the quality of her life. The negative effects are most audible during their breakup scene, the scene that closes the film itself. David first coldly insists that she would eventually "forget herself and call me a 'nigger,'" and after an unconvincing retraction of that accusation insists that being with her would jeopardize his commitment to decolonization. Thus rejected as a privileged bigot who would "be in my way," Mavis in turn accuses him of being unfeeling and power hungry: "People don't count with you, nothing counts with you but power. You use people, you climb on their backs." While she, too, immediately retracts her accusation, and both attempt halfheartedly to defend themselves, the damage is clearly done. Mavis declares an impasse, degrading herself one last time ("You're right and I'm wrong. I'm wrong and you're right"); they decisively part company (David: "That's the end is it?" Mavis: "Yes, that's the end"); and the nasty portraits they have painted of one another linger as the most unambiguous sentiments about each the film has to offer.

Offscreen evidence further attests that *Island*'s "new" interracial package was thoroughly mired in "old" rhetorics of miscegenation. In a single prerelease spread on Belafonte, for example, producer Darryl Zanuck, Joan Fontaine, and the story's author, Carter Barber, all paint the story's black male subject in classic Hollywood strokes. Zanuck, Barber reports, asked Belafonte "to delete allusions in his night-club act to love scenes with the blonde Joan Fontaine."[39] And while the actress herself is quoted as having been "a little bit flattered" that such an "attractive performer" would be "saying . . . that we play a love scene," she also declares: "I tell you this—there is no physical contact between us."[40] Following this disavowal, Barber nonetheless goes on to explain Fontaine's open fascination with the actors' racial difference: "Belafonte's color, which richens as he grows more intense, settled Miss Fontaine on accepting the role. 'I was interested in the contrast between his darkness and my fairness. That meant there'd automatically be a certain electricity.'"[41] And no sooner have Barber's own words thus conjoined with those attributed to Fontaine to compound one set of racial clichés with yet others—fetishistically fixating on race as a matter of skin and "color" that reflects something of the soul within to "automatically" prompt "certain," sexualized, relations and readings, and so forth—than the author goes on to characterize Belafonte as "a sensitive man [who] tends to discern racial subtleties and slurs where none may exist." To exemplify, he recounts a story in which Fontaine reports Belafonte's having gotten "'perfectly furious with me one day when I caught him in a mild fib and said he looked like a child who'd just been caught stealing watermelons.'" Proffering this as the only example of the alleged oversensitivity, Barber assumes it necessary to explain the actor's anger: "The expression smacked of a southernism to [him], evoking a picture of a pickaninny and an overseer." In the course of just this one-page story, then, Belafonte is cast by colleagues and the press as by turns a black beast (who must be censored in his own nightclub act), a fetishized exotic, a "pickaninny," and, after all of that, an inappropriately "sensitive" black radical. Consider that the film recapitulates nearly each of these caricatures, and there is little wonder in Belafonte's ultimate denunciation of the film as a "stinking . . . terrible picture based on a terrible best-selling book."[42]

Extrafilmic evidence also points to ways in which the film was used to contain the white woman as well as the black man. The morning after the film's Los Angeles premiere, *Variety* reported:

> Joan Fontaine, [whose] character . . . has a "mixed" romance with Harry Belafonte, disclosed yesterday she has received a flock of letters protesting her playing the role.
>
> . . . Said the star: "I've gotten terrible letters. . . . Most of the letter-writers termed me unprintable, filthy names. One of the letters had 'KKK' on it.
>
> "I think this is part of an organized drive. . . . Strangely, none of the letters is from the south. They come from such states as New Jersey, Ohio and Pennsylvania. . . . Some of the letters defend my playing such a role, and tell me not to be upset."[43]

The reported letters are disturbing in and of themselves for their rearticulation of history and myth. And the studio's handling of them—assuming the story is true, all the more so if it is not—seems to have capitalized on that very tradition. While Fontaine's statement implies that she had been receiving such letters over time, the fact that she only went public about them on the day of the premiere suggests that the display of the racially assaulted white woman was thus timed to help publicize the film. This publicity was further embellished by her arrival at Grauman's that evening under the protection of police escort, for all the cameras and reporters to see.[44] Hence, with the "KKK" letter writers taking the position formerly scripted for black men, and the cops riding in spectacularly to rescue her, the staging of the premiere thus retraces the very traditions of spectacle, narrative, and cultural belief upon which the hate mail presumably depends.[45]

There is evidence that images of potent black masculinity and contemptuous white femininity were also key to the film's African American reception. Several examples arise in coverage by the *Pittsburgh Courier*. Sharply announcing the restraints put on Belafonte, a front-page headline declares, "Belafonte's Lips 'Sealed'!"; a pointed double reference to his part in the kissless screen romance and to the studio's command that he not discuss Fontaine "in any public statements he makes about the film—however discreet these statements might be."[46] Whereas the white press reported Belafonte's response to this command as "hurt, but not surprised," in one case, frustrated but capitulating, in another, the *Courier* casts the story as a revocation of Belafonte's freedom in its initial headlines ("Belafonte Silenced by Studio! Told to 'Keep Quiet'") and follows up a week later, on the front page, to reassert his independence: " 'Why Should I Keep Quiet?—Belafonte.' "[47] The second story reports that "the celebrated singer actor is not obeying their order. . . . 'No one can prevent me from speaking my mind.' " He proves as much again when he declares in *Ebony*: " 'I definitely think that the movie industry has a policy which prohibits love-making and kissing between interracial couples."[48]

Courier readers are thus amply set up for critic Dizzy Rowe's discussion of the film's New York premiere the following month, and its amused anecdote of resistant spectatorship: "Mrs. [Julie] Belafonte, escorted by Sammy Davis Jr., since hubby was on tour, got the last laugh from the final scene at the 'Island in the Sun' premiere. After all, she's white, he married her, and it was a big joke to watch writers put words into his mouth as a prominent man afraid of the consequences of intermarriage! Most viewers of both races sat with their mouths open trying to figure just what the producers were trying to get across."[49] Confounding this story of debunking reception on the left side of the page is yet another response on the right that calls *Island* "the most forward step in film making," one that "attacks the Negro white question with head-on words and shows Negroes on a basis of equality never before seen in a major film."[50] This review takes pleasure especially in "the power and glory of Belafonte." He is "loved by a white woman whom he rejects. And with powerful words defeats a white man in a moving political rally [articulating] the plight, ambitions and hopes of black people which should have long since been said to the world through the medium of the screen." Hence, the very same racial-sexual representation that could provoke some segregationists and win over others could simultaneously prompt critical interracial laughter *and* black pride in a potent "race man."[51]

Not unlike the film itself, such treatments of it thus variously conjure, revise, contain, and resist notions of black manhood as a threat to white culture via a white woman, and variously contain her as by turns victim, ward, and reject of the Klan, police, and Boyeur/Belafonte, respectively. That she should require such treatment, and that audiences might enjoy it, is multiply set up by accounts of Fontaine's on- and offscreen exchanges with Belafonte. While readers of the *Mirror-News* would have read of her "watermelon" comment months before the premiere, *Courier* readers would also hear him openly deny any interest in kissing her and joke that working with her closely had made him, literally, ill.[52] That his character is understood also by the white press as the one conscripted to put her down is indicated by a review in *Time*, which otherwise had sympathetic words only for the cinematographer: "Belafonte's biggest job . . . is evading the clutches of a white cargo named Mavis . . . , obviously too old for him."[53]

As Mavis watches a plane carry the film's other interracial couples off to England in the last scene, she asks, "In a girl's case . . . does it work the other way around? I mean, Denis Archer marries Margot, Euan marries Jocelyn, but when it's the other way around, does it make any difference?" David replies, "Out here, yes." He begins to explain: "If I were to walk in[to a room] with you, or a girl like you as my wife . . ." He can only shake his head. By contrast, "Maybe the men looking at Margot at some party in Bloomsbury, or some literary tea, well they'd envy Denis Archer. Their own wives look sort of dull when she walks into a room." While David's explanation invokes intersecting codes of race, gender, and class, most telling as we turn to consider the couples the film sends off into the future is that the litmus test for acceptability is imagined as the visual display of a man's woman. We know full well (David's ellipsis suggests) what the consequences are when a white woman's image and a black man's claims to it threaten white male onlookers. The new twist here is the notion that with a shuffling of the interracial cast that makes the "husband" white and the "wife" not, those same onlookers might take pleasure in imagining themselves in a newly enviable masculine position.

The film has by this point borne out this theory for nearly two hours, in part by its ongoing display of middle- and upper-class women on a sunny island with an announced shortage of available men. And the whitest of these women do, in fact, look "sort of dull," as they are typically draped in pale pinks, blues, and grays that accentuate their whiteness and often wash them out entirely. By contrast, Dandridge's Margot Seaton limbos in a bikini top and sarong, fully reclines on her lover's bed in the middle of the day for us to view (with him) from head to toe, and regularly bursts forth in low-cut dresses of bright yellow, orange, and red (fig. 5.12). The liminal racial status of Collins's Jocelyn Fleury is visually insinuated as well, long before the news that outs her father's racial secret, in multiple exposures of her body that mark her visually and sexually as being much closer to Dandridge than to the other white women. Not only is hers the most revealing outfit of her gal pal trio upon their opening arrival from the beach, but her nearly black hair and freshly tanned skin are markedly darker than those of her blonde and redheaded companions. As the film continues, the buxom Collins is wrapped in dresses and bathing suits that are far tighter and brighter and reveal far more than those worn by the other white actresses, and often she exclusively wears bright whites that seem to simultaneously accentuate her claims to whiteness and signal their potential falsity in the emphasized darkness of her skin by contrast.[54]

This extra visual attention given to women of color is utterly in keeping with their narrative status as well. For the film's potent mix of doubt and contempt about the state of white womanhood is regularly met, at another extreme, by delight in women of color for the very attributes the whitest women seem, at least momentarily, to resist. Not only is Margot Seaton visibly circulated at parties as a prized erotic object of black and white male looks, for example, but immediately following Mavis's lament on the uselessness of rich white women like herself, Margot's white date, Denis Archer, eagerly takes her back to his "writing studio" to confess his love. While he describes his hillside hideaway as having been a "summer house, where governors' wives did their sewing," in this and future scenes it will be transformed into their love nest, where he adoringly watches Margot dance and recline while she in turn listens intently and responds enthusiastically. (Of his book about the island, she insists, "This is the best thing you've ever done. . . . It's so true and so good, that it hurts!") Rather explicitly, then, the film offers comfort to a new generation of white men by replacing an older, domesticated generation of white wives with a younger, more passionate type of black mistress. That the second is also happy to take on a permanent position is made clear not only by Margot and Jocelyn's final departure with their men for England, but by Margot's unambiguous response to Denis's news that he must leave the island: "Where you go, I go."[55]

While the very same interracial romances that make racial boundaries somewhat of "a guessing game" thus also work to contain the most certainly black men and all women, and to refortify at least some confidently white men, they also lead to possible solutions to the larger crises of vision detectable from the outset. This is particularly vivid during Jocelyn and Euan's tryst at Belfontaine. Although her father's black ancestry has yet to be revealed at this point, after it is and she discovers she is pregnant, this will turn out to have been the first of many nights Jocelyn will fear might have produced a "black man in the House of Lords." And the interracial coding of this encounter will continue even after her mother privately alleviates Jocelyn's fear with the confession that she is, in fact, the "completely English" offspring of an extramarital affair, because Jocelyn chooses to keep her mother's secret for the time being. But it is the specific textual conditions of her first sexual encounter with Euan that make it of particular interest.

Alone at the family plantation while others are off at carnival, Jocelyn and Euan enjoy a leisurely afternoon of tea and admiration, for the place as well as each other. First he, and then the two of them together, gaze out at the view from the house. He remarks, "I hate leaving here. Your brother is very lucky to have a place like this all to his own." When it is time to leave, they discover the car will not start and the phone lines have been cut. Although the camera alone glimpsed a masked black man sneaking about the premises upon their arrival, they quickly suspect "carnival" trouble. They are noticeably apprehensive at the prospect of a night alone under such conditions—drums beating in the distant village—until Euan pours a calming set of cocktails, and the mood, music, and interracial occupancy of the place quickly change. As they plan food and room arrangements, Jocelyn goes dreamy with desire and reveals her wish since childhood to sleep in one particular room at Belfontaine. When she wins the room in a coin toss, she presses her fingers deep into Euan's arm, and they approach the long-fantasized space with a fade to black. While the film, unlike the novel, does not tell us this is Jocelyn's first time, the heavy-handed spatial metaphor delivered through Collins's feverish performance make it easy enough to imagine, and the final swell of violins insistently recodes the lovers' former fear of penetration from without into an emphatically pleasurable anticipation of Jocelyn's within.

In a curious revival of the (still not-yet avowed) sexual pleasures of the old plantation, this night of potentially interracial passion momentarily holds out the promise of restored sexual and scopic regimes at Maxwell's dying abode. For the scene not only sets the stage for potent forms of desire and sex but with them reawakens the trope of a potent gaze from the plantation, linking Euan's pleasure in the vista to his admiration of the woman Maxwell failed to see in the opening scene. At one point, waiting for Jocelyn to join him, he heads outside to take in the magnificent view that beckons from beyond the porch, and his gaze is literally wedded to that view in a dissolve (fig. 5.13). Later, in the very same location with the porch columns emphatically framing the view beyond, they step outside together to take in the moon, at his suggestion (fig. 5.14). In the second moment Euan's eyes fix instead on Jocelyn, reorienting them finally toward the bedroom. To be certain, these are views from this house we never see with the beleaguered Maxwell, but they imagine the possibility of a restimulated white male look here with the aid of what will for Euan come to be understood as an interracial romance. And yet, as if even Jocelyn's sun-bronzed, virginal passion were not enough to make long-term occupancy viable here, the scene that directly follows the fade-to-sex has already transported the couple the next morning to the modernist interior of her parents' house closer to town. There Euan proposes marriage, paving their way toward Bloomsbury or some other elite London suburb, by David Boyeur's account, as if to better ensure his place as the envy of men with "dull" white (white) wives.

The film offers a different domestic solution for Maxwell, one that arrives in the form of a dream that literally saves his life. Buckling under the strain of his guilt for having murdered Hilary Carson, he contemplates suicide in his master bathroom when Sylvia arrives in the adjoining bedroom with a bottle of champagne and the vision of a life beyond their stifling existence at Belfontaine. As Maxwell stands before the mirror with his gun half raised, his wife lets go of an earlier wish for the elite life that awaits Jocelyn in "London, the big house, being Lady Templeton," and

FIG. 5.12. White spectators, on screen and off, are invited to enjoy the erotic spectacle of a white man's black lover (Dorothy Dandridge).

FIG. 5.13. A night of potentially interracial passion stirs up remarkable views from the plantation.

FIG. 5.14

shares a new one as we watch her undress: "I saw a film the other day about a town in New England. New England, that's where I'd like to live, New England. The characters in the film had a little house and it had a wonderful kitchen with all sorts of gadgets. With a kitchen like that you don't need servants. That's how I'd like to live. Not in some big old house built hundreds of years ago and getting dressed for a lonely dinner. You see, that's the sort of woman you married." Appearing to listen from the bathroom, Maxwell turns his head toward the bedroom at the line "That's how I'd like to live" and smashes the mirror with his gun when Sylvia has finished (see figs. 5.4–5.7). Although he immediately turns himself in, forestalling any immediate actualization of the dream described, the head of police has repeatedly assured him of a short sentence for the guilty man who confesses of his own accord. If we can, as invited, imagine an eventual future for Maxwell, Sylvia's suburban fantasy is surely it.

Coming just after the scene in which Jocelyn learns the news that will allow her to go and be Euan's wife in England, and just before the ones in which Margot declares her dedication to Denis (wherever he goes) and David and Mavis vilify one another, it is as if the old, rotting ground has been cleared enough for Sylvia, and the film, to begin dreaming anew on Maxwell's behalf. And, although her still white-looking husband has been recently outed as having a black grandmother, in keeping with the interracial maneuvers dissected here, the glimpses Sylvia conjures for him sketch a domestic order where gender, not race, maps the dominant structure. For as quickly as we can envision Sylvia's "sort of woman" in her gadget-filled kitchen, so do we know the same "little house" brings with it literal and figurative spaces for Maxwell—manning the yard, reading the paper in the living room, or watching TV. Sylvia's fantasy of a "New England" in America thus not only dreams of a kind of (almost) white flight where they can bury their colonial secrets, I would suggest, but also begins to envision a model of identity and difference ideally suited to overcoming Maxwell's multiple problems under the old regime. For the suburban fantasy, with its strict regulation of gendered and racial positions within and without the home, would seem to lift the burden from the (weakened) master at the (crumbling) center of power, space, and vision—as per the plantation model—and disperse but also secure male power through a replicated structure in which many husbands authoritatively reside, but none with the sole burden of anchoring the structure himself. Even as this makes the fantasy of a singular, originating gaze all but impossible, it nonetheless offers the condolences of discrete, if downsized, domains of authority.

Island in the Sun thus demonstrates that even as the fifties interracial film confronts the end of dominant racial regimes, it nonetheless clings—

as if all the more desperately—to faith in sexual difference as the last stand, if not the natural bedrock, of identity and social hierarchy. What other films reveal more clearly is that this desperate faith is itself frequently also a symptom of profound anxieties about sustaining and enforcing differences of sex. Such anxieties are often so severe, the readings to come will suggest, that these films can also be read to tolerate, even cultivate, sexual transgressions of racial boundaries in order to fiercely reassert dominant orders of gender and heterosexuality.

When All the Men Are White and Most All the Women Are Not (Or, Bringing Home an Ubangi When Agnes Moorehead Is Your Mother)

As my reading of *Island in the Sun* has already begun to suggest, if all women are by definition visible in classical Hollywood cinema, women of color paired with white men in the fifties are set up to be excessively so—through costumes, mise-en-scène, dialogue, and an assortment of narrative excuses.[56] They are professional, amateur, and spontaneous performers (*Sayonara, China Gate, The King and I, Island in the Sun, The Searchers, Imitation of Life*); models (*Mohawk, The Far Horizons, The World of Suzie Wong*); habitual skinny-dippers (*Night of the Quarter Moon*); mute visions of tropical loveliness (*South Pacific*); and otherwise emphatically racialized for spectacular effect (*Love Is a Many-Splendored Thing, The Searchers, Tamango, Touch of Evil*). As if to counterbalance the visible strains besetting the also ample population of white male spectators (*Sayonara, China Gate, The Far Horizons, Island in the Sun, Imitation of Life*); peeping toms (*Sayonara, The Far Horizons, Night of the Quarter Moon*); painters (*The World of Suzie Wong, Mohawk*); photographers (*Night of the Quarter Moon, Imitation of Life*); and surveyors (*The Far Horizons, Kings Go Forth*), these films conjure their hypervisible women of color as if predisposed to that condition, often on display as if by some innate or uncontrollable force.[57] What that force can do for white men can also be quite spectacular.

The hypervisible woman of color often functions in these films to register possible challenges to the dominance of white male vision, only to then facilitate its restoration. This is especially vivid in *Far Horizons*. Soon after a striking image of Sacajawea (Donna Reed!) looking out from the bow of Lewis and Clark's ship as the eyes that lead it, the film cuts to Clark (Charlton Heston) rendering maps—a gesture that transforms her "native" vision into his "civilized" text. And when Sacajawea later happens upon Clark looking through one of his surveying devices, she immediately recognizes the value of his visual equipment. "You take great care with these tools of yours," she observes. "We use them to make maps, pictures of the river," he explains. "These pictures, they're important?" she asks, then answers, "Oh yes, I guess they're more important than we are." Just as soon as the conversation has hammered the value of surveying into our heads, it grafts this political vision to sexual ones. Sacajawea worries: "They will come here. They will bring their women and they will stay. . . . They are beautiful, the women of your people?" Clark appeases her: "Some of them. Just like some Indian women." Just as the romantic music begins, the precious tools fall overboard, but Sacajawea proves her devotion to Clark and his mission by diving in to rescue them. Emerging from the ship's cabin soon after in a dress fashioned from found cloth (her own clothes still wet from the swim), she immediately seeks Clark's approval. He tells her, "It's very pretty," but proceeds to "fix it up a little," improvising a necklace, a belt, a torn "hem," and a "ribbon" salvaged from the scrap. Pleased with his creation, he takes a further liberty: "You look more like a Mary Jane than Sacaja . . . Sacajawea. That name is going to give me a lot of trouble. Do you mind if I call you Janie?" Pleased when he tells her "it means beautiful," she happily accepts her new name as well as her new image. The combined effect is not so much to whiten her but to emphatically feminize her: she still looks like Donna Reed in brownface and primitive clothing, but the makeover at once makes her more visible and implies that she is prone to be seen in this way, waiting to be fully revealed through a white man's desirous look. The all-male crew peeping on it reinforces the imagined success of "Janie's" feminine display and the white man's masculine vision.[58]

Exposing the excessive circumstances that give way to such representations is the frequent scenario at the opposite extreme: a white man occupies the place of seeming vulnerability, and his relation to a woman of color is his best chance at refortifying himself, often in face of the "calculating, suffocating, and thoroughly undesirable" white women who prowl these films.[59] Variations of this strain are evident in *Kings Go Forth, Sayonara, Love Is a Many-Splendored Thing, The Searchers, Mohawk, Band of Angels, Touch of Evil,* and *The World of Suzie Wong,* but *Night of the Quarter Moon* paints its stock characters in the most exaggerated of strokes: a white man of privilege suffers chronically from war trauma, is plagued by a castrating white woman (a mother in this case), and finds a dreamy lover of color who is hopelessly devout and perpetually hypervisible in ways that offer his greatest hope for recovery.

This film opens with a young woman being viciously harassed in her own home, and an extended flashback soon unfolds the history of her recent interracial marriage. Her now-husband, and former POW, Roderic ("Chuck") Nelson originally fell in love with Ginny (Julie London) on a convalescent trip to her native Mexico, where she told him in no uncertain terms that she is "one-quarter" black. He avowed his love regardless, married her, and moved her to his native San Francisco. Subsequently his mother, Cornelia Nelson (Agnes Moorehead), although at first delighted by the news of a daughter-in-law, was appalled to learn of her racial background. When the film returns us to the present, we find Cornelia seizing the opportunity of Chuck's being held by police (after fighting off his wife's harassers) to play on his weaknesses and destroy his marriage. She pressures her psychically fragile son, keeps him drugged and isolated, and uses her power of attorney (established when Chuck was in Korea) to sue for annulment on his behalf on the grounds that Ginny concealed her racial identity. In court Ginny's lawyer argues that Chuck must have known the truth because he regularly saw her skinny-dip before they were married. When he rips at her dress to offer visual proof, the extraordinary display fortifies Chuck to defy his mother's influence and reclaim his wife (see fig. 3.1). While the racial claims of this scene, as discussed in chapter 3, are among the most remarkable in this book, the full force of its simultaneously gendering effects are best understood in the context of the anxious conditions that give rise to it.

On the one hand, Ginny and Chuck's relationship clearly epitomizes the paradigm of women of color restoring the potency of the white male subject and his look. Although the film demonizes the racist punks who openly ogle and harass Ginny through her living room window, it provides an assortment of textual supports for Chuck, his brother Lex, and the spectator to view her in much the same way. In addition to her revealing wardrobe, the subplot of her habitual skinny-dipping marks the terms of Chuck's desire from the start. When he first happens upon her, swimming in the daylight, she asks him to look away, only to emerge from behind a bush as a freshly groomed spectacle, sporting tight shorts, a blouse tied between her breasts, and miraculously fresh makeup and dry, styled hair. Assumedly remarking on the ancient statues we have yet to see, but looking at Ginny, Chuck asks with delight, "This place is really old, isn't it?" She replies, "Oh, about two thousand years I guess." The timing of this exchange, following Ginny's latest exposures in "this place" and Chuck's visible pleasure therein, textually punctuates, even commemorates, those "really old" traditions of gender and spectacle so emphatically paraded.

On the other hand, however, also in keeping with the late fifties interracial films, this classical constitution of white masculinity and vision vis-à-vis a woman of color is shown to mask a far more unstable one. Just as the commemorative sights and lines just detailed are delivered, Ginny proceeds to set up an easel and paint the statues in the ancient landscape. Not unlike the image of Sacajawea guiding the ship, the image of Ginny as landscape painter signals the male subject's less than full command in the visual field. But that lack of mastery is far more anxiously accentuated in this case when Ginny inquires about Chuck's experience in Korea: "You were in a prison camp, I guess you got used to it." "Used to what?" he asks. "Doing nothing," she replies. With these words Ginny clearly strikes a nerve. Chuck becomes furious, insisting that he "did plenty . . . cleaned up their filth . . . buried their dead!" His defensive delivery sharpens the portrait of a man tormented by the possibility of his own proximity to "nothing" and distance from reliably phallic forms of "plenty." Underscoring the point, it is precisely during and after this exchange that Ginny's visual mastery is emphasized in shots with her at the easel as Chuck stands behind her, closer to the ancient ruins.

Chuck's unstable relation to classical masculinity is again buffered at the end of this scene, as it was by Ginny's nude swim and sexy reappearance at the beginning, when she accepts his apology for the outburst and we move immediately to a scene of Chuck's nighttime voyeurism. Here the "really old" cinematic arrangement is fully restored as the camera positions us to share his look at her, first swimming and then climbing out of the water with the moonlight illuminating her flesh at a distance. Ginny's father interrupts Chuck but offers a paternal blessing to further validate the classical codes of gender and vision the scene restores on Chuck's behalf ("That's quite all right, nothing to see from here. Besides, I didn't think you were that kind"). When we see him watching Ginny swim after this point, it will be in the open light of day, and she will not ask him to look away; and, suffice it to say, we will never again see her at her easel.

The exposure of Chuck's past and present instabilities is also buffered by the framing device that precedes the extended flashback: the film begins not with Chuck as prisoner or patient, or with Ginny as painter, but with her displayed alongside paintings that decorate the walls of their suburban home. Indeed, the opening scene is dedicated to elaborating Ginny's hypervisibility. In the film's first diegetic shot the camera slowly moves in to capture her and her cleavage as she prepares to hang one of the paintings, a stylized rendering of men in sombreros. The immediate association of that image with the dark-haired woman in a leopard-print robe introduces Ginny as a spectacle marked by an as of yet unspoken cultural difference. This display quickly leads to her harassment with the sudden crashing of a rock through her front window, and the filmic syntax of the attack further recapitulates her extreme visibility. Shots alternate between views of Ginny placed behind a picture window and the looks directed at her by her harassers and neighbors gathered to watch. Later at the police station, one father argues in the boys' defense, "That woman came to the window half undressed, exposed herself. Naturally the kids got excited." Although the film depicts the "kids" as violent, racist punks, it nonetheless has facilitated their assaultive looks and deeds by presenting her from the start as almost nothing but excessively visible.[60]

This representation of Ginny continues throughout the film. When the cops question her following the attack, photographers burst into the interrogation room and begin to flash, demanding "some cheesecake, let's take a look at those legs! . . . You might make Hollywood. . . . Come on, give us a break. You just might make six o'clock TV." In the flashback, her arrival with Chuck in San Francisco is also attended by eager photographers. One asks, "You're from Hollywood, Mrs. Nelson?" She answers, "Oh no, I'm from Mexico." Thus announcing that attractive women of color are easily confused with Hollywood "cheesecake," *Night of the Quarter Moon* perpetually articulates the equation.[61]

Well before the courtroom climax, then, it is apparent that this film's central "race" problem is fundamentally constituted as a sexual one. That Ginny's hypervisibility is desperately needed to restore her fragile husband is evident not only from his increasingly undeniable displays of lack but also from her mother-in-law's nearly caricatured rendition of the castrating white woman. Indeed, it is the extreme gender "dysfunction" at Nelson manor that demands the extraordinary "racial" spectacles evinced from Ginny.

The wealthy Nelson family is absent any sign of a father, and the mother who heads it is endlessly accused of having too much power and wielding it at her sons' expense. Chuck and his brother, Lex, frequently lament her intrusions, and when Chuck brings Ginny home, Cornelia inspects her with a silent, admiring eye. She quickly deems her an acceptable Oedipal substitute—"She is lovely, Roderic, prettier than I ever hoped to be"—but in the excitement of the moment in which he proposes a toast to christen "the new SS Roderic Nelson" (by which he means Ginny), Lex lets it slip that Mother has softened her strict criteria for daughter-in-law material. Cornelia's joy is exposed as relief that her son has managed to bring home a girl, "any girl," as she says, "I don't care whether she has two heads and comes from Ubangi." A dissonant blare of the sound track punctuates the unintentionally apt racism of the comment, but that comment also signals this mother's concern that her boys behave like (straight) boys. And, while the film here points the finger at Cornelia, she in fact speaks the decidedly racial and sexual truth of the film itself: for, like so many of the films in this period, this one goes to considerable extremes to restore its broken white boy and deliver him as a proper "man," even if that means pairing him with a woman, if not from Ubangi, from Mexico by way of Portuguese Angola.

That said, the "any girl" solution is neither painless nor automatic in this film, thanks in no small part to Chuck's mother. Her interference begins relatively benignly during the flashback when she enters the film via telephone to interrupt the amorous honeymooners, and a demonstrably aroused Chuck in particular. But her intrusions soon escalate when she discovers, as Ginny later teases him, "poor Chuck, he *did* bring home an Ubangi." After the morning paper announces "Social Leader's Bride Revealed as Quadroon," the phone rings again, and the prying maternal voice chides, "You're a sick boy, Roderic, a very sick boy." With her help he really does become sick in a matter of scenes.

Soon after this extended flashback, Cornelia arrives at the police interrogation that prompts it and takes the opportunity of her son's visible weakness to orchestrate his mental breakdown and a lawsuit against his beloved. She asks to be left alone with him, and the terms of the interrogation dramatically shift. Chuck begins the scene coherent and defiant, but by its end he is weeping, shivering, and utterly disoriented. Facing the team Cornelia has brought with her (a doctor and Lex, a lawyer), Chuck at first jokes, "OK, who goes first? In Korea they start by giving you a candy bar, maybe a cigarette." When he senses Cornelia's usual disregard for his desire, he attempts to leave but faints and then falls to the floor. Seizing the moment, she orders the doctor to sedate him and pressures him to admit that Ginny lied about "her background." Through slow motion, blurred point-of-view shots, manipulation of the interrogators' voices, and music that further signals Chuck's confusion, we see the effects of the drugs, the questioning, and the harsh light the interrogators shine into his face. This culminates in the literal transformation of Cornelia et al. into Chuck's Korean torturers, as his view of the former surrounding him dissolves into images of the latter in the same configuration.[62] His resistance now utterly destroyed, Chuck hears his mother's demands as the soldiers' and finally submits, "All right, I'll admit it, I'll admit it." His unspecified admission thus coerced, Cornelia takes him home and begins the annulment proceedings.

At one level, this conflation of Cornelia and Chuck's Korean torturers so manifestly puts the blame on mother for her son's disintegration that it becomes impossible not to see her as the ultimate target. At another, so castigated, she goes on to speak the deep fears I would again argue the film in fact shares. Never speaking explicitly in terms of race (only "background"), she instead invokes the name of the absent father ("If only your father were here now") and articulates Chuck's failure as having put the familial legacy, and his relation to it, in jeopardy: "What does a mother say to a son in a situation like this. . . . Does she remind him of his obligation to his family, to society?" While the whiteness of that "obligation" is implicit, Cornelia's expression of it as a matter of phallic identity understands that a patriarchal structure is also at stake: interracial marriage is a problem for her, and is ultimately refashioned as a solution by the film, because it affects the structure of the family and its standing within the social order. That money and property are thus also at stake is intimated by Cornelia's invocation of "background" and by repeated inscriptions of her within her white mansion at "Bay's End" behind iron gates and large, plantation-style columns. In short, the film registers the overlap of threatened racial, sexual, and economic territories through their defense by the much-maligned white mother. And, in turn, it perpetually operates as if the solution—to Chuck's mental health problems, to the racism and classism that threaten to destroy his marriage; in effect, to all social and psychic crises depicted—is simply to overcome the castrating powers of yet another "white bitch." The epithet is not yet used in a film from 1959, but the imagery and narrative clearly lay the ground for it, projecting the multiple conflicts at issue onto the white woman in a kind of racialized misogyny that implicitly imagines her positive opposite to reside in some "good" (nonbitchy) form of femininity that is decidedly not white. And so we return to Ginny—and, by extension, Margot Seaton, Sacajawea, Suzie Wong, and the rest.

By Chuck's own testimony, Ginny is indeed his cure-all. Dismissing the significance of her being "one-quarter" black during his recovery/courtship in Mexico, he insists, "I'm one-quarter a lot of things—coward, hero, jerk, mental case." He then immediately credits her for his newfound health: "Look at that, steady as a rock. You know, I couldn't hold a glass in that hand when I came here. What did it? The sun? Fresh air? Sleep? Uh-uh, a girl named Ginny." Thus renewed, he soon marries her. But this sexual script is itself already tied to a racial one. For Chuck's declaration has in fact been prompted by Ginny's attempt to discuss her racial heritage. Having announced that her grandmother "was pure Portuguese Angolan," she fears the message has not sunk in: "You haven't heard a word I've said. You know, Chuck, Portuguese Angola isn't in outer space, it's on the west coast of Africa. . . . We lived there 'til my mother died. She was much darker than I am. . . . Chuck I'm one-quarter." Establishing the disclosure the lawsuit will deny, this scene also reveals how Chuck dismisses it: "So you're one-quarter, like the moon was the first night I kissed you." With this effective replacement of "quadroon" with "quarter . . . moon," a displacement imported to the film's title, Chuck articulates the operative textual movement in the film from her racialized body to his gendered vision.

This movement is most pronounced in the courtroom climax. Managing to escape the sanitarium in the final reel, Chuck nonetheless begins this scene going along with his mother's bogus claim (because Ginny's cousin has convinced him that the marriage will only bring his wife misery). But Ginny will have none of this and adamantly testifies to their mu-

tual love. Her lawyer sets out to prove that Chuck still loves her, and that
he had full knowledge of her racial identity all along. After first establishing that he watched her swim naked during their courtship and thus
"couldn't have been misled into thinking that [her] tan was all the result
of the sun," he dramatically rips Ginny's dress from shoulder to hip to
prove that "those parts . . . normally covered by a bathing suit were the
same color as the rest." What we can now see is that this scene's contorted racial-visual logic—that people of color don't tan but have distinct
racial identities indelibly and evenly printed across the surface of their
bodies—works precisely to restore the uncertainty of gender identity and
its classical scopic regime. Not only does the formerly lethargic Chuck
declare his love, as the lawyer had planned, but the imagined instantaneous legibility of Ginny's racialized body, significantly of "those parts
. . . normally covered by a bathing suit," causes him to bolt upright and
resume the position of masculine authority and proprietary vision that
had so stubbornly eluded him.[63] Taking the paradigm to its wildest extreme, such remarkable visual tactics suggest that the white male look,
and the authority and self-determination it formerly signified, are so radically destabilized that they can only regain their force and position in relation to a (racialized, feminized) surface thoroughly unquestionable in
its specularity.

With Chuck and Ginny reunited in the film's final shots, driving off in
a taxi through the streets of San Francisco, the film marshals interracial
romance once and for all to exorcise the earlier images of gender discord.
This is signaled by the presence of supporters gathered outside the courthouse to wave on the happy couple and the absence of the white mother
who remained prominent throughout the trial (where she characteristically lied on the witness stand). With Cornelia finally removed, her original assessment of Ginny now resonates even more clearly as the film's
own determination to replace the white mother and restore the troubled
patriarchy she so emphatically signified with a "prettier," "lovel[ier]"
daughter-in-law of color.

FEMME FATALE BECOMES WHITE ORCHID

While not *all* white women in the late fifties interracial films are as relentlessly wicked as Agnes Moorehead's Cornelia Nelson, many conspic-
uously transgress traditional boundaries. In addition to those who follow
husbands, fathers, and sons across national and cultural borders (e.g.,
Mohawk, Island in the Sun, Sayonara, Touch of Evil, A Majority of One
[1961]), some travel abroad as professionals in their own right (*South Pacific, The King and I, The White Orchid,* and *The Inn of the Sixth Hap-*

piness [1958]), working in ways that challenge gender conventions both foreign and domestic. Although the king of Siam calls his children's imported schoolteacher "Mrs. Anna," her pupils call her "Sir" because she is "scientific, not like lowly women."[64] The same American nurse who cannot sustain the impulse to "wash that man right outta" her hair in the South Pacific nonetheless dresses up as one, and much to the troops' liking, when she performs for them in drag.[65] And after sending for a photographer to join him in the jungles of Mexico, *The White Orchid*'s archaeologist is sorely disappointed with the woman who arrives, assuming the job to be by definition a man's: "I need a guide and I need a photographer. . . . *obviously* I can't take a woman!" To prove herself, the so-rejected woman simultaneously defies a strict local custom that forbids women from seeing certain male performers and overturns extradiegetic traditions of gender, vision, and spectacle when she surreptitiously photographs a partially undressed man through an open window that she opens even wider for an optimal view. Such activity further reveals why white women tend to be outnumbered in these films by women of color, and why when they do appear, they too are frequently managed through interracial affairs. As we will consider in this section, this sometimes means their being worked over on the model of their more obedient and visible Hollywood sisters of color. When this fails, as we will see in the next section, men of color can be conjured to facilitate more radical treatments.

The white woman's failings and her competitor's advantages are particularly evident in triangles that hold out two alternate objects of white male desire, one white and one not. In *Mohawk*, for example, a landscape painter is so inspired by the Iroquois women who happily pose for him that they transform his commissioned genre; Jonathan (Scott Brady) remarks that with them in sight he has to make an extra effort to ensure that there's "at least one tree in the background of each" painting. By contrast, the white woman's image is explicitly reviled in the film's opening scene. When Jon's fiancée and her aunt arrive for a visit, their stagecoach driver, having just compared Mohawks to poisonous snakes, scoffs at their attention to the younger woman's appearance: "When a woman puts on her war paint, she's more dangerous than any Mohawk."[66] The alternative that the (non-Mohawk) woman of color offers to the more-than-poisonous white one is most pronounced in Jon's relation to Onida (Rita Gam), his favorite indigenous model. As she intermittently massages his back and promises to know how to please a man, Jon proposes marriage. And to her response that she is not smart enough to be his wife, he replies, "May the Lord protect me from a brainy woman!" Later, when an argument between them prompts her to defiantly command, "Kill me!" he shoots back, "I'd rather paint you!" This ongoing chain of associations not only establishes the native woman as more desirable/paintable than the white one but also suggests that in loving/painting the former, the white man can evade the "brainy," "dangerous" designs seemingly inescapable with the latter. Not surprisingly, Jon passes up his last chance to reunite with his white fiancée and chooses Onida for good.

Although Clark and Sacajawea separate at the end of *Far Horizons*, her knack for being a certain kind of woman is similarly used to measure, and in this case overtly instruct, the white woman. After their expedition successfully reaches the Pacific to declare all territory covered U.S. property, Lewis, Clark, and Sacajawea return to Monticello to report to the president and face the fallout of the romance plots. Having been wooed by Clark before his voyage, Julia Hancock (Barbara Hale) is devastated to learn of his love for Sacajawea. This triangle peaks in a set of scenes that differentiate two kinds of women, contrasting their styles of spectacle and femininity in particular, and setting us up for the film's ultimate trade-in of Julia's for Sacajawea's.

The first of these scenes features the two women alone in Julia's bedroom, preparing for an upcoming party and facing the critical feminine question of what to wear. Early shots feature a modestly clad Sacajawea (in braids, leather fringed shift, beads, etc.), inspecting Julia's vanity table on the left, with Julia in the background at right in her sizable, well-stocked closet. Marking the excess of the white woman's wardrobe, Sacajawea asks in amazement, "These are all yours?" With a hint of doubt Julia replies, "I know it's rather silly. . . . Don't worry, your dress is lovely." This visual contrast is then fused to a comparison of their conceptions of a woman's role, defined precisely in its relation to a white man. Sacajawea asks pointedly, "The wife of a white man, what does she do?" Like many other white women in fifties Hollywood cinema, Julia herself seems unsure about the answer to this question: "That's a little hard to explain. She does have certain social duties, but these can be easily learned." She continues in earnest, as if this is the true core of things: "She runs her husband's home, entertains his friends, tries to make him happy and successful and proud of being married to her." Noticeably concerned about her own ability to fulfill this role, Sacajawea studies Julia carefully throughout this speech. Julia concludes: "Most important of all, she must love him very much." Doubting herself, Sacajawea questions, "But this is not enough?" Now clearly doubting herself, too, Julia replies, "I don't know." In the face of this confusion, Sacajawea offers her own philosophy of marriage, one Julia and the film seem to admire at this critical moment as much for its certainty as for its conventional simplicity: "Among my people there is not so much to learn. A woman cooks for a man, works in the fields and has the babies, that is all." Affirming Sacajawea's model, Julia insists, "I think that is quite a bit, don't you?"

Having thus established Sacajawea as bankable wife material over and against Julia with her doubts and confusion, the exchange culminates in Julia's discovery of Clark and Sacajawea's romance. Bowing out of the triangle, wounded but sacrificial, Julia offers her rival the dress she has been admiring during their conversation, symbolically ceding her position in the domain of spectacle as well as matrimony.

Shortly after this scene we discover that Sacajawea has chosen neither to wear Julia's dress nor to become the white man's wife. Yet her departure and Clark's discovery of it are orchestrated so as to uphold her model of femininity as the ideal for Clark, Julia, and the spectator. Indeed, the film rivets Julia, and the comparison between the two women, to the interracial lovers' separation. Julia transcribes Sacajawea's parting letter to Clark and initially reads it aloud to him after its author has left. This reading of the letter, and the camera's cutting back and forth between Julia and Clark as she does so, effectively makes her the letter's recipient as much as him. And the letter's content and Julia's emotional response to it clearly indicate that Sacajawea remains the film's ideally devoted, even "natural," woman, and that her textual purpose has been not simply to support Clark and his territorial project but to guide the white woman, too, instructing her in the "simple" arts of a white man's wife.

As the decade advances, hopes for thus remodeling the white woman seem to weaken, and more and more frequently white men and their lovers of color choose—or, by this reading, are perhaps more obliged—to stay together.[67] *Sayonara*, set in Japan during the Korean War and just prior to the lifting of restrictions prohibiting U.S. servicemen from interracial marriage, takes the occasion as an opportunity for an extended meditation on the comparative gender identities of white American women and Japanese ones. As Gina Marchetti has argued, the film "questions national and racial boundaries on one level, [but] also affirms and solidifies very conservative notions of gender identity and sexuality on another" (132). While Marchetti lays out the narrative means by which this dual operation takes place, the film also offers particularly rich examples of how such representations are deeply intertwined through visual representation.

Sayonara's comparison of women is explicitly introduced in one of its earliest scenes, and is overtly staged there and throughout the film in terms that overtly question the status of, and relations among, heterosexual desire, gender identity, specularity, and vision. When a fatigued pilot, Lloyd Gruver (Marlon Brando), arrives for his military vacation at a U.S. base in Kobe, he meets his buddy-to-be, Joe Kelly (Red Buttons), and the two quickly exchange photographs of their respective girlfriends. Lloyd builds his up before sharing it ("I believe that maybe you forgot

what an American girl looks like. . . . First of all, an American girl."),
only to be deflated when he accidentally shows a picture of his "girl"
with her mother. Kelly retorts, "Kind of beat up, ain't she?" Lloyd
quickly produces a second photograph sans mother, and we look on with
them through a close-up at the photo of a young white woman in a white
bathing suit. Joe reacts, "She really does something to a bathing suit."
Lloyd agrees: "She has an enormous capacity to fulfill [sic] a bathing
suit." This verbal strutting of the gaze is quickly tempered when Joe displays a photo of his Japanese girlfriend, Katsumi (Miyoshi Umeki),
wrapped modestly in a kimono. Lloyd initially responds, "She looks like
a smart girl." The implied insult becomes pointed and ugly when Joe announces his determination to marry Katsumi, even if it requires giving up
his American citizenship. Appalled, Lloyd barks, "Go ahead and marry
that slant-eyed runt if you want to, it will serve you right." But here the
former elevation of the "American girl" over the Japanese one comes to
a halt, preparing us for the reversal that will soon ensue for the remainder of the film. When Joe angrily defends himself against Lloyd's insults
and accusations that he's "crazy," he insists, "I am crazy, I'm in love
crazy. . . . Maybe [you don't understand that] 'cause you don't feel as
strong about your girl as I do about mine." At this Brando's brash character falls silent, the first of many signs of his ambivalence about the (still
unnamed) white woman. What is more, an earlier suggestion that Lloyd's
fatigue was caused primarily by doubts about the war and his own role
in it is now effectively supplanted by what will clearly become the film's
primary concern, the meaning and status of gender and sexuality for
Lloyd and men like him in a changing postwar world.

The next scene confirms Lloyd's ambivalence with his sarcastic reaction to his girlfriend's surprise visit. Delivered as a gift from her father,
the general, Eileen Webster (Patricia Owens) awaits Lloyd in the back-
seat of her father's car. Upon discovering her—decked out for the
evening, again in picture-perfect, form-fitting attire—Lloyd declares, "I
forgot what an ugly girl you got here. . . . That dress is terrible! . . . It just
goes in and out . . . just awful!" She has just traveled the globe to see him,
but he cannot stop himself from belittling her. And this is not for her lack
of effort to please and arouse. To Lloyd's sarcastic greeting Eileen know-
ingly replies, "It's meant to go in and out. I go in and out." While the
conflicts that soon end this relationship will be elaborated in scenes to
come, what is striking already in these early ones is the degree to which
the white woman's conventionally eroticized image and the white man's
look at it fail to guarantee what they used to. In this context, Lloyd's accusation that Joe "forgot what an American girl looks like," and implicitly what those looks are supposed to do to a man, comes to sound increasingly like an expression of Lloyd's and the film's own anxieties.[68]

Although such anxieties are thus introduced with the men in question, the film retroactively, as Marchetti writes, "puts the blame on women—namely, on [Lloyd's] fiancée Eileen" (132). The problem with Eileen, we come to learn, is that even though she wants to be Lloyd's curvy lover, she has some funny notions about gender and heterosexuality. This is most explicit in a conversation that implicitly breaks them up. It begins with her questioning why they have yet to marry and peaks in her open rejection of conventional (military) marriage: "You'll never tuck me away in the corner of some little town. Go ahead and be the greatest general in Air Force history, but love me too!" The conversation has several waves in which she expresses her concerns, he attempts to minimize them, and she is compelled to speak them again more forcefully. Explicitly rejecting "a family like our fathers . . . and mothers have," Eileen explains these concerns as the result of "doing a lot of thinking," "thinking too much." Read in the context of anxieties pervasive throughout this period, Lloyd seems to speak for all the good old boys dismayed at the white woman's transformations of late when he finally stops trying to appease her and resigns, in Brando's thickly laid attempt at a Virginian accent: "Sometimes I look at you and I don't understand you. I don't know what's going on in your brain. Sometimes I think I don't even know who you are." The imagined futility of attempting to figure the white woman out is sealed in her response that closes the scene: "Maybe you don't. Maybe you never will."

In keeping with our original glimpses of this relationship, however, Eileen is dubious of more than the constraining life of "a white man's wife," posing the problem as a question of what a *man* wants: "I guess all I'm trying to say is, and I really mean this, Lloyd, if what you want is a family like our fathers have and promotion in the Air Force and position in society, like our mothers have, and you marry me because I'm pretty and smart and have guts and will know the ropes, then I don't think you ought to marry me." Lloyd then confirms that the problem comes down to why and how he wants a woman: "I want a wife, I want a family, a home, in America. And every time I think about having a home like that, I think about having it with a girl like you." For Eileen this is the final straw: "What do you mean a girl *like* me? I'm me! Oh, Lloyd, it's me you've got to love. Oh, Lord, haven't you ever felt like grabbing me and hauling me off to a shack somewhere?" Eileen thus never rejects being an object of male desire, or having "a family, a home" per se. What upsets her is being desired only as a type, "a girl like . . ."; she wants to be desired particularly, passionately, as "me!" Insofar as Lloyd's desire for her was itself (unsteadily) introduced in relation to the swimsuit image of a nameless "American girl," her ultimate refusal of such an identity signals a crisis not only for this relationship but also for the classical cinematic regime of fulfilling male desire. While this refusal certainly could invite significant questions about the state of female subjectivity, the film that follows, like most in this chapter, is preoccupied instead with what it means for guys like Lloyd.

Eileen's defiance of conventional assumptions about gender and desire extends to the domain of spectacle and performance when she takes Lloyd to see Kabuki. There she expresses interest in cross-dressing practices not just in Japan but in educated pockets of the United States (Lloyd: "Kabuki, isn't that the place where there's no dames and the men play all the women's parts?" Eileen: "Yes, like they do at Princeton.") As she reads the program aloud, guiding him through foreign matters he clearly finds disturbing, her own educated diction and openness are continually contrasted to Brando's performance as a ruffled southern boy as they exchange lines like the following:

> LLOYD: She wouldn't be half so ugly if she didn't stick her face in that flour barrel.
> EILEEN: She?
> LLOYD: Well, whatever it was. You got me.
> EILEEN: He's a male actress. It says here they've been trained since childhood to have the grace of a woman, yet the power of a man.
> LLOYD: Oh my word!

When they go backstage afterward to meet the "male actress," Nakamura (Ricardo Montalban), Eileen states plainly, "I find myself coming to be intrigued by everything in Japan." She will pursue such gender-bending intrigues, in the form of Nakamura, after she and Lloyd break up.

It is only after all this trouble with white femininity *and* white masculinity is so clearly announced that Lloyd revokes his original pronouncement against interracial desire and pursues it with a vengeance. And his primary encounters with Japanese women work repeatedly to establish their aptitude for deindividuated forms of spectacle and servitude. After Joe marries Katsumi, Lloyd visits their home and is thoroughly charmed by the way she perpetually bows and tends the men: "This is all right, boy, this is cute, this is nice. . . . Listen, boy, she's just as cute as a bug!" We are invited to respond in kind, watching the "cute" scene to the sounds of romantic music and the woman's sweet humming from the kitchen.

Although less immediately subservient than Joe's, Lloyd's Japanese object of affection, Hana Ogi (Miiko Taka), is similarly introduced in another classically feminine role. Lloyd first sees the performer when his friend Captain Mike Bailey (James Garner) takes him to watch the "bitchy boshi," a bridge over which her all-female troupe, Matsubayashi, travels twice daily. Or, as Mike explains it, "*Boshi* is Japanese for bridge, and we call this particular one the 'bitchy boshi' because there's so much lovely stuff that goes over it." Mike takes Lloyd out for this visual treat just after he has confided the return of periodic existential doubts: he admits that he himself contemplates "a whole different way of life" than the one his father assumed for him and generally ponders the conditions of (un)happy masculinity: "The unhappiest men I know are those who were forced into something they got no inaptitude [*sic*] for." Mike and the film then immediately answer this ambiguous confession with the pleasures to be had at the bridge: "Hey, come on, the goods are on display!" The visual consumption of these "goods" thus works to put down the voiced suspicion that conventional gender structures might be failing to satisfy white men as well as white women.

As Lloyd and Mike happily watch the procession of dozens of women, Lloyd's facility with such attractions is highlighted when Mike points out to his buddy, "There's Tameko-san, the one you saw me with." The point-of-view shot of nearly identically clad girls at a considerable distance makes it impossible to imagine how one could be distinguished from the rest, but Lloyd manages: "Yeah, little one in pink." (Mike confirms: "Yeah, that's the one.") This rather miraculous feat of visual detection, which does not appear to be playing for a laugh, thus confirms Lloyd's proclivity for finding a singular object of desire amid a seemingly indistinguishable mass or type. This is momentarily complicated when his interest is piqued by the only one in the troupe who is noticeably different from the rest, Hana Ogi, standing out for her androgynous look in Western slacks, turtleneck, and plumed fedora. But her initially unconventional appearance will soon be traded in for traditions very much to Lloyd's liking.

Lloyd's spectatorial therapy continues in the next scene at a Matsubayashi performance he and Mike watch eagerly from the front row. The women perform a musical revue, from which we see fragments of no less than twelve numbers. Each has a particular aesthetic, but as a whole these numbers are marked by lights and lanterns, a seemingly endless parade of costumes, and the ongoing motif of the women's bodies perpetually veiled and revealed—behind props (fans, parasols, hats, feathers, etc.) within numbers, and by the alternation of revealing and concealing outfits within and across them (short kimonos, long kimonos, partially see-through kimonos, tuxedos, hot pants, etc.). When Mike asks his friend if he follows the (evidently absent) plot, Lloyd sarcastically grins and answers, "Yeah, there's nothing wrong with the plot!" Translating the remark into Lloyd-like terms slightly closer to the feminist film theories that would confirm his evident visual pleasures: "With spectacle like this, who needs plot!"

Lloyd's relation to Hana Ogi, the performer featured at the center of the stage and chorus line in most of these numbers, develops in keeping with these introductions. At first he routinely watches her from a distance, much as he and Mike originally spied her from the bushes. While the paradigm of the woman of color functioning as "superior" spectacle to the more troubling images of the white woman clearly operates, the significant complication here is that Hana Ogi and her troupe also perform in drag, and she herself is frequently seen in masculine attire, at times awaited by adoring female fans. While her cross-dressing, like Nakamura's, at once marks potential subversions of dominant ideologies of gender and sexuality, as Marchetti argues, it is also used to overcome them.[69] For Lloyd makes Hana Ogi give up the theater and her male costumes and wholly embrace being, as he calls her, "a really fine-looking woman." When Katsumi initially tells him that Hana Ogi will never break the code that prevents members of her troupe from talking to men, he boasts, "Well honey, I'm here to tell you, it's gonna happen." His bravado is justified at their first private meeting, where he finds the formerly androgynous figure in traditional Japanese attire, waiting for him silently with downcast eyes.[70] Not long into their relationship she further resists the strict sexual codes of her profession, confessing, "I am tempted, with you I could become a woman, and a mother, and I could love you."[71] Thus, while the white woman loudly resists being a generic feminine type, the professional Japanese performer chooses to trade in all her other roles for precisely the one Lloyd wants, and in so doing further restores him to being the type of man who can command such conventional performances.

Even when white women are not thoroughly replaced by women of color in these films, they can be figuratively "colored" through a kind of racialized taming that remakes them on the model of their exotic-erotic counterparts. This is sometimes implicit in the casting of white actresses in the roles of docile butterflies and "passionate" mulattoes (e.g., *Love Is a Many-Splendored Thing, Band of Angels, Kings Go Forth, Night of the Quarter Moon*). It also occurs through associative and sometimes even literal "tinting" of diegetically white female bodies and costumes—as noted earlier with Joan Collins in *Island in the Sun*—and/or via exposure to racially or ethnically "other" lovers and landscapes. At the end of *The Searchers*, it is curious to see Ethan Edwards suddenly halt his fierce obsession to kill his abducted white niece and, instead, when he finally tracks her down, sweep her up in a nearly romantic embrace. Yet this change of heart makes textual sense when we compare the cowering female captive in Comanche garb to the aggressively literate, looking, and demanding white women who await Ethan and his nephew back at the homestead.[72] Other racialized transformations of the white woman are less explicit but equally effective in reasserting her conventional cultural and filmic functions. A final telling example returns us to the treatment of a white female photographer in Mexico in *The White Orchid*, following her bold reversal of classical codes of gender and vision.

The evolution of this film's title song points to the white woman's transformation from a dangerous "femme fatale" to a "sweet" white flower. The former name is used to title an early version of the song and, in its lyrics, to repeatedly name the woman in question:

> Like the orchid blowing now
> White of skin aloof somehow.
> Slender form and fragrance sweet
> Are you my femme fatale.
>
> Like the siren Xtabay,
> For whom men forever sigh
> and forget their daily life,
> You tempt me femme fatale.
>
> I know it must be
> If I gain your love
> I'm doomed then to die.
> Yet I don't ask why.
>
> Femme fatale, you are my love,
> Sun and moon and stars above;
> Darling never mind the stall,
> Just kiss me, femme fatale, femme fatale, femme fatale.[73]

While this version renders its subject beautiful but also distant and emphatically deadly, in the film we hear portions sung in Spanish and only at the very end a brief refrain in English that significantly revises the earlier lyrics to rename the former "femme fatale" as "dearest white":

> Like the orchid blooming now
> White of skin aloof somehow.
> Slender form and fragrance sweet
> Are you my dearest white?
>
> I know it must be
> If I gain your love
> I'm doomed then to die.
> Yet I don't ask why.
>
> Dearest white . . .[74]

Although the risk that attends attraction to this woman is not entirely erased by this version, it is noticeably softened. And this transformation, and the shift from the Spanish to these revised English lyrics in the film's final moments, is thoroughly in keeping with the film's representation of

Kathryn Williams (Peggy Castle). For Spanish-speaking Juan (Armando Silvestre) she will literally lead to death, but in the process and its aftermath she will become, for English-speaking Bob (William Lundigan), an all the more "dear" and "white" specimen of femininity.[75]

After their one and only kiss, Kathryn makes it clear that she showed interest in Juan only to keep him on as the expedition's guide, and hence to remain in close contact with Bob, and even make him jealous. And her plan succeeds. Yet, despite this explicit disavowal, the brief interracial romance is in fact crucial to the film's (re)configuration of Kathryn vis-à-vis Bob. Just as we see Juan pollinate the white flowers on his plantation by hand to produce vanilla (probably for export), so do his romantic encounters with Kathryn ultimately produce a newly visible, desirable, white woman for the white man.[76]

This process is particularly noticeable after the expedition needs to shed some weight. While Bob insists on keeping the photographic and sound equipment to record his archaeological findings, Kathryn agrees to leave behind her two suitcases. The stakes of this sacrifice become clearer after they arrive at Juan's plantation and he directs a woman there to provide Kathryn with a fresh change of clothes. Initially, the resident woman is shocked to discover that the white woman's "pantalones" are not on loan "from the senor" but are in fact her own; but when Kathryn reemerges from this female exchange, her tightly wrapped hairstyle has been shed along with the pants, and her hair, blouse, and skirt all now flow freely in a "Mexican" style that is also more classically feminine. Bob's response indicates as much, as he whistles at her new look in a compliment she decodes to mean that she looks "more like a woman." Relations between the white man and woman are so strained, however, that more dramatic machinations are required to put them back together. Unconvinced by Bob's attempt here to mend the rift between them since his initial objection to having been assigned a female photographer ("Oh, a woman!" he first groaned), Kathryn slaps him and runs to Juan. Fulfilling his role in the interracial triangle, Juan interrupts his pollination procedures to praise the beauty not just of her new garments but of "what's in the dress."

When the expedition continues, the most critical matters quickly escalate in visual terms. After Bob's tape recorder is inadvertently broken, Kathryn exclaims, "At least we still have our photographic equipment!" As the visual becomes the primary register for recording Bob's findings, it further signifies his vulnerability: Kathryn still wields the camera, and, as Juan warns, they are under "constant observation" by the natives. But both the white woman's and the white man's relation to vision and power are dramatically reconfigured in the jungle. When Kathryn tries to take a picture there, she is surrounded by the hidden observers who seize her camera, take her and the rest of her party into captivity, and prepare her for sacrifice to the gods. And while Kathryn is thus swiftly moved from her threatening place behind the lens to the ultimate position of "native" woman as ceremonial spectacle, Bob momentarily appears as another of this chapter's highly vulnerable white male subjects when he and Juan are bound together in a hut.

With this telling glimpse of a white man again at risk at the scene of a white woman's captivity, however, the film fashions a particularly remarkable rescue scenario wherein Bob simultaneously frees himself and restores classical visual relations. For his means of escape is, literally, his destruction of the rolls of film that inscribe Kathryn's photographic vision: in close-up we watch her film burn while he positions the ropes that bind him over its flames. With impeccable timing, his release occurs at precisely the moment the chief rips off Kathryn's ceremonial robe atop a Mayan pyramid. Once free of the ropes, Bob waits a moment to let the film become entirely engulfed (lest any trace remain) and uses the flaming mass to set fire to the village. After rescuing Kathryn, and (most amazingly) finding her camera hidden in a cranny of the enormous pyramid's steps, he takes a final moment to look back at the burning village and snap a photograph. Thanks to the sacrifice of this village, and Juan's soon to come, the restoration of the white male gaze, white female spectacle, and the "proper" racial and gendered possession of the photographic apparatus is complete.

After Juan sends the white couple away to safety, we hear with them the distant screams of his offscreen attack, and Kathryn cries out, "Oh, Bob!" as she collapses into him.[77] The racial process that first made her "more like a woman" thus now effectively tints her "white white," reinstating that tradition of the excessively visible and vulnerable representation of white womanhood that works, perhaps above all else, to secure its opposite in white men. Put otherwise in the larger context of this chapter, the white woman need not be permanently browned or temporarily "tanned," so long as her whiteness and femininity finally make *him* look more like a man.

THE LAST (BLACK) MAN AND (WHITE) WOMAN ON EARTH

It is precisely the fatigue of dominant ideological and cinematic forms in the fifties, I have been arguing, that triggers their often relentless rehearsal and revision. Yet, as we have also seen, these films can rarely excise, and routinely call attention to, the palpable sense that formerly controlling subjects and institutions have come to some kind of end. While both tendencies are evident throughout the sensational plots and spectacles discussed throughout this chapter, nowhere are the terms in question pressed to such extremes as in *The World, the Flesh, and the Devil*. Set in the aftermath of a nuclear war, this film imagines the near end of the world itself and focuses on a cast of only three survivors—a black man, a white woman, and eventually a white man—who find themselves in an intense interracial triangle plotted within the dramatic landscape of an otherwise deserted (but strangely intact) Manhattan. More precisely, while the white man is absent for the better part of the film, and is sick with radiation poisoning when he finally arrives, the (healthy) black man devotes himself to projects of cultural preservation and restoration that carefully tend to, and arguably refortify, the positions to which the white man eventually returns. These projects climax most dramatically in the radical re-formation of the white woman and her image. And here, as elsewhere (e.g., *Island in the Sun, The White Orchid, Touch of Evil, The Searchers*), the man of color who does so much gender work is nonetheless finally repositioned in ways that dramatically revoke and revise the masculine privileges temporarily allowed him.[78]

This film's preoccupations with visual and spatial formations of identity and difference are first emphasized by representations that cinematically evoke meditations on the social position of black masculinity from Ralph Ellison's *Invisible Man* and Richard Wright's *Native Son*. The film charts the lonely ascension of Ralph Burton (Harry Belafonte), from being an underground tunnel worker in Pennsylvania (where he was trapped when the catastrophe struck) to becoming a self-proclaimed "mayor" of New York who not only commands a penthouse view of the city but also restores electrical power and wiring to make it, or at least his block of it, visible in the night sky. But this ill-timed ascension is by no means automatic. When Ralph arrives in the abandoned city, his subjection within and beneath white urban space is vividly marked. Searching for others on foot, he is dwarfed by towering buildings that loom over him: the camera pins him beneath and amid them from extreme high and low angles; compositions fix him within intersections and deep, receding vanishing points; and point-of-view shots crane our necks up and around with his, once in a low-angle pan that sweeps nearly the entire circumference of his view up at the enormous structures that surround him (figs. 5.15–5.17). This early passage of the film vividly signifies the enduring

---

FIG. 5.15. In a deserted Manhattan, Ralph Burton (Harry Belafonte) fears a white gaze in the high-rises above him. *The World, the Flesh, and the Devil* (1959).

FIG. 5.16

FIG. 5.17

FIG. 5.18. On his first trip to the rooftops, Ralph assumes the position of the gaze that formerly haunted him.

power of white regimes of vision and space to encode and enforce black subjection, even when the white people themselves have apparently vanished. Ralph voices as much in his own conflicted desire for, and paranoia of, white eyes watching from the windows above him. He cries out desperately, "Come out! Come out! You're all crazy? What are you hiding from me for? I know you're there, and staring at me! I can feel you staring at me! Come out!"

After breaking him all the way down, the film sends Ralph literally up to the very top of the empty buildings that first haunted him—to live, work, play, and look. Just after he listens to tapes at a radio station confirming the doomed fate of this and other cities, he makes his first and pivotal trip to the rooftop to survey the landscape from a position of vision he formerly feared (fig. 5.18). He then begins a regime of industriousness and mechanical wizardry to revive the radio transmitter, an electrical generator, and an assortment of other technologies. That this work signifies a new production of self is made explicit when Ralph floods his street with light for the first time and plays with his own giant shadow. Although he playfully names and recognizes this self-produced self-image ("Hello, Burton!"), the ironic negativity that underwrites this momentary jubilation—being the mayor of a dead city at the end of the world—is marked in the literally negative image of self as shadow and the marionette-like movements he performs with his body. As Ralph later poses the question, "Why should the world fall apart to prove what I am and there's nothing wrong with what I am?"

Despite such tormenting legacies, Ralph unquestionably assumes his new function as possibly the last man on earth to be one of cultural preservation. When, after they become friends, Sarah Crandall (Inger Stevens) asks why he is filling his apartment with piles of books, he responds, "Somebody has to save them"; in the final sequence he declares, "I'll save things, whatever I can. That's why I'm alive." This pronouncement resonates with his most unlikely role as the preserver of dominant racial ideology. Despite the love that grows between them, it is Ralph who will refuse Sarah's advances.[79] To her suggestion that they live in the same building, he mutters abruptly, "People will talk." As the film's press materials curiously explain it, "As a man dedicated to preserving what is best of civilization, he must also preserve what is worst."[80] Ralph is so relentlessly pressed into such service that it is also largely through him that the film attempts to preserve not only the racial and sexual ideologies of dominant culture but also the related dominant visual regimes at risk throughout these films.

In keeping with so many depictions of masculinity detected in this chapter, Ralph's too is noteworthy for the intensity of both its fragility and its attempts at refortification. On the one hand, his vulnerable psychic state is readily detectable—as when he brings home a pair of mannequins for companionship, for example, and throws one off his balcony in a paranoid outburst. On the other hand, the film also uses him to affirm the potency of a more ordinary masculinity. This is evident in the routine "maleness" of Ralph's industrious behavior. An exemplar of do-it-yourself-ism, he spends much of the film draped in a well-equipped tool belt as he scrambles about ladders and fixtures, tinkers with gadgets and wires, and ferries things home in his no-nonsense pickup truck. Such images seem in part to answer contemporary anxieties about the conditions and practices of masculinity by asserting the masculine potentials of domestic life. Ralph's penthouse becomes an elaborate workshop and playhouse, filled with (among other things), a blowtorch, a searchlight, a ham radio, and an electric train set that runs from room to room. This train, combined with rescued paintings that fill most all the walls, toys with the conventional floor plan, blurring spatial distinctions like those between living room and bedroom, public and private. Ralph even reconfigures the meaning of "kitchen," haven of gendered determinacy, by dropping the dishes out the window instead of washing them. Thus freeing himself of so-called women's work, he calculates with his slide rule the number of years before the pile of broken plates will reach his window and force him to relocate.

But the potency of Ralph's masculinity, especially as conjured at moments that emphasize his blackness, is marshaled most dramatically to transform Sarah—from an unseen, lurking force in her initial appearances in the film, to a visibly desiring subject and object of desire, to a literally and psychically mutilated creature. Ralph is cast as the catalyst of each phase of Sarah's transformation, and all this transpires before the white man's arrival on the scene, as if to elaborately reconfigure it, and her, to facilitate his return.

While Sarah first hides in the shadows, unseen even by the camera, she becomes increasingly visible as she becomes increasingly close to Ralph. Although she will confess having watched him since his arrival in the city, her image is withheld from us, too, until just after his first survey of the landscape from on high, a juxtaposition that ties his symbolic transcendence to his function vis-à-vis the white woman. And while our first glimpse is confined to a close-up of pale feet in dark flats, as she trails him she is cloaked in a long, dark coat and is usually photographed from a distance. We only first see Sarah's face distinctly in close-ups and medium shots when Ralph first sees her. And, insofar as she inadvertently reveals herself through a scream (when he hurls his mannequin from the balcony) and a shout of "Don't touch me!" (when he then catches a glimpse of her in the street), Ralph's ability to expose her is itself tied to fantasies of black male violence. Sarah's fear quickly turns to desire, but Ralph's effect on her is much the same: when we next see her after they meet, she is returning from a "shopping" trip with new dresses and a makeover.

The pivotal scene of Sarah's transformation begins with the greatest visual affirmation of Ralph's newly masterful position: a shot of the city from above (fig. 5.19), which is then revealed to be Ralph's point of view with a cut to him looking out from the penthouse balcony where he and Sarah are seated (fig. 5.20). While his two prior rooftop gazes at the city were set up through shots of his approach to that surveying position, this time he already occupies it before we arrive, as if his claim to it no longer requires textual preparation. And the scene takes off from this peak to undertake a radical reconfiguration of the white woman. That her image is what will soon be most at stake is foreshadowed already in the painting of a female figure that hangs between and deeply behind them at the back of the apartment.

This afternoon begins with a series of refusals and rejections. After Ralph dismisses Sarah's proposal to move in downstairs, she criticizes his know-it-all attitude and grows increasingly upset by his emotional distance. When he advises that she ought to get busy, like him, she snaps back that she is "free, white, and twenty-one" and should be able to do as she pleases. His full response is delayed, but the tension immediately intensifies. Soon she breaks down, fixating ultimately on the fact that she will never marry: "There's nobody to marry anybody." Ralph takes himself out of the running when he insists that he will find "somebody" (else) for her to marry and perform the service himself. This comforts Sarah momentarily, and their mutual affection is again visible, but the social legacies brewing not far beneath the surface vividly return when she announces she needs a haircut.

Ralph is visibly disturbed by this request, and even when he agrees to it, his hacking humor signals trouble to come: he grabs a large handsaw and raises it before her, saying, "Let's get at it." A dissolve shows him moments later with a more appropriately sized pair of scissors, but he is still noticeably anxious as he clicks them open and closed. The butchering that ensues, the film nonetheless insinuates, is provoked by the white woman's own desire. She first watches him with her hand mirror and announces, "I've got my eye on you." As Ralph begins cautiously, Sarah forcefully commands, "Cut!" When he snips just a bit at the ends, she insists with a grin, "Be brave! . . . More than that!" So pushed, he swiftly

---

FIG. 5.19. An afternoon lunch with Sarah (Inger Stevens) begins with Ralph taking in his remarkable view.

FIG. 5.20

FIG. 5.21. The haircut that butchers Sarah's image.

FIG. 5.22. Ralph and his gaze dominate the newly devastated white woman.

cuts a large chunk, and the hacking begins. As he haphazardly plunges the scissors into her thick hair, chopping at random angles and lengths, she watches in the mirror—wincing, squirming, and anxiously fingering the hair that remains (fig. 5.21). Stunned, she finally cries, "It isn't weeds you know."

While this scene renders the black man's experience ambiguously opaque (the top half of his face is cropped out of a key close-up, for example, in which he gently blows away the blonde locks that have fallen onto his hand), it is unequivocal in its transformation of the white woman and her image.[81] Indeed, in a film, and an era, that clearly wants to allow for some new kinds of interracial connection, it is a striking return of the image of the black beast conjured precisely to mutilate the white woman. For Ralph clearly destroys the spirit that initially voiced Sarah's desires, along with her literal self-image. She falls silent as soon as the first aggressive cut is made and never fully recovers her former confidence. After Ralph abandons the haircut, the scene continues with a conversation in which her butchered head is prominent. Sarah is seated now so as to appear almost adjacent to that female portrait that hangs on his wall, and we can now clearly recognize it as a Modigliani that stretches and twists a woman's head and neck in his typical style. Ralph at first watches her from the back of the room and then (after putting on his manly tool belt) hovers over her, dominating visually and spatially the woman ultimately reduced to tears (fig. 5.22). He admits his anger at her "free, white, and twenty-one" comment and lectures on the racial barriers between them. But, with Sarah juxtaposed to the Modigliani and under Ralph's assaultive gaze for almost two full minutes in this shot, the film visually insists that even more than that has been at stake. Ralph's potent vision and position so prominently demonstrated at the outset of the scene can now be read as having been evoked, even cultivated, to render Sarah another tortured image in his collection.

These new relations painfully mark Ralph and Sarah's remaining time alone. When we next see her, waiting on her end of the phone as his rings without answer, she stands in a dimly lit room with her hair covered by a scarf, reminding us of her bandaged but unhealed wound. In what initially appears to be a gesture of reconciliation, Ralph invites her to a birthday party in her honor with a front-page headline he has printed for the occasion, but the celebration becomes a ruse whereby he and the film lavishly solicit Sarah's desire only to deny it. When she arrives in a formal gown and a new short hairstyle she has managed to shape attractively, Ralph at first delights her. He welcomes her with a searchlight on the street and pretends at once to be maître d', waiter, cook, and entertainer at a fancy restaurant, playing music he has pressed on vinyl for the special event. Yet when the meal proper begins, and she asks the waiter to ask the performer to join her when his number is finished, he replies, "Mr. Burton isn't allowed to sit with the customers."[82] With Ralph's un-flinching enforcement of segregation, leaving her alone at this "party," the many signs of his mastery on display (the searchlight, the record, etc.) seem now marshaled only to destroy the pleasures he has invited her to take. The jubilant sense of self announced upon her arrival—"I'm *the* Sarah Crandall, and it's my birthday. I'm here! Ring out proud bells!"— is so devastated by his repeated rejections that she finally walks out.

It is at this point in the film, with Sarah now desperate for intimacy on almost any terms, that the white man, Ben Thacker (Mel Ferrer), finally arrives. Sarah spots him on a boat in the harbor, and although she and Ralph have been free of illness (against all odds), in keeping with the fragility of white men seen throughout this chapter, it is Ben who col-lapses almost as soon as they meet. After Ralph and Sarah nurse him back to health (Ralph getting credit for the antidote that makes the criti-cal difference), Sarah finds with Ben the possibility of romance that Ralph has denied her. But the triangle quickly intensifies into rivalry, and the black man's position vis-à-vis the white woman, space, and vision is again rewritten.

The new stakes are particularly graphic on an evening in which the trio has gathered to socialize. Not unlike the afternoon that began with Ralph's point-of-view shot of the city, this scene opens with the point of view of a spectator watching a newsreel on a screen set up in his living room (fig. 5.23). But whereas Ralph previously held sole claim to the re-verse shot that identified the diegetic source of the masterful look, here the reverse shot shows the two men seated on either side of Ralph's pro-jector near the center of our screen (fig. 5.24). Sarah is seated slightly below them and off to the right, making her sight line distinctly off from the central one that both men, and the onscreen projector, clearly share. Redrawing the visual terms even more emphatically, the newsreel images they watch are of two sorts: the launching of a rocket and a bathing beauty contest that features a cavalcade of white women posing for the camera and onscreen male photographers vying to snap them (figs. 5.23 and 5.25). In other words, the two primary signifiers of Ralph's symbolic mastery—images of technological achievement and images of white women—are here reiterated by films (and film technology) that Ralph himself has salvaged. But the same material, which Ben also consumes, now signifies competing male claims.

This rivalry clearly functions to Ben's advantage. Not only does Ralph's sexual denial of himself and of Sarah leave her hungry for male company, but just as Ben finds himself in a prime seat on Ralph's spectatorial couch *because* of Ralph's symbolic achievements, so too has Ralph opened up a prime space for another man in the text of the film itself. Ralph's function as the textual source of Ben's access to classic cinematic forms of male privilege is visually encoded after their screening has ended and Sarah has left the room. In a new seating arrangement in which the men face off, Ralph sits in front of his projector on the left while Ben on the right sits twiddling his cane (signifier of his residual phallic impairment), and between them returns the Modigliani (fig. 5.26). In the context of Ben's increasing pursuit of Sarah, this image not only reiterates the men's sexual rivalry but also, in its movement from Ralph and his projector, to the Modigliani, to Ben and his cane, suggests a chain of access: Ben's relation to that tortured female image is possible only because of Ralph's presence as the one who has produced and sustained it.[83]

When Ralph earlier promised Sarah that he would find "somebody" to marry her, he added, "only you can't be too particular. You'll have to take what you get." His words prove true on both counts: he does keep Ben alive so Sarah can have him, but to be with him, we come to see, is to scrape the bottom of the barrel. When she has yet to fully yield as Ben wants her to, in part because she seems to really love Ralph instead, he threatens her with rape: "I could force you, it would be easy. All the Boys Scouts out of town. Should I force you, is that the way?" With tactics like this, little wonder the white man needs some textual support. When a viewing position comparable to Ralph's and threats of sexual violence fail to get him what he wants, Ben challenges Ralph to a duel, but one in which he assumes a striking advantage. For after he breaks into a gun shop to arm himself and delivers bullets to his rival, he heads to the overdetermined rooftops to hunt Ralph down in the streets below. In an extended sequence in which they travel many blocks, the visual syntax from Ralph's arrival to the city returns, as he runs through the streets attempting to dodge a gaze that is now literally embodied. In no uncertain terms, Ben madly reclaims the visual and spatial position of superiority, and Ralph is resubjected to the position of a black man watched from above (figs. 5.27–5.28). At the very end Ben descends to the street and takes the hand Sarah offers him, linking him to her and Ralph, who holds her other hand, in the final shots (fig. 5.29). Finally, then, Ben's status remains the most ambiguous—his violent will to power exposed but also suddenly, inexplicably, abandoned and forgiven—but Ralph's claims to the penthouse point of view have been unquestionably overturned.

FIG. 5.23. The rivalry between men, overtly staged as a matter of vision.

FIG. 5.24

FIG. 5.25

FIG. 5.26

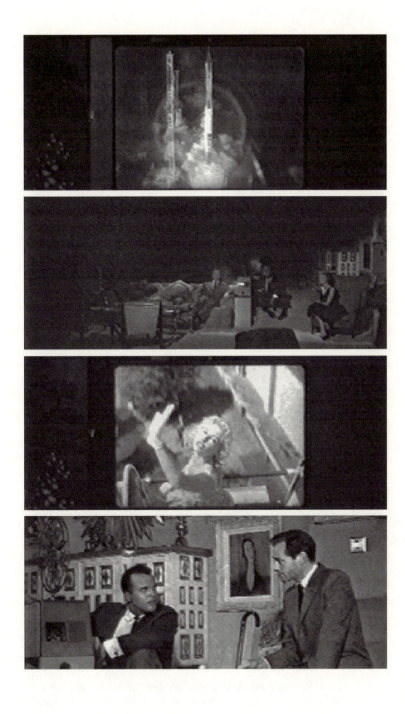

The final shot of the film watches the trio from on high as they walk into the deep vanishing point rendered by the lines of the street and surrounding buildings. While the distant onscreen subjects are for the moment subordinated to a look afforded only to the spectator, this dramatic final image, overlaid with a title that zooms out to declare it "THE BEGINNING," suggests that the future rests not only on a very particular interracial union, between men through the woman, but on the film's dramatic articulations of these as relations of vision and space (fig. 5.30).[84]

DEFERRED VISIONS OF THE FUTURE

This chapter has demonstrated palpable, widespread tension between vivid indicators that dominant forms are on the verge of collapse and the tenacious drive of those forms to revise and (attempt to) restore. This is poignantly encapsulated in the fact that one of Belafonte's own critical responses to *Island in the Sun* was *The World, the Flesh, and the Devil*—the first film to come out of his own company, Harbel Productions. Although Belafonte was reportedly "through with problem pictures about interracial relations" in the sensational summer of 1957, and would become dissatisfied with *The World, the Flesh, and the Devil* at some point in production, the fact is that that film at once held out the promise of an opportunity to defy the limits of the cycle he had helped make popular and intensified those limits with its relentless visual plotting of subject positions.[85]

Looking back on all this from another vantage point, the tremendous force of the textual mechanisms at work is further suggested by the fact that Gregory Peck's Atticus Finch and Spencer Tracy as Sidney Poitier's soon-to-be-father-in-law are the Hollywood white men popular culture *remembers* as having negotiated American miscegenation fantasies in the civil rights era, not the deranged and desperate subjects of the late 1950s. And yet, when we do remember the wild schemes then required to even partially, anxiously suspend miscegenation taboos, as well as their considerably mixed reception, it becomes all the more apparent that classical forms were precisely *not* commanding faith. Despite spectacular efforts to the contrary, the futures of this chapter's "recovered" white men—an amputee, a recovering mental patient, and sundry killers, rapists, and

---

FIG. 5.27. The conventional visual-racial order is forcibly, albeit madly, restored.
FIG. 5.28
FIG. 5.29. Down in the street, the white woman and the black man unite.
FIG. 5.30. Walking into the future, the momentary interracial couple quickly becomes a trio.

THE BEGINNING

heavy drinkers among them—are iffy at best. My larger purpose, then, has been to bring to our attention the ways in which such chronic vulnerabilities coexist with—call forth and yet are by no means fully mended by—the powerful cinematic forms also perpetually on display. To make sense of both trends and their simultaneity in this period, we might conclude that even as such classical Hollywood forms repeatedly showed themselves to be insufficient in the face of manifold social and psychological challenges, they continued to significantly shape the forms of change imaginable.

Most salient here are the ways the fifties films repeatedly articulate the end of old, excessively racial orders (plantations, colonies, etc.) through newly, excessively gendered ones. While suburban migration in postwar U.S. culture has been understood in part as a refusal of anything approaching interracial desire, for example, it is at times imagined in these texts as a means of escape for the mixed and tinted unions that survive.[86] In addition to Sylvia's dream of a "little house" in New England, Chuck and Ginny's finally restored faith in each other and the law make it easy to imagine that as they drive away from the courthouse at film's end they go in search of a more accommodating neighborhood in which to recreate the suburban love nest with which the film began. And what better place in 1957 than the suburbs to accommodate Lloyd Gruver's desire for "a wife, . . . a family, a home, in America, . . . a home like that"—a place where his formerly androgynous lover could finally "become a woman, and a mother" in no uncertain terms. And even if the setting of *Far Horizons* prohibits any literal image of ranch homes or picture windows, Donna Reed's Sacajawea nonetheless invites us to imagine a kindred space where the wives of white men "simply" cook, do housework, and have babies.

That these films repeatedly end with only partial, incomplete hints of such relocations is an appropriate place for us to close as well. At one level, the withholding of images of the future clearly reminds us of the transitional status of these fantasies as they seek to navigate profoundly complicated, incomplete forms of cultural change. At another, as I have suggested, hints of a selectively integrated suburbia suggest that the future could perhaps best be imagined in dominant culture at this point in visual and spatial terms more akin to television than classical cinema. In light of the film industry's own notorious period of crisis in the face of televisual competition, it is again not surprising that such a future would be withheld. For despite the manifold crises on display throughout these films, what they regularly assert instead in their finales is the kind of grand vision afforded by Hollywood cinema. After David Boyeur has fully rejected Mavis Norman, the images that close *Island in the Sun*, reminiscent of its opening, begin just behind him as he heads down a dirt road at sunset; but a significant distance opens up between the camera's look and David's as he walks into the distance, leaving the camera itself in the final position of authoritative vision just before a closing shot of the map with which the film began. Similar are the final separations of the camera from characters who have competed for alignment with it in *The Searchers* final gaze at Ethan walking into the desert, and *The World, the Flesh, and the Devil*'s bird's-eye shot of the interracial trio walking into the deep horizon of an empty Manhattan street. And it is perhaps fitting to end here with the final aerial shot from *South Pacific* that captures the newly formed interracial family on their terrace atop what looks like their own private little island (a high-rent suburb in the South Pacific?). While it is not unique to these films or this period to end with a look that no character shares, in context these finally, emphatically, cinematic images—images that flaunt the scale, color, perspectives, and locations obtainable through a Hollywood image—reveal the eye of a camera further straining to assert itself. To end with this observation is by no means to grant final authority to Hollywood conventions but to register again the excesses of their anxious repetition.

CHAPTER SIX

Guess Who's Coming to Dinner with Eldridge Cleaver and the Supreme Court, or Reforming Popular Racial Memory with Hepburn and Tracy

HANDCUFFED, 1967/68

In light of the intertwined legacies of history, fantasy, and representation examined in this book, it is fitting, if not obligatory, to close these chapters by considering what it means that the first Hollywood film to unequivocally reject the miscegenation taboo was a Tracy and Hepburn film that would go on to become the most popular interracial text of its era, and arguably of the late twentieth century.[1] The question becomes all the more intriguing when we recognize that *Guess Who's Coming to Dinner* (1967), was in fact one of three tremendously influential interracial texts to appear within less than a year. Just months before the release of the instantly celebrated and ridiculed screen verdict on the subject, the Supreme Court in June of 1967 handed down its decision, *Loving v. Virginia*, that finally rendered laws prohibiting interracial marriage unconstitutional. And not long after the film's December release, Eldridge Cleaver, then minister of information for the Black Panther Party, published a collection of boldly personal and political essays that meditate extensively on fantasies of interracial sex that had marked his experiences as a young black man; that book, *Soul on Ice* (March 1968), quickly became a widely discussed and debated best-seller.[2] While *Guess, Loving,* and *Soul* thus form a trio of authors, agendas, and implied audiences that could hardly be more different from one another, together they cut across a wide swath of popular culture to suggest that dominant American legacies of miscegenation were being confronted more directly than ever before. This in turn makes all the more consequential the terms and conditions under which those legacies were publicly avowed and (still) repressed.

While Cleaver exposed multiple forms of racial, sexual, and economic oppression regularly embedded in dominant fantasies and practices of interracial sex, the Court remained virtually silent on such histories in the *Loving* decision, and *Guess Who's Coming to Dinner* could not see its way to openly admitting them but also could not manage fully to avoid them. Yet despite their varied thresholds of cultural knowledge and amnesia, this chapter will argue that these texts demonstrate a shared ability to divest conventional commitments to racial hierarchy secured through the miscegenation taboo only by reasserting rigid conventions of gender and sex. What is more, by reevaluating *Guess Who's Coming to Dinner* in this context, I invite us to take seriously not only how that film so successfully masked the most critical histories of the phobia it allegedly renounced but also how central were classical cinematic forms of vision, space, and spectatorship to that project.

Each of the three texts in question could be said to revolve around one or more mixed couples who function as highly condensed figures within which a range of social categories and conflicts converge. In a period marked at once by the felt limits as well as the successes of the civil rights movement, local and global crises over the Vietnam War, the resuscitation of the women's movement, and various countercultures, divergent attempts to rethink and refashion such couples find in them the means to rearticulate shifting notions not only of race and gender but also of class and generation. Indeed, they repeatedly demonstrate the increasing difficulty of extricating each of these terms and identities from the others. Whereas Cleaver's text critiques some of the powerful effects of that condensation, the more mainstream liberal texts from Hollywood and the Court compound it by insisting on the singularity of the racial questions these couples pose. This is apparent in the film when Spencer Tracy's character sums up the difficulties his daughter and her fiancé will face as the result of their "pigmentation problem." Reducing the dilemma to color, this formulation both clouds the complex meanings of "race" at issue and masks the film's use of this couple to simultaneously navigate contemporary anxieties about gender, sex, class, and the generational divide.

Even a brief, introductory glance at *Guess* quickly reveals the much more complex constellation of differences tangled and untangled in and through its primary couple. Joey (Katharine Houghton), as Matt and Christina Drayton (Spencer Tracy and Katharine Hepburn) tellingly call their daughter, is "a very determined young woman" who wears pants, travels to Hawaii alone, suddenly brings home a black fiancé, frankly expresses her interest in sex with him, and demands that her parents immediately declare their approval of her imminent marriage. Yet she also continuously demonstrates that in the eyes and company of Dr. John Prentice (Sidney Poitier), who alone insists on calling her Joanna, she is delighted to melt and mold her independent spirit into the supporting role of wife, second in its devoted performance only to the one Hepburn plays to Tracy's aging, but still firmly ruling, patriarch.[3] And while this gender drama of taming spunky Joey into the more docile Joanna is tended to through the more talked about "pigmentation" plot, the class conditions that underwrite any possibility of integrating the very white Drayton home are unmistakable: in the extravagance of their mansion overlooking San Francisco Bay; in the black maids who keep it running and get the eponymous dinner on the table; and in John's working-class parents who arrive as decidedly temporary guests, as if to assure that this proposed mixing need not seriously threaten the class structure upon which the Drayton household clearly rests. Finally, although viewers catching the film on cable decades later would be hard-pressed to recall from the film itself *either* that the city in which it is so visibly located was widely known that year as host to the "Summer of Love" (and its public celebrations of sex, drugs, and rock and roll) *or* that loud calls for "black power" had been coming from just across the bay the Drayton home so spectacularly surveys, the dramatic day that marks the temporal sweep of the film's plot is nonetheless punctuated by vivid, albeit highly constrained, eruptions of those highly charged places and times.

The multiplicity of cultural revolutions thus stirring amid the allegedly singular "pigmentation problem" is implied at the outset in the film's literal announcement of the new couple. When Matt Drayton makes his first appearance, arriving home one afternoon not long after his daughter and her new fiancé, his maid, Tillie (Isabell Sanford), greets him at the door and declares, "Mr. Drayton, all hell done broke loose now!" This early line becomes a sort of framing device for Matt's and the film's "extraordinary day" when he recalls it at the opening of his climactic speech that tries to put it all back together at the end. That a similar "all" is at risk in the interracial couples treated by Cleaver and the Court is evidenced to varying degrees in their texts as well, where those couples also function as the textual means through which several kinds of difference are mutually formed, and must be mutually refashioned.

Of the three texts it is *Soul on Ice* that most explicitly articulates such interlocking structures and the ties that can bind them through dominant fantasies of miscegenation. Cleaver insists that the social and psychic injuries that ensue from those fantasies, especially the "sickness between the white woman and the black man," "must be brought out into the open, dealt with and resolved," and that "all of us, the entire nation, will be better off if we bring it all out front."[4] As he analyzes this culturally produced "sickness," a larger model of identity and difference gradually emerges. This model, which he refers to as "myth" (163), even as he clearly understands it to have profoundly real effects on American psyches and institutions, posits identity in U.S. culture as organized simultaneously around two intersecting binary axes; male-female and black-white. For Cleaver, this results in four distinct positions—white man, white woman, black man, and black woman—each of which is defined in opposition to the others.[5] After describing the dominant scripts of these four mythic characters (scripts that are multiply marked by fantasies of interracial sex), a fictional character whose voice is rhymed with the author's reflects:

> All this is tied up together in a crazy way which was never too clear to me. At one time it seems absolutely clear and at other times I don't believe in it. It reminds me of two sets of handcuffs that have all four of us tied up together, holding all black and white flesh in a certain mold. (162–63)

Understanding these "two sets of handcuffs" as racial and sexual difference intertwined, the metaphor resonates deeply with the representations at issue throughout Cleaver's book, as well as my own. For it envisions a structure wherein the position of any one of those raced and gendered subjects "tied up together" necessarily affects, or is affected by, the position of each of the others. Based on what we know from the representational "handcuffs" charted in the present study, we could explain the alternating clarity and craziness the character associates with this "mold" as following, on the one hand, from the relentless terms of identity and relation it commands and forbids, and, on the other, from the dizzying complexity of the permutations that can arise as one or more of the handcuffed subjects has cause to move.

This chapter seeks to analyze that tightly regulated movement as charted within and across *Loving v. Virginia*, *Soul on Ice*, and especially *Guess Who's Coming to Dinner*. Cleaver's double handcuffs—which his own conceptions of labor invite us to triple if we disentangle race from class, and which multiply and divide yet further when we factor in the calls for generational change implicit throughout his text—serve as a particularly apt metaphor with which to do so at a moment so marked by the multiple "movements" of the late sixties. For certainly it was in part the intersection and collision of those movements, combined with the shattering violence of race riots, assassinations, and a gruesome war, that created the era's particular sense that all was, in fact, breaking loose. And it is important for this project that Cleaver's metaphorical handcuffs speak not just of ideological constructs but of lived and psychological experience, molding not only social positions but also the vulnerable "flesh" of human beings and their innermost conceptions of self, other, difference, and relation.[6] Cleaver's evident desire to break free demands for him both an explicitly political project, as represented by his work with the Panthers, and a process of self-dissection and psychic reassemblage that is also vividly enacted in the pages of his book.[7] So, too, even if under more guarded terms, *Loving*'s defense of the right to marry as "fundamental to our very existence and survival" and *Guess Who's Coming to Dinner*'s "what-would-you-do-if-your-daughter . . ." premise also figure their treatments of interracial intimacy as attempts to address the social questions such intimacy has always opened onto at the most deeply personal of levels.[8]

It is precisely because of the simultaneously social and psychological significance these texts still hold, "for all of us, the entire nation," that this chapter queries the terms and conditions under which they boldly confronted the legacies of miscegenation handed down to them—from the courts, from Hollywood, and from experiences of everyday life. In short, this chapter asks, what are the implications of Cleaver's metaphorical "handcuffs" for the textual production of popular American memory, and forgetting, in these unprecedented interracial texts of 1967 and 1968?

From Miscegenation to Marxism

Before turning to the conditions under which Hollywood and the Supreme Court renounced codes against miscegenation, it is useful to further mine Cleaver's more radical reckoning of those codes' functions and effects. For his text not only speaks of a black male experience that is all but impossible to see in the white texts but also keenly moves between starkly personal reflection on his own preoccupations with white women and equally stark analysis of the larger social structures those preoccupations enact and resist.

Early in *Soul on Ice*, Cleaver tellingly relates his own intellectual history as having been marked by a pivotal shift from obsessions with miscegenation to a new obsession with the writings of Karl Marx and other "readings into the history of socialism" (16, 12). He locates this shift just after a " 'nervous breakdown' " in the wake of Emmett Till's murder in Mississippi, precipitated by the following event:

> One day I saw in a magazine a picture of the white woman with whom Emmett Till was said to have flirted. While looking at the picture, I felt that little tension in the center of my chest I experience when a woman appeals to me. I was disgusted and angry with myself. Here was a woman who had caused the death of a black, possibly because, when he looked at her, he also felt the same tensions of lust and desire in his chest—and probably for the same general reasons that I felt them. It was all unacceptable to me. I looked at the picture again and again, and in spite of everything and against my will and the hate I felt for the woman and all that she represented, she appealed to me. I flew into a rage at myself, at America, at white women, at the history that had placed those tensions of lust and desire in my chest. (11)

While the culpable "history" here named gets variously elaborated throughout the essays that follow this first, it will prove central to Cleaver's ongoing analysis of interracial desire and the identities articulated through it that the announced cure to the breakdown set off by the white woman's picture is his discovery of Marx (12). Reading Marx, "although he kept me with a headache," "was like taking medicine" and "diverted me from my previous preoccupation: morbid broodings on the black man and the white woman" (12). This transformation narrative is complicated by the fact that such "morbid broodings" would not disappear: by his own account Cleaver would go on to rape white women after release from the prison term being served at the time of the breakdown; then, back in prison, he would write this essay that famously confesses, and less famously but emphatically renounces, his earlier performance of interracial rape as "an insurrectionary act" (14).[9] Nonetheless, that Cleaver's own narrative emphasizes this turn in his thinking from "morbid broodings" over miscegenation to curative "headache[s]" over Marx, and that his writings suggest that turn to have marked something more like a junction between two conceptual paths he would continue to move between, strikes to the heart of his insistence throughout *Soul on Ice* that a series of social hierarchies—namely, those of race, gender, sexuality, and class—intersect to form the peculiar handcuffs of social and psychic life in the United States.

Although Cleaver does not expound on the relations between his preoccupations with miscegenation and Marx, reverberations between those two lines of his thought are amply detected throughout the book. Certainly a Marxist critique of capitalism informs Cleaver's implicitly black nationalist critique of the civil rights movement, and, as we will see, his analysis of the psychosexual dimensions of America's "racial caste system" is equally imprinted by class consciousness (189).[10] At the same time, his attention to the "double handcuffs" and his critique of dominant miscegenation fantasies that reproduce them emphasize in ways Marx obviously does not that the classical U.S. imaginary articulates and legitimates dominant economic relations through a fantasmatic regime that is relentlessly sexed and raced.

Although Cleaver at times seems to conflate race and class, his understanding that race functions in part to sustain a class structure is occasionally made explicit by, and is always implicit in, his interlocked foursome.[11] He discusses this at length in two of the major analytical essays from the final section of the book, "White Woman, Black Man." We first learn of the mythic four in the opening chapter to that section, "The Allegory of the Black Eunuchs," where they are introduced by "the Lazarus" (the character who describes the double handcuffs) as he tries to explain his sexual obsession with white women to a group of younger black men. Lazarus begins his explanation with a raced and sexed model of identity inherited from slavery, where the meaning of "white" and "black" are free and enslaved, respectively: "I know that the white man made the black woman the symbol of slavery and the white woman the symbol of freedom. Every time I embrace a black woman I'm embracing slavery, and when I put my arms around a white woman, well, I'm hugging freedom" (160). As Lazarus's narrative continues, the free-enslaved dichotomy is elaborated further as a mind-body dichotomy that in turn reflects and enforces a labor relation. All these meanings conjoin to script the handcuffed cast of four. As Lazarus tells it, "The white man wants to be the *brain* and . . . wants us to be the muscle, the *body*" (162, original emphasis). He therefore "turned himself into the Omnipotent Administrator and established himself in the Front Office. And he turned the black man into the Supermasculine Menial and kicked him out into the fields." This understanding of black defined as body and labor leads Lazarus to explain its feminized version in "the myth of the strong black woman," "self-reliant Amazon . . . Aunt Jemima." And because each of these positions has both a sexed and a raced opposite, that myth is also "the other side of the coin of the myth of the beautiful dumb blonde" (162). The white woman's form of disembodiment and distance from labor is not a preponderance of "brain" but a gendered deformation of it: she is a "weak-minded, weak-bodied, delicate freak . . . on a pedestal" (162).

Cleaver further elaborates this mythic foursome in a more direct, analytical voice in the next essay, "The Primeval Mitosis," and here his miscegenetic and Marxist visions most clearly converge. Three elements of this convergence are especially pertinent to the chapter at hand: (1) Cleaver's understanding of the primacy of representation and fantasy to dominant American structures of racism; (2) his attempt to reverse the trajectory of dominant American fantasies of miscegenation by exposing the intertwined hierarchies of class and gender, as well as race, routinely secured by miscegenation rhetoric; and (3) his deep commitment to conventional forms of sexual difference, even as he seeks to radically critique and reconceptualize dominant orders of race and class.

The first of these speaks to the way *Soul on Ice* articulates not just a complex set of social structures but a complex regime of representation in popular American culture. For while Cleaver's vocabulary implies his handcuffed foursome to be a direct product of slavery, it is better understood as a later descendant of that history as rewritten by late nineteenth- and twentieth-century representations. His figuration of the "Supermasculine Menial" as pure body, even pure penis in some passages, does not match up with historical accounts of a system that regularly denied black men any such potent claims, but it does of course describe revisionist representations of black masculinity throughout white culture after the Civil War.[12] Indeed, readers of my own chapters will recognize the reverberations between Cleaver's metaphors (white minds vs. sexualized black bodies, "delicate" white women vs. "Aunt Jemima[s]," etc.) and the dominant cinematic representations of difference excavated here.[13] So powerful are his insights, in fact, that *Soul on Ice*'s contribution to a then-struggling civil rights movement arguably lies as much in its understanding of the power of popular representation to shape and deform identity as in its analysis of the sexual and economic structures of American racism.

Second, the Marxism of Cleaver's miscegenation critique, if you will, leads him to expose, or at least reverse the trajectory of, the veiled leaps that typically organize the logic of dominant miscegenation fantasies. Whereas those fantasies loudly police "race" while effectively (though more quietly) regulating class and gender relations as well, Cleaver's "morbid broodings" lead him to consider not only the racial but also the sexual and class work performed in the interracial fantasies he has at times internalized. In his discussions of various permutations of (hetero)desire between blacks and whites (black men for white women, white women for black men, etc.), he typically understands such desires to be driven by a given subject's wish to acquire or align with forms of privilege or potency denied his or her own raced-classed-sexed position. *Soul on Ice* thus insists on the necessity of recognizing this utterly intertwined series of hierarchies in any attempt to cure the social "sickness" symbolized by the miscegenation taboo.

Equally crucial to Cleaver's transformative vision, although seemingly at odds with his intersectional critique, are its rigidly sexed and gendered limits. For although his desire to dismantle dominant structures of race and class is palpable throughout the book, he not only is committed to the most conservative terms of sexual difference but uses them to fundamentally organize his conception of race-class revolution and a world beyond it.[14] These conditions are most explicit, and excessive, in the penultimate chapter, "The Primeval Mitosis." After beginning with a series of provocative quotations on the nature of gender and sex, the chapter continues in Cleaver's own words, seemingly inspired by the likes of Darwin and Plato: "The roots of heterosexuality are buried in that evolutionary choice made long ago in some misty past . . . by some unknown forerunner of Homo sapiens. Struggling up from some murky swamp, some stagnant mudhole, some peaceful meadow, that unknown ancestor of Man/Woman, by some weird mitosis of the essence, divided its Unitary Self in half" (177). This feverish mixture of origin stories continues, and Cleaver spins it to craft a theory of the "dynamic magnetism of opposites—the Primeval Urge—which exerts an irresistible attraction between the male and female hemispheres, ever tending to fuse them back together into a unity in which the male and female realize their true nature" (177). This language of the "true nature," "biology," and "essence" that yield the "eternal and unwavering motivation of . . . man and woman" continues for several paragraphs and undergirds the entire chapter (177). And its purpose, we soon discover, is to provide the "unwavering" force that will guide us toward, and finally offer the "optimal conditions" of, "a Classless Society": "Man's continual striving for a Unitary Sexual Image, which can only be achieved in a Unitary Society, becomes a basic driving force of the Class Struggle, which is, in turn, the dynamic of history. The quest for the Apocalyptic Fusion [of male and female] will find optimal conditions only in a Classless Society, the absence of classes being the *sine qua non* for the existence of a Unitary Society in which the Unitary Sexual Image can be achieved" (177–78).

While words like "fusion" and "Unitary" might suggest a desire to overcome classical sexual binaries, no such overcoming is ever articulated. Instead, the language works to relentlessly shape, and sex, the book's movement toward race-class liberation. While the second sentence of the passage just cited could be read to privilege class struggle as the primary goal, which then makes possible the conditions for "the Unitary Sexual Image" (Cleaver's idealized "fusion" of male and female), the first more startlingly suggests a heterosexual impulse that is not only prior to but a "driving force of the Class Struggle" and "history" itself.[15] Little doubt remains, then, as to which forms of difference Cleaver seeks to reconceive, and which will forever determine us from the "misty," "murky" "mudhole" of primal "Man."[16]

The book's intertwined vision of revolution and sexual determinism is also implicit in its overall structure, composed of essays that chart a racially shifting sequence of hetero-couplings that resolve with an open letter, "To All Black Women, from All Black Men."[17] Here the author declares a sexual reunion of black men and women as the means, simultaneously, to forge a black utopia and to resurrect black masculinity. While this letter openly recognizes the violence of slavery to black women, it continues to make tremendously gendered demands of them:

Across the naked abyss of negated masculinity, of four hundred years minus my Balls, we face each other today, my Queen. I feel a deep, terrifying hurt, the pain of humiliation of the vanquished warrior. . . . I fear I will fail unless you reach out to me, tune in on me with the antenna of your love. . . . Let me drink from the river of your love at its source, let the lines of force of your love seize my soul by its core and heal the wound of my Castration, let my convex exile end its haunted Odyssey in your concave essence which receives that it may give. Flower of Africa, it is only through the liberating power of your *re*-love that my manhood can be redeemed. (206–7)

Amid the desperation so described, the writer clings to sexual difference as the one thing that can give not only comfort but also shape (his "convex exile" seeking her "convex essence") and purpose to a masculine body and soul otherwise broken, impotent, frozen. Closing the letter, and the book, with a final image of a new racial community built from heterosexual union—with imagery and language that surprisingly echoes *The Birth of a Nation*'s final vision, even as it overthrows its white supremacy—Cleaver finally calls: "Put on your crown, my Queen, and we will build a New City on these ruins" (210).

Repeatedly, then, sexual difference functions as a kind of absolute limit in this self-consciously revolutionary text—the one order of difference it thoroughly depends on amid its embrace of a series of radical transgressions and dismantlings. Cleaver announces as much when he writes: "All men must have [a male 'self-image'] or they start seeing themselves as women, women start seeing them as women, then women lose their own self-image, and soon nobody knows what they are themselves or what anyone else is—that is to say, the world starts looking precisely as it looks today" (94). Strikingly, as we will soon see, it is precisely such deep commitments to phallocentrism and heterosexuality accompanying visions of racial progress that make this popular, "radical," black treatment of interracial sex from 1968 most akin to its more mainstream white counterparts.[18]

The Memory of *Loving*

After Cleaver's fierce reckoning with dominant American legacies of miscegenation, even with its rampant sexual essentialisms, the Supreme Court's could hardly seem tamer. And, I suggest, this is not simply the product of an admittedly jarring shift from Cleaver's baldly sexual and political language to the formal distance and legal obligations of juridical prose. Rather, both *Loving*'s deferred history and its textual details suggest further the terms and conditions under which laws against interracial marriage could be denounced and divested by dominant white culture. Especially noticeable, following Cleaver, are the Court's silences on the sexual and economic injuries historically legitimated by those laws, and the sexual straightjacket that holds together the destabilizing decision.

As legal historians tell the story, the Supreme Court's reluctance to address the matters at stake in interracial marriage laws was particularly palpable in the thirteen years prior to *Loving*, when the Court "bypassed four opportunities to rule on the constitutionality of miscegenation statutes before it finally faced the issue squarely in *Loving*."[19] The Court first refused to review *Jackson v. Alabama* just months after the original ruling in *Brown v. Board of Education* (1954) by denying certiorari, "the most effective way to weed out unimportant cases," even though "*Jackson* involved a federal question of the magnitude that would ordinarily warrant the Court's acceptance of it."[20] Its second and third refusals came in late 1955 and early 1956, respectively, when it first sent *Naim v. Naim* back to Virginia and then, upon its return, dismissed it on the grounds that it was "'devoid of [a] properly presented Federal Question.'"[21] In the words of two different legal scholars, the reasoning of the first gesture was "not well grounded on facts," and the second was "ludicrous."[22] The fourth pass came considerably later, in 1964, when in a case involving interracial cohabitation, not marriage (*McLaughlin v. Florida*), the Court found in favor of the cohabitants, and even went so far as to overturn the logic that had been essential to prior defenses of antimiscegenation marriage statutes, but refused to extend the new logic to marriage.[23]

This avoidance is typically interpreted as an act of caution in the wake of *Brown v. Board*. An unidentified justice was "reported to have said": "'One bombshell at a time is enough.'"[24] But precisely where or how another one might have gone off, for whom and in what form, is not exactly a simple question. In a history of the Court's ongoing avoidance of miscegenation cases, Chang Moon Sohn reveals that two very different constituencies were not ready for the Court to hear the question. On the one hand, as one might expect, "the fear of Southern whites that educational integration would eventually lead to interracial marriage" was audible immediately after *Brown* in the "mongrelization" rhetoric of White Citizens Councils, and in the public charge of Virginia's attorney general, Eugene Cook, "that *Brown* was the Court's way of paving the road for an attack on state miscegenation statutes" (155). But the National Association for the Advancement of Colored People (NAACP) and its then director-counsel, Thurgood Marshall, were also firmly against such an attack throughout the middle to late fifties, or at least refused to take part in it.[25] Marshall in particular "was much afraid that any [such] attack . . . so soon after *Brown* would enrage . . . Southern feeling, which in turn would have an adverse effect on school integration" (134). Sohn further problematizes such explanations with the record of the Court's own hesitations and a 1965 Gallup poll that, although confirming stronger antimiscegenation sentiment in the South (by blacks and whites), reported that "48% of [all] Americans approved of . . . laws making interracial marriage a crime."[26] Such details again remind us how intensely fraught were the historical circumstances within which the

Court was asked to consider the practices and beliefs embedded in these laws.

But what should we make of the decision that finally did reject them? Through a reading of the legal history behind *Loving*, Adrienne D. Davis has called it a "legally radical decision" because it struck down laws that had worked to "promote and maintain the racial and gender caste order of slavery."[27] Without denying such radical implications and progressive effects of the landmark decision, my close reading of the decision itself, in the larger context of this chapter's examination of popular memory being forged in the period, approaches *Loving* from a different vantage point. Being careful to avoid legal claims well beyond my expertise, as a critic of miscegenation rhetoric my analysis of *Loving* leads me to two by now rather simple but nonetheless significant observations: (1) even as it boldly indicts the "White Supremacy" of antimiscegenation laws, the decision remains silent on the histories of institutional oppression and exploitation they sanctioned; and (2) its final championing of marriage serves not only to affirm a normative sexual order but arguably to restabilize orders of class and race implicitly at risk in the decision.

After an introduction, the first of *Loving*'s two numbered sections provides the primary argument that the statutes in question violate the Fourteenth Amendment. The Court here extends its logic in the interracial cohabitation case a few years earlier, now fully rejecting earlier defenses of the marriage statutes that held them to be valid because they punished black and white parties equally: "The Equal Protection Clause requires the consideration of whether the classifications drawn by any statute constitute an arbitrary and invidious discrimination. The clear and central purpose of the Fourteenth Amendment was to eliminate all official state sources of invidious racial discrimination in the States."[28] These criteria then serve as the explicit grounds for the decision against Virginia: "There is patently no legitimate overriding purpose independent of invidious racial discrimination which justifies this classification. The fact that Virginia prohibits only interracial marriages involving white persons demonstrates that the racial classifications must stand on their own justification, as measures designed to maintain White Supremacy" (11). This final explanation echoes the Court's opening commentary in this section. There it rejected a prior Virginia ruling a little more than a decade earlier, which had "concluded that the State's legitimate purposes were 'to preserve the racial integrity of its citizens,' and to prevent 'the corruption of blood,' 'a mongrel breed of citizens,' and 'the obliteration of racial pride,' *obviously an endorsement of the doctrine of White Supremacy*" (7, emphasis mine). At the beginning and end of its main argument in *Loving*, then, the Court unflinching names "White Supremacy" as the cause and intended effect of the laws in question.

Because the rhetorical force of the decision so rests on this indictment, a consideration of its part in shaping the meaning and memory of interracial history would seem to beg the following questions: What explicit or implicit meanings of "White Supremacy" does *Loving* offer? And, in turn, how does it effectively interpret the miscegenation statutes for the legal record? Such questions quickly arise in the present context because, although the Court clearly argues that the statutes legitimate acts of "arbitrary and invidious discrimination" and white privilege, how exactly they do so—with what particular logics, mechanisms, or effects—is virtually impossible to discern from the decision. The meaning of "White Supremacy"—or, more precisely, how Virginia's marriage statutes seek to maintain whites as superior to other races—is only, at best, implicit.

While the condemnation following the earlier Virginia ruling cited here might be read to suggest that the statutes maintain white privilege by regulating whiteness as an exclusive social territory (e.g., " 'preserv[ing] the racial integrity of . . . citizens' "), the Court never says as much. What it does do, in the introduction, is invoke language that more explicitly reduces the terms and territories at stake, as we have seen elsewhere, to color. This comes with a citation of the Virginia court's assertion of a kind of divinely segmented global palette whose discrete, pure colors dare not be "mix[ed]": " 'Almighty God created the races white, black, yellow, malay and red, and he placed them on separate continents. And but for the interference with his arrangement there would be no cause for such marriages. The fact that he separated the races shows that he did not intend for the races to mix' " (*Loving*, 3). The Supreme Court is of course here citing a segregationist vision it will flatly reject. Nonetheless, this language of race as color lingers in *Loving* without comment. And when the Court later cites from its own concurring opinion in *McLaughlin*, it affirms more directly the notion that racial discrimination is reducible to color bias: "Indeed, two members of this Court have already stated that they 'cannot conceive of a valid legislative purpose . . . which makes the color of a person's skin the test of whether his conduct is a criminal offense' " (11). More important, coming near the climactic end of section I, as the last sentence of the paragraph immediately preceding the one that will deem Virginia's laws to be "measures designed to maintain White Supremacy," this rejection of a legal test based solely on skin color textually resides as the nearest thing to an explanation of how, precisely, such measures operate or might be detected.[29]

While the Court of course had every reason to reject discrimination keyed to skin color, what becomes increasingly noticeable from our vantage point is the virtual silence on the manifold forms of power (social, economic, sexual, and psychic) historically secured beneath this surface rhetoric. The one muted trace of that history comes and goes quickly in

Loving, and is entirely without elaboration. Sandwiched between a sentence that tallies the number of states then with similar laws still in place (16) and two more that discuss Virginia's Racial Integrity Act of 1924 from which "the present statutory scheme dates," we read: "Penalties for miscegenation arose as an incident to slavery and have been common in Virginia since the colonial period" (6).[30] Although this unspecified relation to slavery is not explained, a footnote directs us to a "historical discussion of Virginia's miscegenation statutes" in a contemporary law review. Yet the inquiring reader who seeks out that bulky article will find nowhere in its detailed history of criminal codes and punishments any discussion of their social or economic origins or effects, in relation to slavery or otherwise. The article urges the Court to overturn the remaining statutes on Fourteenth Amendment grounds, but of those statutes' historic function it says only: "It is possible that the original miscegenation bans served a legitimate purpose at a time when Negroes were essentially an alien part of the community"[31] This is the sole source the Court offers to the reader of *Loving* should she want to learn something about the history of the laws at issue.

For readers suspecting, as I did, that the Court's silence must at least partly be explainable by the terms with which the case was presented to it, the written arguments filed by the Lovings' attorneys could not be more startling. While the Court's decision alone would lead us to think that those attorneys argued the case only as a matter of Equal Protection and Due Process, what we find in their brief to the Court is that before turning to those arguments they argued in great detail, and with very different footnotes, exactly what is most significantly absent from the Court's opinion; namely, that miscegenation laws were "originally passed primarily for economic and social reasons as means to foster and implement the institution of slavery" and continued to "perpetuate and foster illicit exploitative sex relationships [of the sort for which they were] explicitly designed."[32] And the appellant's brief gets very specific about how exactly the laws worked toward these ends. Under slavery, it explains, when slaves "intermixed to a considerable extent" with "indentured white servants" who "usually served out a seven-year contract while the Negro or Indian might be enslaved for life," "slaveowners wanted protection from the loss of their slave property through intermarriage with a free white" (16–17). And laws that rendered "illegitimate [the children born of] Negro slaves and white masters," and determined the slave or free status of such children "according to the condition of the mother . . . according to some historians, led to intentional slave breeding by slave-owners" (17). The brief goes on to claim that these laws continue to function as "the State's official symbol of a caste system" (28), citing in support one of the very texts the Court itself cited in *Brown v. Board*.[33]

Yet, whereas in that earlier case the Court had cited directly Gunnar Myrdal's *An American Dilemma* (among other texts) about the psychological effects of segregation, *Loving* takes up none of that book's claims, extensively reprinted for it in the appellant's brief, about relations between miscegenation taboos and social hierarchies.[34] This omission is particularly noteworthy since Myrdal digs beneath precisely the superficial explanations referenced in *Loving*. As the brief cites him: " 'The great majority of non-liberal white Southerners utilize the dread of 'intermarriage' . . . to justify discriminations which have quite other and wider goals than the purity of the white race. . . . what white people really want is to keep the Negroes in a lower status.' "[35]

As one reads pointed, elaborated claims like these leaping out from the pages of the appellant's brief, the Court's silence in *Loving* on anything like the mechanisms of sexual and economic exploitation embedded in the laws at issue only becomes louder and louder. Insofar as the Fourteenth Amendment arguments required the determination of "invidious" racial distinctions, the brief would seem to offer ample material. More to the point, that *Loving* refers to none of it suggests that even in 1967 the Court could boldly condemn antimiscegenation laws so long as the specific forms of power and oppression legitimated through them not be named.[36] Whatever the causes and intentions that produced that silence— and one can imagine a variety of them, including a pragmatic desire in the ever more explosive racial climate of the late sixties not to detonate, unnecessarily, the *atomic* bomb of this history spoken in the fullest sense—looking back at the history of memory in question, the decision now appears symptomatic of, and helps us understand, the ways in which mainstream American culture managed to keep the cultural meanings of the taboo at bay, even as it sought to dismantle it.

Also relevant to the larger shaping of history and memory in question is the way the Court supplements its arguably incomplete treatment of racial institutions in section I with a thorough embrace in section II of the institution of marriage. Technically, race and the Fourteenth Amendment are still at issue, as the Court (like the appellant's brief before it) argues Virginia to be violating due process by racially restricting "the freedom of choice to marry" (12). But the end of the opinion thus provided shapes and seals the terms under which the Court confronts American legacies of miscegenation in several significant ways.

In tone and content, there is a palpable sense of relief in section II at having maneuvered through the most difficult matters of slavery, segregation, and white supremacy in the minefield that was section I, emerging with the renewed certainty and simplicity of affirming "one of the 'basic civil rights of man' " (12). In part, this works to conclude the deci-

sion in a voice that compounds the silences here detected with a re-
sounding call for among the most personal of liberties:

> The freedom to marry has long been recognized as one of the vital personal
> rights essential to the orderly pursuit of happiness by free men.
>
> Marriage is one of the "basic civil rights of man," fundamental to our very
> existence and survival. To deny this fundamental freedom on so unsupportable
> a basis as the racial classifications embodied in these statutes . . . is surely to
> deprive all the State's citizens of liberty without due process of law. The Four-
> teenth Amendment requires that the freedom of choice to marry not be re-
> stricted by invidious racial discriminations. Under our Constitution, the free-
> dom to marry, or not marry, a person of another race resides with the
> individual and cannot be infringed by the State. (12)

In addition to the obvious maleness of the named subjects of freedom,
striking in our context is the language of essence and origin that here nat-
uralizes the institution of marriage.[37] The Court not only cites case precedent when it declares marriage as among the "basic civil rights of man"
but in its own words, repeatedly—and not wholly unlike its black nationalist counterpart—declares its "vital," "essential" function, "fundamental to our very existence and survival." Such language leaves little
doubt as to the structuring function here granted the sexed, and sexing,
institution. *Loving* thus not only reminds us that the real problem with
color blindness is its muteness about institutionalized forms of inequality
and exploitation; it also suggests once again that as the rigid borders and
binary distinctions of one system of difference are increasingly challenged, the language of another is ready at hand to provide closure and a
renewed sense of order.

THINKING OF THE SELF AS A MAN

In some respects, after the preceding examination of the terms with
which its more expressly radical and conservative liberal contemporaries
avowed and disavowed American legacies of interracial sex, those of
Guess Who's Coming to Dinner come as even less of a surprise. Looking
and sounding more like the Warren Court than Eldridge Cleaver, Spencer
Tracy, as we have seen, sums up the young couple's dilemma as "a pigmentation problem," reducing the matter to a language of color that
avoids histories of exploitation and privilege nonetheless evident in his
hilltop mansion with seemingly all-white interiors and all-black servants.[38] And the history that seems to both surface and fade with the texts
just considered reminds us that such avoidance is already significantly

structured into the Hollywood text by casting the couple in question as a black man and a white woman. For even as this pairing implicitly confronts white culture's most popular, violent fantasies of miscegenation, it also allows for the continued forgetting, in effect, of *What Happened in the Tunnel* and on the plantation.[39]

In addition, the precise way the plot poses its central question—will the interracial couple's parents accept them?—sets the problem up as a conflict of husbands versus wives, mothers versus fathers, and its solution utterly depends on the nostalgic casting of Tracy and Hepburn, the aging star couple who had helped make the "battle of the sexes" a classic Hollywood subgenre.[40] Yet while the conventionality of such Hollywood rhetoric can make it difficult to immediately recognize the full reach of its impact in this case, the payoff of having traced similar rhetoric in the contemporary, nonfilmic texts—I hope—is that we are now better positioned to consider *Guess*'s particularly cinematic contributions to the larger histories of memory, identity, and representation in question. I approach this here first by examining how the film's narrative enacts the wider cultural tendency to tolerate, at times even celebrate, the opening up of formerly restricted racial institutions only by refortifying sexual ones. Then, in the final section, I consider how this most popularly remembered text of the chapter's trio elaborates this gesture in sometimes startlingly exact, revised but also consequently familiar, visual and spatial terms.

The centrality of sexual difference to this film is quickly demonstrated by the regularity with which contemporary reviewers understood it to be, at bottom, a Tracy and Hepburn movie. The nostalgia that saturates such accounts is compounded by the fact that *Guess* was the couple's first on-screen reunion in nine years and would also be their last. Fans knew before seeing the film that Tracy had died soon after shooting it, intensifying the already emotionally charged experience of watching him in a role in which he finally declares openly his passion for the woman long known as the primary but officially unrecognized woman in his life. So powerful was the performance, the reviews repeatedly insist, that even those who hated the film would love Tracy and Hepburn. Writing for *Life*, Richard Schickel judged *Guess* "false," "unbelievable," and "dishonest," but of the star couple he rejoiced: "They bicker fondly together in their patented manner, and for me, at least, their performances in this movie are beyond the bounds of criticism."[41] A reviewer at the *New Yorker* effectively describes the counterbalancing act detectable in many more reviews: "The movie insidiously charms us into ignoring its defects, and for this the credit must go to a superb cast."[42] While this praise is not exclusive to them, the reviewer makes it clear that Tracy and Hepburn are his shinning favorites: "When, at [the film's] climax, he turns to her and tells her what an old man remembers having loved, it is, for us who are permitted to overhear him, an experience that transcends the theatrical."

The film itself provides ample cause to take such responses seriously. In addition to the particular charms of this particular star couple, central to the text are several sexually differentiated elements grafted to them. The father's rule, the mother's delicate handling of him, and the house designed around them (with his bay-view study, paintings presumably from her art gallery decorating the interior walls, etc.) all provide a palpable sense of order and stability to a situation that nonetheless signifies the potential for significant social and personal upheaval. But clearly the most hallowed and central patriarchal structure of all is the father of the bride. For his "blessing" is the authoritative judgment around which the entire film revolves and without which, by the film's logic, everything really *will* fall apart. Indeed, most everything in the film—the content and structure of the plot, familial happiness, the marriage itself, and the political statement it will make—hinges on the white father's decision. *Guess* thus explicitly registers, elaborates, and responds to its presumably racial "problem" by translating it and its solution into decidedly gendered terms. When John battles his own father (Roy E. Glenn Sr.) near the end, championing his right to live as he chooses, his fierce speech climaxes with a line that not only reduces race to color but finally shears away both of those to suggest that sexual difference is now the only difference that should matter: "*Dad, dad,*" John pleads, "you think of yourself as a colored man, I think of myself as a *man.*"[43]

Equally revealing is the fact that amid the many deliberations of this marriage, there is little, if any, real discussion of race. Characters repeatedly remark on the match being unexpected and a "shock," and a few comments are made to the effect that others will make it difficult for the couple and any children they might have. Yet, while we see Matt debate with John about whether blacks have "a special sense of rhythm" and announce to Christina his astonishment that a black mailman could produce such a fine son (a doctor for the World Health Organization, a distinguished scholar, etc.), we hear none of the specific feelings or fears that make him initially object to his daughter's marrying a black man, even though he does so openly, almost immediately, and until the film's last scene. While it is not surprising that a proudly liberal Hollywood film would not make a "hero" like Drayton/Tracy speak the ugliest white phobias of miscegenation, such silences nonetheless signal the patriarchal plot's relative muteness on racial matters, despite its alleged preoccupation with them.

This reticence might be productively compared to the Court's apparent choice, albeit under very different circumstances, to not dig too deeply into the causes and practices underlying "White Supremacy" in *Loving*.

For while that case obviously had considerably more authority and intent to change social institutions, the Hollywood film also made popular a message many still were not ready to hear. And yet in so doing, it too inadvertently perpetuates the amnesiac effect the miscegenation taboo worked to secure in the first place, when it denied and secured social and economic territories staked out by "race" by displacing their defense onto a terrain feigned to be purely personal and sexual. And in *Guess* it would seem especially unthinkable to remember such structural histories, since the (beloved) Draytons' identity and position so clearly depend on forgetting them. (To John's parents, Matt introduces Tillie, in her maid's outfit waiting to serve before the food gets cold, as "a member of this family for twenty-two years.") It thus goes without saying in this film, but is glaringly visible even before conventions of sex and gender can step in to work out the details, that any racial accommodations this family can make are only possible so long as they in no way disturb its class status. But keeping that condition as unspoken as it is intact, in a kind of romantic rewriting of *Birth*'s interracial rape plot, *Guess*'s patriarchal plot nonetheless secures the white man's authority over the white woman and her black lover by having the first finally declare that the *only* thing that matters is the love and regard of two individuals for each other.

That said, and despite the overpowering centripetal force whereby all textual paths lead back to Matt Drayton/Spencer Tracy in anticipation of his final speech, in addition to the prospect of a black son-in-law *Guess* registers several potential forces that could, and in some other parts of the universe already do, seriously challenge the old white man's authority in ways the film itself does not.

The film's only references to contemporary black liberation struggles are channeled through Tillie and played for laughs in a not-so-modern minstrel style. Watching from the kitchen as John and Matt confer on the terrace, she muses loudly, "Civil rights is one thing, but this here is *somethin'* else!" Catching John unawares as he changes clothes in the guest room, she dresses him down as "one of those *smooth*-talkin', *smart*-ass niggers just out for all you can get, with your *black* power and all that other trouble-makin' nonsense!" Railing on, she threatens, "You bring any trouble in here, and you just like to find out what black power *really* means!" The sense in this scene of the eruption of something otherwise contained is amplified by the camera's sudden tilt to a jarring canted angle, the only such deviation from standard framing conventions in the film. Linking the excessive performance here demanded of Isabell Sanford to a tradition of "faithful servants" dating back to *The Birth of a Nation*, James Baldwin described Tillie in this scene as "prepared to protect her golden-haired mistress from the clutches of this black ape by any means necessary."[44] What his linguistic play signals, in part, is the textual reversal whereby the film denies and discredits black nationalism by applying its terms to a force here deemed purely sexual.

Less hysterical, but arguably even more contained, are the film's brief glimpses of youth culture. Never so explicitly named as "civil rights" or "black power," flower power might be said to silently flash upon the screen in the image of Joey's pale hand reaching into and across a medium shot of John's dark face (as he looks out across the city) to tuck a daisy behind his ear (fig. 6.1). Although the image of the clean-cut pair chatting on the terrace of her parents' palatial residence could hardly be more unlike stock imagery of hippies hanging out in the park and in the streets that summer, the daisy here commences a brief glimpse in this sequence of a nonetheless modern romance, marked not only by the emphasized difference in skin tones but also by Joey's tomboyish plunking down on a stool with knees apart as the two tease and confide in one another (fig. 6.2).[45] Yet, with a zoom-out we realize this image is being watched from inside the house by Christina, and then also by Matt, and soon what began as the image of a new kind of love is read by, and compared to, the image of Tracy and Hepburn (fig. 6.3). As we watch the older couple standing together, Christina describes how moved she is to see Joey so happy, and the film offers us the promise that older form(ula)s of romance will eventually move the old man to accept the young couple.

Far more pronounced than these fleeting eruptions of civil rights and counterculture are the feelings of old age and conservatism they breed in a man like Matt Drayton. This is most explicit in a scene in which Matt, insisting that he and Christina get out of the house before the dinner party begins, takes her for a drive that ends up at Mel's Drive-In. Even here, where Matt is literally surrounded and confronted by youth culture, it appears exceedingly tame—short-haired, neatly dressed kids hang out in shiny cars, and a gum-chewing carhop serves coffee and ice cream. Nonetheless, this is the setting within which the film elaborates the question of Matt's age—first through a didactic scenario in which the cranky old man comes to like an unexpected new flavor of ice cream, and then through his confrontation with a young black driver whose car he blindly backs into. Matt's sense of generational assault is palpable as the other driver shouts, "Stupid old man! You ought to be put away in a home or something!"

What makes this didactic scene especially interesting in our context is the way it tends to its evident anxieties about the aging white patriarch with nostalgia for an earlier history of the classical (Hollywood) couple. Before Matt has to suffer new flavors and ageist name-calling, the drive-in setting prompts Christina to reminisce about her own early marriage as she thinks about what lies ahead for her daughter. The scene's gender politics are made plain when she remarks, "The work he's doing is so im-

FIG. 6.1. Joey Drayton (Katharine Houghton) tucks a daisy behind the ear of her fiancé, John Prentice (Sidney Poitier), with a view of the bay in the background. *Guess Who's Coming to Dinner* (1967).

FIG. 6.2. Joey and John talk on the terrace.

FIG. 6.3. Christina Drayton (Katharine Hepburn) looks on, as does her husband behind her.

portant. She'll be able to help him with it and share in it. It's the best break any wife can have." Less obvious is the way the scene revises the history it invokes. Watching Hepburn and Tracy alone, framed side by side, we are invited to read the scene as a celebration not just of Matt and Christina's good old days but of Tracy and Hepburn's. Grinning sweetly, with a classically Hepburnesque delivery, Christina muses, "You know, for us it's all been great, but, you know what was the best time of all? It was in the beginning when everything was a struggle and you were working too hard and worried and sometimes frightened. And there were times when I felt, when I really *knew* that I was a help to you. That was the very best time of all, for me." In light of how set up we are to imagine ourselves to be reminiscing (with her) about this classical Hollywood couple as we once knew it, what is remarkable is how thoroughly this narrative rewrites it. For despite their capitulations to normativity, this team's early films were "battles" of the sexes precisely for their preoccupation with female independence—hence the dilemma of the first such film, *Woman of the Year* (1942), about the early stages of a relationship and a marriage in which a man feels eclipsed by said woman's fame and success. The sexual conservatism of the 1967 film thus not only works to stabilize gender relations for its own senior and junior couples, offering the revised portrait ultimately as a model for Joey and John, but in doing so goes so far as to deny and rewrite the gender discord of the 1940s, and the "classical" couple of the Tracy and Hepburn comedies. And these considerable efforts to revive and rewrite conventional terms of sexual difference work in turn to establish the safest possible context within which to confront the question of the white patriarch's decline.[46]

Further evidence of this lies in the fact that the drive-in sequence's romantic nostalgia not only mitigates a crisis of age but also follows immediately after Tillie's mocking invocation of "the Reverend Martin Luther King" and is edited into two segments so as to bookend the scene of her threats to John and his "black power."[47] Thus although the multiple challenges to Matt's authority are still clearly in the air, the nostalgic mode and wifely reassurances of the drive-in scene also soften the sharp verbal edges and visual angles of Tillie's defense of the white family's only daughter.

While conservative gender rhetoric thus works to manage looming racial and generational threats, it also clearly reinvigorates the dominant sexual order in the course of the film. For although we hear not even a fleeting utterance of "feminism" or "women's lib," there are signs of female forces beyond Matt Drayton's control. Joey asserts her own determination, and at least the hypothetical possibility of female political power (in the further diluted form of a second thought), when she tells her father of her decision to marry John: "You couldn't stop me . . . even if you were the governor of Alabama, I mean if Mom were." And, in his climactic speech, after Matt first describes Joey as "a very determined young woman, much like her mother," within moments he reveals his intolerance even for her timid response to the news that John has secretly given the deciding vote about their marriage to her parents. When she turns to John and muses gently, "You didn't? What a funny thing to do," her father snaps: "Joey, this may be the last chance I ever have to tell you to do anything. So I'm telling you: shut up!" While this invocation of the end of paternal authority announces the fear that the young woman really *could* escape patriarchal control (even as it also tries to excuse the father's abuse of the power he clearly still has), the force with which the film has put Joey's entire future in Matt's hands, and defined her "best break" as becoming a dutiful wife (Joanna) to John, suggests again and again that this particular fear has been effectively put to rest.

THE LAST (?) GASP OF THE GREAT WHITE SPECTATOR

While *Guess*'s heavily gendered narratives thus work overtime to replot multiple lines of difference and power, it is in the articulation of vision and space that these plots, and those of Cleaver and the Court, most dramatically collide. Specifically, the film's struggle to overcome racial prejudice provokes troubled meditations on a series of aging classical Hollywood forms, namely, the classical white male hero; regimes of vision and space organized around him; and the "great white" spectator invited to see and be situated in analogously privileged ways. When analyzed in this regard, *Guess Who's Coming to Dinner* further demonstrates that Hollywood fantasies of miscegenation are central not simply to narrative structures that regulate the interlocked movement of dominant American identities but also to a range of cinematic forms through which those identities are visually produced and reproduced. So much so, in fact, that it is not an exaggeration to say that just as the most popular miscegenation film of American cinema's first half century relentlessly codified a set of cinematic "handcuffs" in its persistent interarticulation of vision and difference, so the most popular miscegenation film of that cinema's second half century was equally preoccupied with the aging limits, and potential (im)mortality, of those classical cinematic forms.

That classical cinema was itself a key subject in *Guess Who's Coming to Dinner* is indicated in part by the fact that reviewers regularly equated, as if interchangeable, its leading star couple, the classic screwball sex comedies they were known for, and the "magic" of Hollywood at its best:

The magic (nothing less) which Tracy and Miss Hepburn had engendered in all of the previous screen outings, together works again.[48]

Unfortunately . . . their [Tracy and Hepburn's] presence . . . reminds us of how really wonderful pictures like *Woman of the Year* and *Adam's Rib* were.[49]

Spencer Tracy's final film and moreover a last teaming with Katharine Hepburn qualifies, all other considerations aside, as must-viewing for anyone who has ever cared about movies.[50]

At times the very same critics extended such commentary further, and less kindly, to read the film as an indicator of the exhaustion of virtually every register of Hollywood style. One described it as a "comfortably old-fashioned picture, set in the comfortably old-fashioned upper-middle-class milieu of soundstage decor," but despite these comforts was left with "the nagging uneasiness . . . that the problem has not really been confronted or solved, but only patronized."[51] Arthur Knight begins his review with the ominous declaration: "Revivals of old movies reveal a disconcerting fact. . . . The sets, the costumes, even the style of acting— all are dead giveaways, an idiosyncratic response to the way things are despite determined effort to create a vision of how they might have been."[52] And *Newsweek*, after declaring the young couple "a pair of pop-ups from some children's book on tolerance" and the film's treatment of the issue "an absolute antique," advances further: "In technique, too, the film might have been made a decade or two ago with its painted sunsets, sclerotic photography, glaucomic process shots and plastic flowers pummeled by floodlights."[53]

As these dismissive, occasionally vituperative, critiques accumulate alongside the nostalgic ones, a decidedly conflicted portrait of Hollywood cinema emerges. Excessive but exemplary in its movement between these extremes was *Newsweek*. Immediately following the diseased portrait of the film's visual style just cited, in that very same paragraph, it suddenly finds redemption in terms so lavish they must be read for full effect:

No matter though, when Tracy and Hepburn are on screen doing their lovely stuff for the last time together; when she comes on like a fugitive from an old Red Cross poster, a slash of crimson fabric on her shoulder and the old Supergirl gleam in her eye, when she screws up that screwy smile and shrugs that tomboy shrug and seems to be saying, "What the hell, life, you can do your worst but we'll still survive," and he stands there next to her looking grim and granite-good inside, with a face so full of valleys and crags that a space probe would find it unfit for landing.

When Tracy tries and fails to recall some newfangled flavor of ice cream he recently enjoyed, a teen-age temptress at a drive-in serves him fresh Oregon boysenberry sherbet. He tongue-tips it dubiously. "This isn't the stuff." Suddenly his face erupts with joy. "But I like it!" *That* is vitality and also good writing, scenarist William Rose's apt metaphor for the changes in life that the old folks must learn to accept [original emphasis]. And when Tracy gives his blessings to the lovers in a noble speech that was written as a melodrama's climax and may now serve as an artist's epitaph, when he says his say about youth and yearning and whether an old, white-haired man is necessarily a burned-out shell who can no longer remember the passion with which he has loved a woman, *then everything wrong with the film is right and we can see, through our tears, that the hero we worshipped was just what we always knew he was, an authentically heroic man* [emphasis mine].[54]

Coming just after the pan of *Guess*'s "pop-up" book tolerance and "glaucomic" visuals, this encomium is striking for the way it enacts, as well as states, the power of "Spence and the Supergirl" to put "right" the political and aesthetic flaws so harshly enumerated at the outset. Indeed, the power of the dynamic duo is so great that it grips the critic of tired Hollywood forms to interpret the didactic ice cream parable as "good writing"! Nonetheless, the crisscrossing rhetorics of aging and "vitality" that riddle both the scorn and the praise suggest that *several* classical Hollywood institutions—its style, its classical couple, its "granite-good" hero—are showing their age, albeit some more gracefully than others. (The publicity still beneath the text, of a sash-draped Hepburn combing the old man's hair, like a little boy's, visually reiterates the effect.)

The film itself further articulates the join between the aging classical style and the aging classical hero that the reviews tend to split apart. What is more, in that join there is further evidence that another subject being at once challenged, mourned, and nostalgically resurrected in the course of the interracial drama is that classical position from which the Hollywood spectator has been invited to see and interpret—not unlike Tracy's "authentically heroic man" who finally sees the light from his hilltop view overlooking the bay. And the film is startlingly literal in its enactment of such concerns. Not only do plot and cameras literally revolve around the aging patriarch gazing sternly about his house as he contemplates whether to tolerate the unexpected vision of his daughter with a black man, but the space in which this drama unfolds is crucial to that process. It is fitting, then, that the studio spared no expense to build what it touted as "one of the largest single sets in Hollywood history," designed "like a real house, all rooms connecting."[55] Save for a few strategic outings, the Draytons' remarkably situated modern mansion and the placement and circulation of bodies within and around it for the

better part of an afternoon and evening serve as the literal and metaphorical space wherein the film works out the conditions under which this
couple can come together and the interracial dinner party can finally take
place.

James Baldwin first recognized how deeply this film's racial project de-
pended on its representation of space:

> The setting of *Guess Who's Coming to Dinner* is the key. We are on the heights
> of San Francisco—at a time not too far removed from the moment when the city
> of San Francisco reclaimed the land at Hunter's Point and urban-renewalized the
> niggers out of it. The difficult and terrified city, where the niggers are, lives far
> beneath these heights. The father is in a perfectly respectable, perhaps even ad-
> mirable profession, and the mother runs an art gallery. The setting is a brilliant
> re-creation of a certain—and far from unattractive—level of American life.
> And the black doctor is saying, among other things, that his presence in this
> landscape (this hard-won Eden) will do nothing to threaten, or defile it—
> indeed, since in the event that he marries the girl, they are immediately going
> to the Far East, or some such place, he will not even be present. One can
> scarcely imagine striking a bargain more painless; and without even losing a
> daughter, who will, merely, in effect, be traveling, and broadening her educa-
> tion; keeping in touch via trans-Pacific telephone, and coming home to San
> Francisco from time to time, with her yet more various, toddling, and exotic
> acquisitions. (70)

To this I would add that the film goes out of its way not only to establish
that the black man will not threaten to occupy or claim white space but
also that he will not threaten to challenge or disturb that position of mastery held out by it, that position from which the world below is looked
at, contemplated, judged, and represented (Drayton runs a newspaper).
In question are not only the authority and principles of a classical Hollywood hero like Matt Drayton but the position of the white spectator who
has long been invited to imagine himself, or herself, as the occupant of a
similarly privileged place.

Before we turn to analyze the enormous energy the film spends to establish, embellish, worry over, and preserve such places and the vistas
they afford, another outside view helps to establish the larger cultural positions and relations at stake. For the same writer whose account of America's interlocked "handcuffs" of difference could be said to have its own
implicit spatial analysis (the abstraction and remove of the "Omnipotent
Administrator," the mired bodies of blacks, etc.) invoked related terms in
a 1968 interview, there tying them explicitly to white spectatorship:

> At the present stage, the majority of white people are indifferent and compla-
> cent simply because their own lives have remained more or less intact and as

remote from the lives of most blacks as the old French aristocracy was from "the great unwashed." It's disturbing to them to hear about Hough burning, Watts burning, the black community in Newark burning. But they don't really understand why it's happening, and they don't really care, as long as *their* homes and *their* places of work—or the schools to which they send their children—aren't burning, too. So for most whites, what's happened up to now has been something like a spectator sport. There may be a lot more of them than there are of us, but they're not really involved.[56]

Immediately resonant here is the way Cleaver's description of a mainstream white political position is so explicitly tied to a simultaneously visual, spatial, and psychic one. So "remote" from black life and black rebellion, the relation of whites to the fires and what they represent is one of a spectator who is not disinterested but whose position and interests are imagined to be wholly dislocated, and thereby distinct, from the scene of racial struggle.

The possibility of this state of affairs—the possibility for white Americans to imagine themselves removed from racial battles, even from "race" itself—surely depends on a long history of segregation, hierarchy, and exclusion. At the same time, as we have seen repeatedly, the history of moving-image culture and the spectatorial positions it solicits and affirms in particular play a notable role in this process, rendering those physical, social spaces of white seclusion (the suburbs, "the hills," etc.) into widely disseminated, subjective experiences of whiteness ("remote," untouched, etc.).

The new variation on this theme for the present chapter is that, while Cleaver and, later, Baldwin openly expose and resist such literal and figurative architectures, Hollywood demonstrates mainstream culture's capacity to sustain them *even as* it calls for a liberal renunciation of white supremacy. Cleaver suggests how this is possible when he claims that "any liberality [the Omnipotent Administrator] might show . . . is itself a part of his lust for omnipotence. His liberality is, in fact, charity"(180). It is not, Cleaver implies, a renunciation of the privileged position but a benevolent gesture bestowed from it. While such terms might be used, polemically, to describe the Supreme Court's righteous but indistinct decree against white supremacy, they are excessively, graphically inscribed in Matt Drayton's final denunciation of those "bastard[s]" who would oppose the young couple's marriage. For, as we will see, this denunciation occurs precisely at the moment when his place at the critical, elevated center of the text has been utterly sealed through plot, editing, camera work, lighting, and the arrangement of bodies in his expansive white living room on the hill.[57] To understand the full significance of these textual terms, a sketch of those they answer is first in order.

The most persistent visual trope in *Guess Who's Coming to Dinner* is the view of San Francisco Bay. Not only is the Draytons' home designed to showcase a breathtakingly wide, panoramic sweep of that view, but it guides the camera, and even the script, from start to climax. The film opens with a quiet shot of the sky in which an airplane at a distance comes slowly closer and louder as the names of the film's stars appear above it at left. The title slowly unfolds in larger letters beneath the ("United") plane—each word projected separately, slowly, to draw out the question ("GUESS . . . WHO'S . . . COMING . . . TO DINNER"). The anticipatory silence is dramatically filled in the cut to the second shot with a sudden swell of the hokey theme song ("You've got to give a little, take a little, let your poor heart ache a little . . .") and the revelation of the dramatic backdrop against which this narrative of compromise will transpire—a dazzling display of San Francisco and its bay spreading out beneath and beyond the plane. Although we do not yet see who, seated inside it, is enjoying this view from on high with us, that ambiguity will turn out to be a thoroughly appropriate beginning to the film that ensues.

The first few scenes to follow elaborate the visual terms put in question by the arrival of the interracial couple we soon meet. While the pair is repeatedly marked as a spectacle in and of itself (the object of prying looks by the camera, a cab driver, and a nosy employee of Joey's mother's), the possibility of John's assertion of a look of his own quickly arises. As they drive into the city from the airport, another dramatic display of the skyline is revealed (again punctuated by a sudden musical swell), this time from the freeway. Their first stop, at Christina's art gallery, then explicitly introduces Joey's family as being in the business of elite visual culture. And the question soon posed is, What will John's relation to that culture be?[58] Although at first uncertain about some of the modern pieces on display, he proves a quick study. When the couple starts to leave the gallery, moments after Joey has explained a puzzling, blinking piece to be a "kinetic sculpture," John turns back with a knowing grin to switch it off, thus demonstrating his ability to manipulate, as well as appreciate, abstract art.

These preliminary setups are in effect just light warm-ups to the dramatic visual contest that ensues once John enters the Draytons' bay-view home. Although marked as a visual object right up to his approach to the front door (when, to Joey's amusement, he puts on her wide-brimmed straw hat to free his hands for suitcases and tipping), this status changes almost immediately upon entry. A brief stop in the foyer establishes the professional differences between the blacks who serve and are served here, as Joey introduces "Dr. John Prentice" (in a suit and tie with briefcase) to "Miss Matilda Binks" (in a maid's uniform), and then asks "Tillie" to bring them lunch on the terrace. Having made that crucial distinction (in a film in which racial integration is possible so long as it remains disconnected from class equity), the film moves to introduce John first to the Draytons' home, then to Christina, and finally to Matt. And these scenes serve to introduce the visual and cinematic stakes at issue as much as the more obvious racial ones.

As the histories and theories explored in previous chapters would lead us to expect, even though Matt Drayton's gaze across the bay is finally insisted upon as the most controlling gaze in the film, the troubles that plague him with his daughter's interracial engagement are repeatedly represented as potential encroachments upon that entitled view. Even before Joey has finished ordering lunch in the foyer, John's desirous eyes are drawn off screen to the living room, into which he quickly moves and begins to look around. With hands clasped behind his back, neck and eyes craning forward, he quietly but deliberately strides about, peaking into corners and adjoining rooms to admire the extravagant expanse of well-appointed living space.[59] Joanna grins and leans against a piece of furniture as he does so, silently inviting him to enjoy this perusal of her native milieu (fig. 6.4). That she, in a yellow-trimmed shift at his right, is rhymed with one of the female figures, also standing and in yellow, in a painting that hangs to his left, makes literal the parallel between John's new relationship to the white woman and to this luxurious white space and its many visual attractions. That John likes what he sees is evident by the look on his face, and his childlike response to Joey's query of "You like it?": "It's bu-tee-ful!"

After allowing John, and the spectator, this initial orientation to the interior, Joey excitedly offers up the prime viewing spot just outside: "Come out and look from the terrace!" As the couple heads in that direction, we can see that the living room John has surveyed is lined by a bank of picture windows, but at this point only partial glimpses of the bay appear through windows and trees. And just as they move through the open glass door to the terrace, John's look swerves in the opposite direction. In midstride he suddenly stops, turns back to stare and squint in the direction of the foyer, and calls out a long, "Heeeey, who's that?" (fig. 6.5). The camera answers with a point-of-view shot that traces his look back to its new object, a young black woman in a miniskirt. Further registering John's interest, a quick pan follows her as she steps out from behind a partly opaque glass partition, and a zoom-in draws closer for a head-to-toe inspection (fig. 6.6). While the racial politics of this look have been critiqued, its timing is also key.[60] For, in rerouting it, the film inclines John toward a sexual, "black," kind of looking at precisely the moment he has been invited to take in the prized, white-owned view.[61] And this deferral of his consumption of the view from the terrace is extraordinarily effective. After John stops, Joey does, too, resting her arms

FIG. 6.4. Upon his arrival at the Draytons' hilltop mansion, John takes a look around.

FIG. 6.5. He is distracted on the way to one view by another.

FIG. 6.6. Dorothy (Barbara Randolph), the distracting object of John's look.

on either side of the door frame to confirm the pull of the distraction: "That's Dorothy. Isn't she a knockout?" But even after she drags John outside in mock jealousy, we do not return to their original destination. When the camera cuts to follow them, still walking and giggling, their position and direction have entirely changed: they walk not toward the vista but with their backs to it, on the other end of the terrace, heading toward Matt's study.[62] Whether they have already gone to see the view, without us, or have forgotten about it entirely (along with the continuity editor) is unclear. In either case, the effect is the same: many scenes will ensue before we actually see John gaze out at the much-discussed view, and when he does so, the territory will be much more extensively marked.

It is not until Matt Drayton appears, indeed, not until the belated moment in which he realizes John's relation to his daughter, that the visual turf in question is finally, fully revealed. When Christina arrives, at first stunned by what John here calls "a rather shocking pair," the trio moves to sit down on couches in front of the picture window. Although the view is still obstructed and out of focus, we can occasionally glimpse pieces of it behind them for the first time (fig. 6.7). But the equation between the news of this couple and the status of the view is undeniable when Matt arrives moments later. First, with Christina, the couple returns to the terrace to enjoy Tillie's sandwiches, and presumably the view originally offered with them. But again the camera manages to take us there without revealing it, instead framing the trio's conversation tightly, with the house in the background (fig. 6.8). Because John proposes breaking the news to the soon-to-arrive father gently, when Matt appears the newcomer is introduced simply as a doctor Joey met in Hawaii. Thinking nothing of this, Matt quickly excuses himself to make a golf date. But halfway through the living room he does a slow double take, and we can see the larger meaning of John's presence start to dawn on him. In a cinematographic gesture that almost seems too elaborate to be unconscious, it is only upon Tracy's performance of this recognition, turning himself 180 degrees to return to the terrace and reinspect John and the situation (exactly undoing the course of the swerve that originally drew John's look back from the doorway), that the camera is finally set free of its former constraints: for only after turning entirely around with Matt, all in the movement of a single shot, does the camera move back out to the terrace to finally reveal the long-withheld view (figs. 6.9A–6.9C).[63]

At the end of its dramatic rotation, this shot lands on a static setup of Matt and John standing side by side against the backdrop of the view between them. That they represent two competing positions of authority is further suggested by the placement of Chris and Joey, seated in the foreground in front of them (with their backs to us) as if to watch their respective men. After John initially explains his relation to Joanna, a shot-

FIG. 6.7. John and Joey at their first meeting with her mother.

FIG. 6.8. Getting acquainted on the terrace.

reverse-shot series capturing the men's exchange is anchored in Matt's point of view but is also marked by John's and the camera's considerable height above him. Matt then sits down and is rendered alone in a medium close-up, seated in front of the view. The visual authority connoted by this reframing and the black-rimmed eyeglasses that stand out from Tracy's white-haired head is simultaneously put into question by his half-loosened tie (interrupted in the double take) and the baffled looks that wash over his face (fig. 6.10).

With the visual-racial-patriarchal territory thus carefully marked, one final condition must be met before the black man is finally allowed to gaze directly at the view: he must relinquish all authority in the matter of his future with, or without, the white man's daughter. Annoyed and disturbed by the scene on the terrace, Matt retires to his study, where he calls his secretary to research John's background. After Christina joins him, John knocks and announces that although "Joanna doesn't know it,

FIG. 6.9A. Matt Drayton (Spencer Tracy) does a double take.

FIG. 6.9B. The view of the bay is finally revealed for the first time as Matt returns to the scene on the terrace.

FIG. 6.9C. Two men, one vista.

FIG. 6.10. A baffled father takes in his daughter's interracial news.

and I don't see any reason she should," he has decided that "unless you approve . . . there won't be any marriage." When Matt bristles at this as an "ultimatum," John reassures him it is not, and leaves as politely as he entered. Christina then makes it clear that she cannot disapprove, leaving the ball entirely in Matt's court.[64]

Only now does the film allow John a clear and direct look at the remarkable landscape: when the next scene begins, we finally see him, in a close-up, gazing out across the bay in contemplation. As the reader will recall from the ensuing scene described earlier, John's long-awaited look from the terrace is nonetheless fleeting and contained almost as forcefully as it was withheld: by the spectacle-rendering daisy Joey soon tucks behind his ear (see fig. 6.1); by her desirous look that pulls him in the opposite direction (see fig. 6.2); and eventually by the zoom-out from this romantic scene that exposes diegetic voyeurs to be watching the "problem" couple along with us (see fig. 6.3). The "origin" of the zoom is first identified in Christina's look from the study, but the camera then further reveals Matt standing behind her and also watching the couple on the terrace. And it is at the moment of *that* knowing gaze from Matt's study, after John's has so fully surrendered, and as Christina speaks tearfully of her pride in her daughter's happiness, that the film has established the visual terms, as well as the romantic ones, under which Matt will eventually accept the marriage.

For all that, the film has in effect only just begun at this point, and much anguish now ensues over the question of whether or not the "broken down old phony liberal"—as an old friend teasingly calls him—can sustain our faith in the justice of his vision.[65] It is only now, in fact, with these primary visual terms and conditions established, that the many forms of difference and authority in question get seriously discussed, or seriously erupt, in the hours between lunch and dinner: in Tillie's "civil rights" and "black power" outbursts from the kitchen and guest room; in the sexual confidences Joey shares with her mother in her childhood bedroom ("He wouldn't [have sex]. I don't think he could have been in much doubt about my feelings, but he just wouldn't"); in Matt's bafflement in the garden that a "colored mailman's son" could be so successful, etc. In short, having amassed the central cast on and around the terrace in the opening scenes to establish the critical terms and issues, the film then scatters it about the house's many spaces to address the couple's manifold implications.

The afternoon's negotiations carefully set up for the film's climactic dinner party. That it arrives on the scene of a visual crisis as well as a patriarchal one is detectable in one last dramatic view from the terrace taken in before the guests arrive. Having returned from their ice cream outing at sunset, Matt and Christina argue bitterly in the foyer as a vivid orange glow saturates the wall behind him. Despite her nostalgic invocation of a young couple's good old days, he now makes it clear that he has no intentions of relenting and accuses her of "not behaving in her [daughter's] best interest." For the spectator who has been invited to embrace the women's romantic terms, Matt's flaming anger now threatens a tragic ending. After he storms up the stairs, the theme song returns in a minor key, with painfully slow and dissonant modulations. Christina strolls somberly, pensively, through the glowing living room, as if pulled toward the garish light streaming in from outside. The camera follows her attentively as she passes the empty dinner table and begins to remove her coat and scarf, at times pulling in close enough to reveal Hepburn's uncontrollable shake. The details are apt, because the scene contemplates the painful possibility that the pairing of Tracy and Hepburn might not be enough, that the man really is too "old" and too "phony" to come around. Christina clearly worries as much, her eyes filling and finally bursting in the scene's final shot. And this tormented performance is staged around the view that glows now as if on fire. We see it, with her, first through the windows, and finally as she gazes deliberately out from the edge of the terrace at the intensely dark, orange scene—by far the film's most extraordinary and excessive use of color (figs. 6.11–6.12). While previous scenes were shot with bright, shadowless lighting that brought everything sharply into view ("sclerotic photography"?), this is the sequence of "painted sunsets" and "glaucomic process shots." The subject and timing of such an afflicted visual style, therefore, precisely grafts the film's crisis of faith in the Hollywood hero to the evident crisis of the visual conventions typically attached to him.

The sense of impending tragedy persists as the guests begin to arrive. Christina breaks down with the first, Monsignor Ryan (Cecil Kellaway), urging him to go upstairs and reason with her husband. Matt's own loss of control is evident in his fumbling struggle to get dressed as he refuses to listen to his old friend's reason. Yet his real estate continues to function steadily without him. Upon her arrival Mrs. Prentice (Beah Richards) immediately comments, "What a lovely home. . . . You have such a magnificent view." In a gesture that will initiate the choreography of negotiations soon to transpire, Christina invites her out to see it. When Matt just then joins the party, he barks at his wife, "The view? What in the hell are you talking about?! What view?!" Even granting his understandable preoccupation with the film's central "problem," the momentary amnesia of this utterance—in this house, in this film—has the distinct ring of negation (in the psychoanalytic sense), announcing by way of denial something that in fact matters very much.

A series of critical conversations follow. On the terrace the mothers discuss their husbands' stubborn disapproval; the fathers confer in Matt's

FIG. 6.11. A troubled Christina is drawn to the view.

FIG. 6.12. As tears well up in her eyes, Christina, fearing an impending tragedy, takes in the fiery sunset.

study; and in the living room the monsignor worries with John that his relationship, and his fiancée, will soon be destroyed. Later, also on the terrace, John's mother first voices her support to her son, prompting him to confide his newfound passion; she then confers with Matt. Again in the all-male space of the study, John and his father face off. And upstairs, oblivious to it all in a room still marked by her childhood, an ecstatic Joey giddily packs, blind even to her mother's visible dread. Compounded, these scenarios again suggest the importance of space and patriarchy to deciding the future of the interracial couple—as if the Drayton home just needs to be large enough, well-designed enough, to accommodate all of these negotiations. And the trope of the view continues to play a central role. First in the conversation between the two mothers, then in the one between mother and son, and finally with Mrs. Prentice and Mr. Drayton, the most passionate and tormented exchanges are staged against the (artificial) backdrop of city lights shimmering over a dark bay.

With the first two of these pairs, initial looks at the bay turn inward for face-to-face conversation. But the third is captured mostly in a disjointed set of profiles, Mrs. Prentice's in the foreground at left looking off screen toward the house at right, and Matt's behind her looking in the opposite direction toward the bay (fig. 6.13). As his eyes remain mostly fixed on the view, she gives a stunning, speech proposing with an unexpected directness that what is ultimately at stake is not the young lovers' races but the fading perception and sexuality of their aging fathers:

> What happens to men when they grow old? Why do they forget everything? I believe those two young people *need* each other like they need the air to breathe in. Anybody can see that by just looking at them. But you and my husband are—you might as well be blind men. You can only see that they have a problem. But do you really know what's happened to them? How *they* feel about each other? I believe that men grow old. And when sexual things no longer matter to them, they forget it all, forget what true passion is. If you ever felt what my son feels for your daughter, you've forgotten everything about it. My husband too. You knew once, but that was a long time ago. Now the two of you don't know. And the strange thing for your wife and me is that you don't even remember. If you did, how could you do what you are doing?

The power of this speech is registered in part by Matt's profound silence and by the fact that he will require several more scenes of contemplative gazing to muster a response. As that response will partially admit, the woman's words clearly resonate. In addition, for this spectator, especially from the perspective of the end of this book, there is real poignancy in witnessing, at once, the old white man being forced to confront his own impotence and a black woman so fiercely and yet somehow humanely delivering the truths she seems here to tell in a film that otherwise wants little of them. This is, to be sure, a far cry from the kind of historical reckoning we might want at this point. Even so, insofar as this scene's encounter between a black woman and a white man is staged as a momentary flash of destabilizing sexual truth, it is interestingly of apiece—albeit on a different emotional register—with its distant filmic ancestor from 1903 with which I began this study. Here the "truth" has shifted with the times and, arguably, flashes a good bit longer and harder than that of *What Happened in the Tunnel*. But it again announces the vulnerabilities and instabilities that perpetually haunt even the most privileged figures of popular American cinema, even amid some of their most classical appearances. All of this, then, helps as well to make further sense of the stridency with which Matt and the film will finally respond.

In keeping with the visual rhetoric the film has already established by now, the staging of Mrs. Prentice's speech makes it evident that the sexual potency she puts into question is also bound up with the wider, more symbolic forms of authority under discussion in this chapter. For Matt's

FIG. 6.13. As Mrs. Prentice (Beah Richards) speaks of old men and their fading perceptions, Matt listens while gazing out at the view.

FIG. 6.14. Matt ponders the situation . . .

FIG. 6.15. . . . and finally sees the light.

gaze at the view remains troubled throughout the speech and is then featured in not one but three more sequences intercut with scenes inside the
house, each of which carefully follows and focuses on him as he paces
and stares at the landscape (fig. 6.14). The third of these culminates in a
zoom-in to a close-up of his gaze again fixed on the view, at a distinct
moment of recognition: he blinks, nods to himself, and mutters "I'll be a
son-of-a-bitch" before turning to deliver his verdict inside (fig. 6.15).

Upon the film's release critics regularly read Matt's climactic speech as
not simply the best thing about the film but a memorial to Spencer Tracy
himself and his command of his craft, even in the face of death. The *Hollywood Reporter* noted that it took five days to shoot because "the old
trouper was so ill . . . he couldn't work more than two or three hours a
day." But deeming "that last speech alone" worthy of "a posthumous
nomination," it asserted, "Spence dying outacts most actors in the best of
health."[66] The *New Yorker* cast the performance as a kind of self-
conscious tribute: "The very words that he spoke were written for him
deliberately as 'last' words"; and "being aware that it was the last picture
he would ever make [Tracy] turned his role into a stunning compendium
of the actor's art; it was as if he were saying over our heads to generations
of actors not yet born, . . . 'Here is how to dominate a scene by walking
away from it.' "[67] Such claims of immortality so tightly join "Tracy," his
performance, and his role—the "vitality" of each invigorating the others—that it sometimes becomes impossible to pry them apart: "His final
performance was just exactly what it should be: a sincere, concentrated,
honest portrait of a sincere, concentrated, honest man who might as well
have been Spencer Tracy."[68] Despite the suggestion that "Spencer Tracy"
could be the model, or real ideal, behind such a "portrait," all signs point
to its origins in a wider series of Hollywood traditions.

First and foremost among these is that "authentically heroic man," the
one who finally emerged in the course of Tracy's speech as "the hero we
worshipped . . . just [as] we always knew he was." This tradition of "authentic" masculine authority is described by another reviewer as "conviction," championed as "that basic and supreme gift" of the Hollywood
actor: "He was at all times what he said he was. . . . If he is not who he
says he is, than [*sic*] he is an actor reading lines. Tracy was never, never
that. His 'great American eagle face,' looking more than ever like something hewed in oak, had become part of that conviction. He did not start
with it; it grew from within."[69] The quoted epithet comes from Joey, who
uses it to describe Matt, not Tracy, when he stares fiercely but refuses to
be read.[70] And this is a facial expression we see repeatedly, especially in
the sequences of Matt alone looking out from the terrace before he delivers his final speech. That the kind of man and look it refers to are further
bound up with an even wider range of classical Hollywood values and
forms is suggested when another review not only deems Tracy the master

of the film but oddly imbues him with the organizational principles of classical Hollywood narrative itself: *Guess* is "the late great actor's picture and he dominates it with his vitality and the *clarity and logic of his presentation.*"[71]

The devout tones with which such classical Hollywood aesthetics are regularly celebrated in these texts ("worship," "transcend[ence]") turn decidedly biblical in a short trade piece on the film's lighting design, entitled "Fiat Lux" (Let There Be Light).[72] Invoking the first words of God himself, the divine illumination of the phrase is here doubly apt. As intended, it referred to a technological miracle in which, to accommodate the "unique circular shot, seldom attempted indoors," heavy arc lights were raised such that "all lighting [was] suspended from . . . catwalks" and could be "alternately dimmed and intensified by remote control." And, fittingly, the scene that inspired such divine stagecraft was the old master's all-knowing speech, a speech staged to position him not simply as the object of all lights and looks but as the commanding subject out from whom everything else would appear to radiate. Indeed, the film presents Matt's final words as more powerful than those of the priest invited to this difficult party precisely for his gift, as Christina puts it, for expressing "beautiful thoughts." Monsignor Ryan confesses to John's parents that the tools of his trade, soothing words for "nearly every human condition," have failed him here: "I'm completely stumped. There's simply nothing I can say." Mrs. Prentice concurs, silencing her husband, and at this very moment the film cuts to Matt's flash of recognition that will lead him to finally speak his mind at length.

The "personal statements," as Matt calls them, delivered to all assembled guests and residents, and Tracy's knowing delivery, clearly seek to redeem the "authentically heroic [Hollywood] man" earlier put into question. The logic of Matt's turnaround is rather sudden, but is brought on, he explains, by a deeply felt response to Mrs. Prentice's claim that he has lost all connection to forms of sexual desire he once knew, "that like her husband I'm a burnt-out old shell of a man who cannot even remember what it's like to love a woman the way her son loves my daughter." Having run through several others, he adds that "this is the only statement presented to me all day with which I am prepared to take issue." His objection leads him first to insist, "Old? Yes. Burnt-out? Certainly. But I can tell you, the memories are still there. Intact, indestructible." And those memories serve as the means by which he now recognizes that "the only thing that matters is what they feel, and how much they feel, for each other. And if it's half of what we felt, that's everything." The lump in his throat verifies the authenticity of his claims, further confirmed by tears welling up in all the women's eyes. What is more, the power of this romantic sentiment renews the voice of liberal conviction. Of those who would still object, Matt further insists, "Screw all those people!" Now it is only "some bastard" who would make a case against them, and "knowing what you two are, knowing what you two have, knowing what you two feel," the only thing worse than getting married "would be if you didn't get married." Having thus said his piece, he pauses, and barks once more, "Well, Tillie, when the hell are we going to get some dinner?" The terms and conditions under which this interracial dinner party can finally be seated are thus made clear with a swell of sentiment for conventional marriage that handily tops the Supreme Court's. And this one is expressly delivered as a white patriarch's final words over all racial, sexual, and socioeconomic others.

Significantly, the only history Matt's long-anticipated speech invokes is his own asserted memory of an intensely potent masculinity, and the sequence cinematically commemorates the visual-spatial command long associated with such a figure. The speech begins with, and is anchored by, the image of the eagle-eyed sage holding forth: he stands at the center of a medium close-up, his sensible glasses framing the eyes cast out and downward in the direction of the diegetic spectators seated before him (fig. 6.16). Through reaction shots and shots that include the backs of his onlookers' heads in the foreground, all other eyes, like ours, are riveted upon him at the centerpoint where their looks converge. In each case, these looks reflect back to him the reach and force of his gaze and knowing presence (fig. 6.17).

This effect intensifies as the speech unfolds. In a reconfiguration of the original arrangement of players on the terrace, now in the living room Matt faces the view while Joey and John, seated, watch him quietly with their backs to it. When Matt speaks of his passionate memories of Christina, she at times looks on from his side, positioned as affirming witness and inspiring vision—akin to the Modigliani hovering over her shoulder (fig. 6.17).[73] The cinematographic climax occurs when Matt stands directly in front of John and Joey to announce his verdict in their favor. Looking sharply down at them, he announces that they will "have no problem with me," but adds that they will be "up against . . . a hundred million people right here in this country who'll be shocked, and offended, and appalled at the two of you." When the speech takes this social turn, the camera begins to turn as well, starting with a directly frontal full shot of Matt that then slowly pivots around him (fig. 6.18). The revolving camera soon cuts in for a close-up, still slowly encircling its subject, but now pivoting our look in an orbit entirely focused on his (fig. 6.19). And this insistence on the commanding centrality of Matt's judgment and determined gaze occurs exactly as his speech becomes most righteously liberal, urging the couple to "cling tight" against people's "prejudices, and their bigotry and their blind hatreds and stupid fears." When the camera's slow revolution finally halts, it lands on Matt in profile as he looks off screen to the right, in the direction of John and Joey and the view behind them, eyes cast

FIG. 6.16. Matt begins the speech that will deliver the heavily anticipated judgment.

FIG. 6.17. All eyes focus upon him.

FIG. 6.18. The camera begins to rotate around him.

outward with as much determination as his vocal delivery of the line that here implores them to "say 'screw all those people!'" (fig. 6.20). With a few more reaction shots to register the pride, respect, and welling tears of the onscreen audience, to conclude the speech the camera returns to the medium close-up with which it began. Only then does it break away for a long shot that captures all parties—smiling, rising, and moving toward the dinner table. Following them, the camera finally settles just outside the dining room, behind Matt at the near head of the table. Now, after all the machinations described, and with the affirmed couples and temporary guests seated appropriately and Tillie serving her way around the table, our look is positioned closest to his to acceptingly survey the new family snapshot so neatly laid out before it (fig. 6.21).

The formal terms in question thus emphatically mark the political, historical, psychological, and cinematic limits of the interracial acceptance the film is so proud of at the end. For, despite its evident crises of faith in the conventions in which it ultimately still wants to believe, *Guess Who's Coming to Dinner* made popular for decades to come a set of forms whereby the legacy of white supremacy represented in the miscegenation taboo is selectively renounced from a position of white, patriarchal privilege that nonetheless further secures itself by retaining its noticeable remove from the territorial battles at issue. In terms that fully resonate with those in which the taboo was cinematically codified in 1915, in other words, interracial desire is only speakable, and visible in 1967, when those who have the most to lose are still finally positioned as if telling and seeing the story, surveying and projecting the field in which it appears as if they have no part to play but that of liberal judge or benevolent father.

Looking Out from My Own Hilltops

As a white writer at times absorbed in the details of my own impassioned visions and at times pulled back to see all that I have surveyed—and as one who grew up in the hills across the bay from the Draytons, no less—I know firsthand how white people with good intentions can fail to see themselves in the racial picture. Just as I would hope that my own failures to fully divest from these and other forms of authority and privilege do not invalidate the work I have attempted here, so I would not want to vitiate the value of the unprecedented embraces of interracial love considered in this chapter. Instead, my aim has been to learn from their all too familiar limits also on display. In that spirit, it seems appropriate to conclude by asking what more it tells us about Hollywood cinema and American culture generally that the most popular miscegenation film of the late twentieth century would so obviously, almost obsessively, assert the power of its visibly aging white, affluent, patriarchal gaze?

FIG. 6.19. The camera's rotation continues . . .

FIG. 6.20. . . . and stops as the speech climaxes.

FIG. 6.21. *Guess* closes with a new family snapshot, taken from Matt's end of the table.

In the context of film studies, the almost unbelievable predictability of this gaze demands attention. While film historians have worked with great care in recent decades to correct earlier traditions of film theory and analysis that would have perhaps too quickly confirmed *Guess*'s cinematic fantasies of mastery and authority, this study has tried to show that even as we rightly resist methodological determinism, there is still much to learn from historically sensitive engagements with, and revisions of, the modes of inquiry made possible by that earlier body of scholarship.[74] At one level, the relentless textual forms and tremendous popularity of films like *The Birth of a Nation* and *Guess Who's Coming to Dinner* vividly remind us what (in part) inspired those admittedly too "predictable" theories of vision and spectatorship in the first place.[75] At another, insofar as the forms studied here perpetually complicate those theories—emerging from utterly unexpected predecessors; interlocking one set of differences with yet others; baldly exposing the anxieties they at times seem so desperate to keep at bay; continually transforming in the face of historical change; exhausting and revising in seeming perpetuity— they beg us to recognize the considerable flexibility, ambivalence, and telling intricacies of such a seemingly limited repertoire of representations. Such an understanding of "classical" Hollywood forms helps us to account for their ongoing ability not only to negotiate change and resistance but also to be genuinely moving, as well as genuinely maddening, despite their seeming predictability.

Approaching the question finally in the context of a contemporary culture in which we still struggle to cope with the legacies of slavery and segregation, the ultimate lesson perhaps is that in order to continue to repair the damages implicit in dominant screen fantasies of miscegenation, we need not only to remember the complex social histories they have worked to displace and disavow but also to recognize the consequential positions we can assume in the very processes of consuming, producing, and even renouncing, the fantasies as well as the histories. Joining and expanding the alternative screen histories that lie beyond the scope of this book's reach, and at times finding popular audiences for their more independently minded visions, some of the most provocative contemporary American filmmakers are certainly on to this. Often knowing very different things in very different ways, films like *Far from Heaven* (Todd Haynes), *Lone Star* (John Sayles), *One False Move* (Carl Franklin), *The Watermelon Woman* (Cheryl Dunye, 1996), *Jungle Fever* (Spike Lee), *Bulworth* (Warren Beatty), and *Daughters of the Dust* (Julie Dash, 1991) passionately provoke us to confront our own spectatorial relationships to the dominant fantasies. Only by persistently doing so, this book leads me to suggest, can we hope to ever safely forget them.

Notes

1. The continual erasure of Ron Goldman's murder only demonstrated further the centrality of miscegenation fantasy to the media coverage.

2. The case generated some, if not enough, critical reflection, and in it the media coverage was repeatedly linked to the silent epic long associated with the birth of American cinema itself. See especially Ann DuCille, *Skin Trade* (Cambridge, Mass.: Harvard University Press, 1996), 136–69, and Toni Morrison, ed., *Birth of a Nation 'hood: Gaze, Script, and Spectacle in the O. J. Simpson Case* (New York: Pantheon, 1997). In the second volume Morrison and Patricia Williams are particularly insightful on the narratives and critiques that did and did not take place.

3. In *Playing the Race Card: Melodramas of Black and White from Uncle Tom to O. J. Simpson* (Princeton, N.J.: Princeton University Press, 2001), Linda Williams interrogates responses to the Simpson case by tracing a history of "racial melodrama" behind it. Defining this as an ongoing, popular mode of representation in American culture whereby we determine virtue by sympathizing with racially marked victims, Williams argues that the racial schism in belief around the case can be understood as the clashing of what she calls the "Tom" and "anti-Tom" traditions: blacks were moved by the story of a suffering black man framed by police, and whites by the story of a white woman being assaulted by a black beast. While her readings are often brilliant and persuasive, I am hesitant to accept the notion—not that Williams entirely does—that one's race fully determines which set of images one is likely to be swayed by, or that racial belief is as singular as her model might sometimes imply. Although my own memory is, granted, neither innocent nor fully reliable, I remember my own reaction to the case as something more like a shifting, contradictory process whereby I sometimes wanted to believe he did not do it and sometimes wanted to believe he did.

4. The lack of visible or audible resistance does not mean there was none, although in light of recent outrage at the Simpson case and the considerable noise in the theater, it was striking that I heard no one object to the film's ugly resurrection of the fantasy of the black rapist.

5. The other state was Alabama, which began efforts to end its ban soon after South Carolina, and did so in a state election in 2000. "The 2000 Elections: South," *New York Times*, 8 November 2000, B8.

6. "Bedroom Doors, Battle Lines," *Columbia (S.C.) State*, 6 February 1998, A1.

7. Ibid., A10.

INTRODUCTION
WHAT HAPPENED IN THE TUNNEL AND OTHER OPEN AMERICAN SECRETS

1. The word "miscegenation" first appeared in a pamphlet from 1863 written anonymously by two Democratic journalists, D. G. Croly and George Wakeman, as if from the point of view of radical Republicans, to ridicule abolitionist politics. Despite this and other objectionable histories, I use the word in part as a reminder of the vexed history of fantasies and practices it conjures. The word also resonates with that part of this project that interrogates fantasies of interracial desire not only as ones that play with racial and sexual boundaries (the Latin roots being *miscere*, "to mix," and *genus*, "race") but also with those as fantasies of (a) nation. On the Croly and Wakeman pamphlet, see George M. Fredrickson, *The Black Image in the White Mind: The Debate on Afro-American Character and Destiny, 1817–1914* (New York: Harper and Row, 1971), 171–74, and David R. Roediger, *The Wages of Whiteness: Race and the Making of the American Working Class* (London: Verso, 1991), 155–56.

2. Louis Althusser identifies precisely those things we take to be "obviousnesses" as the products of ideology. "Ideology and Ideological State Apparatuses (Notes towards an Investigation)," in *Lenin and Philosophy and Other Essays* (New York: Monthly Review Press, 1971), 171–72.

3. "Is It Still Taboo for Blacks and Whites to Kiss in Movies?" *Jet*, 27 April 1998, 32.

4. Especially interesting is that Denzel Washington's concerns to please black female viewers and white male ones can be met simultaneously by refraining from on-screen romances with white women. The implication that particular representations of interracial desire, or their repression, can serve multiple pleasures and politics will prove instructive. "Is It Still Taboo for Blacks and Whites to Kiss in Movies?" 35–36.

5. For a long time film scholars only occasionally treated the subject in readings of particular films or, in passing, in larger studies of African Americans in cinema (e.g., Ed Guerrero, *Framing Blackness: The African American Image in Film* [Philadelphia: Temple University Press, 1993]; Mark Reid, *Redefining Black Film* [Berkeley and Los Angeles: University of California Press, 1993]; Thomas Cripps, *Slow Fade to Black: The Negro in American Film, 1900–1942* [London: Oxford University Press, 1977]; Cripps, *Making Movies Black: The Hollywood Message Movie from World War II to the Civil Rights Era* [New York: Oxford University Press, 1993]; Daniel J. Leab, *From Sambo to Superspade* [Boston: Houghton Mifflin, 1976]; and Donald Bogle, *Toms, Coons, Mulattoes, Mammies and Bucks: An Interpretive History of Blacks in American Films*, new expanded edition [New York: Continuum, 1993]). Gina Marchetti wrote the first book-length treatment of interracial desire in film, focused on Asians and Caucasians, *Romance and the "Yellow Peril": Race, Sex, and Discursive Strategies in Hollywood Fiction* (Berkeley and Los Angeles: University of California Press, 1993). Interracial screen fantasies have since continued to receive more attention. See especially Sharon Willis, *High Contrast: Race and Gender in Contemporary Hollywood Film* (Durham, N.C.: Duke University Press, 1997); Jane M. Gaines, *Fire and Desire: Mixed-Race Movies in the Silent Era* (Chicago: University of Chicago Press, 2001); and Linda

Williams, *Playing the Race Card: Melodramas of Black and White from Uncle Tom to O. J. Simpson* (Princeton, N.J.: Princeton University Press, 2001).

6. The fast-growing body of work on the topic beyond film studies includes (only partially) Martha Hodes, *White Women, Black Men: Illicit Sex in the 19th-Century South* (New Haven, Conn.: Yale University Press, 1997); Hodes, ed., *Sex, Love, Race: Crossing Boundaries in North American History* (New York: New York University Press, 1999); James Kinney, *Amalgamation! Race, Sex, and Rhetoric in the Nineteenth-Century American Novel* (Westport, Conn.: Greenwood, 1985); Werner Sollors, *Neither Black nor White Yet Both: Thematic Explorations of Interracial Literature* (New York: Oxford University Press, 1997); Jean Walton, *Fair Sex, Savage Dreams: Race, Psychoanalysis, and Sexual Difference* (Durham, N.C.: Duke University Press, 2001); Robyn Wiegman, *American Anatomies: Theorizing Race and Gender* (Durham, N.C.: Duke University Press, 1995); Joel Williamson, *New People: Miscegenation and Mulattoes in the United States* (New York: Free Press, 1980); and Robert J. C. Young, *Colonial Desire: Hybridity in Theory, Culture and Race* (London: Routledge, 1995).

7. Nick Browne, "Race: The Political Unconscious of American Film," *East-West Film Journal* 6, no. 1 (1992): 5–16.

8. Michael Rogin, *Blackface, White Noise: Jewish Immigrants in the Hollywood Melting Pot* (Berkeley and Los Angeles: University of California Press, 1996).

9. I borrow this language from Sharon Willis, whose important book on race, gender, and Hollywood also considers how "social identities are not accidentally or occasionally inflected by each other but, instead, are mutually constituting" (*High Contrast*, 179).

10. While the phenomenal success of *Birth* far exceeds that of *Guess Who's Coming to Dinner*, in addition to its oddly enduring status in the decades since, the latter was the second-highest-grossing film of 1968, was nominated for (all of the) major Academy Awards of 1967, and received them for Best Actress and Best Original Screenplay. Both films were on the American Film Institute's 1998 list of the hundred best American films of all time. That *Guess* came in next to last on the list suggests the AFI makes no great claims to its aesthetic achievement but, one imagines, includes it for having brought the civil rights movement to the screen—a choice that reaffirms the cultural status of the Tracy-Hepburn film. Cobbett S. Steinberg, *Film Facts* (New York: Facts on File, 1980), 25, 241.

11. The language of "intersection" to describe the convergence of constructions, and experiences, of race and gender (as well as other forms of difference) comes from Kimberlé Crenshaw. See her "Mapping the Margins: Intersectionality, Identity Politics, and Violence against Women of Color," in *Critical Race Theory: The Key Writings That Formed the Movement*, ed. Kimberlé Crenshaw, Neil Gotanda, Gary Peller, and Kendall Thomas (New York: New Press, 1995), 357–83.

12. Robin Wood implies as much in a reassessment of *Mandingo*. After the section heading "Miscegenation," he declares: "If *Mandingo* is the greatest Hollywood film about race [which he has announced plainly he believes it to be], it is because it is also about sex and gender." "*Mandingo*: The Vindication of an

Abused Masterpiece," in *Sexual Politics and Narrative Film: Hollywood and Beyond* (New York: Columbia University Press, 1998), 267.

13. *The Bodyguard* (1992), *Jungle Fever*, *Mr. and Mrs. Loving* (1996), and *Othello* (1995).

14. That this story codes the interracial couple as a particularly spectacular subject is further suggested by the fact that the only other story in the issue with a similarly repetitive and voluminous visual layout is on a fashion show.

15. Lips touch in only one of the images (and even then the couple is laughing and the contact is partial), and only in two others are lovers poised to kiss.

16. Although *Jet* targets black readers, this particular cover—which I spotted at an upscale grocery store in the South with predominantly white shoppers and predominantly black clerks—casts a relatively wide net at the checkout stand with its simultaneous flashing of black and white, male and female stars, and a titillating interracial topic.

17. In a related reading I came to after drafting this one, Sharon Willis queries the media's reception and production of the primary interracial couple from *Jungle Fever* after the film's release. She asks, "How does that film get reduced to an icon, like the one offered on *Newsweek*'s cover (June 10, 1991)? This staged image posed Snipes and Sciorra . . . in a highly theatrical embrace" (*High Contrast*, 158). Her answer situates the icon in the context of an image culture that structures all controversial subjects "as punctual spectacles [in which] social issues take on a dramatic—or melodramatic—shape that is designed to suggest swift and effective resolution" (159). When that structure takes up race in particular, she argues, it facilitates "the dominant culture's 'passion of ignorance'" about the subject (159).

18. Here I take up a line of inquiry first posited in *"Race," Writing, and Difference* (Chicago: University of Chicago Press, 1985), edited by Henry Louis Gates Jr. Whereas that work and much that has followed since ask us to critically theorize and historicize "race" as it has been formed through various writings, I will pursue the cinematic ramifications of the inquiry to ask what it means to read "race" in and through the cinematic image. While I invoke such quotation marks at moments when it is especially important to remember the fictive, discursive character of the categories in question, they are always implicit. At the same time, equally important to this book are the profoundly real and consequential effects that can follow from such cultural fictions.

19. As Willis puts it, "If the dominant media kept trying to read *Jungle Fever* as a failed ethnography of interracial relationships, it overlooked the possibility that the film might perform another ethnography, an ethnography of the dominant white gaze" (*High Contrast*, 179).

20. The interracial relationship between a working-class white man and a professional black woman might have a future after the film, but Flipper's final embrace, punctuated by a scream of "No!" that reverberates after the film has ended, emphasizes the refusal that marks his renewed commitment to Harlem. For black men, the ending seems to say, that is a commitment that demands the reimposition of intraracial desire.

21. For an analysis of the scholarly tradition that celebrates Griffith in a troubled relation to his racist film, see Clyde Taylor, "The Re-birth of the Aesthetic in

Cinema," in *The Birth of Whiteness: Race and the Emergence of U.S. Cinema*, ed. Daniel Bernardi (New Brunswick, N.J.: Rutgers University Press, 1996), 15–37.

22. Tom Gunning and André Gaudreault characterize early cinema as a "cinema of attractions," calling attention to the ways it flaunts its exhibitionism. Gunning, "The Cinema of Attraction: Early Film, Its Spectator and the Avant-Garde," *Wide Angle* 8, nos. 3/4 (1986): 63–70.

23. Jane Gaines reads *Tunnel* this way: "The historical asserts itself in every interracial sexual encounter. . . . If this early film fragment is finally incoherent on the subject of interracial sexuality, this merely signals the calculated oblivion of white society. . . . This is the audience that, all the while it plunks down its money to see *What Happened in the Tunnel*, still, in the end, would not want to *know* what happened on the train" (*Fire and Desire*, 89). Sharon Willis theorizes the perpetual linkage of interracial sexual fantasy and repression itself in a contemporary context, suggesting things have not changed all that much: "From time to time, this borderline case . . . emerges, or perhaps erupts, as a point of fascination and urgency, but it seems to be repressed just as suddenly. It is as if the dominant culture needed to maintain interracial sexuality as its 'repressed,' permanently ready to return, however briefly" (*High Contrast*, 159). She goes on to suggest that this perpetual return and disappearance serves as a mechanism of containment, pretending to address the "issues" that in fact are only silenced or reduced by the structure she diagnoses.

24. I am indebted here to Carol Clover and Adrienne Davis for conversations very early and quite late in this project, respectively, that were crucial to my recognition and articulation of this historical narrative. Indeed, Clover saw what *Tunnel* threatened to show sooner than I did, and Davis confirmed and significantly strengthened my sense of our culture's having forgotten it. In a manuscript in progress I received just before finally completing this one, Davis articulates the eclipsing of the one interracial pair (what she calls "the slavery paradigm") by the other ("the apartheid paradigm" of segregation) in the popular imagination, before turning to her primary subject, the history of law under slavery that "secured black women *as* sexual property, at the same time excluding them from rights *to* property." Reflecting on the contemporary status of these legacies, she notes of the common cultural assumption that, in effect, the significance of "miscegenation" inheres primarily in the "interracial sexual regulation [of] black men and white women" that it "has decreased somewhat since President Jefferson's biological connection to the Hemings family has been proven. Still, it is telling that there has not been nearly as much publicity or discussion as the depth and degree of denials of their relationship might have suggested." Adrienne D. Davis, "*Loving* against the Law: The History and Jurisprudence of Interracial Sex" (forthcoming).

25. The tie between the train passenger and the film's spectator would have been even more vivid for those who saw the film in the exhibitionary space of the Hale's Tours that "took the form of an artificial railway car . . . combin[ing] auditory, tactile, visual, and ambulatory sensations to provide a remarkably convincing illusion of railway travel." Raymond Fielding, "Hale's Tours: Ultrarealism in the Pre-1910 Motion Picture," in *Film Before Griffith*, ed. John Fell (Berkeley and Los Angeles: University of California Press, 1983), 117. According

to Charles Musser, in 1906 *Tunnel* was "advertised . . . in the trades . . . with this purpose specifically in mind." *Before the Nickelodeon: Edwin S. Porter and the Edison Manufacturing Company* (Berkeley and Los Angeles: University of California Press, 1991), 264. But the links between trains and cinema in play do not end there. In the decision that gave us "separate but equal" only seven years prior to this film, the space of the train car was envisioned as potentially imposing the "enforced commingling of . . . races." Brook Thomas, ed., Plessy v. Ferguson: *A Brief History with Documents* (Boston: Bedford Books, 1997), 42, 50–51. These convergences further bring into relief how two new technologies that provided radically new forms of spatial and temporal mobility, trains and cinema, were also quickly used to legislate difference and constraint. On trains and early cinema more generally, and "sexual and/or racial movements" in *Tunnel* in particular, see Lynne Kirby, *Parallel Tracks: The Railroad and Silent Cinema* (Durham, N.C.: Duke University Press, 1997, 99.

26. See Judith Mayne, "Uncovering the Female Body," in *Before Hollywood: Turn-of-the-Century Film from American Archives*, ed. Charles Musser and Jay Leyda (New York: American Federation of the Arts, 1987), 63–67; Mayne, *The Woman at the Keyhole: Feminism and Women's Cinema* (Bloomington: Indiana University Press, 1990), 173–74; Lauren Rabinovitz, *For the Love of Pleasure: Women, Movies and Culture in Turn-of-the-Century Chicago* (New Brunswick, N.J.: Rutgers University Press, 1998); Miriam Hansen, *Babel and Babylon: Spectatorship in American Silent Film* (Cambridge, Mass.: Harvard University Press, 1991), 39; and Kirby, *Parallel Tracks*.

27. Jacqueline Stewart, *Migrating to the Movies: Cinema and Black Urban Modernity* (Berkeley and Los Angeles: University of California Press, forthcoming), chap. 2.

28. As Kirby puts it, "The women can laugh at the man because everyone can laugh at the black woman—an assumption entirely taken for granted by the film and the society in which it was produced" (*Parallel Tracks*, 99). Mayne specifies the visual terms of that assumption when she writes that the man "kisses the 'wrong' woman, the inappropriate object of spectacle" ("Uncovering the Female Body," 66). In a later text she adds, "If [the women's] laughter suggests a resistance to the authority of the male look, it is a resistance that is nonetheless locked into the hierarchy of subject and object, a hierarchy doubly inscribed through sexual and racial difference. The women's laughter is possible only within a firmly established structure of self and other" (*Woman at the Keyhole*, 173–74).

29. Hazel Carby locates a black feminist critique of such logic from the late nineteenth century, the period that gives rise to this film. Discussing insights from Ida B. Wells in particular, Carby writes, "Black women were relegated to a place outside the ideological construction of 'womanhood.' That term included only white women; therefore the rape of black women was of no consequence outside the black community." "'On the Threshold of Woman's Era': Lynching, Empire, and Sexuality in Black Feminist Theory," in Gates, *"Race," Writing and Difference*, 308–9.

30. See Rabinovitz (*For the Love of Pleasure*) for a reading of female movement in this film and related turn-of-the-century representations.

31. Chang Moon Sohn, "Principle and Expediency in Judicial Review: Misce-

genation Cases in the Supreme Court" (Ph.D. diss., Columbia University, 1971), 10.

32. Phil Brown, "Black-White Interracial Marriages: A Historical Analysis," *Journal of Intergroup Relations* 16, nos. 3 and 4 (fall/winter 1989–90): 28.

33. Sohn, "Principle and Expediency," 10, 12.

34. The antimiscegenation statutes that existed in many states from the 1600s "insured the perpetuation and projection of the slavery system . . . [since] the sexual coupling of Whites with Blacks . . . threaten[ed to] obscure . . . the racial barriers crucial to a caste-based system of slavery." Kenneth James Lay, "Sexual Racism: A Legacy of Slavery," *National Black Law Journal* 13, nos. 1–2 (spring 1993): 167. On property and antimiscegenation law, see also Peggy Pascoe, "Race, Gender and Intercultural Relations: The Case of Interracial Marriage," *Frontiers*, 12, no. 1 (1991): 5–18; Eva Saks, "Representing Miscegenation Law," *Raritan* 8, no. 2 (1988): 39–69; and Patricia J. Williams, "On Being the Object of Property," *Signs: Journal of Women in Culture and Society* 14, no. 1 (1988): 5–24.

35. Carby, "'On the Threshold of Woman's Era,'" 309.

36. This is not to suggest that they were consumed by all viewers in the same ways. While my primary aim in this book is to begin to understand the representational history of these fantasies in popular American film, that history is complicated yet further by equally complex histories of film reception and exhibition. My research at times addresses some of that extrafilmic history, but more work on the complex relations that can obtain between filmic representations and their consumption is very much needed. One important source for investigating alternative readings to those invited by the Hollywood texts is the very different history of interracial fantasies in African American cinema, another complex history well beyond the scope of this book. Several scholars have recently made great strides in that field, especially as it continues to be rediscovered in the silent and early sound period. See, for example, Jane Gaines, *Fire and Desire*, and her earlier essay "Fire and Desire: Race, Melodrama, and Oscar Micheaux," in *Black American Cinema*, ed. Manthia Diawara (New York: Routledge, 1993), 49–70; Charlene Regester, "Black Films, White Censors: Oscar Micheaux Confronts Censorship in New York, Virginia, and Chicago," in *Movie Censorship and American Culture*, ed. Francis G. Couvares (Washington, D.C.: Smithsonian Institution Press, 1996), 159–86; Stewart, *Migrating to the Movies*, chaps. 6, 7; Pearl Bowser and Louise Spence, *Writing Himself into History: Oscar Micheaux, His Silent Films, and His Audiences* (New Brunswick, N.J.: Rutgers University Press, 2000); J. Ronald Green, *Straight Lick: The Cinema of Oscar Micheaux* (Bloomington: Indiana University Press, 2000); and Pearl Bowser, Jane Gaines, and Charles Musser, eds., *Oscar Micheaux and His Circle: African-American Filmmaking and Race Cinema of the Silent Era* (Bloomington: Indiana University Press, 2001).

37. Ruth Frankenberg, *White Women, Race Matters: The Social Construction of Whiteness* (Minneapolis: University of Minnesota Press, 1993), 240.

38. I am thinking here of Freud's reflections on the lack of "logical relations between the dream-thoughts," specifically the lack of connections as indicated through conjunctions like "because" and "although," the common reshuffling of

"chronological sequence," and the confounding of causal relations, all of which require "the restoration of the connections which the dream-work has destroyed . . . to be performed by the interpretive process." Sigmund Freud, *The Interpretation of Dreams* (1900), in *The Standard Edition of the Complete Psychological Works of Sigmund Freud*, trans. James Strachey (London: Hogarth, 1953), 4:312–16.

39. Jane Gaines similarly analyzes lynching: "The central economic concern is shifted onto the sexual, or the threat to real property gets transposed as the threat to symbolic property—White womanhood. But . . . it is not the taboo *sexual* thought that is repressed, it is the *economic* motive that is unspeakable. Sex (even when there was none) was historically asserted and 'money' was denied." Gaines, "Fire and Desire," 54 (original emphasis).

40. My thinking here is indebted to Kaja Silverman's work on ideology and subjectivity, specifically her claim that ideological belief is secured through investments in the psychosexual. Like any period's "dominant fiction," she argues, our current one of the patriarchal family "not only offers the representational system by means of which the subject typically assumes a sexual identity . . . but forms the stable core around which a nation's and a period's 'reality' coheres." Kaja Silverman, *Male Subjectivity at the Margins* (New York: Routledge, 1992), 34, 40.

41. Pinpointing a related divided belief, Robin Wood finds untenable the claim that children of interracial couples "will have difficulty in 'belonging,'" arguing that "such irrational rationalizations are mere cover-ups for a more profoundly irrational distaste for close intimate contact with a skin of a different color, a distaste to which it is difficult to admit precisely because one *knows* it to be irrational" ("*Mandingo*," 269, original emphasis).

42. Frankenberg's 1986 interview with a young woman who "considered herself politically progressive" further maps the fantasy's reach. She "claimed that white women had good reason to be afraid of Black men because 'let's face it, they are only a few generations out of the jungle.'" Not unlike Ginny, this woman would go on to question and qualify her statement ("Who knows whether that's really the reason. I only just thought of it") (*White Women, Race Matters*, 80).

43. At the outset of his investigation of interracial literature, *Neither Black nor White Yet Both*, Werner Sollors cites a host of instances of censorship of interracial literature by groups like the Catholic Church, New York City censors, and the estate of Margaret Mitchell (4–5). Particularly relevant to the current study is the Book-of-the-Month Club's demand that Richard Wright revise original scenes of *Native Son* to soften and excise particular details of Bigger Thomas's relation to Mary Dalton, whom he first encounters in the original text on a movie screen. While the implications of this revision are vast, for the moment I would simply note that the original novel (and, in displaced form, the revision) scripts a sexualized cinematic look—a look both solicited and criminalized by conventional cinematic practice—as that which begins Bigger's fateful relation to Mary Dalton. This signals again the high cultural stakes of interracial desire at the movies. My thanks go to Pamela Barnett for sharing her knowledge, and even her notes, on the relation of the restored original text to the revised one.

Chapter One
The "Agony" of Spectatorship at Biograph

1. Throughout the text I refer to the American Mutoscope and Biograph Company as Biograph, as it was officially renamed in 1910. All films discussed in this chapter were produced at Biograph, unless otherwise noted. Tom Gunning, *D. W. Griffith and the Origins of American Narrative Film* (Urbana: University of Illinois Press, 1991), 3.

2. Daniel Bernardi has also questioned "the relationship between narrativization and racial articulations in Griffith's Biograph films," arguing that Griffith's development of narrative forms "utilizes stylistic techniques—from composition to editing—to articulate an ideology of race that positions 'whites' as normal and superior and 'non-whites' as deviant and inferior." "The Voice of Whiteness: D. W. Griffith's Biograph Films (1908–1913)," in *The Birth of Whiteness: Race and the Emergence of U.S. Cinema*, ed. Daniel Bernardi (New Brunswick, N.J.: Rutgers University Press, 1996), 104.

3. Hazel V. Carby, " 'On the Threshold of Woman's Era': Lynching, Empire, and Sexuality in Black Feminist Theory," in *"Race," Writing and Difference*, ed. Henry Louis Gates Jr. (Chicago: University of Chicago Press, 1985) 309.

4. *Moving Picture World* (hereafter cited as *MPW*), 13 March 1915, 1586 (emphasis mine).

5. Bederman makes this claim explicitly in the context of social and political challenges posed by "working class and immigrant men, as well as middle-class women," to which I would add more specifically the racial and ethnic conflicts enumerated earlier, which she elsewhere suggests are also central to negotiating the white, middle-class male anxieties she identifies. Gail Bederman, *Manliness and Civilization: A Cultural History of Gender and Race in the United States, 1880–1917* (Chicago: University of Chicago Press, 1995) 15.

6. Here I draw not only on Laura Mulvey's seminal thesis on the dominance of a sadistic, voyeuristic male gaze in Hollywood cinema ("Visual Pleasure and Narrative Cinema," *Screen* [1975]; rpt. in Laura Mulvey, *Visual and Other Pleasures* [Bloomington: Indiana University Press, 1989], 14–26), but also on subsequent challenges to, and complications of, theoretical equations between masculinity, looking, and mastery, on the one hand, and femininity, spectacle, and passivity, on the other. While I will address specific critiques as they become pertinent, I sometimes refer to the dominant feminist film theoretical model as generally applicable to classical cinema. I do so not to deny important exceptions to that model but because it remains profoundly useful for understanding how classical cinema regularly, even if not always, constitutes and enforces sexual difference. For a wide range of critiques and revisions in addition to those cited later, see Diane Carson, Linda Dittmar, and Janice R. Welsch, eds., *Multiple Voices in Feminist Film Criticism* (Minneapolis: University of Minnesota Press, 1994); Steven Cohan and Ina Rae Hark, eds., *Screening the Male: Exploring Masculinities in Hollywood Cinema* (London: Routledge, 1993); and Linda Williams, ed., *Viewing Positions: Ways of Seeing Film* (New Brunswick, N.J.: Rutgers University Press, 1995).

7. I take this formulation from Kaja Silverman, whose elaborations beyond

Mulvey's original thesis deeply inform the conceptual terms of this and the following chapter. Most crucially, Silverman develops Mulvey's diagnosis of classical cinema's attribution of castration to the female image by differentiating anatomical from symbolic castration. Silverman marshals this distinction to argue that what Hollywood cinema classically disavows and projects onto women is not the fear of not having a penis but rather the fear of not having fullness of being or self-presence. According to Silverman, it is that symbolic wound, or "lack" (not a physical one), which all subjects undergo with the entry into language, but which classical masculinity disavows and projects onto women in order to make and sustain its claims to mastery and privilege. Hence, classical cinema's tendency to equate masculinity with potent vision and femininity with passive spectacle becomes one of the cultural means through which such claims are championed and sustained. Silverman, *The Acoustic Mirror: The Female Voice in Psychoanalysis and Cinema* (Bloomington: Indiana University Press, 1988), 1–71.

8. Eileen Bowser, "Racial/Racist Jokes in American Silent Slapstick Comedy," *Griffithiana* 53 (May 1995): 35–43.

9. In the first, when a white man climbs up the wall of a white woman's house to pursue her, her black maid puts her hands over his eyes and kisses him nearly a dozen times. In the second, a series of lovers—young and old, black and white—rendezvous under the same tree, only to mix up in the end such that an old white man mistakenly takes the hand of a young black woman to the amused audience of all the other players. Like the visually impaired kisser of *The Mis-Directed Kiss*, this old man requires the aid of his glasses to recognize his error.

10. I cite this non-Biograph example because it so demonstrates the extent to which the white man's failure is visually conceived, even as it branches out to the domain of linguistic puns. This is further evident in the film's setup of the men before the woman arrives at their home/workshop replete with telescopes.

11. Griffith got a job as an actor at Biograph in 1908, where he was also credited for writing a few films before and after he began directing, also in 1908. The ascription of authorship for *Mixed Babies* to him comes from Cooper C. Graham, Steven Higgins, Elaine Mancini, and João Luiz Viera, (*D. W. Griffith and the Biograph Company* [Metuchen, N.J.: Scarecrow Press, 1985], 18), who explain that "it is impossible to determine with any degree of certainty whether an individual submitted an outline, a synopsis, or an actual script" (7). Whatever precise form it first took, *Mixed Babies* nonetheless testifies to the fact that the preoccupation that so significantly marked his directorial oeuvre was visible even at the earliest stage of his career.

12. This figuration of black women is literalized by *What Happened in the Tunnel*'s rewriting of *Love in a Railroad Train* (1902), replacing the earlier film's switch from a white woman to a baby's bottom with a switch from a white woman to a black one.

13. Jacqueline Stewart reads such black servants as part of a larger tendency of early cinema to "figure ... the 'problem' of modern, urbanized Negroes around their changing and/or improper relation to their roles as laborers," hence "register[ing] the fact that African Americans circulate more freely in the marketplace, and in various work spaces." Stewart, *Migrating to the Movies: Cinema*

and Black Urban Modernity (Berkeley and Los Angeles: University of California Press, forthcoming), chap. 2.

14. Kaja Silverman, *Male Subjectivity at the Margins* (New York: Routledge, 1992), especially 125–56.

15. As Stewart puts it, "It is ridiculous that these white men cannot see the overdetermined markers of Blackness (darkness of skin, costume) that are immediately apparent to the spectator" (chap. 2).

16. The white male look was by no means systematically afforded the status of the gaze in early cinema, but such fantasies certainly were entertained there. See Lucy Fischer, "The Lady Vanishes: Women, Magic, and the Movies," in *Film Before Griffith*, ed. John L. Fell (Berkeley and Los Angeles: University of California Press, 1983), 339–54; Linda Williams, "Film Body: An Implantation of Perversions," *Ciné-Tracts* (1981); repr. in *Narrative, Apparatus, Ideology*, ed. Philip Rosen (New York: Columbia University Press, 1986), 507–34; and Judith Mayne, *The Woman at the Keyhole: Feminism and Women's Cinema* (Bloomington: Indiana University Press, 1990), 157–222. Lauren Rabinovitz has more recently challenged earlier claims about the continuity between early and classical articulations of sexual difference, arguing that in the early period "a woman may be a voyeur in some circumstances, and she may even control looking, but only and always within carefully circumscribed situations" (*For the Love of Pleasure: Women, Movies and Culture in Turn-of-the-Century Chicago* [New Brunswick, N.J.: Rutgers University Press, 1998], 85). Further complicating desires to ascertain singularly gendered models for singular periods in film history, the same could be said of classical cinema, albeit under even more regulated terms. Feminist work on horror cinema has been especially instructive in this regard. See Carol J. Clover, *Men, Women, and Chain Saws: Gender in the Modern Horror Film* (Princeton, N.J.: Princeton University Press, 1992); and Rhona J. Berenstein, *Attack of the Leading Ladies: Gender, Sexuality, and Spectatorship in Classic Horror Cinema* (New York: Columbia University Press, 1996).

17. Especially suggestive in this regard is Linda Williams's argument that melodrama is not just a genre but "the fundamental mode of popular American moving pictures . . . the foundation of the classical Hollywood movie," a mode that "move[s] us to pathos for protagonists beset by forces more powerful than they and who are perceived as victims" in a "relatively feminized victimhood . . . identified with virtue and innocence." "Melodrama Revised," in *Refiguring American Film Genres*, ed. Nick Browne (Berkeley and Los Angeles: University of California Press, 1998), 42–43.

18. This is the only Biograph film never released in the United States, due to censors' objections. The censorial history is reported in an appendix in Graham et al., *D. W. Griffith and the Biograph Company*.

19. The catastrophic excess of *The Heart of an Outlaw* is matched by that of *Broken Blossoms*, wherein the mother's death is not explained and the incest is only implied, but the father's murder of his child is brutally explicit.

20. Cf. Nick Browne, "Griffith's Family Discourse: Griffith and Freud," In *Home Is Where the Heart Is: Studies in Melodrama and the Woman's Film*, ed. Christine Gledhill (London: British Film Institute, 1987), especially 226, 233.

21. Frantz Fanon describes white woman as symbolizing "white culture, white

beauty, white whiteness." *Black Skin, White Masks,* trans. Charles Lam Markmann (New York: Grove, 1967), 63. Mary Ann Doane invokes this passage in her discussion of white women in Hollywood in "Dark Continents: Epistemologies of Racial and Sexual Difference in Psychoanalysis and the Cinema," in *Femmes Fatales: Feminism, Film Theory, Psychoanalysis* (New York: Routledge, 1991), 244. Eileen Bowser, ed., *Biograph Bulletins, 1908–1912* (New York: Farrar, Straus and Giroux, 1973), 4. Because the Biograph publicity sheets for each film are reproduced on a single page, I typically provide page citations for each one only with my initial introduction of it.

22. The double spelling ("half breed" and "half-breed") comes from the original text.

23. There is some discrepancy in the literature over whether or not Griffith directed *Tavern-Keeper's Daughter.* While Graham et al. report that he did (*D. W. Griffith and the Biograph Company,* 21), according to Eileen Bowser, production records show it was shot before his directorial work had begun (*Biograph Bulletins,* viii). Regardless, it is clearly in keeping with the kind of work he was immersed in at Biograph. And insofar as my interest in that work is more concerned with its articulations of wider cultural discourses than with individual authorship, the precise authorship of this particular short, or this particular publicity sheet, is not of ultimate importance.

24. Bowser, *Biograph Bulletins,* 1. Interestingly, it is not the white girl but a male Gypsy who is beaten in this film, and hence prompted to kidnap her in revenge. While this beating passes rather quickly and in long shot, Biograph's publicity describes how the bourgeois "husband . . . with a heavy snakewhip lashes the Gypsy unmercifully, leaving great welts upon his swarthy body." This will resonate in the discussion to come of the preoccupation with male suffering in the Indian and Civil War films. Indeed, *Dollie* could be said to anticipate the shift I will elaborate there from fantasies of suffering male bodies to fantasies of suffering female ones.

25. Nick Browne has written that "development of [narrative] cinematic language was, from the very start, linked to a particular subject matter," and by his account "this subject was the family—typically the threat of its dismemberment either by loss of a child or by the death, separation, or violation of a parent" ("Griffith's Family Discourse." 224). Thus, "with Griffith's first film, *The Adventures of Dolly,* . . . either the formal and technical advances in cinema as a medium are introduced, or their meaning is normalised, by reference to some family drama" (224). Reminding us that such forms are not unique to Griffith or the United States, the British *Rescued by Rover* (Cecil Hepworth, 1905) similarly deploys the "gypsy" motif to spatially map a bourgeois child's abduction and return.

26. Gunning notes that the threat of Griffith's intruders "was occasionally intensified by making him (or her) a different race or nationality. . . . But outsiders do not pose the only threat to family harmony. A major source of conflict comes from characters who violate their proper family roles. In 1908 this usually meant adultery (or its suspicion), or a conflict between parents and children (usually over a daughter's choice of a husband)" (*D. W. Griffith and the Origins of American Narrative Film,* 141). Further in this discussion of "the economics of family

harmony" he addresses the frequent closing of films with the family embrace (142). Although Gunning does not interpret it as such, his account suggests that although racial difference is not always "the problem" to be overcome in these films, difference of some kind is. For even when there is not an intruder who is somehow differentiated from the family, the politics of sexual difference that are meted out through "the economics of family" are fundamental to the films' narrative and cinematic organization.

27. Bowser, *Biograph Bulletins*, 47.

28. Ibid., 11.

29. I do not mean to ignore the specificity of distinct racial, ethnic, and class differences, but rather to consider the meaning and effects of the ways Griffith's replication of the chase scenario in film after film conflates them.

30. *MPW*, 19 June 1909, 834 (emphasis mine).

31. Bowser, *Biograph Bulletins*, 59. While the *Bulletin* repeatedly refers to the invader as a "negro," the film introduces him at a black bar in which most other patrons are much darker than he, and a sign on the wall nominates "Black/Tans" as the intended guests of an upcoming dance. In addition to the light-skinned "negro" thief, we also see a light-skinned woman in this scene who ostentatiously enters the bar on the arm of a dark-skinned man. Hence, already in *The Girls and Daddy* we find not only the fantasy of the black man chasing white women but the further formulation of that fantasy in the guise of ambitious, and dangerous, mulattoes who both imply past acts of miscegenation and forebode future ones. At the same time, it should be noted that these characters are not used to publicize the film; instead, the experience emphasized to attract viewers is that of the endangered white girls. The image featured on the *Bulletin* is of one sister fighting off her (racially unclear) attacker, and the bold caption above it advertises the "Exciting Experience of Two Brave Girls."

32. Bernardi reads the shot mentioned here as "rhetorically linking the pursuit of the blackface burglar with the fright and virtue of the white girls" ("The Voice of Whiteness," 122).

33. Clover, *Men, Women, and Chain Saws*, especially 21–64, 166–230.

34. Tom Gunning has unearthed a history of texts (several films and a play) behind this one in which the male figure cannot stop the assault of his loved ones as he hears it over the phone; instead, "the telephone torments him with distance and impotence." Gunning reads such "nightmare[s] of masculine impotence" in the context of "a specifically modern agony . . . the suffering made possible through [technology's] 'annihilation of space and time.'" Tom Gunning, "Heard over the Phone: *The Lonely Villa* and the deLorde Tradition of the Terrors of Technology," in *Screen Histories: A Screen Reader*, ed. Annette Kuhn and Jackie Stacey (Oxford: Oxford University Press, 1998), 223, 222.

35. Prophetically, this was the Gish sisters' first role at Biograph, auditioned for and landed, the story goes, at their first meeting with Mr. Griffith. Richard Schickel, *D. W. Griffith: An American Life* (New York: Simon and Schuster, 1984), 176.

36. Even so, the enemy revealed to the spectator is the family's "slattern maid" aided by her also slattern male friend, and the intruders of *The Lonely Villa* are also marked as working-class.

37. Eileen Bowser, *The Transformation of Cinema, 1907–1915*, History of the American Cinema 2 (Berkeley and Los Angeles: University of California Press, 1990), 173.

38. Bailey Millard, "Indian Brides Who Have Made Their Husbands Rich," *New York Times*, 8 May 1910, 12.

39. Bowser, *Biograph Bulletins*, 5.

40. Immediately before its doubly gendered description, the *Bulletin* just cited describes "the aboriginal American" as "a most noble creature."

41. "The Vogue of Western and Military Drama," *MPW*, 5 August 1911, 271.

42. Richard Abel, *The Red Rooster Scare: Making Cinema American, 1900–1910* (Berkeley and Los Angeles: University of California Press, 1999), 160, 172.

43. Even when I do not use them, quotation marks are always implicit when I use terms like "Indian" and "red" to describe identities constructed by white fantasy and representation. And it gets even more complicated. In this chapter, for example, it is especially problematic to refer to a white identification with whites dressed up in racial masquerade as simply a "cross-racial" identification.

44. As Abel discusses in another context, writers in *Moving Picture World* argued for and against the "accuracy" of Hollywood depictions of Indian character and culture as early as 1909. We should also note that Native Americans appealed to Washington as early as 1911 in protest of Hollywood misrepresentation. Wild West, "Accuracy in Indian Subjects," *MPW*, 10 July 1909, 48; "Kalem Indian Stories Popular," *MPW*, 25 June 1910, 1099; "The 'Make-Believe' Indian," *MPW*, 4 March 1911, 473; Richard V. Spencer, "Indians Protest against Indian Pictures," *MPW*, 8 March 1911, 581; "Indians War on Films," *MPW*, 18 March 1911, 581; "Indians Grieve over Picture Shows," *MPW*, 7 October 1911, 32; W. Stephen Bush, "Moving Picture Absurdities," *MPW*, 16 September 1911, 773.

45. Wild West, "Accuracy in Indian Subjects," 48.

46. Bowser, *Biograph Bulletins*, 31.

47. Ibid., 118.

48. "The Englishman and the Girl," *Variety*, 26 February 1910.

49. Bowser, *Biograph Bulletins*, 169.

50. Resonating with Abel's larger argument about the genre's place in a cinematic project of Americanization, this film's deployment of "The Englishman" in a U.S. context further suggests concerns with national forms of masculinity. While Wilberforce's whimpiness works in part to fortify American masculinity by contrast, the fact that the Americans must dress up in Indian masquerade to act out a more threatening version of masculinity further suggests the psychic proximity of all the white men, inviting us to read the newly arrived Englishman as a kind of proto-American and the production of a fully fledged American manhood as requiring the multiple performances staged within the film. Such a reading invites a consideration of literary traditions in which American national identity emerges through what Michael Rogin has called fantasies of "Indianization." And the historical and representational location of the Biograph Indian films between such literary traditions and the dominant film tradition of Hollywood to

follow further suggests a reading of them as a pivot between, as Rogin argues it, the privileged fantasies of Indianization in the former and of blackface in the later. *Blackface, White Noise: Jewish Immigrants in the Hollywood Melting Pot* (Berkeley and Los Angeles: University of California Press, 1996).

51. A white male body is again the body in jeopardy in *Fate's Interception* (1912), a Western that is not an Indian film but that follows a similar plot to *A Romance of the Western Hills*. After a betrayed "Mexican" girl asks a Mexican friend to kill her white lover, she has a change of heart and rushes to stop the murder. This film, however, dreams up a particularly racist rescue device in which the Mexican avenger who lies in wait in the white man's room blows out the flames of gas lanterns to hide in the darkness but fails to turn off the gas and inadvertently kills himself.

52. *Elderbush Gulch* was completed in May 1913 and released in March 1914 (Graham et al., *D. W. Griffith and the Biograph Company*, 210). Bowser writes: "By 1913 the amateur scriptwriting public was informed that Indian scenarios were not wanted by the studios. They were considered . . . an exhausted vein. . . . People were interested in action, thrills, mystery, and happy endings, not tragic heroes" (*Transformation of Cinema*, 176–77). This shift in public tastes could be read as another sign of the shift I am examining in this chapter from film fantasies that feature male suffering to those that assert male power.

53. Bowser, *Biograph Bulletins*, 465.

54. Ibid., 457.

55. It is perhaps this very representational flexibility that allows *The Red Girl* (1908) to use the same generic repertoire (interracial romances, captivities, chases) to elaborate a story about variously raced and independently minded women. After a series of female adventures, this film closes with a denouement shot of a happy interracial couple of "girls," the "Red Girl" of the title and Kate, "a girl miner" (Bowser, *Biograph Bulletins*, 19). Also pertinent here is Abel's discussion of female viewers reportedly enthralled with the genre and a little-known group of early Westerns featuring "'cowboy girls'" (171, 282 n. 145). Although I have not been able to see these films, such implicit and explicit forms of cross-gender identification—in the heart of the genre most assumed to be undoubtedly "masculine," no less—further resonate with the textual turns pursued throughout this chapter.

56. Bowser reports an increase in Civil War films from "at least a dozen . . . in 1908, twenty-three . . . in 1909, thirty-two in 1910, with a leap to seventy-four in 1911, only fifty-eight in 1912, another leap to ninety-eight in 1913, and just twenty-nine in 1914" (*Transformation of Cinema*, 177).

57. On this shift see also Scott Simmon, *The Films of D. W. Griffith* (Cambridge: Cambridge University Press, 1993), 117.

58. The transitional status of these films is marked in part by their visible similarities to *Birth*, with their scenes of troops heading off to war, battle sequences, and, of course, scenarios of Southern victims trapped in houses surrounded by Northerners and other undesirables.

59. Bowser, *Biograph Bulletins*, 162.

60. Ibid., 126.

61. This embrace will be one of the visible residues of the Biograph prehistory

in *Birth,* where Walthall will again return as a weary Confederate veteran to his mother's outstretched arms.

62. Bowser, *Biograph Bulletins,* 349.

63. This transformation of character echoes the quick changes detected earlier in the Indian films, again pointing to the genres' shared fantasmatic terrain.

64. Bowser, *Biograph Bulletins,* 219.

65. Scott Simmon considers the literary tradition of cross-gender identification in Civil War literature in the context of Biograph films (*Films of D. W. Griffith,* 120–21). See also Elizabeth Young, *Disarming the Nation: Women's Writing and the American Civil War* (Chicago: University of Chicago Press, 1999).

66. In *Swords and Hearts,* Old Ben rescues the white patriarch from the burning estate, and a similar rescue of a child occurs in *His Trust* (1911).

67. The dutiful black servants in the films under discussion are close relatives to those of the more familiar Griffith Biograph films *His Trust* and *His Trust Fulfilled* (1911), films Rogin discusses at some length in his related treatment of the uneven history of gender in Griffith's work, "'The Sword Became a Flashing Vision': D. W. Griffith's *The Birth of a Nation,*" in *"Ronald Reagan," the Movie, and Other Episodes in Political Demonology* (Berkeley and Los Angeles: University of California Press, 1987), 190–235. This essay was very influential to my own thinking here, and I engage it more directly in the next chapter.

CHAPTER TWO
THE MIXED BIRTH OF "GREAT WHITE" MASCULINITY AND THE
CLASSICAL SPECTATOR

1. Randy Roberts, *Papa Jack: Jack Johnson and the Era of White Hopes* (New York: Free Press, 1983), 61. Dan Streible reconstructs the extended London quotation as bracketed here from almost a dozen different sources in *Fight Pictures: A History of Boxing and Early Cinema* (Washington, D.C.: Smithsonian Institution Press, forthcoming), chapter 7. Subsequent references to Streible will be to this manuscript. See also his "Race and the Reception of Jack Johnson Fight Films," in *The Birth of Whiteness: Race and the Emergence of U.S. Cinema,* ed. Daniel Bernardi (New Brunswick, N.J.: Rutgers University Press, 1996), 170–200. I also am grateful to Streible for generously sharing his expertise in conversation.

2. Streible, *Fight Pictures,* chapter 7.

3. Ibid. Alternatively, Streible shows Johnson's success to have been a great source of "race pride" for African Americans, and both he and Al-Tony Gilmore (*Bad Nigger! The National Impact of Jack Johnson* [Port Washington, N.Y.: Kennikat, 1975]) consider critiques in the black press (some of which I will discuss) of the dominant, white constructions of Johnson. My emphasis here on the white narratives reflects this book's interrogation of dominant fantasies of miscegenation.

4. These dates mark victories in heavily publicized fights with Tommy Burns (26 December 1908), Stanley Ketchel (16 October 1909), Jim Jeffries (4 July 1910), and Jim Flynn (4 July 1912). Streible documents the reception of these fights, and their films, in detail.

5. Refusing to fight Johnson, Jeffries gave his title away in 1905. Streible cites Jeffries's admission that "the title will never go to a negro if I can help it" (*Fight Pictures*, chapter 7).

6. Gail Bederman, *Manliness and Civilization: A Cultural History of Gender and Race in the United States, 1880–1917* (Chicago: University of Chicago Press, 1995), 1.

7. Streible, *Fight Pictures*, chapter 7.

8. Ibid.

9. The Federation of Church Clubs, for example, was making plans to push a bill with this language in New York. "For a Law to Stop Fight Pictures," *New York Times*, 16 July 1910, 2. See Gilmore for a discussion of local censorship campaigns and bans throughout the country (*Bad Nigger!* 75–93).

10. Finnis Farr, *Black Champion* (Greenwich, Conn.: Fawcett, 1964), 133 (original emphasis).

11. Attempts to ban the Johnson-Jeffries fight films failed in Berlin, but in London they resulted in a resolution denouncing them as "undesirable." According to one historian of international film censorship, the "considerable agitation" regarding the Johnson-Jeffries fight film in England too was "not unconnected with the fact that it showed a Negro defeating a white man." "Berlin to See Fight Films," *New York Times*, 16 December 1911, 4. Neville March Hunnings, *Film Censors and the Law* (London: George Allen and Unwin, 1967), 50.

12. U.S. Congress, Senate, *Cong. Rec.*, 1 August 1912, 9988; U.S. Congress, House, *Cong. Rec.*, 19 July 1912, 9305. Despite that "other" clause, apparently the law was never used to ban anything but films.

13. Roger Marchetti, *Law of the Stage, Screen and Radio* (San Francisco: Suttonhouse, 1936), 113–14 (emphasis mine).

14. On the failure of a bill to ban the exhibition of prize fight films introduced in the House by Representative Smith (R-Iowa) in 1910, Streible writes: "With Jeffries given a chance to win, the all-white, all-male Congress demonstrated it had no desire to pass the Smith bill" (*Fight Pictures*, chapter 8).

15. U.S. Congress, House, *Cong. Rec.*, 1 July 1912, 8551.

16. U.S. Congress, House, *Cong. Rec.*, 19 July 1912, 9305.

17. Ibid. (emphasis mine).

18. Gilmore, *Bad Nigger!* 75–79.

19. Ibid., 83, quoting the *Chattanooga Times*, 7 July 1910.

20. Marchetti explains that prize fight films were still illegal as late as 1936, despite the fact that by then prize fights were "legal in almost all of the states and despite the fact that there is no prohibition on the circulation of vividly detailed and illustrated newspaper accounts or on the blow-by-blow accounts from the ring via the radio, and despite the fact that no ban is placed on the circulation and distribution of scenes in motion picture plays of prize fights, duels, rough and tumble battles as violent and brutal as any 'real' or unstaged contretemps" (*Law of the Stage, Screen and Radio*, 114).

21. Streible, *Fight Pictures*, chapter 7.

22. Johnson's public image is discussed in all texts written about him. He was known not only for his prowess in the ring and with white women (as I will address) but also for dressing extravagantly, showing off, driving fast, and having a

good time. Gilmore cites such characteristics in explanation of his book's title, *Bad Nigger!* (13).

23. The recent exception is Gail Bederman, who so recognizes the centrality of masculinity to the Johnson phenomenon that she invokes it, as partially cited earlier, to begin (and illustrate the cover of) her book on racialized turn-of-the-century struggles over conceptions of manhood. While her contextualization of the phenomenon has been extremely helpful to my analysis of its filmic components, her analysis emphasizes the (re)fortification of male power through racial discourse, while in this case I find that power also significantly envisioned at risk in racial terms

24. The circulation of one story about Johnson's penis in particular, of him wrapping it in gauze bandages prior to public displays, suggests that such mythologies continue. Seizing on it, as I have here, as an indicator of the questions of masculinity at stake in the Johnson phenomenon, Bederman writes that he "actually wrapped his penis in gauze to enhance its size . . . flaunting his genital endowments for all to admire" (*Manliness and Civilization*, 8). Her citation locates the story in two earlier scholarly accounts, Gilmore's *Bad Nigger!* and Roberts's *Papa Jack*. Roberts, it turns out, cites Gilmore for the story. And Gilmore in turn cites (without specifying a page number) Robert H. deCoy's *Jack Johnson: The Big Black Fire* (Los Angeles: Holloway, 1969), a book that claims on its cover to be an "uncensored biography." But deCoy recounts the story (60) in ways that complicate its subsequent interpretation as evidence of Johnson as sexual powerhouse and agent provocateur. On the one hand, the source of the story is uncertain, as deCoy's is a popular, celebratory biography riddled with quotation marks but no citations. On the other hand, if the story is accurate, what has been minimized in the translations is deCoy's contextualization, which introduces it as Johnson's "mock[ing]" response to "'perverted curiosities'" that surrounded him at a moment when he was known to be involved with two different white women—curiosity exhibited in the form of gossip, pornographic comics depicting him "with an oversized, out of proportion penis, in grotesque positions with little white virgins," and onlookers who "flocked to the [boxing] camp for a sight of his oversized member" (59). Moreover, while that context is at least alluded to in claims that he "played on" white fantasies (Gilmore, *Bad Nigger!* 14) or "actively used them to position himself" (Bederman, *Manliness and Civilization*, 8), what drops out of the retellings altogether is deCoy's assertion that the gauze act was "one accommodation he would live the rest of his life to regret" (60). The erasure of such regret, and the profound limits it would seems to signify, thus seem to still haunt our stories about Johnson.

25. The autobiography, on the other hand, offers five half-page stills from the Johnson-Jeffries fight, each of which variously displays, visually and through captions, the range of skills and strength demonstrated in Johnson's victory. John Arthur Johnson, *Jack Johnson Is a Dandy: An Autobiography* (New York: Chelsea, 1969).

26. One of these, an advertisement from the 1970 film *The Great White Hope*, explicitly illustrates my claim that these pictures of Johnson loving white women come to take the place of those of him beating white men. The ad features a photo of James Earl Jones, as Johnson, with his massive arms encircling Jane Alexander,

playing his (composite) white wife, about the neck, and the caption above them reads: "He could beat any white man in the world. He just couldn't beat all of them." The only sense to be made of the text from the photo below it is that the white woman is, in effect, the one "white man" he couldn't beat. Reprinted in deCoy, *Jack Johnson*, between 256 and 257.

27. Gilmore, *Bad Nigger!* 98.

28. Lee Grieveson reads these parallel regulations of Johnson and his films together to argue that "concern with disciplining the movement of a . . . black body through social space . . . became enmeshed with the regulation of moving pictures" more generally. Lee Grieveson, "Fighting Films: Race, Morality, and the Governing of Cinema, 1912–1915," *Cinema Journal* 38, no. 1 (1998): 40. On Johnson's prosecution, see his biographers previously cited and David J. Langum, *Crossing over the Line: Legislating Morality and the Mann Act* (Chicago: University of Chicago Press, 1994), 179–86.

29. Roberts, *Papa Jack*, 146.

30. U.S., Congress, House, *Cong. Rec*, 11 December 1912, 503.

31. Chang Moon Sohn, "Principle and Expediency in Judicial Review: Miscegenation Cases in the Supreme Court" (Ph.D. diss., Columbia University, 1971), 21–22. U.S. Congress, House, *Cong. Rec*, 11 December 1912, 502.

32. U.S. Congress, House, *Cong. Rec.*, 11 December 1912, 502.

33. Sohn, "Principle and Expediency in Judicial Review," 20–23.

34. Gilmore, *Bad Nigger!* 85.

35. *Chicago Broad Ax*, 9 July 1910, cited in ibid.

36. While critics have commonly assumed *Birth* to be based on Dixon's novel *The Clansman* (1905) and its predecessor, *The Leopard's Spots* (1903), Russell Merritt claims there is "no evidence that Griffith ever read *The Leopard's Spots*" and argues that Griffith was working with the stage version of *The Clansman*, also written by Dixon, but unpublished, as well as the novel. "Dixon, Griffith, and the Southern Legend: A Cultural Analysis of *The Birth of a Nation*," in *Cinema Examined*, ed. Richard Dyer MacCann and Jack C. Ellis (New York: Dutton, 1982), 173.

37. *Chicago Broad Ax*, 9 July 1910, cited in Gilmore, *Bad Nigger!* 86.

38. Although I am interrogating collective rather than individual fantasies, Freud is nonetheless influential to my thinking about how "beating" and "loving" can become interchangeable in fantasy, and about how the roles of beater and beaten can undergo manifold castings and recastings to suit various psychic ends. Sigmund Freud, "A Child Is Being Beaten" (1919), in *The Standard Edition of the Complete Psychological Works of Sigmund Freud*, trans. James Strachey (London: Hogarth, 1986), 17:179–204.

Linda Williams recently reads American interracial beating fantasies in a wider historical sequence. Beginning with the image in *Uncle Tom's Cabin* of a white man beating a black man (the "Tom" image), she moves between it and the image of a black man assaulting a white woman (the "anti-Tom" image) in popular texts of the last two centuries. My analysis here could be described as an excavation of layers beneath the anti-Tom tradition (because my texts emerge *after* slavery, the white cultural fear is of white vulnerability, not, as in Stowe's novel, the vulnerability of enslaved blacks). This material clearly complicates Williams's assertion that in the first decades of American film the "spectacle of a black man beating a white man was not publicly tolerated"—a claim she pins to the ban on Johnson fight films without regard to their initial popularity. *Playing the Race Card: Melodramas of Black and White from Uncle Tom to O. J. Simpson* (Princeton, N.J.: Princeton University Press, 2001), 86. Whereas the fantasy of the white man being beaten tends to disappear with her two models, it could be read as the place where they join before being displaced onto other bodies.

39. Streible, *Fight Pictures*, chapter 7.

40. Ibid., chapter 8.

41. Ibid., chapter 7.

42. Ibid.

43. Ibid.

44. Ibid.

45. Ibid. Streible documents a considerable industry in still and moving pictures of the Johnson-Jeffries fight, actual and faked, including lantern slide collections "in various levels of price and quality—from Joseph Levi & Co.'s set of twelve views, to Duhem & Hartern's one hundred color slides."

46. Ibid.

47. Ibid.

48. Cf. chapter 1.

49. Streible, *Fight Pictures*, chapter 8. This dominant image of Johnson, like others, was contested by a variety of resistant ones. Especially striking is Streible's discovery of a revival screening of the Johnson-Jeffries film in black Chicago in 1915 that the *Chicago Defender* read "not as a rebuttal to Willard's supporters but to Griffith's." Charlene Regester reads Oscar Micheaux's depiction of a black boxer knocking out a white one in *The Brute* (1920) as another black revisitation of Johnson's victories, and one that censors in Chicago were still not willing to tolerate in 1920. "Black Films, White Censors: Oscar Micheaux Confronts Censorship in New York, Virginia, and Chicago," in *Movie Censorship and American Culture,* ed. Francis G. Couvares (Washington, D.C.: Smithsonian Institution Press, 1996), 169.

50. *Cong. Rec.*, 11 December 1912, 503–4. The present chapter was prompted in part by a suspicion that, despite the extensive literature on *Birth*, our analyses of the considerable forces the film musters to position spectators and shape our vision is still incomplete, especially when it comes to understanding: (1) the history of what we might call intersectional modes of address—whereby films attempt to define and solicit our investments in multiple forms of difference (racial, sexual, etc.); and (2) the ways such modes can shift and settle across historical periods. In pursuing such questions, however, I do not mean to ignore critiques made of film critical and theoretical studies of spectatorship, namely, that they fail to account for the diversity of audiences and their interpretations. Rather, I seek to expand our accounts of the "intersected" positions, if you will, that films invite us, sometimes urge us, to imagine and assume. We need such work, I think, *in tandem with* studies of reception and exhibition that often complicate or even defy such textual terms, but nonetheless interact with them, to understand the complex history of relations between films and viewers. For a theoretical discussion of how *Birth*'s modes of address can radically fail when a spectator's knowl-

edge or experience makes its demands impossible, see Manthia Diawara, "Black Spectatorship: Problems of Identification and Resistance," *Screen* (1988); repr. in *Black American Cinema*, ed. Manthia Diawara (New York: Routledge, 1993), 211–20. For accounts of the film's complex, uneven reception, by white and black audiences, see Anna Everett, *Returning the Gaze: A Genealogy of Black Film Criticism, 1909–1949* (Durham, N.C.: Duke University Press, 2001), 59–106; Jane Gaines, *Fire and Desire: Mixed-Race Movies in the Silent Era* (Chicago: University of Chicago Press, 2001), 219–57; Janet Staiger, *Interpreting Films: Studies in the Historical Reception of American Cinema* (Princeton, N.J.: Princeton University Press, 1992), 139–53; Thomas Cripps, *Slow Fade to Black: The Negro in American Film, 1900–1942* (London: Oxford University Press, 1977), 41–69; and Merritt, "Dixon, Griffith, and the Southern Legend."

51. Kristin Thompson dates the developmental phase of classical narrative form from 1909 to 1916. David Bordwell, Janet Staiger, and Kristin Thompson, *The Classical Hollywood Cinema: Film Style and Mode of Production to 1960* (New York: Columbia University Press, 1985), 157, 217.

52. While I do not mean to resurrect the myth of *Birth* as origin of classical cinema, I do mean to take seriously the manifold implications of that mythology and its partial truths (e.g., *Birth*'s unprecedented amalgamation and expansion of classical devices, its symbolic status).

53. Following previews in California and New York, *Birth* premiered in New York on 3 March 1915. *The Cheat* was released in December of the same year. See entries in Patricia King Hanson, ed., *American Film Institute Catalog of Motion Pictures Produced in the United States: Feature Films 1911–1920* (Berkeley and Los Angeles: University of California Press, 1988). Other miscegenation films of the era include *The Octoroon* (1913); *Across the Border* (1914); *Where the Trail Divides* (1914); *The Typhoon* (1914); DeMille's *The Squaw Man* (1914), followed by *The Squaw Man's Son* (1917) and two remakes of the original (1918 and 1931); *The Nigger* (1915); *Madame Butterfly* (1915); *Betrayed* (1916); *The Leopard's Bride* (1916); *Lone Star* (1916); *The Bar Sinister* (1917); and dozens of others into the early 1920s. See entries in Hanson, *American Film Institute Catalog*.

54. While the climactic beating in *Broken Blossoms* is performed by the girl's father, and not the Asian man who loves her, insofar as it is prompted by the father's discovery that the girl has been living with Cheng Huan, it significantly echoes, even as it significantly revises, the classic miscegenation beating fantasies.

55. Of *Birth*, Mary Ann Doane writes: "The white woman . . . act[s] as the textual pivot for the elaboration of a discourse on blackness as economic, political, and, most importantly, sexual threat." *Femmes Fatales: Feminism, Film Theory, Psychoanalysis* (New York: Routledge, 1991), 228.

56. See Angela Y. Davis, "Rape, Racism and the Myth of the Black Rapist," in her *Women, Race and Class* (New York: Random House, 1981), 172–201.

57. Hazel V. Carby, " 'On the Threshold of Woman's Era': Lynching, Empire, and Sexuality in Black Feminist Theory," in *"Race," Writing and Difference,* ed. Henry Louis Gates Jr. (Chicago: University of Chicago Press, 1985), 308.

58. Michael Paul Rogin, " 'The Sword Became a Flashing Vision': D. W. Griffith's *The Birth of a Nation,*" in *"Ronald Reagan," the Movie, and Other*

Episodes in Political Demonology (Berkeley and Los Angeles: University of California Press, 1987), 190–235; Sumiko Higashi, "Ethnicity, Class, and Gender in Film: DeMille's *The Cheat*," in *Unspeakable Images: Ethnicity and the American Cinema,* ed. Lester D. Friedman (Urbana: University of Illinois Press, 1991), 112–39; and Gina Marchetti, "The Rape Fantasy: *The Cheat* and *Broken Blossoms*," in *Romance and the "Yellow Peril": Race, Sex, and Discursive Strategies in Hollywood Fiction* (Berkeley and Los Angeles: University of California Press, 1993), 10–45.

59. Robert Lang, "*The Birth of a Nation:* History, Ideology, Narrative Form," in *The Birth of a Nation,* ed. Robert Lang (New Brunswick, N.J.: Rutgers University Press, 1994), 17.

60. While this plot sketch might seem to leave out the role of the Civil War in the film's first half, I will read that conflict as effectively beginning, by the film's account, with the guerrilla raid on Piedmont.

61. On the centrality of narrative to the fundamental principles of classical Hollywood form, see, for example, Bordwell, Staiger, and Thompson's *Classical Hollywood Cinema.*

62. Not only were the actors' living quarters segregated, but, as Griffith describes *Birth*'s casting in his autobiography, "the decision was to have no black blood among the principals" (*Focus on D. W. Griffith,* ed. Harry M. Geduld [Englewood Cliffs, N.J.: Prentice-Hall, 1971], 41). As Rogin puts it, "no black [actor] could be allowed to manhandle Lillian Gish" ("'The Sword Became a Flashing Vision,'" 225). Instead, Griffith would subjugate black actors to the background roles of extras and black up white men to play out the film's foregrounded fantasies of racialized sex.

63. Quoted by a columnist citing a *Chicago Herald* interview. *New Republic,* 5 June 1915, 105. The columnist criticizes the statement as being "an accusation quite characteristic of the tone of *The Birth of a Nation*" and retorts: "The disgust and anger aroused by this photoplay does not require any predilection for intermarriage."

64. "Capitalizing Race Hatred," *New York Globe,* 6 April 1915; repr. in Lang, *Birth of a Nation,* 165, 164.

65. D. W. Griffith, "Reply to the *New York Globe,*" *New York Globe,* 10 April 1915; repr. in Lang, *Birth of a Nation,* 168. Staiger situates this accusation in the context of multiple claims made for and against the film (*Interpeting Films,* 144).

66. Thomas Dixon also recapitulated *Birth*'s miscegenation rhetoric in his response to the *Globe,* reporting that a review by select clergy commended the film's efforts "to prevent the lowering of the standard of our citizenship by its mixture with Negro blood." "Reply to the *New York Globe,*" 166.

67. As a result in part of early efforts to censor the film, some footage has likely disappeared. Accounts of two scenes in particular—a castration sequence during the scene of Gus's bloody "trial" and murder by the Klan, and concluding images of blacks being sent back to Africa—have long circulated, but the source for both is the recollection of a single viewer, Seymour Stern ("Griffith: I—*The Birth of a Nation*: Part I," special Griffith issue *Film Culture* 36 [spring–summer 1965]: 114–32), whose account has become increasingly questioned, but not de-

finitively discredited. While Russell Merritt claims as further evidence for "the final solution" a title cue sheet for the film at the Museum of Modern Art, the published affirmation of those sentiments by Dixon, and "Dixon's Lincoln in *The Clansman*" ("Dixon, Griffith, and the Southern Legend," 181 and n. 35), Robert Lang has declared that "there is no hard evidence that the film ever actually included shots of a wholesale deportation of American blacks to Africa, although there is some indication that there may have been an intertitle referring to 'Lincoln's solution,' 'Back to Liberia!'" (*"Birth of a Nation,"* 11). Both Jane Gaines (*Fire and Desire*, 236) and Linda Williams (*Playing the Race Card*, 127) simultaneously invoke and call into question Stern's account, a double gesture that seems at this point required. For my purposes, it *is* accurate to say that whether or not the film showed a Klansman plunging his knife at Gus below the frame and "a final flash of the castrated Negro's pain-racked face and body" (Stern, "Griffith," 123–24), after the Klansmen have their way with him, Gus's dead body *is* delivered to Lynch's doorstep in a mutilated state (with "KKK" pinned to it) that evokes the aftermath of a lynching. And even without a literal deportation sequence, the film *does* finally succeed, as Williams puts it, in "flushing" the screen of blackness (120).

68. It is telling that a reviewer at *Moving Picture World* would misremember this scene as ending with "Stoneman kissing the mulatto and with this title: 'Thus the fatal weakness of one man blights the nation'" (13 March 1915, 1586). Stoneman does not kiss Lydia; this is not how the title reads; and the sequence of events is incorrect. Nevertheless, the reviewer has misrecalled the details in a way the film itself invites. While Lydia is depicted in these early scenes as a lowly servant who lusts for power, later in the film, following Lincoln's death and Stoneman's subsequent rise in Washington, she will be depicted as the lady of Stoneman's house. Her foregrounded presence there contributes to the film's eventual characterization of what it dubs the new "Executive Mansion of the Nation" as "this strange house on Capitol Hill." Insofar as Lydia presides as the de facto queen to Stoneman's "uncrowned king," this "strange," because interracial, house on Capitol Hill already threatens to imply a mixed ruling couple and hence a mixed nation. Silas Lynch will later voice this fantasy as his own when, having announced his desire to marry Elsie, he exclaims: "See! My people fill the streets. With them I will build a Black Empire and you as a Queen shall sit by my side." Thus, the film points the finger at Stoneman for sanctioning Lynch's transgressive sexual desires, as much as it clearly blames Stoneman (the Northern "radical") for his encouragement of Lynch's political desires.

69. Significantly, as Rogin also points out, the film here too reverses and denies the power dynamics of the male-female and master-servant relations by making "Stoneman subservient to Lydia" ("'The Sword Became a Flashing Vision,'" 209).

70. I consider the potential fallout of this historical legacy for popular representation in future chapters, especially in discussions of what the Production Code can be read as having worked to repress, in chapters 3 and 4, and of what *Guess Who's Coming to Dinner* did and did not finally confront, in chapter 6.

71. As is evident already, Rogin's reading paved the way for my own in several respects. Identifying "the multiple rescue operations performed by the ride of

the Klan" as bringing together "three converging histories[:] the political history of postbellum America, the social history of movies, and the history of Griffith's early films" ("'The Sword Became a Flashing Vision,'" 191), he read the representations of race and gender in *Birth* and two earlier Biograph films in the context of "the general crisis of patriarchy at the end of the nineteenth century" (198). Yet whereas Rogin ultimately focused on the phallic failure of fathers, both Griffith's own alcoholic one and the symbolic Father of patriarchy more generally, I focus on the cinematic articulation of such concerns and the consequences thereof for popular representation. Rogin (191) cites Griffith's recollection as reported in *The Man Who Invented Hollywood: The Autobiography of D. W. Griffith*, ed. James Hart (Louisville, Ky.: Touchstone, 1972) 89, 28–29.

72. *MPW*, 13 March 1915, 1586.

73. Like all historical "facts" *Birth* draws upon, that the real Pennsylvania senator Stoneman's character was modeled on, Thaddeus Stevens, did in fact have a clubfoot and a wig, and even a mulatto maid and possible mistress, is only significant to a point. Mimi White's analysis of *Birth*'s overt historical references demonstrates that "the use of citation is neither consistent nor sustained. It is an intermittent practice which the film employs to (re)establish its bearings, but which it dispenses with, once having marked its 'authenticity' and 'historicity' in such a manner." White notes such a dispensing of Stoneman's key Stevens-like qualities in particular. Mimi White, "*The Birth of a Nation*: History as Pretext," *Enclitic* (1981/1982); repr. in Lang, *Birth of a Nation*, 216.

74. Russell Merritt notes that "the war episodes [Griffith] chooses to photograph . . . are the ignoble catastrophes of war, not the glorious victories" ("Dixon, Griffith, and the Southern Legend," 180), and he explicitly ties this to the Biograph tradition. Rogin links the two implicitly when he writes that such scenes "compose an ecstasy of pain" ("'The Sword Became a Flashing Vision,'" 211).

75. Readers of the previous chapter will recall that at Biograph white Southern men repeatedly fail the cause due to various combinations of fear, drunkenness, and incompetence.

76. White reads some of the same textual relations I will here to demonstrate the film's privileging of the personal and familial over the national ("*Birth of a Nation*," 219–24).

77. In a letter we read with Ben, Flora signs off "XXXXXX (Kisses)/ Your big/ Sis."

78. In addition to the extreme long shots of Sherman's march (discussed later), we see many long and extreme long shots of troops moving across battlefields and citizens fleeing in the foreground while Atlanta burns in the distant background. The epic quality of these images comes not only from the camera's distance but also from the fiery red tints and split-screen effects, effects that seem to both intensify the chaos and violence of war and to mark it as larger than the ordinary lives elsewhere depicted with soft browns and simpler, more intimate compositions.

79. As will become increasingly significant with the following analysis, these shots also establish a dramatically disembodied vantage point for the spectator.

80. While the 1992 restoration of *Birth* (currently distributed on videotape and DVD by Kino International, and on DVD by Image Entertainment) does not

include the original shot replicated in this flashback, the MOMA print that served as the basis for Robert Lang's meticulous continuity script of the film (and distributed by Republic) does. In that script the shots in question are numbered 334 and 767. From the discrepancy it appears that the 1992 print does not include the actual "death of the second Cameron son" as the missing intertitle describes it but merely alludes to it when news of it reaches his family not long thereafter. Lang, *Birth of a Nation*, 66, 106.

81. The intertitle that immediately follows this scene, and sets up the next one between Ben and Elsie, reads: "Still a North and a South. Pride battles with love for the heart's conquest."

82. Maureen Turim reads this moment as "a subjective framing of history" that is "structurally crucial to the film's ideological slant, for it structures memory as the South's province" (*Flashbacks in Film: Memory and History* [New York: Routledge, 1989], 105, 42). She also notes that the flashbacks through which Ben recounts to other men "a series of outrages" committed by blacks "support . . . the film's racism and . . . nostalgia for Aryan privilege and domination" by giving them the look of objectively recalled fact (42). Turim's analysis invites us to further consider the contrast between the femininity of white, Southern suffering in the one example, versus the masculinity of a flashback that functions to represent historical, white "truth." Readers of chapter 1 will also recognize this scene's resonance with the logic uncovered, but only just begun there, whereby the white "Southern rose" carries the filmic burden of suffering on her brother's behalf.

83. Here I recur to the discussion of feminist film theory I began in chapter 1. Jane Gaines, for one, recognized early on that filmic transactions of men looking at women were never singularly about gender. "White Privilege and Looking Relations: Race and Gender in Feminist Film Theory" (1988); repr. in *Issues in Feminist Film Criticism*, ed. Patricia Erens (Bloomington: Indiana University Press, 1990), 197–214.

84. I first invoked Clover to discuss Griffith's suffering white women in chapter 1. For her account of how the slasher film's young female victim-hero allows the genre's typically young male viewer to enjoy masochistically, see *Men, Women, and Chain Saws* (Princeton, N.J.: Princeton University Press, 1992), 21–44.

85. On the questions surrounding the "missing" castration footage, see note 67.

86. As Robyn Wiegman writes, the black man's "threat to white masculine power arises not simply from a perceived racial difference, but from the potential for sameness." "In the context of white supremacy," she continues, "we must understand the threat of masculine sameness as so terrifying that only the reassertion of a gendered difference can provide the necessary disavowal." *American Anatomies: Theorizing Race and Gender* (Durham, N.C.: Duke University Press, 1995), 90.

87. See Lynne Segal, "Competing Masculinities (III): Black Masculinity and the White Man's Black Man," in her *Slow Motion: Changing Masculinities, Changing Men* (New Brunswick, N.J.: Rutgers University Press, 1990). Doane, reading Fanon, also discusses the ways in which "whiteness . . . relegates black-

ness to . . . corporeality. . . . The black *is* the body, *is* the biological" (224). Approaching this in the context of American national identity more specifically, Robyn Wiegman writes that "in the constitution of the citizen as a disembodied entity . . . the white male was (and continues to be) 'freed' from the corporeality that might otherwise impede his insertion into the larger body of national identity," whereas "for the African-American male subject . . . it was precisely the imposition of an extreme corporeality that defined his distance from the privileged ranks of citizenry" (*American Anatomies*, 94).

88. Too irresistible not to note is a recent story about a filibuster in the actual State House restaged in the film, now composed of predominantly white and male legislators. During a seventeen-hour debate on video poker, the House was filled with sleeping bags, barbecue, and senators "smacking their lips and licking their fingers," and after a night and a day "empty food sacks . . . litter the senators' desks, competing for space with the feet propped up on many." John Reinan, "Senators Work Chops on Barbecue, Bon Mots," *Columbia (S. C.) State*, 27 March 1998, A11.

89. Silverman maintains that no human look is ever equivalent to the mastery of the gaze, but only postures as such in the course of asserting privilege. Male possession of the look, she suggests, has thus been misrecognized in film theory as ownership of the gaze. *Male Subjectivity at the Margins* (New York: Routledge, 1992), 125–56.

90. While my reading of *Birth*'s visual regime is largely influenced by feminist film theory and criticism, more recently it finds close affinities with Richard Dyer's investigation of representations of whiteness: "There is a specificity to white representation, but it does not reside in a set of stereotypes so much as in narrative structural positions, rhetorical tropes and habits of perception." *White* (London: Routledge, 1997), 12. See also his reading of how *Birth* "betrays a feeling that the South is, after all, not quite white enough to give birth to the new white nation." "Into the Light: The Whiteness of the South in *The Birth of a Nation*," in *Dixie Debates,* ed. Richard King and Helen Taylor (New York: New York University Press, 1996), 175.

91. This very scene prompts Doane to reflect that "Blacks will habitually be confined in the Hollywood cinema to providing an environment, a space, 'local color,' a background for the unfolding of white dramas" (*Femmes Fatales*, 230–31).

92. Doane writes: "Whiteness is not a characteristic of the skin but is hyperbolized and ritualized as the white robes of the Ku Klux Klan which function to conceal identities" (ibid., 228).

93. That an inaugural scene of sexual difference (boy and girl under the sheet) is pressed into the service of representing an emerging representational system of racial difference (for Ben and the film) renders particularly vivid Dyer's claim that "concepts of race are always concepts of the body and also of heterosexuality. . . . Heterosexuality is the means of ensuring, but also the site of endangering, the reproduction of [racial] differences" (*White*, 20).

94. The omnipotence of Ben's vision in this scene is underscored by its textual echo of the epic pan from part 1. These two shots share a set-up (a hillside over-

looking a valley) that is replicated nowhere else in the film. The closest exception completes the trio, as I will later elaborate, in the final sequence.

95. The gun-to-the-white-woman's-head trope has a long life in Hollywood, as exemplified in both *Stagecoach* (1939) and *The Searchers* (1956), where we see and hear, respectively, the philosophy that "a bullet in her brain" is better than a white woman potentially being raped by, or even cohabitating with in the second case, a man of color.

96. Even if Klansmen can never literally see as much as we do, their gazelike power is pivotally indicated when their "white spies disguised" (in blackface), assumedly to advance the mission to "disarm all blacks," inadvertently see Elsie at Lynch's window. This virtually miraculous sighting not only offers them and us an exact (masterful) reversal of the captive view she holds within, but without it Ben and the rest of the Klan would have no knowledge of her captivity. Indeed, the discovery happens so quickly that it can cause a rare glitch in the otherwise tight series of causal chains that set the rescue in motion. And yet, if the spectator misses this "disguised" and fortuitous look, which is easy to do, the rescue seems all the more omniscient, as we cannot remember how the Klan knew it needed to get here in the first place!

97. As Kristin Thompson summarizes it, what "underlies the development of the classical system" is "the basic idea of creating the spectator as an invisible onlooker at the ideal vantage point." She elaborates: "The primitive cinema's placement of the spectator at a distance did not always provide the best view for grasping important narrative information. But the omnipresent narration of the classical cinema situates the spectator at the optimum viewpoint in each shot. Staging, composition, and editing combine to move that viewpoint instantly as the action shifts" (*Classical Hollywood Cinema*, 214).

98. Gina Marchetti finds a related kind of movement in *The Cheat*, wherein "the film teeters between masochistic and sadistic positions" for both its Asian male and white female characters (*Romance and the Yellow Peril*, 24). Although I am here arguing for the instability of even what we might presume to be the most stable identity/position—that of the spectator who is most closely rhymed with the white male hero himself—that she finds similar oscillation in another of the classic miscegenation silents clearly resonates with my larger claims.

99. The paradox I have in mind lies in the simultaneous facts that classical narrative discourse typically situates its spectator as the one who sees from "the ideal vantage point," in Thompson's words, and yet always absolutely limits and determines what we see. While these poles are variously indulged across genres, episodes, the trajectory of a plot, and the like, they are arguably always in play to some extent. Christian Metz insists on such a duality in a discussion of classical cinema when he claims that "all vision consists of a double movement: projective (the 'sweeping' searchlight) and introjective: consciousness as a sensitive recording surface," a surface he also describes as "soft wax," *The Imaginary Signifier: Psychoanalysis and the Cinema* (Bloomington: Indiana University Press, 1977), 50. Such descriptions seem especially apt here as they echo the modulating forms of vision held out for us and embodied on screen in the "sweeping" gazes of Ben, the Klan, and the white legislators, on the one hand,

and in the "soft," impressionable objects of vision and suffering epitomized by Flora, Margaret, and Elsie.

100. Linda Williams pinpoints a temporal parallel to this oscillation between the spectator's agony and omniscience, masochism and mastery: "To watch a last-minute-rescue . . . is to feel time in two contradictory ways. Although a rapid succession of shots specifying the physical danger gives the effect . . . of events happening extremely fast, the parallel cutting between [the encroaching danger, the rescuer on his way, and the victim at risk] prolongs time beyond all possible belief. Actions *feel* fast, and yet the ultimate duration of the event is retarded. We are moved in both directions at once in a contradictory hurry-up and slow-down" (*Playing the Race Card*, 33).

101. Cf. note 97.

102. These figurations of us and Ben (et al.) perched at the edge of the sea, like the earlier kindred shots, interestingly echo Thompson's description of the newly ideal spectatorial vantage point in the classical system "on the scene's edge," "directly on the edge of the playing area" (*Classical Hollywood Cinema*, 219, 214). As a result, she explains, "The studios' ideal for authenticity and depth was location shooting itself. With no backdrop to cut off the spectator's view, the location shot could create a considerable sense of depth . . . almost automatically at the edge of the narrative space" (219). Hence, we can read this final move from the obviously projected seascape behind Phil and Margaret to the actual cliff from which we look out with Ben and Elsie as yet another peak in the finale's crescendo of classical cinematic visions.

CHAPTER THREE
"THE UN-DOABLE STORIES," THE "USUAL ANSWERS," AND
OTHER "EPIDERMIC DRAMA[S]"

1. It is tempting already to read the epithet as a memorial to classical cinema's gleaming whiteness. On associations of whiteness and light, see Richard Dyer, *White* (London: Routledge, 1997), especially 82–144.

2. I offer a detailed history of the clause later in this chapter. For now it suffices to say that after being an official suggestion in the Don'ts and Be Carefuls of 1927 and the Production Code of 1930, it was included in the even more powerful Production Code of 1934, where it remained until the mid-1950s. The language cited here can be found in various reprints of the Code, including Thomas Doherty, *Pre-Code Hollywood: Sex, Immorality, and Insurrection in American Cinema, 1930–1934* (New York: Columbia University Press, 1999), 363; Garth Jowett, *Film, the Democratic Art* (Boston: Focal, 1976) 469; and Raymond Moley, *The Hays Office* (Indianapolis: Bobbs-Merrill, 1945; repr., New York: Jerome S. Ozer, 1971), 242.

3. On the Code's regulation of homosexuality, see Vito Russo, *The Celluloid Closet: Homosexuality in the Movies* (New York: Harper and Row, 1981); Andrea Weiss, *Vampires and Violets: Lesbians in Film* (New York: Penguin, 1992); and Patricia White, *Uninvited: Classical Hollywood Cinema and Lesbian Representability* (Bloomington: Indiana University Press, 1999).

4. It is briefly mentioned in some books on blacks in Hollywood, and not at all in others. There is a similar absence in the literature on film censorship, dating back to contemporary critics who singled out other banned subjects. See "Virtue in Cans," *Nation*, 16 April 1930, 441, and a 1940 photograph, "Thou Shalt Not," by Whitey Schafer and used on the cover of Thomas Doherty's *Pre-Code Hollywood*. The mocking photo is crowded with prohibited images (a prostitute, a dead cop, liquor, etc.), but there is no sign of miscegenation. Recent critics like Doherty, Ella Shohat, Robert Stam, and Ruth Vasey have begun to correct the long silence. In his chapter on "racial adventure film[s]," Doherty writes, "The psychic core of the genre is . . . the threat and promise of miscegenation" (254).

5. Of the classical period Gregory Black writes, "No film could be produced or exhibited without PCA approval." This overstates the case by ignoring films produced and exhibited beyond the purview of the PCA's parent organization (the Motion Picture Producers and Distributors of America), but it understates the power the PCA had to shape Hollywood films, as I will consider. Black, *Hollywood Censored* (Cambridge: Cambridge University Press, 1994), 2.

6. Ella Shohat, "Ethnicities-in-Relation: Toward a Multicultural Reading of American Cinema," in *Unspeakable Images: Ethnicity and the American Cinema*, ed. Lester D. Friedman (Urbana: University of Illinois Press, 1991), 234.

7. In addition to Cripps, Nesteby, and Doherty (cited below and above), see Rhona Berenstein on jungle horror in *Attack of the Leading Ladies: Gender, Sexuality, and Spectatorship in Classic Horror Cinema* (New York: Columbia University Press, 1996), 160–97.

8. James Snead names the process whereby blackness is emphatically made to be seen "marking": "Initially because of shortcomings of early lenses and film stocks, but later due purely to the needs of image-making rhetoric—black skin has been over-marked in order to eliminate ambiguity." *White Screens, Black Images: Hollywood from the Dark Side* (New York: Routledge, 1994), 5. See also Brian Winston, "The Case of Colour Film," in *Technologies of Seeing: Photography, Cinematography, Television* (London: BFI, 1996), 39–57; Richard Dyer on the related history of lighting; and Jane Gaines on cinema's relation to mythologies about the body's ability to reveal "race," and the ways in which Oscar Micheaux "refut[es] the . . . ideology of telltale signs," in *Fire and Desire: Mixed-Race Movies in the Silent Era* (Chicago: University of Chicago Press, 2001), 216.

9. Sigmund Freud, *The Interpretation of Dreams* (1900), in *The Standard Edition of the Complete Psychological Works of Sigmund Freud*, trans. James Strachey (London: Hogarth, 1953), 4:141–46.

10. James Hugo Johnston, "Miscegenation in the Ante-Bellum South" (Ph.D. diss., University of Chicago, 1937), 1.

11. Ella Shohat and Robert Stam, *Unthinking Eurocentrism: Multiculturalism and the Media* (London: Routledge, 1994), 160.

12. As Stam and Shohat put it, the clause "forestalled the possibility of a denunciatory counter-narrative from the perspective of people of color, for whom sexual violence by Whites has often been a core historical experience" (ibid., 160).

13. Here come to mind Martha Hodes's, *White Women, Black Men: Illicit Sex in the 19th-Century South* (New Haven, Conn.: Yale University Press, 1997), and

Nabokov's assertion that "'a Negro-white intermarriage which is a complete and glorious success resulting in lots of children and grandchildren' is 'utterly taboo' in literature." Nabokov cited in Werner Sollors, *Neither Black nor White Yet Both* (New York: Oxford University Press, 1997), 4.

14. Dolph Frantz (*Shreveport Journal*) to Adolph Zukor (Paramount), 25 August 1937, *Imitation of Life* (1934) file, Production Code Administration Collection, Margaret Herrick Library, Academy of Motion Picture Arts and Sciences, Beverly Hills, California (hereafter cited as PCA).

15. Ibid. (emphasis mine).

16. Such an interpretation of interracial dancing goes beyond even the PCA's most extreme interpretation of the miscegenation clause, yet an internal memo on the complaint from Louisiana complains in turn that scripts do not indicate the racial identity of dancers. Some years later a venomously racist letter from Minnesota forwarded to the PCA, reacting simply to a film review, objects: "I don't want my children playing with little black——, or going to school with them either. I don't ever want to catch my daughter dancing with a black —— of a —— at a school dance, or any dance for that matter. . . . Go to New York City if you want to see what comes of mixing white with black. See all the white women and black niggers walking the streets; go to the school and college dances and see the mixed dancing. What always follows dancing Mr. Zanuck? Thats [*sic*] right, inter-dating." Roger C. Foss to Zanuck, 12 September 1950, *No Way Out* file, PCA.

17. Ian F. Haney Lopez writes: "It is no accident that the first legal ban on interracial marriage . . . also constituted the first statutory effort to define who was Black" (*White by Law: The Legal Construction of Race* [New York: New York University Press, 1996], 118). And Richard Dyer similarly pinpoints "interracial heterosexuality" as one of the central staging areas of whiteness, since "heterosexuality is the means of ensuring, but also the site of endangering, the reproduction of [racial] differences" (*White*, 25, 20). Michael Omi and Howard Winant "define *racial formation* as the sociohistorical process by which racial categories are created, inhabited, transformed, and destroyed." *Racial Formation in the United States from the 1960s to the 1990s* (New York: Routledge, 1994), 55.

18. Robyn Wiegman, *American Anatomies: Theorizing Race and Gender* (Durham, N.C.: Duke University Press, 1995), 24. Tremendously welcome is Wiegman's attempt to "expos[e] the visible relation that collapses social subjectivity with skin and marks an epidermal hierarchy as the domain of natural difference" (9).

19. Adrienne D. Davis, "Identity Notes Part One: Playing in the Light," *American University Law Review* 45, no. 3 (1996): 705. In both cases Davis reads, from 1806 and 1854 respectively, the scopic rule is one of two methods by which the court attempts to determine racial identity (the other is bound up with ancestry and racial names). This supports Wiegman's claim that no singular racial paradigm dominated in the United States in the nineteenth century.

20. See Sollors on biblical and mythic racial stories (*Neither Black nor White Yet Both*, 32–111); Dyer on varying capacities and interests of Christianity, biology, genealogy, and genetics (*White*, especially 14–30); and Omi and Winant on

the usurpation of biological models with models of ethnicity (*Racial Formation*, 9–23).

21. As per Sollors's "Appendix B, Prohibitions of Interracial Marriage and Cohabitation," 406.

22. This is the title to Sollors's chapter on the subject (112–41).

23. Jefferson to Francis Gray, 4 March 1815, from *The Writings of Thomas Jefferson*, vol. 14, ed. Andrew A. Lipscomb and Albert Ellery Bergh (Washington, D.C.: Jefferson Memorial Association, 1903); repr. in Sollors, *Neither Black nor White Yet Both*, 114.

24. The report's explanation of the "significance of the terms 'black' and 'mulatto'" only substantively begins in 1870. Of previous decades it remarks: "At the censuses of 1850 and 1860 the terms 'black' and 'mulatto' appear not to have been defined. In 1850 enumerators were instructed simply . . . to write 'B' or 'M' in the space on the schedule, to indicate black or mulatto, leaving the space blank in the case of whites." This confirms the logical assumption that the definitional "problem" emerged anew after the end of a property system that had its own legal and extralegal means of ascertaining and asserting racial identity. U.S. Bureau of the Census, *Negro Population, 1790–1915* (Washington, D.C., 1918; repr., New York: Kraus, 1969), 207.

25. Ibid., 207 n. 1.

26. E.g., "Instructions to enumerators make the 1890 classes represent the following proportions: Black, ten-sixteenths or more; mulatto, six to ten sixteenths; quadroons, three to six sixteenths; and octoroons, less than three-sixteenths" (ibid., 208).

27. Immediately following the sentence cited in my previous footnote, a new paragraph explains: "The fractions noted indicate class limits, within which every gradation of intermixture is comprehended, the exact proportion of intermixture in the great majority of cases being in all probability a proportion which can not be accurately stated by any fraction with a small denominator, and ranging by minute gradation, in the aggregate, from an imperceptible trace of white to an imperceptible trace of Negro blood" (ibid., 208).

28. Ibid., 208 n. 1.

29. Ibid. (emphasis mine).

30. Ibid.; see also note 27.

31. As evidenced in U.S. Bureau of the Census, *Fifteenth Census of the United States: 1930, Population*, vol. 2, *General Report Statistics by Subjects* (Washington, D.C., 1933); U.S. Bureau of the Census, *Sixteenth Census of the United States: 1940, Population*, vol. 2, *Characteristics of the Population* (Washington, D.C., 1943); U.S. Bureau of the Census, *Report of the Seventeenth Decennial Census of the United States, Census of Population: 1950*, vol. 2, *Characteristics of the Population* (Washington, D.C., 1953); U.S. Bureau of the Census, *Eighteenth Decennial Census of the United States, Census of Population: 1960*, vol. 1, *Characteristics of the Population* (Washington, D.C., 1961); U.S. Bureau of the Census, *1970 Census of Population*, vol. 1, *Characteristics of the Population* (Washington, D.C., 1973); U.S. Bureau of the Census, *1980 Census of Population*, vol. 1, *Characteristics of the Population* (Washington, D.C., 1983).

32. Indirectly setting the stage for us to consider the mechanisms whereby cin-

ema can constitute race as something *visible*, Eva Saks shows how in the law metaphors of "blood essentialized race" as an internal, inherited, invisible thing, such that the wave of miscegenation law passed during Reconstruction "internalized the feudal economy the Civil War had supposedly ended." "Representing Miscegenation Law," *Raritan* 8, no. 2 (1988): 48.

33. U.S. Bureau of the Census, *Census of Population: 1960*, xliii.

34. U.S. Bureau of the Census, *Negro Population, 1790–1915*, 207.

35. In 1950, for example, the United Nations published a report by an international group of scholars that declared: "The biological fact of race and the myth of 'race' should be distinguished, for all practical social purposes 'race' is not so much a biological phenomenon as a social myth." "UNESCO Report on Race," July 1950; repr. in *States' Laws on Race and Color*, ed. Pauli Murray (Athens: University of Georgia Press, 1997), 546.

36. U.S. Bureau of the Census, *Census of Population: 1950*, 35.

37. Also from the 1950 census report: "Experience has shown that reasonably adequate identification of the smaller 'racial' groups is made in areas where they are relatively numerous but that representatives of such groups may be misclassified in areas where they are rare" (35). These and additional instructions listed in the report's appendix clearly indicate that spatial location is also key to racial naming, an idea I explore filmically in chapter 4.

38. Lauren Berlant, "National Brands/National Body: *Imitation of Life*," in *Comparative American Identities: Race, Sex, and Nationality in the Modern Text*, ed. Hortense J. Spillers (New York: Routledge, 1991), 113.

39. Wiegman also writes about "the ascendancy of a visual regime in which the very framework of 'black' and 'white' designates authentic, natural races" (*American Anatomies*, 41). Segregation practices under and since Jim Crow, she claims, "ha[ve] and continue . . . to situate every subject in U.S. culture within the panoptic vision of racial meanings" (40).

40. On the censorship of *The Heart of an Outlaw*, see chapter 1, note 18. On *Birth*'s censorship, see Gaines, *Fire and Desire*, 219–57; Charlene Regester, "Black Films, White Censors: Oscar Micheaux Confronts Censorship in New York, Virginia, and Chicago," in *Movie Censorship and American Culture*, ed. Francis G. Couvares (Washington, D.C.: Smithsonian Institution Press, 1996), 159–86; and Cripps, *Slow Fade to Black*, 41–69.

41. The Don'ts and Be Carefuls are reprinted in Moley, *Hays Office*, 240–41, and Jowett, *Film*, 466–67.

42. Lea Jacobs has substantially revised the notion, inherited from Raymond Moley, that the PCA was newly empowered to "enforce" the Code in 1934. While Moley asserts, as Jacobs summarizes, that in that year the PCA "had the power to bar a film from exhibition in any theater owned by or affiliated with any member company of the MPPDA" (amounting to "77 percent of the important first-run theaters in the United States") by withholding its seal of approval, Jacobs finds that the PCA was in the business of helping studios acquire the seal, not of denying it, and that its predecessor, the Studio Relations Committee, also "was a vigorous organization," one that "experienced at least moderate success in persuading producers to make changes in films." Thus significantly complicating Moley's account, Jacobs nonetheless maintains "that censorship was

'stronger' after 1934 . . . in a theoretical sense" because after that point the censors took an even stronger hand in effecting "more far-reaching transformation[s] of offensive material." Lea Jacobs, "Industry Self-Regulation and the Problem of Textual Determination," in *Controlling Hollywood: Censorship and Regulation in the Studio Era*, ed. Matthew Bernstein (New Brunswick, N.J.: Rutgers University Press, 1999), 90, 94.

43. "Virtue in Cans," 441.

44. Moley, *Hays Office*, 63. The SRC is also sometimes referred to in the literature as the SRD, the Studio Relations Department. On the often confusing configurations and reconfigurations of staff, duties, and agency names at the MPPDA, SRC, and PCA, see Lea Jacobs, *The Wages of Sin: Censorship and Fallen Woman Film, 1928–1942* (Berkeley and Los Angeles: University of California Press, 1997), especially 27–31.

45. The PCA files often include records of local and state censorship boards. For example, the file on *White Cargo* reports objections to the British version of the same title from 1930 by censors in several states to a scene, as New York reportedly described it, of "views of native girl deliberately pressing legs and body against white man's body." Virginia objects that it "deals in marriage between Whites and Blacks" and thereby "contravenes the racial integrity laws of" that state. Ohio objects to "white man living with native girl," and Pennsylvania calls for extensive cuts of *The Birth of a Nation* in an undated report. Geoffrey Shurlock to Robert Vogel (MGM), 30 April 1942, *White Cargo* file, PCA; W. D. Kelly to Joy, telegram, 22 May 1931, *Never the Twain Shall Meet* file, PCA; and report of local censorship rulings, *The Birth of a Nation* file, PCA.

46. The other section, on "the moral responsibility of the motion pictures," was taken from a document drafted by two prominent Catholics, Daniel Lord, a priest and professor of drama who despised Hollywood vice, and Martin Quigley, an editor of several periodicals, including the *Motion Picture Herald*. See Black, *Hollywood Censored*, especially chap. 2.

47. As Doherty explains, there is "no 'definitive' copy of the Code as adopted in 1930 and enforced thereafter"; instead, "various texts of the Production Code have been reprinted over the years in trade journals, memoirs, and scholarly work," as well as in assorted pamphlets issued by the industry itself (*Pre-Code Hollywood*, 347). While the sources and dates of such reprints tend to be ambiguous, they generally reproduce the miscegenation clause as cited here (cf. note 49). One exception, wherein a reprint of the 1930 Code reverts to the plural "sex relationships," appears to be a mistake. Leonard J. Leff and Jerold Simmons, *The Dame in the Kimono: Hollywood, Censorship, and the Production Code from the 1920s to the 1960s* (New York: Grove, 1990), 285.

48. *A Code to Maintain Social and Community Values in the Production of Silent, Synchronized and Talking Motion Pictures*, Motion Picture Producers and Distributors of America, Inc., 31 March 1930, 5, Herrick Library. This 1930 pamphlet version of the Code is also reprinted in *Prima dei codici 2: Alle porte di Hays* (Venezia: La Biennale di Venezia, 1991), 370.

49. In a trade cover story lambasting the Code as "the motion picture industry's most curious and contrary secret"—"held for more than a decade in . . . concealment, confused the while by intricate devices of expression concealing the

concealment"—Terry Ramsaye complains of the proliferation of summary pamphlets, documents he claims had "no relation to the basic document and purpose of the Code save to evade or afford evasions." Perhaps not surprisingly in a journal edited by Martin Quigley, Ramsaye believes the heart of the Code lies in its "unchanging moral principles," not the "painfully specific" list of subjects. Terry Ramsaye, "The Code Mystery," *Motion Picture Herald*, 7 February 1942, 2–3.

50. AFI interview with Geoffrey Shurlock, as excerpted in *Prima dei codici*, 395.

51. Lord and Quigley's draft of their code is reprinted in Black's *Hollywood Censored*, 302–7.

52. Shurlock interview, *Prima dei codici*, 395.

53. In addition to the objections cited earlier, we find Hays attempting to appease a complaint from Indiana about *Blonde Captive*, an Australian production in which anthropologists allegedly find a white woman living with a native man. While a note atop Hays's letter raises the "question whether this was sent or not," in it Hays assures that he will alert the PCA to watch out for the film and tries to comfort the complainant with the clause itself: "In the meanwhile I wonder if you won't be interested in seeing a copy of our Code which governs American-made motion pictures. In that you will see that the Code specifically prohibits miscegenation." Hays to Dr. Lillian Crockett Lowder (Indianapolis, Ind.), 11 April 1932, *Blonde Captive* file, PCA.

54. Or so we are led to understand from a legal representative of Capital Pictures who, in his lengthy appeal to the PCA's 1942 rejection of a reissue of *Blonde Captive,* takes issue with the logic he claims "Milliken [MPPDA] expressed . . . that there are certain states in the South that have laws prohibiting such marriages." "Appellant's Brief: In the Matter of the 'Blonde Captive,' Capital Pictures Corp. Appellant," undated, *Blonde Captive* file, PCA.

55. As Peggy Pascoe puts it, such laws "were enacted first—and abandoned last—in the South, but it was in the West, not the South, that [they] became most elaborate." "Race, Gender, and Intercultural Relations: The Case of Interracial Marriage," *Frontiers* 12, no. 1 (1991): 6. See Sollors's appendix for specific states and their specific laws.

56. In an appeal to studios to resist "quick profits" from "the injection of objectionable matter or . . . objectionable themes," Hays insists: "This is not a question of morals; it is a question of business." President's Annual Report, 28 March 1927, 69, in *The Will Hays Papers,* ed. Douglas Gomery (Frederick, Md.: University Publications of America, 1986), reel 32, box 0603. While Protestant and Jewish groups vocally objected to Hollywood subject matter, the Catholic Church took the organizational lead with "more than eleven million Church members sign[ing] pledges to boycott offensive pictures." Tino Balio, ed. *The American Film Industry* (Madison: University of Wisconsin Press, 1976), 220.

57. A decline in attendance in the early thirties led studios "to introduce salacious subject matter . . . in an attempt to attract patrons" (Balio, *American Film Industry*, 221). Stories of interracial desire in exotic locales with rac(e)y titles fit that bill exactly. So suggest the files of projects from plays like *White Cargo, Congai, The Shanghai Gesture,* and *Lulu Belle.*

58. While such modifications seem to have occurred gradually, punctuated by

multiple meetings and press releases, the two major revisions to the miscegenation clause noted previously are documented by a series of stories in the trades and an interview with a former censor, as well as pamphlet copies of the Code itself. See "Prod'N Code Gets Modern Touch," *Variety*, 9 September 1953, 1+; "Movie Code Changes Due," *Hollywood Citizen-News*, 4 January 1954; "Majors 'Loosen Up' Prod'N Code," *Variety*, 14 September 1954, 1+; "Pix Code Gets Liberal Face-Lift," *Variety*, 12 December 1956, 1+; "Production Code Liberalized," *Hollywood Reporter*, 12 December 1956, 1+; Barbara Hall, *An Oral History with Albert E. Van Schmus* (Beverly Hills, Calif.: Oral History Program, Herrick Library, Academy of Motion Picture Arts and Sciences, 1993), 184–86; "A Code to Govern the Making of Motion Pictures the Reasons Supporting It and the Resolution for Uniform Interpretation" (Motion Picture Association of America, Inc., 1930–55); "The Motion Picture Production Code" (Motion Picture Association of America, Inc., December 1956).

59. Henry Popkin, "Hollywood Tackles the Race Issue," *Commentary* 24, no. 4 (1957): 354.

60. Richard S. Randall, "Censorship: From *The Miracle* to *Deep Throat*," in Balio, *American Film Industry*, 436.

61. From an annual report to the producers two years into his tenure as PCA director, quoted in Moley, *Hays Office*, 96–97.

62. *Wages of Sin*, 23. (See also note 42.) Annette Kuhn similarly argues that censorship is not simply a one-way prohibition or repression but "the interactions of certain processes and practices." *Cinema, Censorship and Sexuality, 1909–1925* (London: Routledge, 1988), 6–7. While I want to retain the formative, constructive sense of these practices that the language of "censorship" runs the risk of stamping out, I nonetheless still use that language—in part because it is cumbersome to refer to the actors at the PCA as "self-regulators" and in part because the miscegenation clause was so expressly written as a prohibition.

63. Jacobs, "Industry Self-Regulation and the Problem of Textual Determination", 91.

64. Cf. note 45. The PCA suggests marriage as a means to appease Ohio state censors in a case where their regular sanction of relations between white men and "brown" women in the South Seas (discussed later) also applies. W. D. Kelly to Joy, telegram, 22 May 1931, *Never the Twain Shall Meet* file, PCA.

65. Hays wire re *The Love Mart*, 1928, cited in Auster's "Memorandum for Mr. Breen re—MISCEGENATION," 13 March 1934, *Imitation of Life* file, PCA; James Wingate to A. M. Botsford (Paramount), 6 July 1933, *White Woman* file, PCA.

66. This does not, as it might at first seem, contradict my claim that in classical Hollywood cinema, as in popular twentieth-century American culture more generally, the most denied interracial relation is that between white men and black women. For the loud policing of black men and white women (and the relative silence on the subject of white men and women of color that typically accompanies it) replicates dominant culture's preference for the myth of the black rapist to the history of the white one.

67. For example, in 1901 Arizona deemed marriages between "persons of Caucasian blood . . . with Negroes, Mongolians or Indians . . . null and void";

and Oregon in 1902 similarly prohibited marriages between "any white person [and] any negro, Chinese, or any person having one-fourth or more negro, Chinese, or Kanaka blood, or any person having more than one-half Indian blood" (as cited in Sollors, *Neither Black nor White Yet Both*, Appendix B, 402–3).

68. U.S. Bureau of the Census, *Census of Population*, 1920, 10–11.

69. U.S. Bureau of the Census, *Negro Population, 1790–1915*, 207.

70. Review of *I Live for Love, Motion Picture Daily*, 1 October 1935.

71. Breen to J. J. McCarthy (MPPDA), telegram, 5 June 1936, *Last of the Mohicans* (1936) file, PCA.

72. Whereas the PCA was often reticent about scripts taken from popular Broadway shows, for example, Breen reports to Hays that *Last of the Mohicans* "is an excellent audience picture based on the classic novel." He uses the literary cachet of such texts as a means to canonize Hollywood itself when he procures copies of the film script of *Ramona* "to go to the English classes at Notre Dame University." Breen to Hays, 31 July 1936, *Last of the Mohicans* file, PCA; Breen to Joy (20th C.-Fox), 7 October 1936, *Ramona* file, PCA.

73. C.R.M. [Charles R. Metzger], synopsis, 14 April 1936, *Last of the Mohicans* file, PCA.

74. Synopsis, 11 April 1928; synopsis, 8 June 1928; and synopsis, 31 July 1936, *Ramona* file, PCA.

75. Synopsis clustered with correspondence of May 1929, *Congai* file, PCA.

76. Interoffice memo from F. L. Herron to Hays, 9 January 1930, *Congai* file, PCA. The PCA is also concerned about a series of issues it implicitly links to "miscegenation," including the woman's loyalty to her "native" lover, her disloyalty to her white lover, and "the general disparagement of the White Man and of civilization as opposed to the jungle and jungle emotions." Interoffice memo from Lamar Trotti to Maurice McKenzie, 9 January 1930.

77. Doherty reports Olga J. Martin to have been Breen's secretary at the PCA (*Pre-Code Hollywood*, 47); she describes her own book about that agency, *Hollywood's Movie Commandments: A Handbook for Motion Picture Writers and Reviewers* (New York: H. W. Wilson, 1937), as "based on the facts gathered from the 'inside'" (5).

78. Martin, *Hollywood's Movie Commandments*, 178.

79. Joy to Hays, 20 January 1932, *Congai* file, PCA (emphasis mine). This letter also appears in the files of *Lulu Belle* and *Shanghai Gesture*, though without the typo of the double "four."

80. Resume, 24 October 1929, *Shanghai Gesture* file, PCA.

81. Martin says as much. Of "perversion; miscegenation; sadism; incest; impotency; the sale of women; the details of harem life; and white slavery," she writes: "Stories or pictures having these subjects for their main themes can rarely be changed without completely rewriting the plot" (*Hollywood's Movie Commandments*, 151).

82. According to Pascoe, state laws to prohibit interracial marriage "by the 1860s . . . call [it] *miscegenation*" ("Race, Gender, and Intercultural Relations," 6).

83. Jay Sanford Tush (International Film Exchange) to F. S. Harmon (MPPDA), 14 July 1939, *Shanghai Gesture* file, PCA (emphasis mine).

84. Julia Kelly (MPPDA) to Joy, 28 July 1932, *Madame Butterfly* file, PCA.

85. Joy to Kelly, telegram, 22 July 1932, *Madame Butterfly* file, PCA.

86. Toni Morrison, *Playing in the Dark: Whiteness and the Literary Imagination* (New York: Vintage, 1992), 7.

87. When such questions implicitly arise, as we will see in the next chapter, they can provoke extraordinary anxiety and attention. A recent letter to the editor suggests that this cultural blind spot is becoming increasingly exposed. Of a story on the revelation that tennis player Alexandra Stevenson is the illegitimate daughter of former basketball star Julius Erving, a writer from Connecticut notices that Stevenson is first described as "a black woman" and then as "the daughter of a white mother," and asks, "Why is this young woman black if she is the child of one black and one white parent?" "Mixed Messages," *New York Times*, 11 July 1999, Y25.

88. Cited in Auster memo, 13 March 1934, *Imitation of Life* file, PCA.

89. Although Breen's letter does not specify, he appears to be reviewing Universal's version of the film produced in 1928, which would put the original film itself prior even to the Don'ts and Be Carefuls.

90. Breen to Maurice Pivar (Universal), 16 May 1939, *Uncle Tom's Cabin* file, PCA.

91. Memo for the files, 14 November 1956, *Band of Angels* file, PCA (emphasis mine). The cited paragraph is followed by the studio's more permissive suggestion that one sequence "might contain a sex affair which would then be treated with an adequate voice for morality and a sense of shame on the part of the two principles, and would result in their marriage at the end of the picture." That the film itself leaves open the possibility of premarital sex does not annul the larger point evidenced by the memo, that sex under slavery is the sorest spot of all at the PCA.

92. Hays cited in Auster memo, 13 March 1934, *Imitation of Life* file; W. D. Kelly telegram to Jason Joy, 22 May 1931, *Never the Twain Shall Meet* file; Carl Milliken (MPPDA) to William M. Pizor (Capital Pictures), 13 July 1942, *Blond Captive* file: all PCA.

93. James Fisher, synopsis of *Aloha Oe* (later *Aloha*), 2 October 1930, *Aloha* file, PCA; Joy to Rogell, 3 October 1930, *Aloha Oe* file, PCA.

94. Joy to Phil Goldstone (Tiffany Productions) [reporting Ohio Board of Censor cuts to *Aloha*], 20 February 1931, *Aloha* file, PCA. Another letter reporting cuts from the New York Board of Censors writes the line as "Look, that one's almost a blonde now." Joy to Goldstone, 8 April 1931, *Aloha* file, PCA. I have not found a print of this film to verify the actual dialogue.

95. Dyer, *White*, 48.

96. Davis argues that the scopic rule not only "establishes as legal standard the individual judges' perceptions of racial distinction" but in so doing "safeguard[s] . . . a white subject position" in and through the law ("Identity Notes," 706).

97. E.g., Analysis of Film Content, 26 March 1951, *Show Boat* (1950) file, PCA. Cf. note 24.

98. Maurice McKenzie memo to Hays, 7 July 1930, *Congai* file, PCA. The scope of the claim is later reduced from the universe to the industry when Joy tells

Paramount that other studios found "the subject . . . too far beyond the pale for anyone to attempt to put it on the screen." Joy to Schulberg, 14 January 1932, *Congai* file, PCA.

99. See Wiegman on the regular cultural "equation between the idea of 'race' and the 'black' body" (*American Anatomies*, 21).

100. On the dynamics of exclusion and inclusion that use blackness to produce and fortify whiteness, see Harryette Mullen, "Optic White: Blackness and the Production of Whiteness," *Diacritics* 24, nos. 2–3 (summer–fall 1994): 71–89.

101. Regarding a 1939 proposal of *Heart of Darkness*, Breen advised: "In treating . . . scenes with this native girl, please take care to avoid any possible inference of miscegenation, in line with the Code requirements for that subject." While the file does not specify further, and the script never made it to the screen, the caution presumably derived, per Conrad's novel, from the relationship between Kurtz, a British colonist, and an unnamed African woman. "African" thus serves as the unspoken middle term that weds "black" to "native." Breen to J. R. Mc Donough (RKO), 15 December 1939, *Heart of Darkness* file, PCA.

102. Wilson, resume of activities, 3 May 1930, *Never the Twain Shall Meet* file, PCA (emphasis mine).

103. Analysis Chart, 11 August 1942; PCA to Mayer (MGM), 12 November 1941, *White Cargo* file, PCA.

104. PCA to Mayer, 15 October 1941, *White Cargo* file, PCA (emphasis mine).

105. Analysis Chart, 11 August 1942, *White Cargo* file, PCA.

106. *Variety* described it as another "lurid tale . . . of white men done in by liquor and half-caste sirens of dark lands" (15 September 1942; clipping in *White Cargo* file, PCA).

107. PCA to Mayer, 12 November 1941, *White Cargo* file, PCA (emphasis mine).

108. The appellant's brief cited earlier (the only objection to the miscegenation clause I found in the PCA files) explicitly refuses the notion of racial "blood." Arguing in detail against a prohibition it situates in the context of Jim Crow, the KKK, and even the ban on "a prize fight between a colored and a white man," the brief insists: "*It is not a biological question. That theory has been exploded. The American Red Cross disposed of [it] when the blood donors of the colored race brought the issue to the fore*" (original emphasis).

109. Wilson, resume of activities, 3 May 1930, *Never the Twain Shall Meet* file, PCA.

110. Shurlock to Robert Vogel (MGM), 17 March 1958, *Night of the Quarter Moon* file, PCA. It is striking how increased silence on matters of race in this period is matched by an even more voracious policing of the female body. In file after file the PCA says little to nothing about race, but it endlessly warns of "the need for the greatest possible care in the selection and photographing of the dresses and costumes of [what they habitually call] your women." This mantra can be found, for example, in the files of *Show Boat* (1950), *White Orchid, Far Horizon, Intruder in the Dust*, and *No Way Out*.

111. Cripps, *Slow Fade to Black*, 124–27; James R. Nesteby, *Black Images in American Films, 1896–1954* (Lanham, Md.: University Press of America, 1982), 117.

112. Nesteby 117.

113. The proximity of the 1920 films to that of 1919 is marked by their shared star, Richard Barthelmess. But his recasting from *Broken Blossoms'* broken "yellow man" to *Idol Dancer's* broken (by drink) white lover also indicates the reshuffling of erotics and color I will explore later in the new genre.

114. As Ruth Vasey reads it, "In view of American film's preoccupation with heterosexual relations, it is not surprising that colonial attitudes most commonly found expression in the movies through the politics of sexual dominance. The inevitable response . . . was the banning of interracial affairs in every context except that of the politically innocuous Pacific Ocean." "Foreign Parts: Hollywood's Global Distribution and the Representation of Ethnicity," in Couvares, *Movie Censorship and American Culture*, 223.

115. The language of "blood" here will be one of the things to dissipate from the genre in the years to come, but this emphasis on the visual establishment of difference, as we will soon see, will significantly remain.

116. Analyzing "the white heroine's racial mobility" in jungle horror, Rhona Berenstein describes that figure as "a mediator between the worlds of the white and the black man. [She] has an interstitial role. She poses a threat of interspecies and interracial union and introduces the possibility that the darkness attributed to the 'out there' of the jungle also inhabits the 'in here' of the white domain" (*Attack of the Leading Ladies*, 169).

117. *Birth* projects the white man's "weakness" for black women as a strictly Northern condition.

118. Michael Rogin has convincingly argued the first of these projections, and I explore it and propose the second in chapter 2.

119. The "white man who loves the native girl" in *Paradise Isle* is a "blind painter" no less, "seeking the only doctor who can restore his sight." "Paradise Isle," *Variety*, 28 July 1937; clipping in *Siren of the South Seas* file, PCA.

120. For example, first hearing Dorothy Lamour's character speak in *Jungle Princess* (1935), the white man asks, "Is that all you know is baby talk? And Malay baby talk at that? Say, what sort of a girl are you anyway?" See also *Her Jungle Love*.

121. *Variety*, 19 March 1938, *Her Jungle Love* clippings file, Herrick (emphasis mine).

122. Hence the trade description of Lamour as "No. 1 sarong-wearer of the Hollywood tropics." "*Her Jungle Love*," *Hollywood Reporter*, 19 March 1938.

123. "At the Rialto" [*Jungle Princess* review], *New York Times*, 24 December 1936; in *Jungle Princess* file, PCA (emphasis mine).

124. "*Mutiny on the Bounty*," *Variety*, 11 November 1935 (emphasis mine).

125. Martin writes: "The union of a member of the Polynesians and allied races of the Island groups with a member of the white race is not ordinarily considered a miscegenetic relationship" (*Hollywood's Movie Commandments*, 178). "The Code intention is to characterize as a miscegenetic union any relation be-

tween the white race and the black race and in most cases also between the white and yellow races. Consequently unions between natives of other than these races with whites would not for Code purposes, be considered 'miscegenation'" (209).

126. *Variety* notes that one "makes no pretense of being a serious study of the East-meets-West problem" and reports "a little of the west versus east in the romantic angle" in another. *"Paradise Isle," Variety* 28 July 1937; *"Her Jungle Love," Variety*, 23 March 1938.

127. The use of the word "native" throughout the PCA's writings on South Sea Island films is another indicator of their proximity to fantasies strictly regulated against in territories where the PCA regularly interchanged that word with "black." Synopsis by K. S. Johnson, 28 August 1932 ("Received" 6 April 1934); Breen to Mayer, 19 April 1934, *Mutiny on the Bounty* file, PCA.

128. Breen to Mayer, 26 December 1934, *Mutiny on the Bounty* file, PCA.

129. Ibid.

130. *"Mutiny on the Bounty," Variety*, 28 October 1935. Breen repeatedly warns, for example, that "the meeting and mating of Christian and Maimiti should not explicitly show that they spent the night together." Ibid.

131. Breen to Mayer, 26 December 1934, *Mutiny* file, PCA (original emphasis).

132. Breen writes: "We presume . . . your camera angles and distances, as well as . . . use of loin cloths and flowers, will meet the requirements of the Code." Breen to Mayer, 27 February 1935, *Mutiny* file, PCA.

133. Joy to Al Rogell (Rogell Productions), 3 October 1930, *Aloha Oe* file, PCA.

134. Ibid. (original emphasis).

135. "RED WOMAN: Paramount . . . advised they would use the title, 'Behold My Wife.' The title RED WOMAN would probably not be acceptable in this office." J. Kelly to Hazel Plate (PCA), 6 November 1934, *Behold My Wife* file, PCA.

136. A reviewer *does* dare speak the color of this love's name, a "pleasing romance of a white man and a brown maiden." Yet that utterance remains firmly within the confines of the color discourse, describing the "native girl" only as "brown" or "dusky and childlike," in the last case yoking the genre's optics of "dusky" skin to its equally central preference for dependents. *"Paradise Isle," Hollywood Reporter*, 1 July 1937, clipping in *Siren of the South Seas* file, PCA.

137. In light of this conclusion, remarkable is the fate of one of the original "un-doables," *Lulu Belle*. Although at one point *Lulu Belle* was a code word for Code trouble (in 1932 Hays wrote of *Marquita* that RKO must "mak[e] the picture conform to the Code [and] not hav[e] it 'Lulu Bell' [*sic*]"), it was finally approved in 1948 after multiple revisions by multiple studios. Universal proposed transforming the lead character "from a negro wench in Harlem . . . into a French harlot, thus removing the idea of miscegenation"; later "she is a wild child of nature" whose antics erupt in "a savage scene" and finally "a scene of jungle terror"; and at Warner Bros. she becomes "a part-Creole-part-French-Canadian girl . . . in a night club in New Orleans." But in the Columbia script finally approved, the only notation under "Race" on the PCA's review form is "Negro Waiters." What is more, cast in the role of the originally black character was Dorothy Lamour, queen of the assimilable "tan," playing her as a dark brunette with a dark

mole on her face, flashy costumes, and gaudy jewelry. This example further suggests that Hollywood's malleable signifiers of color can attach to particular stars and spread with them beyond generic confines. Hays to Joy, 24 June 1932; Hays to R. H. Cochrane (Universal), 1 November 1930; synopsis of *Lulu Belle* from Zehner (Universal) to Wingate, 6 December 1933; Memo for the files re: Lulu Belle, Warner Bros., 5 April 1940; and Analysis Chart, 10 February 1948: all in *Lulu Belle* file, PCA.

CHAPTER FOUR
PICTURIZING RACE

1. The plot follows the rise of a white widow on the profits of her black maid's pancake recipe, focusing on the relationships among these single mothers, Bea Pullman and Delilah, and their respective daughters, Jessie and Peola. While the film shows no hetero "sex relationship" between whites and blacks, Bea and Delilah arguably function as a couple (Delilah cooks, cleans, and rears Bea's child during the day and rubs her feet at night), yet a reading of this relationship as "miscegenation" was well beyond the sensibilities of the PCA censors. On the "radical female homosociality" that underlies this and related films, including *Pinky*, see Patricia White, *Uninvited: Classical Hollywood Cinema and Lesbian Representability* (Bloomington: Indiana University Press, 1999), 154, 165. White cites Judith Butler and Lauren Berlant as "among the few commentators to read lesbian connotations in *Imitation of Life*" (153), Butler (on the 1959 remake) in "Lana's 'Imitation': Melodramatic Repetition and the Gender Performative," *Genders* 9 (1990): 1–18, and Berlant in "National Brands/National Body: *Imitation of Life*," in *Comparative American Identities: Race, Sex, and Nationality in the Modern Text,* ed. Hortense J. Spillers (New York: Routledge, 1991), 110–40.

2. Hays (President, MPPDA) to Robert H. Cochrane (Universal), 18 May 1934, *Imitation of Life* (1934) file, Production Code Administration Collection, Margaret Herrick Library, Academy of Motion Picture Arts and Sciences, Beverly Hills, California (hereafter cited as PCA).

3. Breen to Universal, 9 March 1934, as cited in Hays to Universal, 18 May 1934 (emphasis mine); and [unsent] Breen to Universal, 9 March 1934, *Imitation* file, PCA (emphasis mine). "Not sent/to be rewritten" is written across the top of the second letter cited here, and Hays appears to be quoting from the revision (itself not in the file) in the first.

4. Hays to Universal, 18 May 1934, *Imitation* file, PCA (emphasis mine).

5. [Unsent] Breen to Universal, 9 March 1934. That Breen transposes the clause's main term and the explanatory ones that the Code puts in parentheses again points to the uncertainty surrounding it at the PCA.

6. Hays to Breen, 20 March 1934, *Imitation* file, PCA.

7. Resume [of meeting with Universal], 9 March 1934; [unsent] Breen to Universal, 9 March 1934; Breen to Zehner (Universal), 20 July 1934; and memo for the files, 9 March 1934: all in *Imitation* file, PCA.

8. Breen to Zehner, 20 July 1934 (emphasis mine).

9. The censors' clarity in ruling on the lynching scene is consistent with the

PCA's ongoing certainty about the pairing of black men and white women. In a staffer's research memo discussed later in this chapter, the one concrete finding made on the miscegenation clause is the 1928 quotation from Hays discussed in chapter 3: "Inadvisable always to show white women in scenes with negroes where there is any inference of miscegenation or social relationship." Memo for the files, 9 March 1934; Breen to Universal, 9 March 1934, cited in Hays to Universal, 18 May 1934; Maurice McKenzie (Exec. Asst. to Hays at MPPDA) to Breen, 3 April 1934; Breen to Zehner, 27 July 1934; Breen to Hays, 3 August 1934: all in *Imitation* file, PCA.

10. Memo for the files, 9 March 1934.

11. Ibid.

12. Breen to McKenzie, interoffice memo, 26 March 1934, *Imitation* file, PCA (emphasis mine). Similar language is used in a résumé from the same file of 9 March 1934.

13. While in the film Delilah says only that Peola's "pappy was a very very light-colored man," Hurst's novel includes references to his "white blood." Yet these, too, are ambiguous. Delilah says he was "mixed up wid plenty of white blood," but a page later adds there was "mostly nigger in mah nigger." The fullest explanation is that Peola's "pap was born of two Virginie darkies, which ain't sayin' dar mayn't have been plenty of white blood in him, down dar whar white blood in nigger veins comes cheaper'n moonshine whisky." Thus, even when the novel speaks of what the film will not, it posits it as being at least three generations prior to Peola, and even then leaves it uncertain. Fannie Hurst, *Imitation of Life* (1933; New York: Harper and Row, 1990), 119, 120.

14. Memo re "Material Submitted to This Office but Not Scheduled for Immediate Production," 2 April 1934, *Imitation* file, PCA (emphasis mine).

15. Breen to Universal, 9 March 1934, cited in Hays to Universal, 18 May 1934 (emphasis mine).

16. Again marking the PCA's uncertainty, the word is incorrectly typed "myscegenation," then corrected by hand. J. B. Lewis to Breen, interoffice memo, 10 March 1934, *Imitation* file, PCA (emphasis mine).

17. I. Auster, "MEMORANDUM FOR MR. BREEN re—MISCEGENATION," 13 March 1934, *Imitation* file, PCA.

18. As we know from files like *Shanghai Gesture, Madame Butterfly, Congai,* and *Lulu Belle,* considered in chapter 3, it is inaccurate insofar as films had been made, and discussed by the PCA and its predecessor, that dealt with interracial sex relationships. However, as will become increasingly apparent, insofar as the definition of "miscegenation" implicitly at work in evaluations of *Imitation of Life* was entirely different, it makes sense that the staffer could not find precedents in the Code mirroring the "present problem."

19. A future threat is again suggested when Breen writes that Peola's passing as an adult "brings in the possibility of miscegenation." Although this is typically ambiguous, the context suggests that Peola's passing could lead to her union with a white man. Breen to Universal, 9 March 1934, as cited in Hays to Universal, 18 May 1934.

20. Confusion between desire and identification is also not surprising from psychoanalytic perspectives that understand the first to be predicated upon the

second. As Kaja Silverman puts it: "identity and desire are so complexly im-bricated that neither can be explained without recourse to the other." *Male Sub-jectivity at the Margins* (New York: Routledge, 1992), 6. For discussions of cross-racial identification in particular, see Eric Lott, *Love and Theft: Blackface Minstrelsy and the American Working Class* (New York: Oxford University Press, 1993); Harryette Mullen, "Optic White: Blackness and the Production of Whiteness," *Diacritics*, 24, nos. 2–3 (summer–fall 1994): 71–89; and Michael Rogin, *Blackface, White Noise: Jewish Immigrants in the Hollywood Melting Pot* (Berkeley and Los Angeles: University of California Press, 1996).

21. McKenzie to Breen, 3 April 1934.

22. Miscellaneous correspondence from PCA staff members: Breen to Univer-sal [unsent], 9 March 1934; memo for the files, 9 March 1934; Breen to Lewis, interoffice memo, 10 March 1934; Breen to Hays, 22 March 1934; "Material Submitted to This Office but Not Scheduled for Immediate Production," 2 April 1934; McKenzie to Breen, 3 April 1934; Breen to Universal, 9 March 1934, cited in Hays to Universal, 18 May 1934; Breen to Hays, 7 June 1934; and Wingate to McKenzie, 26 June 1934: all in *Imitation* file, PCA.

23. "The color black [is] repeatedly overdetermined, marked redundantly, al-most as if to force the viewer to register the image's difference from white images. . . . Marking is necessary because the *reality* of blackness or of being 'colored' cannot always, either in films or in real life, be determined." James Snead, *White Screens, Black Images* (New York: Routledge, 1994), 5.

24. Memo for the files, 9 March 1934.

25. Daniel J. Leab, *From Sambo to Superspade* (Boston: Houghton Mifflin, 1976), 109.

26. Jacqueline Stewart offers a prior history to such devices: "Fair-skinned Blacks (who might be interpreted as racially mixed) are repressed in the earliest films; light-skinned Blacks do not appear regularly until the transitional period, when their appearance (the way they look *and* why they are featured) can be nar-rativized and explained, usually in a drama set during the remote but familiar context of slavery." *Migrating to the Movies: Cinema and Black Urban Moder-nity* (Berkeley and Los Angeles: University of California Press, forthcoming), chap. 2.

27. It appears that the decisive moments transpired off the record, in meetings between the PCA and Universal, including some with then studio head Carl Laemmle Jr. Even as the film was going into production, the PCA wrote to the Hays Office in New York: "This script presents indirectly the subject of misce-genation. . . . the matter is still open." When Breen sent another "grave" warning to Universal a month letter, cautioning against the use of black dialect as well as the lynching scene and the unspecified "inflammable racial question," it sparked a flurry of meetings and impassioned letters that clearly reflect the studio's out-rage at Breen's exacting regulation. As a result, Hays reminded Breen that Uni-versal's Vice President Cochrane "is one of the most splendid men in the busi-ness," with his "heart absolutely in the right place." Breen then tried to make amends with yet another letter and handily approved the film itself in November. Wingate to McKenzie, 26 June 1934; Breen to Zehner, 20 July 1934; resume, 26 July 1934; Breen to Zehner, 27 July 1934; resume, 27 July 1934; Cochrane to

Breen, 27 July 1934; Hays to Breen, 28 July 1934; Breen to Cochrane, 31 July 1934; Breen to Zehner, 14 November 1934: all in *Imitation* file, PCA.

28. "Miss Colbert looks like a million, giving the character a superb treatment and wearing gowns that will make the femme fans gurgle and gasp in admiration." *Hollywood Reporter*, 3 November 1934, clipping in *Imitation* file, PCA.

29. Leab, *From Sambo to Superspade*, 109.

30. Hurst, *Imitation of Life*, 62.

31. In an essay to which I am deeply indebted, Valerie Smith similarly isolates the camera's articulation of Bea's movement and Delilah's "stillness" as signs of their respective economic and social positions. "Reading the Intersection of Race and Gender in Narratives of Passing," *Diacritics* 24, nos. 2–3 (summer–fall 1994): 47.

32. As in Douglas Sirk's 1959 version of the film, Delilah, desperate for work and happy to serve, volunteers to take care of Bea and Jessie in exchange for a place for her and Peola to stay.

33. Press releases regularly described Beavers as "'a black angel.'" Donald Bogle, *Toms, Coons, Mulattoes, Mammies, and Bucks: An Interpretive History of Blacks in American Films,* new expanded edition (New York: Continuum, 1993), 66.

34. Sandy Flitterman-Lewis reads Bea's repetition of this line, and the film generally, as the expression of a nostalgic desire for "that untroubled unity" of mother and child in "an originary moment . . . isolat[ed] from all social context, from all difference and disturbance." *"Imitation(s) of Life*: The Black Woman's Double Determination as Troubling 'Other,'" *Literature and Psychology* 34, no. 4 (1988): 48.

35. As we will see, the white women's debt is visually inscribed in the neon Delilah hovering over this scene.

36. Moments later Bea bumps into a frozen Delilah, standing statuelike in the pose solicited but never dismissed by her mistress. Bea chuckles at Delilah's "failure" to understand that the moment has passed, yet Delilah's indefinite pose signals all too correctly that this newly fixed image will in fact never end. Lauren Berlant credits the film with a certain self-consciousness in such ironies. She claims that "the grotesque hyper-embodiment of Delilah in this sequence violates her own and the film's aesthetic codes: I feel certain that her graphic decontextualization is specifically designed to allude to and to ironize Aunt Jemima, in her role as a site of American collective identification" ("National Brands/National Body," 125). While the film clearly alludes to Aunt Jemima, I am arguing that this scene's excessive aesthetic codes are thoroughly in keeping with a larger visual logic established throughout the film. Hence, I read them not as "interference with the Aunt Jemima in Delilah" but rather as cinematic elaborations of the "fantasy condensed in the face and history of Aunt Jemima" that Berlant identifies in the novel's production of the Delilah logo (125, 122). Especially relevant is Berlant's isolation of the novel's construction of Delilah as the teacher of "Jemimesis," "who trains 'imitations' or 'replicas' of herself in the 'University of Delilah'" where she teaches "how to commodify the 'mammy's' domestic aura"—a process that further works to free B. Pullman from the limits of corpo-reality (120). I would suggest that in the 1934 film it is the cinematic apparatus

itself that voraciously takes over, and fundamentally alters, this "Jemimetic" role, now teaching all Hollywood viewers how to read "black woman" in and through her filmic image. That said, our critical readings and many others clearly demonstrate that spectators can resist such instruction. On resistant black spectatorship of *Imitation of Life*, see bell hooks, *Black Looks: Race and Representation* (Boston: South End Press, 1992), 115–31, and Anna Everett, *Returning the Gaze: A Genealogy of Black Film Criticism, 1909–1949* (Durham, N.C.: Duke University Press, 2001), 218–32.

37. While the logos imagine the pleasure to be Delilah's own, Bea's coaxing of the "great big" smile and her naming that image as her own desire ("That's it! . . . That's what I want!") make it all the more obvious that the film's incessant projection of the servant's smile is a projection of the master's pleasure.

38. The distinction is important not only for understanding the ways in which new technologies update old racial traditions but also for clarifying their differing stakes. Whereas laws that made slaves out of the offspring of black women and white men worked to fend off potential social and economic claims that "mixed" subjects might otherwise make to white property and privilege, here the potentially unstable site is the sight of the body itself, and the structure in greatest jeopardy is the visual-epistemological system that claims to racially mark it.

39. Both at school and at the store where Peola works, it is the sight of her mother that ultimately outs her. At school Delilah is introduced through the window of the classroom door, an appearance that clearly echoes her introduction in the film. And Peola's visual deviance in the adult passing scene is rendered as a noticeable variation on the theme of Delilah displayed in the pancake shop window: Bea and Delilah find Peola in another shop window, where she appears not as a black mammy/laborer but as a white beauty/cashier. Though clearly not the actual proprietor, like Bea she is positioned (with her back to the window and behind a glass cigar case at the cash register) to take both the erotic gaze and the money of the white male customers.

40. Where we diverge, as my earlier note explains, is on the question of the 1934 film's "solution."

41. Berlant, "National Brands/National Body," 113.

42. The illusion of the unity of racial signifier and signified here contrasts dramatically, for example, with what I suggested in chapter 3 was an untenably visible distance between them that developed in the fractional blood math of the late nineteenth and early twentieth centuries.

43. Again I am thinking of "obviousness" in Louis Althusser's sense of the word as that which clearly indicates the work of ideology. *Lenin and Philosophy and Other Essays* (New York: Monthly Review Press, 1971), 171–72.

44. For a discussion of the history of Aunt Jemima, see Berlant, "National Brands/National Body," especially 122.

45. The phrase is Valerie Smith's ("Reading the Intersection of Race and Gender," 45), in a context I discuss later in this chapter.

46. When Bea pronounces this, after hearing Delilah's story of trying to find work to take care of her unwanted child, Delilah corrects, "Two hundred and forty, yessum," further underscoring the film's emphasis on her bodily form. And just earlier she insists, "I's very deceiving as to proportion, I don't eat like I look,

it's the truth!" Hollywood's extreme investment in the size of this black female body is also exposed in Bogle's account of Beavers's "steady battle . . . to stay overweight" for the sake of her film career, a battle that led to "force-feed diets" and, when that wasn't enough, to being padded and stuffed "to look more like a full-bosomed domestic" (*Toms, Coons, Mulattoes, Mammies, and Bucks*, 63).

47. To say that Hollywood cinema worked, and often worked hard, to make spectators believe in these fantasies is not to say spectators always necessarily did, or do. Anna Everett recently offers ample evidence of multiple, divergent black readings that variously resist and invest in the fictions posited by *Imitation of Life* and *Pinky* (*Returning the Gaze*, 218–32, 307–12). That said, it is striking that of the many responses Everett unearths to the former, none seem to question its ultimate assertion of Peola's racial identity. This in part, no doubt, speaks to the profound social reality racial categories acquire for the people excluded and oppressed through them, despite their having been socially constructed. Yet that very fact and the high stakes involved therein further beg the question of how belief in these categories, especially when they are so openly put into question, is produced and maintained.

48. Memo for the files, 12 December 1929, *Lulu Belle* file, PCA. As explained in the previous chapter, the Studio Relations Committee was effectively the PCA's predecessor.

49. On the revisions to *Lulu Belle*, see chapter 3, note 137.

50. *Focus on D. W. Griffith*, ed. Harry M. Geduld (Englewood Cliffs, N.J.: Prentice-Hall, 1971), 41.

51. Breen to Zehner, 17 October 1935, *Show Boat* (193_) file, PCA (emphasis mine).

52. By the midthirties white actors like Sylvia Sidney (*Madame Butterfly, Behold My Wife!*), Loretta Young (*House of Rothschild, Ramona*), and Charles Boyer (*Shanghai, Algiers*) had frequently starred as Asians and Native Americans. In the case of *Ramona*, for example, critics went so far as to praise the film for the believability of its racial masquerades: "Miss Young makes not only a beautiful Ramona but a believable and winning one. . . . Don Ameche, a well-known voice in radio drama, in his screen debut as Alessandro, the valiant Indian lover, makes a most excellent impression, his rich voice and good diction aiding a fine impersonation. Pauline Frederick is admirable as the domineering Spanish mother" (*Hollywood Reporter*, 12 September 1936).

53. For a discussion of (many) possible reasons why the PCA did not object to *Show Boat*'s central mixed couple, Julie and Steve, played in the 1936 film by two white actors, see Linda Williams, *Playing the Race Card: Melodramas of Black and White from Uncle Tom to O. J. Simpson* (Princeton, N.J.: Princeton University Press, 2001), 178–85. Certainly it would suit the PCA that the film "effectively remove[d] the mixed race woman from the narrative" (185). I would add that, albeit in highly questionable ways, many of the film's interracial musical exchanges assert racial difference to be audible even when it is not visible.

54. Turning back historically for a moment, we find the kinds of demands on spectatorial belief I am addressing here perhaps nowhere so readily demonstrated as in *The Birth of a Nation*. The sway of filmic fictions of race over the "real" racial identities of actors, and the degree to which American cinema has long

commanded belief in those fictions, is vividly demonstrated in a series of shots from *Birth*'s climactic race to the rescue. There we see both (1) white actors in blackface playing the demonized black male villains; and (2) white actors in blackface playing white men who have disguised themselves as black men in order to infiltrate and spy on the "real" blacks. The film thus requires the spectator to juggle two sets of images of white men in blackface but to read them, and believe in them, as two radically different signifiers. If we do not, the foundational fiction upon which the entire film rests (that black men are out to rape white women and overthrow white male power) is put in jeopardy. If we read one set of white men in blackface as in fact white men in blackface, what is to stop us from reading the characters Gus and Silas Lynch as in fact the white actors Walter Long and George Siegmann? The answer, obviously, is a series of cinematic cues put in place to guide our reading of these different masquerades. Remarkable nonetheless is the film's tremendous faith in the spectator's ability to follow, and willingness to accept, the multiple layers of racial fiction it manufactures.

55. This film also pushes the passing narrative mostly off screen. The one exception is when Pinky and her white lover embrace when he still believes her to be white.

56. Memo for the files, "Re Quality," 31 March 1948, *Pinky* file, PCA. The PCA's warnings that the film might be censored locally were borne out in a case that made it all the way to the Supreme Court. After an appellate court upheld the conviction of a film exhibitor in Marshall, Texas, for showing the film without a license from his local censorship board, the high court's decision stated simply, "The judgment is reversed," citing (among others) its decision in the *Miracle* case just days before granting motion pictures the protection of free speech under the First Amendment. *Gelling v. Texas*, 343 U.S. 707 (1952). For an analysis of the legal case, see Cindy Patton, "White Racism/ Black Signs: Censorship and Images of Race Relations," *Journal of Communications* 45, no. 2 (1995): 65–77.

57. The appellation comes from Thomas Cripps, although Harmon seems at the time to have actually been located at the PCA's parent organization, the Hays Office (MPPDA) in New York. Thomas Cripps, *Making Movies Black: The Hollywood Message Movie from World War II to the Civil Rights Era* (New York: Oxford University Press, 1993), 239. "Some Comments and Suggestions re *Pinky*," Harmon to Jason Joy (20th C.-Fox), 18 March 1949, *Pinky* file, PCA.

58. This unrealized revision imagines the racial truth to be spoken by Pinky's black grandmother. Although she is reticent ("Jedg, does I hav ter tell it?" "Fo de Lawd, I knows awright but I hates ter tell"), the lawyer and the judge press the maternal figure to (again) verify the younger woman's invisible identity. "Some Comments and Suggestions re *Pinky*."

59. Zanuck to Harmon, 30 March 1949, *Pinky* file, PCA.

60. The case was made in the form of a legal brief, filed (presumably only at the PCA) on behalf of Capital Pictures, appealing the PCA's refusal to approve the redistribution of an Australian-made documentary due to its (alleged) discovery in the last reel of a "white woman living with [a] native aborigine, and admitting to the parentage of [a] half-caste child." Carl Milliken [MPPDA] to William M. Pizor (Capital Pictures), 13 July 1942, *Blonde Captive* file, PCA. While the PCA file leaves no record of what, if anything, came of this appeal, the

PCA would surely not soon forget its pointed claims: "Paragraph 6, Section II, of the Production Code is contrary to and in conflict with every progressive principle of our country, and is repugnant to the cardinal principle of democracy." Situating the clause in the context of the Civil War, Reconstruction, and Jim Crow, the brief argues its obsolescence as "day by day in the progressive steps of our country we are eradicating, annulling and vitiating these various unfair and reactionary laws." Comparing the clause's insistence on "racial barriers" to "the theory of the race problem advocated by Nazi Germany," the brief urges the PCA to join the ranks of those "champions of minority rights [citing recent acts by FDR and the Supreme Court] agitating for the strict enforcement of our laws and the guarantees thereof to the colored race": "the motion picture industry which is in the vanguard of progress . . . should not be a party to the discrimination, nor promulgate same in its code." Appellant's brief, undated, *Blonde Captive* file, PCA.

61. Zanuck's reply to Harmon itself figures the issue as one of differing forms of knowledge and belief. He writes: "I know that you have more knowledge and are more sensitive to this whole problem from the Southern point of view, but I am inclined to believe that the larger good will accrue by making this a picture dealing with tolerance rather than injecting the illicit miscegenation angle." Significantly, he reports "hav[ing] consulted the Negro representatives of many different Negro points of view, and without exception they have objected to the suggestion of miscegenation." Zanuck to Harmon, 30 March 1949, *Pinky* file, PCA.

62. It came in second to *Jolson Sings Again*. The film also earned Academy Award nominations for its lead actress, Jeanne Crain, and for both supporting actresses, Ethel Waters and Ethel Barrymore. Cobbett S. Steinberg, *Film Facts* (New York: Facts on File, 1980), 21, 218.

63. Joy to Breen, 2 March 1949, *Pinky* file, PCA. This letter seems to have put momentary PCA anxieties to rest. After the PCA's initial decision to "leave the matter entirely up to the studio," upon reviewing the script a year later Breen significantly tightened up: "We strongly urge that you avoid physical contact between Negroes and whites, throughout this picture." Joy's reply insisted on the PCA's earlier green light, as well as on "a great deal of research" and "careful and exhaustive planning" on the studio's part, and its "belie[f that] these [physical] contacts [are] absolutely necessary to the power of the story," "contacts [that] will be as tender and as restrained as any that we've ever put on the screen." It ended with the emphatic line about the white actress ("Incidentally, you know, of course, that the actress . . . will in fact be a white girl"). Although the file does not reveal which argument(s) persuaded Breen, all objections disappear from the paper trail after this point, and only weeks later the very same Breen forwards Harmon's impassioned plea for a full confession to Zanuck. Memo for the files, 31 March 1948; Breen to Joy, 28 February 1949; Joy to Breen, 2 March 1949; all in *Pinky* file, PCA.

64. Donald Bogle reads the casting of Jeanne Crain as Pinky as effectively whitening "her 'interracial romance' with actor William Lundigan," and soliciting greater sympathy from white viewers (*Toms, Coons, Mulattoes, Mammies, and Bucks*, 152). More curiously here, James Snead claims that the casting of the "roles of mulatto black women passing for white [with] white actresses [func-

tions] to make sure that a visual ambiguity does not compound an already difficult conceptual leap" (*White Screens, Black Images*, 5). This lack of visual ambiguity would seem nonetheless considerably complicated at the multiple points
when this film unambiguously insists that the (white-looking) character is essentially "black." While my reading focuses largely on the potential ruptures of
knowledge posed by light skin, the film's (second) director, Elia Kazan (brought
in to replace John Ford), reportedly worried that Jeanne Crain might be "too
white—'white in her heart' even" (Cripps, *Making Movies Black*, 236). The
depth model implied by such language, and its troubled relation to the surface,
will become increasingly significant as my reading unfolds.

65. Although the film codes this as a "positive" project of racial uplift, and
sets us up to be relieved that Pinky frees herself of a man eager to erase her history, for me the film's conservatism is belied by the fact that Pinky's "options"
are posed in such extreme binary terms: live with an unlikable man who would
have you deny your heritage *or* stay on the plantation to live out the dying wish
of your (grandmother's) white mistress. Ralph Ellison, for one, would seem to
agree. Describing the "basic and unusually negative assumptions about Negroes"
in four films from 1949, he sums up the conflict that structures *Pinky* with the
question: "Should Negro girls marry white men or—wonderful non sequitur—
should they help their race?" Ralph Ellison, "The Shadow and the Act," *Shadow
and Act* (1953; New York: Random House, 1994), 277; cited in Everett, *Returning the Gaze*, 307. When Zanuck sent an early version of the script to the
NAACP, multiple voices there objected to it, too, one deeming it "a bid for complete submission on the part of colored people." NAACP correspondence to
Zanuck, cited in Alan Gevinson, ed., *American Film Institute Catalog: Within
Our Gates: Ethnicity in American Feature Films, 1911–1960* (Berkeley and Los
Angeles: University of California Press, 1997), 777. More recently, Mark Reid
has interpreted the film as one that "valorizes a racially dualistic world, [such
that] Pinky cannot celebrate her mixed racial background." *Redefining Black
Film* (Berkeley and Los Angeles: University of California Press, 1997), 45; and
Rogin has contrasted the segregationist ending and its ultimate refusal of identificatory fluidity for Pinky to the integration permitted Jewish men in contemporary films like *Gentleman's Agreement* (1948) and *Home of the Brave* (1949), reflecting a Hollywood opposition he maps back to *The Jazz Singer* "between the
Jew who can change his identity and the African American who cannot change
hers" (*Blackface, White Noise*, 221).

66. As Kaja Silverman writes in *Male Subjectivity*, reading and quoting
Althusser, "Ideological belief . . . occurs at the moment when an image which the
subject consciously knows to be culturally fabricated nevertheless succeeds in
being recognized or acknowledged as 'a pure, naked perception of reality'" (17).

67. Sigmund Freud, "Some Psychological Consequences of the Anatomical
Distinction between the Sexes" (1925), trans. James Strachey, in *Sexuality and
the Psychology of Love,* ed. Philip Rieff (New York: Macmillan, 1963), 187; and,
in the same volume, "Fetishism" (1927), trans. Joan Riviere, 214–19.

68. Ralph Ellison initially declares utter disbelief, for all viewers, writing of
Jeanne Crain's performance: "No one is apt to mistake her for a Negro, not even
a white one." But then, immediately complicating this claim with something that

sounds like it must entail divided belief, he continues (of this and three other films): "And yet, despite the absurdities with which these films are laden, they are worth seeing, and if seen, capable of involving us emotionally. . . . It is here precisely that a danger lies. For the temptation toward . . . sharing in their emotional release is apt to blind us to the true nature of what is unfolding—or failing to unfold—before our eyes. As an antidote" for white viewers prone to respond with a "profuse flow of tears," he recommends watching such a film "in predominantly Negro audiences" to break the spell with the critical laughter of black disbelief. Ellison, "The Shadow and the Act," 280, discussed in Everett, *Returning the Gaze*, 308–9.

69. Sigmund Freud, "Splitting of the Ego in the Defensive Process" (1938), trans. James Strachey, in *Sexuality and the Psychology of Love*, 222. Homi K. Bhabha describes skin as "the most visible of fetishes, recognized as 'common knowledge' in a range of cultural, political and historical discourses, [one that] plays a public part in the racial drama that is enacted every day in colonial societies." *The Location of Culture* (London: Routledge, 1994), 78. Bhabha invokes the notion of skin as fetish to query the forms of "splitting and multiple belief" that subtend "the particular regime of visibility deployed in colonial discourse" (81). The present examples make such splittings all the more apparent and raise the question of what happens when skin, the subject's own or another's, fails to uphold its "common knowledge" function.

70. Christian Metz, *The Imaginary Signifier: Psychoanalysis and the Cinema* (Bloomington: Indiana University Press, 1977), 45. Feminist film theorists have critiqued Metz for his appropriation of Freudian concepts of divided belief without acknowledging their utter entanglement in the Freudian corpus to questions of sexual difference. See especially Jacqueline Rose, "The Cinematic Apparatus," in *The Cinematic Apparatus,* ed. Teresa de Lauretis and Stephen Heath (New York: St. Martin's, 1980), 172–86, and Kaja Silverman, *The Acoustic Mirror: The Female Voice in Psychoanalysis and Cinema* (Bloomington: Indiana University Press, 1988), 1–41. My own position at the moment is itself somewhat divided: on the one hand, I am thoroughly indebted to this feminist tradition; on the other hand, as I attempt to theorize the role of the cinema in the constitution of racial knowledge, I find Metz's formulations particularly resonant. In borrowing from him in this way, however, I do not mean to perpetuate his original blindness. It is by no means coincidental that the subject upon and through whom racial identity is most coercively worked out is female, and that the methods by which she is made to be "black" often borrow and extend classical cinematic means of constituting femininity through articulations of narrative, visibility, space, and voice.

71. That this last fence is falling over also could be read to already signal, as discussed later, the multiple breakdowns of the racial order entertained in the film.

72. Characters repeatedly recognize this, and Miss Em's insipid cousin blurts it out: "I had heard you were light, but I had no idea, why, you're practically white!" Alone with Miss Em, she adds, "She's whiter than I am!"

73. Ephraim Katz, *The Film Encyclopedia*, 2nd ed. (New York: Harper-Collins, 1994), 301.

74. As I argue elsewhere, *The Searchers* (1956) similarly invites speculation about miscegenation through its refusal of details. Susan Courtney, "Looking for (Race and Gender) Trouble in Monument Valley," *Qui Parle* 6, no. 2 (1993): 114–17.

75. The incomplete trailer of *Pinky* before the film on the 1994 FoxVideo videotape begins with a shot from the assault scene, emphasizing the critical significance of that exchange.

76. On related logics in *Imitation of Life* (1959), see Marina Heung, "'What's the Matter with Sara Jane?' Daughters and Mothers in Sirk's *Imitation of Life,*" *Cinema Journal* 26, no. 3 (spring 1987): 21–43.

77. Patricia White reads the film's "lesbian familial model" as producing "a quiet travesty of patriarchal inheritance" (*Uninvited*, 164).

78. While this formulation emphasizes the construction of the subject within the film, it will become increasingly apparent that I take this orchestration of space to also be productive of a subjective position for the spectator, as one who knows with and beyond *Pinky*.

79. That the construction of Pinky's racial identity regularly engages classical cinematic tropes for constructing gender is indicated in part by the tendency of her voice to be textually marked as embodied (breathy, screaming, etc.) and inserted into textual recesses (the cabin, her inner voice, etc.), much in the way Silverman demonstrates the female voice to be typically kept at a distance from positions of discursive authority (*Acoustic Mirror*, 42–71).

80. I am grateful to Herman Gray for pushing me to recognize the extent to which the process I am describing produces whiteness as well as blackness. Insofar as whiteness is conjured as that position for whom blackness becomes visible and known, this is another example of the dominant white logic whereby "whites are those who have such knowledge, but are themselves less readily the object of it." Richard Dyer, *White* (London: Routledge, 1997), 20.

81. The *Hollywood Reporter* raved over precisely the film's ability to make spectators identify with Pinky's plight: "Neither white man nor Negro can appraise 'Pinky' without thinking earnestly: 'What would I do under the same circumstances?'" 30 September 1949, clipping in *Pinky* file, PCA. This response was precisely what Zanuck had hoped for. Defending the script against the NAACP's harsh critiques, he argued that in 1948 "a motion picture which deals with the Negro minority in the United States must be above all things nonpropagandist. All it can hope to do, at its boldest, is to make the white majority experience emotionally the injustice and daily hurts suffered by colored people." Zanuck to Walter White, as cited in Gevinson, *American Film Institute Catalog,* 777.

CHAPTER FIVE
OUT OF THE PLANTATION AND INTO THE SUBURBS

1. After his failed legal attempt to block a new city integration policy, Arkansas governor Orval Faubus called out the National Guard on 2 September 1957 to surround Central High School and prevent nine African Americans from

attending. Nearly a month later, President Eisenhower took control and sent additional troops to enforce the policy and protect the new students. A military presence remained throughout the school year. Sean Dennis Cashman, *African-Americans and the Quest for Civil Rights, 1900–1990* (New York: New York University Press, 1991) 137–41.

2. "Hollywood's Summer Films Tackle Some Sweaty Topics with Varying Success," *Life*, 22 July 1957, *Island in the Sun* production file, Margaret Herrick Library, Academy of Motion Picture Arts and Sciences, Beverly Hills, California. Hereafter documents reviewed in the clippings files at the Herrick Library, where they often do not include complete citation information, are cited as Herrick. Unless otherwise noted, such documents were found in the production file of the film in question.

3. Henry Popkin, "Hollywood Tackles the Race Issue," *Commentary* 24, no. 4 (1957): 354.

4. Befitting the conflicted character of its lot, *Love Is a Many-Splendored Thing* was nominated for Academy Awards for Best Picture, Best Actress (Jennifer Jones as William Holden's Eurasian lover), and color cinematography but was also singled out by the *Harvard Lampoon* for "Best Reason for Closing the Open Door" and "Most Embarrassing Interlude." Other highs: *The King and I* was the second-top-grossing film of 1956, nominated for nine Academy Awards, and won five; *Island in the Sun* was the eighth-highest-grossing film of 1957; in 1958, *South Pacific* was the seventh and *Sayonara* the third, the last winning four Academy awards; in 1959, *Imitation of Life* was the fourth-top-grossing film, and *The Inn of Sixth Happiness* made almost half as much at thirteenth; *West Side Story* took no less than ten Oscars in 1961 and came in a very high-grossing second in 1962; Nancy Kwan drew crowds two years in a row, with *The World of Suzie Wong* grossing the sixth-highest profits of 1961 and *The Flower Drum Song* the ninth of 1962; and although marking a period just beyond the one under consideration here, both *Mutiny on the Bounty* and *To Kill a Mockingbird* were nominated for Best Picture in 1962 (beat out by *Lawrence of Arabia*), the first coming in at sixth in sales and the second at eighth. Many of these high grossers were also among the *Lampoon*'s ten worst films of their respective years (e.g., *Bhowani Junction, Island in the Sun, South Pacific,* and *Mutiny on the Bounty*). Cobbett S. Steinberg, *Film Facts* (New York: Facts on File, 1980), 22–24, 226–35, 335–39.

5. While the Supreme Court delayed ruling on the constitutionality of anti-miscegenation laws in the wake of reactions to *Brown v. Board* in 1954 (see chapter 6), local bodies weighed in on both sides of the issue. Many western states repealed their intermarriage laws in the late fifties and early sixties, and several southern ones upheld theirs. See Werner Sollors, *Neither Black nor White Yet Both* (New York: Oxford University Press, 1997), Appendix B. Meanwhile, for example, the Reformed Church approved intermarriage among its "pro-integration moves" ("Mixed Marriages OK'd!" *Pittsburgh Courier*, 27 June 1957); and the Duke University Women's College delegation sponsored a similar bill in the North Carolina Student Legislature, which passed ("Students OK Mixed Union," *Pittsburgh Courier*, 23 November 1957). Despite such "new" attitudes, reading through the popular black press in the period makes it evident that, as one writer

put it about a week after *Island*'s premiere: "Miscegenation is nothing new under the sun." Jo Black, "Can You Tell? . . . Negro or White?" *Pittsburgh Courier*, 22 June 1957, 4. Despite dominant white America's assertions to the contrary, published knowledge of such history sometimes took the form of remembering famous black men like Frederick Douglass and Jack Johnson who had married white women but also did not shy away from the exploitative sexual legacy of slavery. See "Famous Negroes Married to Whites," *Ebony*, December 1949, 20–28; Baker Morten, "The Lowdown on Miscegenation," *Pittsburgh Courier*, 10 August 1957, mag. sec., 4.

6. More direct ties between Hollywood's interracial texts and wider cultural ones are also visible. A front page from the *Chicago Defender* features the headline "Klansmen Flog 10 in Alabama: NAACP Asks for Florida Probe," and just beneath that a photo of Belafonte and another story from Florida, "Racists Protest 'Island in the Sun,'" 24 August 1957, 1. Reversing the order of importance, a headline from the *Pittsburgh Courier* reads, "Belafonte's Lips 'Sealed'!" (a double entendre discussed later) and is oddly echoed in a smaller one below it: "King Tells NAACP: 'Let Me Speak,'" 15 June 1957, 1. And *Motion Picture Herald* writes of *Night of the Quarter Moon*: "This racial melodrama comes along at a time when such subject matter is gaining considerable public attention, both on the screen and in daily news bulletins. For this reason, shrewd showmen will find . . . more than a fair share of exploitable angles that should pay off" (21 February 1959, Herrick).

7. "Toward the end of the decade the tendrils of culture, clan, and tribe grew so intricate, even tortured, in their view of race relations that they seemed mannerist." Thomas Cripps, *Making Movies Black: The Hollywood Message Movie from World War II to the Civil Rights Era* (New York: Oxford University Press, 1993) 281.

8. "Hollywood's Summer Films Tackle Some Sweaty Topics"; "Island in the Sun," *Hollywood Reporter*, 13 June 1957, Herrick.

9. "Band of Angels Dated," *Mirror News*, 10 August 1957, Herrick. Another reviewer declared the film "so bad that it must be seen to be disbelieved. . . . Look away, look away." "Old Kentucky Hash," *Newsweek*, 29 July 1957, Herrick.

10. Douglas Robinson, "Hollywood Vista: Two Features Involving Negroes Make Progress Toward Screen—Addenda," *New York Times*, 15 December 1957, Herrick.

11. "Night of the Quarter Moon," *Cue*, 7 March 1959, Herrick.

12. Rob Roy, "Roy Writes of New Hits," *Chicago Defender*, 1 November 1958, 18; and "Nat Cole, Julie London, Barrymore Star in Film on 'Interracial Theme,'" *Chicago Defender*, 14 February 1959, 19. An even more politicized celebration of a somewhat less objectionable film is this: "A film like 'Kings Go Forth' should prompt U.S. citizens to press forward more rapidly toward the goal of the real democracy in our nation about which they preach to the rest of the universe." "South Won't Like the Film Version of 'Kings Go Forth,'" *Pittsburgh Courier*, 21 June 1958, 22.

13. Segregationists predictably opposed intermarriage, but opinions varied among civil rights advocates as to its relevance in debates over integration. Such variation, and the regular linkage of our films to such debates in the popular

press, is visible in a sidebar on the subject accompanying an *Ebony* cover story, "Why I Married Julie," by Harry Belafonte, keyed to the release of *Island in the Sun* (also reviewed in this issue). Under Belafonte's discussion of the social implications of his marriage to a white woman, a caption proclaims: "Prominent Negro Leaders Answer Question: Does Interracial Marriage Hinder Integration?" Most of the writers, activists, religious leaders, and entertainers quoted reject the conflation of integration and interracial marriage as an obfuscation of the movement's demands for equal rights with private matters of sex and friendship. Some nonetheless maintain that interracial marriage could "hasten" or "help . . . integration." *Ebony*, July 1957, 90–91.

14. Prior to the release of *Kings Go Forth*, producer Frank Ross, "who frankly admitted that he was not in favor of miscegenation," is reported as saying that in the white press the film would be "advertise[d] . . . as a tender love story set against the backdrop of war. In the Negro press, however, it is probable that they will utilize the miscegenation theme." This dual campaign might also explain why a black press agent was hired for the film ("Hollywood Vista"). Ads for *Night of the Quarter Moon* suggest similar tactics were used in the Spanish-language press. One features a full view of Julie London's exposed back and ripped bra, while a man attempts to cover her. A caption over them declares, "No me importa el color de su piel . . . ella es mia!" The same image is used in the English ad, but a black square covers the exposed bra under the single word "Exposed!" Much smaller captions announce, in rhetoric familiar from the South Sea Island films, "A tropical night, . . . a beautiful girl, . . . what man would stop to ask questions?" Undated Spanish-language publicity sheet and ad from the *Hartford Times*, 28 May 1959, Herrick.

15. Popkin, "Hollywood Tackles the Race Issue," 354.

16. Ibid.

17. Joan Fontaine is quoted as saying, "The audience will have to decide how much interracial passion there is in the movie." Carter Barber, "Belafonte a Dramatic Vanguard for Negro Achievements," *Mirror-News*, 18 April 1957, 12, Herrick.

18. "'Sun' Lures Dixie Fans," *Pittsburgh Courier*, 13 July 1957, 21. This story, which also notes that these developments are encouraging signs to the industry for related films in production, ran a month after another claimed the film had been "banned in every Southern state and . . . created the fear that some borderline states in the North may follow suit." "Controversy Still Rages Over Interracial Movie," *Pittsburgh Courier*, 16 June 1957, 20. The same paper later reports a Warner Bros. announcement "that despite incidents of protest against their controversial 'Band of Angels,' . . . the film will be shown in 100 important cities in Texas, Louisiana and Mississippi." "100 Southern Cities to See Racial Movie," *Pittsburgh Courier*, 3 August 1957, 21.

19. Groups and individuals worked to have the film blocked by local theaters (including at least two northern ones), the U.S. military, and the South Carolina state legislature, and the film was in fact banned in at least two southern cities (Memphis, Tennessee; and West Memphis, Arkansas). "'Sun' Boycott Try Fizzles in Mples [Mich.]," *Variety*, 14 June 1957, Herrick; "Dixie Segregationists Attack 'Island in Sun," *Variety*, 4 April 1957, Herrick; "The Storm over Belafonte,"

Look, 25 June 1957, 140; "Memphis Bans 'Sun' as Too Frank a Pic on 'Miscegenation,'" *Variety*, 8 July 1957, Herrick; "'Sun' Goes Down in West (Memphis), Traditional Haven of Banned Pix," *Variety*, 12 August 1957, Herrick.

20. "Racists Protest 'Island in Sun,'" *Chicago Defender*, 24 August 1957, 1; Masco Young, "The Grapevine," *Pittsburgh Courier*, 7 September 1957, 23; "Movie Men Fight Ban on Race Pix," *Pittsburgh Courier*, 28 September 1957, 23. The film was also banned for six years in the Bahamas because it was "believed by many to be the implied locale of events detailed in the novel and the film." "Nassau's Delayed ('57) Interracial 'Sun' Pic," *Variety*, 20 November 1963, Herrick.

21. As David Halberstam summarizes Friedan's findings, "She had tapped into a great reservoir of doubt, frustration, anxiety, and resentment. The women felt unfulfilled and isolated with their children. . . . As she wrote later: 'It was a strange stirring, a sense of dissatisfaction. . . . Each suburban wife struggled with it alone. As she made the beds, shopped for groceries, matched slipcover materials, ate peanut butter sandwiches with her children . . . lay beside her husband at night—she was afraid to ask of herself the silent question—'Is this all?'" *The Fifties* (New York: Villard Books, 1993) 598, 595–96, citing Betty Friedan, *The Feminine Mystique* (New York: Norton, 1963), 11.

22. Steven Cohan, *Masked Men: Masculinity and the Movies in the Fifties* (Bloomington: Indiana University Press, 1997), 6.

23. Ibid. On ambivalent filmic representations of gender and sexuality in a decade remembered for its normative familial images, see also Nina Leibman, *Living Room Lectures: The Fifties Family in Film and Television* (Austin: University of Texas Press, 1995).

24. "Famous Negroes Married to Whites," 22.

25. "The Storm over Belafonte," 142. Even Belafonte's own account is accompanied by a photograph of Julie serving him at the table with a caption that stresses her domesticity ("Why I Married Julie," 94).

26. "Eartha's My Little Sun-Tanned Daughter," *Pittsburgh Courier*, 21 May 1960, 24.

27. Nat King Cole is pictured with his African American wife, but the copy reports a hug between him and Marlene Dietrich. Sammy Davis Jr. is pictured in a separate photo from that of a glamorous young British "Lady" who, according to the text beneath the pictures, was slated to work for him but whom he had yet to meet. "Across the Colour Bar," *Daily Mail*, 30 May 1960, Davis clipping file, Herrick.

28. The claims here uttered by Gable/Butler/Bond reverberate multiply with those made by Birmingham clergy six years later in their objection to "untimely" acts of civil disobedience. As Dr. King famously refutes them, "We know through painful experience that freedom is never voluntarily given by the oppressor; it must be demanded by the oppressed. Frankly, I have yet to engage in a direct-action campaign that was 'well timed' in the view of those who have not suffered unduly from the disease of segregation. For years now I have heard the word 'wait!' It rings in the ear of every Negro with piercing familiarity. This 'Wait' has almost always meant 'Never.' We must come to see, with one of our distinguished jurists, that 'justice too long delayed is justice denied.'" Martin Luther King Jr.,

"Letter from Birmingham Jail," *New Leader*, 1963; repr. in *Documentary History of the Modern Civil Rights Movement*, ed. Peter B. Levy (Westport, Conn.: Greenwood, 1992), 111.

29. As will become increasingly relevant, Gable's own reading of what ties *Band of Angels* to *Gone with the Wind* downplays race and emphasizes gender instead: "The only similarities . . . are that both have Civil War backgrounds and in both I'm forced to deal with a stubborn woman." Hazel Flynn, "Gable Returns to Dixie," *Beverly Hills Citizen*, 7 August 1957, 5, Herrick.

30. Brian Henderson's argument that *The Searchers* uses its story about whites and Native Americans to work through contemporary questions about relations between whites and African Americans is also useful for thinking about the wide range of interracial pairs depicted in this period. Henderson, "*The Searchers*: An American Dilemma," *Film Quarterly* 34 (winter 1980–81): 9–23. When we shift the focus of analysis from the status of "the other" depicted to the negotiations of whiteness and white privilege, the commonalties between the various narrative and cinematic strategies deployed become particularly evident.

31. The troubled relation of Mexican detective Mike Vargas to visual mastery is signaled early on, when he is nearly splattered with acid by a member of the crime family he is working to prosecute: though Vargas ducks the burning liquid, it comes quite close and lands on a poster of a burlesque dancer instead, linking Vargas's vulnerability to that of the classical female image. Vargas continues for the better part of the film decidedly not seeing and not knowing what is happening to his wife, Susan. Just before she is harassed in her motel room, chased by a flashlight beam from a man across the street as she undresses, we see Mike in the street below; he is close enough to see what happens but does not. Later when he calls to check on her in another motel room, the one in which she will soon be sexually assaulted, he is framed in a composition with the blind woman whose phone he has borrowed, an association that makes his inadequacy, as husband and cop, all the more apparent. He will arrive on the scene too late with a flashlight that illuminates nothing but the evidence of her attack and later will drive directly below the balcony from which she screams for help, again not seeing her. And although the film will ultimately grant Quinlan the authority of having had an accurate hunch about the man he frames for murder, the uncertainty of his methods and equipment is repeatedly exposed. In the scene that leads to his demise, for example, although he sees Vargas sneaking about Tana's home, he is so drunk that he does not believe his own eyes. With male vision thus thoroughly failing its protagonists, the film stages the final showdown as a sonic one wherein Vargas pursues Quinlan and his verbal confession with a tape recorder. This also illuminates why, according to Stephen Heath, "the two fundamental figurative modes of the narrative action" in the film's textual system are "the telephone and . . . the look." Stephen Heath, "Film and System: Terms of Analysis, Part II," *Screen* 16, no. 2 (1975): 96.

32. Resonant here are the visual terms with which Tom Engelhardt diagnoses the end of a certain national narrative in this period, "a saga of expanding liberties and rights that started in a vast, fertile, nearly empty land whose native inhabitants more or less faded away." *The End of Victory Culture: Cold War America and the Disillusioning of a Generation* (New York: HarperCollins,

1995), 4. In the Hollywood version of this saga, "as the enemy bore down without warning from the peripheries of human existence . . . the viewer, inside a defensive circle of wagons, found himself behind the sights of a rifle" (4). Although "the Japanese attack on Pearl Harbor fit the lineaments of th[e] story well," its vision ceased "*in a blinding flash* over . . . Hiroshima that left Americans more bereft than they could then have imagined. . . . the story that had helped order their sense of history for almost 300 years proved no longer sustainable . . . ; *victory and defeat, enemy and self, threatened to merge*" (5–6, emphasis mine).

33. Of the many films I will not discuss in detail, and one that my readers are perhaps most likely to expect, is Douglas Sirk's remake of *Imitation of Life* (1959). That it is not so easily mapped through the tropes I detect here speaks in part to the ways in which it puts conventional representations of race and gender into question, even as it also at times reproduces them. At the same time, in keeping with my larger argument here, that film, too, is even more anxious about gender than its 1934 predecessor, even as it becomes ever more self-conscious and critical about the construction of race. Nonetheless, I leave it out of the present discussion (1) because it has received such fine, exhaustive critical attention already (see notes in chapter 4); and (2) because my efforts in this chapter are focused on excavating the representational work of the more common, and less discussed, tropes I find in this period.

34. The rape scene erupts early on, when Maxwell grills Sylvia about the imagined lover. Growing increasingly accusatory, he finally rips at her dress and forces aggressive kisses. When she pulls away and yells for him to stop, he refuses, muttering that women get tired of making love in the same old routine, and the scene fades to black.

35. Maxwell identifies Carson's cigarettes as "Egyptian," coding even this imagined sexual rivalry, and in effect the film's main plot, with a hint of miscegenation. This figurative racial coding will become literalized and reversed when the Fleurys' black ancestry is exposed and Maxwell finally confronts Carson, who will then declare that he "wouldn't take something from someone like you with a tarbrush rubbed across his face." This remark pushes Maxwell to strangle Carson while madly repeating: "Tarbrush, tarbrush, tarbrush!"

36. On these and related visual conventions for creating a "white" point of view, see Richard Dyer, *White* (London: Routledge, 1997), especially 37–39.

37. Belafonte released his first album in 1954, and with two more in 1956 "he hit the really big money in record sales. He leads the pack in this country's current trend to calypso music—in fact, *Variety* . . . reports that he has in large part caused it." Jeanne Van Holmes, "Belafonte Gives It All He's Got," *Saturday Evening Post*, 20 April 1957, 75.

38. Her first appearance in the film seems primarily dedicated to announcing this. Dropping off Sylvia and Jocelyn after a trip to the beach, she asks if they need help unloading and then sits in the car with no intention of helping, amused with herself as she tells Jocelyn to "call somebody"—presumably one of the many servants we hear about (but never see) at the Fleurys' mansion. Later, when David takes her to see a black village, she appears at best like an amused tourist and at worst like a careless outsider defiling another culture.

39. Barber, "Belafonte a Dramatic Vanguard," 12.

40. Ibid. *Ebony* reports Fontaine's attitude quite differently, quoting her as saying, "'At least I have made them agree that Harry and I can drink out of the same coconut. . . . But they insist no kissing, and that we give one another up.'" "Island in the Sun," *Ebony*, July 1957, 36. In addition to the coconut, there is in fact some extremely fleeting, modest "physical contact" between them in the film. He lifts her off a bus by the waist and lightly guides her by the arm, and each of them once grabs the other by the arm—once in a moment of tenderness and later in a flash of anger. *Ebony* also reports the British press's charge that "Hollywood censors had made their pressure felt on the interracial love scenes," and Cripps concurs: "Surely the makers were made skittish by the baleful eye of the PCA" (*Making Movies Black*, 264). I found no record of this, although that does not rule out the possibility.

41. Barber, "Belafonte a Dramatic Vanguard," 12.

42. "'Sun' A 'Terrible Pic' Says Belafonte, Even Tho 'I Get to Sock James Mason,'" *Variety*, 8 July 1957, Herrick. Although Belafonte's and Mason's characters are fierce rivals throughout the film, no literal "sock" (or any physical contact between them) appears in the final cut.

43. "Cops Guard Joan Fontaine, Poison-Pen 'Sun'-Burn Victim, At Pic's Preem," *Variety*, 14 June 1957, Herrick.

44. That she had received the letters over time is implied when she explains, "I think this is part of an organized drive. After all, the picture hadn't even been released when the letters were written: none of these people had seen it. . . . I've received about 50 thus far from the studio, which forwards them to me." Ibid.

45. That the vulnerability of the image of Fontaine thus produced inhered in her (fair) white womanliness is encoded in the wordplay of *Variety*'s title for the story that reported the scene at Grauman's the following day: "Cops Guard Joan Fontaine, Poison-Pen 'Sun'-Burn Victim."

46. "Belafonte's Lips 'Sealed'!" *Pittsburgh Courier*, 15 June 1957, 1+. That story draws from *Look*'s, which gives the more detailed account of the studio's command cited here. "The Storm over Belafonte," 139. Cf. note 6.

47. "The Storm over Belafonte," 140; Barber, "Belafonte a Dramatic Vanguard," 12; Hazel Garland, "'Why Should I Keep Quiet?'—Belafonte," *Pittsburgh Courier*, 22 June 1957, 3.

48. Although *Ebony* gives Zanuck's denial of this claim the last word on the subject, it rings hollow with his explanation that "there is no scene that calls for kissing." "Island in the Sun," *Ebony* 36.

49. "Theatrical Round-up: Dizzy Rowe's Notebook," *Pittsburgh Courier*, 27 July 1957, 21.

50. "Move On to Continue Making Racial Movies," *Pittsburgh Courier*, 27 July 1957, 21.

51. Recognizing that "ideologies of masculinity always exist in a dialectical relation to other ideologies," Hazel V. Carby has recently interrogated "their articulations with discourses of race and nation in American culture." She is especially concerned that in African American history "the result of the pursuit of 'race consciousness, race pride, and race solidarity' was the emergence of particular social types, among which was the Race Man." *Race Men* (Cambridge, Mass.: Harvard University Press, 1998), 2, 4, 5. Michelle Stephens imports Carby's analysis of the

race man to her own of Belafonte in "The 'First Negro Matinee Idol': Harry Belafonte and American Culture in the 1950s" (paper presented at the American Studies Association convention, Sheraton Hotel, Montreal, 29 October 1999).

Further testifying to *Island in the Sun*'s mixed reception, the same *Defender* story that takes note of its "presenting a pair of love romances without a single kiss being involved" explains the success of the film "at loop's Oriental" in black Chicago as due to the fact that "it is a good theater and not for its romantic intrigue," which the reviewer finds not all that intriguing. Nonetheless, he closes by calling the film, "a step in right direction—for common sense and human treatment of all peoples alike for nation's theater screen." "Chicagoans Like 'Island in the Sun,' But Pooh, Pooh Awe-Inspiring Claims," *Chicago Defender*, 15 June 1957, 8.

52. "'It stands to reason that if a man and woman are supposed to be in love, there is going to be some hugging and kissing. Not that I wanted to kiss Miss Fontaine. She wouldn't be the first woman that I have kissed'" (Garland, "'Why Should I Keep Quiet?'" 3). "'The day we filmed [sharing a coconut] I caught a cold. I guess that's what happens in these interracial situations'" ("Belafonte's Lips 'Sealed'!'" 3).

53. "The New Pictures," *Time*, 24 June 1957: 84.

54. *Variety* deems Fontaine's a "warm characterization," calls Dandridge "a spectacular looker," and notes that "Miss Collins also registers strongly in the looks department." "Island in the Sun," *Variety*.

55. As I explain in the next paragraph, when Jocelyn and Euan head off to England at film's end, he (and the rest of the film's inhabitants) will believe his very tan and now pregnant wife to be of mixed race.

56. Robyn Wiegman's account of how blackness has been constituted as feminine and visible in part through representations of the black female body in earlier texts helps lay the ground for understanding why non-white female bodies are captured as if predisposed to hypervisibility. *American Anatomies: Theorizing Race and Gender* (Durham, N.C.: Duke University Press, 1995), 43–78.

57. Even *Island*'s Margot Seaton, a white-collar worker who comports herself with propriety at work and upscale parties, appears suddenly at carnival as not just one of many revelers but a spectacular sight unto herself, limboing in a scant costume, isolated from the crowd that parts around her. And her display is so much the point here that not only is Hollywood's classical narrative imperative frozen, in Mulvey's terms, but sacred laws of continuity are disregarded. Although the scene ends with Margot headed toward her white boyfriend after catching a glimpse of his disapproving look from a balcony, the implied scene to come never transpires. If she was off to confront his proprietary gaze, all the more reason, we can only surmise, to skip it.

58. Gina Marchetti reads related "Pygmalion fantas[ies]" in Asian-white interracial romances of the fifties in *Romance and the "Yellow Peril": Race, Sex, and Discursive Strategies in Hollywood* (Berkeley and Los Angeles: University of California Press, 1993), 119. Of a scene from *The World of Suzie Wong* in which a white painter angrily rips the Western clothes off his favorite "Oriental" model in the name of authentic "beauty," she writes, "Beneath all this high art posturing . . . is the simple male pleasure of the striptease. Any threat Suzie's sexuality

may pose is stripped away with her clothes" (121). What Marchetti goes on to argue about the representation of Asian women so exposed for white men could be further applied to the representation of many women of color throughout Hollywood, and especially abundant in this period: "The films can uphold both the gender and racial status quo by depicting Asian women as more truly 'feminine,' content at being passive, subservient, dependent, domestic, and slaves to 'love.' The films implicitly warn both white women and women of color to take the Western imagination's creation of the passive Asian beauty as the feminine ideal if they want to attract and keep a man" (116).

59. The adjectives are Marchetti's, who does not exaggerate (ibid., 115).

60. The rock hits Ginny in the head, drawing blood, and the boys hack and rip up plants in the front yard.

61. A pinup generated in the name of the film further demonstrates this. Although its dark-haired actress/model never appears in the film, the pinup displays her with her skirt "caught" on a fence post to reveal her upper thigh. Pinup/publicity photo (?) for *Night of the Quarter Moon*, Herrick.

62. The resonance with *The Manchurian Candidate* (1962) is significant. On that film's, and the period's, intertwined phobias of mom and communists, see Michael Paul Rogin, *"Ronald Reagan," the Movie, and Other Episodes in Political Demonology* (Berkeley and Los Angeles: University of California Press, 1987), 236–71.

63. Freud's fantasy of the instantaneous legibility of sexual difference and its meaning comes to mind, a comparison that speaks to the heart of my argument that when the "natural" orders of sexual difference, especially its vision and visibility, are no longer reliable, those of race are called upon to take up the slack. Hence it is further telling that not just any part of Ginny's raced body, but the sexed ones, provide the crucial sight.

64. Caren Kaplan analyzes the mutual negotiation of gender and empire in " 'Getting to Know You': Travel, Gender, and the Politics of Representation in *Anna and the King of Siam* and *The King and I*," in *Late Imperial Culture*, ed. Román De La Campa, E. Ann Kaplan, and Michael Sprinker (London: Verso, 1995), 33–52. On the male gaze, see Laura Donaldson, *"The King and I* in *Uncle Tom's Cabin*, or On the Border of the Women's Room," *Cinema Journal* 29, no. 3 (1990): 53–68.

65. Marjorie Garber reads "the comic treatment of gender crossing in *South Pacific* [as] in part a displacement of anxieties about the transgressing of racial borderlines." Yet, "it is equally possible . . . to see the racial issues . . . as displacing a greater anxiety about gender, or about policing, or breaching, the borderline between gay and straight." *Vested Interests: Cross-Dressing and Cultural Anxiety* (New York: HarperCollins, 1992), 58.

66. Such sentiments have a history in the Western. In *Stagecoach* (1939) the man-friendly prostitute says of the "Ladies League of Law and Order": "There are worse things than Apaches!"

67. This can be explained in part by the fact that the Code's restrictions against miscegenation were in the process of being softened and ultimately removed throughout this decade. But that fact, too, can be read as an effect of the shifting cultural politics I am analyzing. Moreover, we need more than the

chronology of Code revisions to explain why, in addition to the "new" romances between whites and blacks, romances between whites and Native Americans, Asians, and Mexicans were more likely to ultimately be severed (often by death, sometimes by choice) in roughly the first half of the decade (e.g., *Broken Arrow, The White Orchid, The Far Horizons, Love Is a Many-Splendored Thing, The King and I, The Searchers*) and to survive in the second half and beyond (e.g., *The Vanishing American, Run of the Arrow, China Gate, Sayonara, Touch of Evil, The World, the Flesh, and the Devil, The World of Suzie Wong, A Majority of One*).

68. For Marchetti the swimsuit photograph "represents female . . . sexuality that may be beyond Gruver's power to control" (*Romance and the "Yellow Peril,"* 133). While that is partly confirmed later by the vividness of Eileen's desire, it does not address why the very same kind of male voyeurism that elsewhere in Hollywood cinema functions so successfully to disavow such disturbances markedly fails to do so here—even before the woman appears, and voices her desires, in the flesh.

69. The film minimizes the potential contemporary threats implicit in these theatrical practices in part by repeatedly reminding us of their traditional history. To Lloyd's suggestion that the play "could use a Marilyn Monroe," for example, Nakamura replies, "Unfortunately, Miss Monroes were barred from Kabuki in the seventeenth century." He nonetheless affirms contemporary conventions, adding that he, too, is "a great admirer of Miss Monroe."

70. By the logic of the film, Hana Ogi's male drag could ultimately be read to demonstrate how feminine she *essentially* is, despite her masculine attire. Heavy lipstick always threatens to tip her androgynous look a bit further to the femme side, and her masculine costumes are always quickly superseded by excessively feminine ones.

71. When Lloyd takes offense that her "obligation" to Matsubayashi exceeds (momentarily) her obligation to him, she explains that the troupe rescued her after her father had to sell her, and thus "brought honor back to my family." That the restoration of a father's honor comes through his daughter's permanent obligation to performance is in keeping with my larger reading here, as is the fact that Brando finally convinces her that her "first obligation" is, now, to be with him—"to be man and wife and make some children."

72. I offer an extended reading of this film in "Looking for (Race and Gender) Trouble in Monument Valley," *Qui Parle: Literature, Philosophy, Visual Arts, History* 6, no. 2 (1993): 97–130.

73. Lyrics sent to Breen from Reginald Le Bord (Cosmo Productions), 26 January 1954, *White Orchid* file, PCA Collection, Herrick.

74. Although this last "dearest white" is sung as the beginning of another line, the print transferred to video by Hollywood's Attic (1996) cuts abruptly just after it. It seems likely the stanza would continue with the replacement of "femme fatale" with "dearest white."

75. The reading I am proposing here is of course quickly complicated for and by Spanish-speaking audiences.

76. The white woman's equation with the plantation's white flower echoes *The Birth of a Nation*. And it speaks to this film's ties to, and distance from, the

earlier one that she is now not only *not* the given property of the white man, but that the man of color is brought in to cultivate her as such when the white man seems unable to do so.

77. Juan's final sacrifice serves not only to restore the white couple but also to release Bob of the risk of being surrounded by the invisible eyes that formerly surrounded him.

78. In the case of *Touch of Evil,* I am thinking here more of the men of the Grandi family who surveil, assault, and abduct Susan Vargas than of Charlton Heston's brownface performance as her husband—a more ambivalent role marked by his visual and detective failings as well as his final mastery (cf. note 31), an ambivalence that seems echoed in the racial ambiguity of casting such a white male actor as a Mexican. In Stephen Heath's words, "Vargas is Mexican but *not really*" ("Film and System," 93). For an extended reading of the complex meanings of "Mexican" in this film, and its criticism, see William Anthony Nericcio, "Of Mestizos and Half-Breeds: Orson Welles's *Touch of Evil,*" in *Chicanos and Film: Representation and Resistance,* ed. Chon A. Noriega (Minneapolis: University of Minnesota Press, 1992), 47–58.

79. While the film is very reticent to actually show this love, or allow it to develop, Sarah implies it for her part after an argument when she says, "We haven't said anything about love, have we?" Ralph later admits he loves her but still assumes she should be with a white man. It is only in the final sequence that the two seem to mutually, albeit quietly, acknowledge their feelings, when she begs him to stay and they clasp hands in a close-up. Yet the immediate addition of the white man to this scene again quickly mitigates the image of Ralph and Sarah as a couple.

80. *The World, the Flesh, and the Devil* press kit, Herrick.

81. It is unclear if it is the continued demand for intimacy and/or the relation of subservience that upsets Ralph. Later, when he finally expresses his anger, he yells, "Nobody cuts my hair, I have to do it myself!" The power imbalance is already implied in Sarah's initial joke that she will tip him if he does a good job.

82. In the month before this film's premiere, Belafonte's face appeared on the cover of *Time,* which declared him "at the peak of one of the remarkable careers in U.S. entertainment." This story, like others, singles out the pleasures of Belafonte "for his female fans" in "partially open" shirt and "snug black pants." "Lead Man Holler," *Time,* 2 March 1959, 40.

83. As they sit by the projector, Ben asks Ralph, "There are two of us and only one of her. What are we gonna do about it?"

84. "The end of the picture . . . has the three settling their differences in some unexplained way. . . . Are we to assume that some sort of polygamous arrangement has been worked out, or will the three thenceforth lead entirely sexless lives, thus dooming both white and colored races to extinction?" Review of *The World, the Flesh, and the Devil, Saturday Review* 2 May 1959, Herrick.

85. "Belafonte Nixes More Race Films," *Pittsburgh Courier,* 24 August 1957, 3. Weeks earlier the same paper reported that "the most potent in-personality in the nation," "outspoken Harry Belafonte . . . [r]efus[ed] to continue as the lothario of . . . 'miscegenation' flickers." "Belafonte Tells of Roles He Wants from Hollywood," *Pittsburgh Courier,* 3 August 1957, 21. Cripps cites Belafonte's

great disappointment at *The World, the Flesh, and the Devil*, especially its ending (*Making Movies Black*, 266). And Belafonte's antiestablishment commitments were not limited to these films: "'I hate Madison Ave. and Hollywood and the clichés of American culture. . . .' [I plan] to go on 'resisting the clichés of the social order.'" "Does Belafonte Hate Success?" *Pittsburgh Courier*, 20 July 1957, 22.

86. After the desegregation decision in 1954, "the suburban school promised some relief from the pervasive fear of racial integration and its two presumed fellow-travelers—interracial violence and interracial sex." Kenneth T. Jackson, *Crabgrass Frontier: The Suburbanization of the United States* (New York: Oxford University Press, 1985), 289–90.

Chapter Six
Guess Who's Coming to Dinner with Eldridge Cleaver and the Supreme Court

1. As noted in the introduction, the AFI recently confirmed this film's popular status. And lest we think it derived primarily from the film's novelty, we need only recall that several others voyaged into related territory. Significantly in our context, *Time* hailed the widely acclaimed *One Potato, Two Potato* (1964)—a film that followed the loving relationship of a white woman and a black man, and the story of her losing her daughter from a prior marriage as a result—as the only "100% American" film since *The Birth of a Nation* ("Mixed Marriages at Cannes," *Time* 15, May 1964). Two other notable alternatives from this period are *If He Hollers Let Him Go* (1968) and *The Landlord* (1970). In the first, a rich white man tries to force an escaped black convict to terrorize his white wife, but the escapee and the wife turn against the husband and toward each other. The second—directed by a white man, Hal Ashby, from a novel written by a black woman, Kristin Hunter—looks like an interracial version of Ashby's cult hit *Harold and Maude*, released a year later. Here the rich white kid frees himself from his family by buying and moving into a building in Harlem, where he finds sex, and eventually love, with women he finds there.

2. The book also made Cleaver famous. As one review described later that year, "Today Cleaver is nationally known as the author of *Soul on Ice*, a widely read book of essays, as Minister of Information for the Black Panther Party in Oakland, as a defendant in an upcoming trial for parole violation (which may make him, like his colleague, Huey Newton, a *cause célèbre* among black nationalists and New Left radicals), as candidate for President on the Peace and Freedom party ticket, and as a literary idol of the black nationalists. His face shows up frequently on national television, his statements are widely reported in the press, he is important enough to have inspired the distaste and opposition of Governor Ronald Reagan, and Maxwell Geismar has called him 'one of the new distinctive literary voices.'" Jervis Anderson, "Race, Rage and Eldridge Cleaver," *Commentary*, December 1968, 63.

3. Christina's boyish nickname, "Chris," on the other hand, is used only by her husband, though he and the film, as we will see, clearly have other means of taming her.

4. Eldridge Cleaver, *Soul on Ice* (New York: Dell, 1968), 16, 17.

5. Leerom Medovoi claims Cleaver's "blind spot" is his assumption that these identities and relations are "social truths." "A Yippie-Panther Pipe Dream: Rethinking Sex, Race, and the Sexual Revolution," in *Swinging Single: Representing Sexuality in the 1960s*, ed. Hilary Radner and Moya Luckett (Minneapolis: University of Minnesota Press, 1999), 145. Yet, despite Cleaver's escalating gender essentialism (which I will discuss), his critical reflection on the "myth" (*Soul on Ice*, 162–63) and "social imagery" (183, 189) he discusses, and the transformative aspirations that fuel his book, suggest that *at times* he understand these identities, or at least their racial components, to be mutable social constructs.

6. In a 1969 interview Cleaver described the point in 1957 when "I became serious about the political system and how that related all the way down to the individual." He explains Frantz Fanon's influence on his thinking in related terms: "The most important thing is that [Fanon] describes the consciousness and the situation of a colonized people. [He] was a psychiatrist, so . . . was able to unravel what goes on in the mind of a colonized people." Lee Lockwood, *Conversation with Eldridge Cleaver: Algiers* (New York: Dell, 1970), 82, 90–91.

7. "I started to write . . . [t]o save myself. . . . I had to seek out the truth and unravel the snarled web of my motivations. I had to find out who I am and what I want to be, what type of man I should be, and what I could do to become the best of which I was capable" (*Soul on Ice*, 15).

8. *Loving v. Virginia*, 388 U.S. 1 (1967).

9. For a reading that at last takes seriously the renunciation as well as the "act," see Pamela Barnett, "Desire and Domination: Eldridge Cleaver and Racial-Sexual Politics of the Sixties," in her *Dangerous Desire: Sexual Freedom and Sexual Violence in American Literature since the Sixties* (New York: Routledge, forthcoming). In addition to her manuscript, I am grateful for vital conversations, feedback, and research materials Barnett shared with me as I wrote this chapter.

10. "Integration speaks not at all to the problem of poverty, only to the problem of blackness." Stokely Carmichael, "What We Want," *New York Review of Books*, 26 September 1966; repr. in *Documentary History of the Modern Civil Rights Movement*, ed. Peter B. Levy (New York: Greenwood, 1992), 181–82.

11. Speaking of race and "mixing, 'mongrelizing,' miscegenating," Cleaver writes that "deep-seated fears and emotions . . . are harnessed to social images and thereby transformed into weapons of the Class Struggle" (*Soul on Ice*, 190). Suggesting that social power is also absolutely gendered, he continues: "Race fears are weapons in th[at class] struggle between [white and black men] for control of sexual sovereignty" (190).

12. I am grateful to Adrienne Davis for a conversation in which she saw so immediately how Cleaver's model of black masculinity diverges from slavery's, helping me to articulate its proximity to postbellum popular culture's. Coming to a similar analysis that *Birth* led us to in chapter 2, Lazarus explains that "the black man's penis was the monkey wrench in the white man's perfect machine. The penis, virility, is of the Body. It is not of the Brain . . . the Omnipotent Administrator discovered that in the fury of his scheming he had blundered and clipped himself of his penis" (*Soul on Ice*, 164). The "solution" to this blunder, by Cleaver's account, is that the white man expands the domain of his omnipo-

tence to regulate the black penis, and empower his own, first through a process of control—"The stem of the Body, the penis, must submit to the will of the Brain'" (165)—and, failing that, through lynching and castration.

13. Cleaver discusses the symbolism of boxing as well, describing the politics surrounding Muhammad Ali in terms befitting those of Jack Johnson: "The boxing ring is the ultimate focus of masculinity in America, the two-fisted testing ground of manhood, and the heavyweight champion, as a symbol, is the real Mr. America" (*Soul on Ice*, 84). He soon adds: "Every institution in America is tainted by the mystique of race, and the question of masculinity is confused by the presence of both a 'white' man and a 'black' man" (86).

14. One of the first black feminists to do so, Michele Wallace articulated the masculinist terms of black nationalism in the *Village Voice*: "It took me three years to fully understand that Stokely [Carmichael] was serious when he'd said my position in the movement was 'prone'; three years to understand the countless speeches that all began 'the Black man . . .' did not include me." "A Black Feminist's Search for Sisterhood" (1975); repr. in Levy, *Documentary History of the Modern Civil Rights Movement*, 199–200. Similar rhetoric is detectable in *Soul on Ice* and is especially evident in an interview taken not long after its publication. Never addressing what it does for black women, Cleaver says "for the young black male, the Black Panther Party supplies very badly needed standards of masculinity." Robert Scheer, ed., *Eldridge Cleaver: Post-prison Writings and Speeches* (New York: Random House, 1969), 203.

15. "The psychic core of [a white woman's] sensuality," for example, is described as "the male-seeking pole of her Female Principle" (*Soul on Ice*, 184). Elsewhere this logic sanctions Cleaver's virulent homophobia, including his notorious textual assault of James Baldwin in "Notes on a Native Son" (97–111).

16. And there are more examples. In a 1968 interview, sexual difference and heterosexuality are again joyfully reified as the "natural" modes of difference: "Black or white, the male-female principle is toward unity. Both black and white people have to get out of the bags they're in *to be natural again. . . . everyone needs a new understanding of his total nature*, mental and physical. . . . Only then will *the primary thrust of life—the fusion of male and female*—be freed of sociological obstacles. That's the base of the kind of social system I want to see" (Scheer, *Eldridge Cleaver*, 209).

17. The book's beginning, middle, and end are marked by three very different heterosexual pairs. Key to Cleaver's early self-portrait is his discussion of raping white women. After a section of political essays, we find ourselves in "Prelude to Love–Three Letters," reading very intimate letters between him and his attorney, Beverly Axelrod. For Cleaver and his book this relationship marks a turning point: "You have tossed me a lifeline. . . . There was a deadness in my body that eluded me. . . . since encountering you, I feel life strength flowing back" (*Soul on Ice*, 143). Even as he refuses to name Axelrod's racial identity, he sets us up to read this as an interracial love affair. Not long after confessing his earlier love/hate for white women, he toys with confessing his unlikely object of desire ("How much more incredible is it, then, . . . to fall in love, and with a lawyer!"), and he writes to Axelrod: "We represent historical forces" (20, 150). But the book closes with a more expressly public love letter, "To All Black Women, from

All Black Men," declaring a healing form of intraracial love. While this trajectory begs further analysis, the intertwining of heterosexed forms (of desire, politics, and prose) is striking. In the language of transformative love born with his "lawyer," Cleaver writes in the final chapter: "Such is the magic of a woman, the female principle of nature which she embodies, and her power to resurrect and revitalize a long-isolated and lonely man" (24). Race again disappears in the throes of desire, and only a sexed "principle of nature" has the "magic" and "power" to restore a dying man.

18. Cleaver eventually moved away from his leftist politics to become an active Reagan Republican. "Covering a Controversial Figure: An Informal Survey," *Newswatch Project*, San Francisco State University Journalism Department, 1998, http://www.newswatch.sfsu.edu/Critiques/1998/Cleaver.html.

19. "Once in *Jackson* [*v. State of Alabama*], twice in *Naim* [*v. Naim*], and again in *McLaughlin* [*v. Florida*], the Court repeatedly utilized . . . 'passive virtues'—the power of the Court to decline to exercise the jurisdiction which it is given." Chang Moon Sohn, "Principle and Expediency in Judicial Review: Miscegenation Cases in the Supreme Court" (Ph.D. diss., Columbia University, 1971), 120–21.

20. Sohn continues: "The conclusion is inescapable that the Court was avoiding a case that it would ordinarily have accepted" (ibid., 121).

21. Ibid., 87, 92, 122.

22. Ibid., 122 and, citing Gerald Gunther in the *Columbia Law Review*, 123.

23. The formerly ruling logic, inherited from *Pace v. Alabama,* 106 U.S. 583 (1883), held that miscegenation laws did not violate the Fourteenth Amendment because their discrimination was "directed against the offence . . . and not against the person of any particular color or race."

24. Robert J. Sickels, *Race, Marriage, and the Law* (Albuquerque: University of New Mexico Press, 1972), 4, citing Walter F. Murphy, *Elements of Judicial Strategy* (Chicago: University of Chicago Press, 1964), 193.

25. Until 1964 "the NAACP was doing its best to dissociate itself from any attempt to invalidate miscegenation statutes" (Sohn, "Principle and Expediency in Judicial Review," 133). Marshall was nominated to the Supreme Court the day after the *Loving* case was decided.

26. The Gallup poll measured 30 percent of blacks and 72 percent of whites in support of retaining the laws. Sohn, "Principle and Expediency in Judicial Review," 150, from *Boston Globe*, 11 March 1965.

27. Adrienne D. Davis, "*Loving* against the Law: The History and Jurisprudence of Interracial Sex" (forthcoming).

28. *Loving v. Virginia*, 10.

29. Justice Stewart's brief concurring opinion reiterates the point, again referring to the skin test (ibid., 13).

30. According to Kenneth James Lay, "[T]wenty-nine states [had] statutes still on the books in 1951. In 1964, nineteen states still had anti-miscegenation laws." "Sexual Racism: A Legacy of Slavery," *National Black Law Journal* 13, nos. 1–2 (Spring 1993): 175.

31. Walter Wadlington, "The *Loving* Case: Virginia's Anti-miscegenation Statute in Historical Perspective," *Virginia Law Review* 52, no. 5 (June 1966): 1222.

32. Brief for Appellants, *Loving v. Virginia*, 9, 26.

33. *Brown v. Board of Education*, 347 U.S. 483 (1954), 495 no. 11.

34. Brief for Appellants, 26.

35. Ibid., 27, citing Gunnar Myrdal, *An American Dilemma*, 590–91.

36. The history of the statutes lent the Court a hand. The brief that insisted on the history of exploitation also acknowledged their having been most recently modified by Virginia's Racial Integrity Act of 1924, reflecting the "surge of racial antagonism and intolerance of the 1920's" (ibid., 37). That kind of history, and rhetoric, was what the Court was ready to openly name, citing as it did the act's emergence in a period of "extreme nativism" (*Loving v. Virginia*, 6).

37. In light of the texts that clearly have and have not left their marks on *Loving*, I would further point to a pertinent precursor to this section whose influence we have already considered. For, in that very same law review article to which the Court directed the reader for a (caste- and gender-blind) history of Virginia's miscegenation statutes, we find a concluding plea urging the Court to "now make it clear that bans on interracial marriage have no place in a nation dedicated to the equality of man." Pinpointing the very essence of the issue at stake, it continues: "The fundamental question is whether a man and his wife—and their children—should suffer at the hands of the law because they choose to marry across racial lines" (Wadlington, "The *Loving* Case," 1223). Read in context here, such invocations of "man" as the possessor of the right to marry, and implicitly of the woman he marries, make the gendered terms of the civil rights championed increasingly apparent.

38. See Ed Guerrero, *Framing Blackness: The African American Image in Film* (Philadelphia: Temple University Press, 1993), 77, and Thomas E. Wartenberg, *Unlikely Couples: Movie Romance as Social Criticism* (Boulder, Colo.: Westview Press, 1999), 121. Wartenberg writes that white spectators can "identify . . . themselves as supporters of integration while believing that nothing is required of them to bring it about" (125).

39. Here one could interestingly compare the long-term popularity of *Guess Who's Coming to Dinner* to the long-term trashing of *Mandingo* (1975), the first Hollywood film to depict the routine sexual abuse of black women by white men under slavery, as well as to actually show interracial sex between a white woman and a black man. Robin Wood's case for restoring *Mandingo*'s reputation, as noted in the introduction, rests precisely on that film's confrontation of the complex power dynamics of all such encounters.

40. Wartenberg also recognizes this film's "patriarch[al] strategy for accommodating racial integration" wherein "[r]ather than compromise men's power over women, patriarchy will admit black men to the ranks of the privileged" (*Unlikely Couples*, 120). This follows his general note in the introduction that "[a] film that seeks to subvert the hold of one mode of social domination may inadvertently support that of another" (4).

41. Richard Schickel, "Sorry Stage for Tracy's Last Bow," *Life*, 15 December 1967, 16.

42. "Good Causes," *New Yorker*, 16 December 1967.

43. A vivid testament to the complex history attending such rhetoric is Ernest C. Withers's powerful photograph (taken just months after the film's release) of

African American sanitation workers on strike in Memphis, carrying placards that repeatedly declare: "I AM A MAN." Such an image reminds us of the deeply human and progressive contexts out of which such declarations can emerge. These contexts clearly inform John's remark as well. The photo is reprinted in Thelma Golden, ed., *Black Male: Representations of Masculinity in Contemporary American Art* (New York: Whitney Museum of American Art, 1994), 18.

44. James Baldwin, *The Devil Finds Work* (New York: Dial, 1976), 72.

45. The generational change in the air continues in the next scene when Dorothy, the young black maid, hooks up for a ride with a white delivery boy, and they groove in the driveway to the (not so) funky music emitting from his van. Although another tame image of youth culture, this one nonetheless again equates it with interracial (albeit intraclass) couples.

46. Although Matt is left furious by the confrontation with the young black driver, at scene's end Christina giggles at him lovingly, inviting us to read the old man's loss of control as more endearing than disturbing or pathetic.

47. King's name is offered as a quizzical response when Joey, having invited yet another guest to the party after already having invited John and his parents, asks Tillie, "Guess who's coming to dinner now?"

48. Charles Champlin, review of *Guess*, uncited newspaper, *Guess* clippings file, Margaret Herrick Library, Beverly Hills, California.

49. Schickel, "Sorry Stage for Tracy's Last Bow," 16.

50. Champlin, review of *Guess*.

51. Ibid.

52. Arthur Knight, "The Now Look," *Saturday Review*, 16 December 1967.

53. "Spence and the Supergirl," *Newsweek*, 25 December 1967.

54. Ibid.

55. Production notes, *Guess* file, PCA, Herrick.

56. Scheer, *Eldridge Cleaver*, 175–76.

57. By contrast, *The Landlord* exposes a white man's structural relation to dominant fantasies of miscegenation. When his one-night-stand with a black tenant destroys her marriage and her husband's fragile psyche, he owns up to his responsibility and appears to renounce his former position, taking custody of the child born of the affair (who the mother does not want), giving his formerly coveted building to the black couple he has helped to destroy, and attempting to forge a new kind of interracial relation with an independent woman.

58. Joey articulates the terms under which the film is willing to open up that culture when she explains her mother's "brilliant" plan to put paintings in hotel rooms. The idea, as she tells John, is that "guests get to look at good paintings instead of bad reproductions, the painter gets a chance to make a sale, and mom gets her commission." In other words, the masses can take a peek so long as the profits of those who own and sell are still a priority, and those who cannot afford to buy are clearly marked as "guests" with only temporary access.

59. Also from the production notes we learn that "paintings, valued at more than $90,000, were rented from five leading Los Angeles art galleries to decorate the rooms." *Guess* file, PCA, Herrick.

60. Arguing that the film's visual representation refuses the color blindness defended in the narrative, Wartenberg discusses the "determinedly desexualized

representation of its central love affair" and cites John's eroticized look at Dorothy as the film's overt attempt "to emphasize that John's sexual interest is not limited to white women" (*Unlikely Couples*, 127).

61. Poitier's looks at Joanna are never this overtly sexual. What is more, at the moment of this look he is (presumably) directed to "sound more black," something that happens only when he speaks with other (working-class) African Americans.

62. When John then goes into that study, his look and placement continue to gently toy with the absent white man's. He sits at Matt's desk—also with a view, but also withheld—admiring and fingering a photo of Joey and her mother. As if to again safeguard Matt's position a little longer with a black alternative, Joey teases that she better shut the door "in case Dorothy walks by."

63. Frame enlargements of this film were not possible. Left, then, with the choice of either not including images for this chapter's culminating visual argument or reproducing frame grabs of a "reformatted" image (no widescreen version of the film is available on VHS or DVD), I opted for the second. One of the unfortunate effects is that these images minimize the grand sweep of the view (as, of course, does the size of the reproductions). I run these risks to give my reader a chance to glimpse for herself (sort of) the evidence for my claims.

64. Christina here makes explicit both Matt's liberal hypocrisy and the film's inability to articulate racism beyond the language of "color": "The way she is is just exactly the way we brought her up to be. We told her it was wrong to believe that the white people were somehow essentially superior to the black people, or the brown or the red or the yellow ones. People who thought that way were wrong. . . . That's what we said. And when we said it, we did not add, 'but don't ever fall in love with a colored man.'"

65. This name is given him by Monsignor Ryan, another of the dinner guests, upon learning of Matt's reaction to Joey's engagement.

66. James Bacon, *Hollywood Reporter*, 6 December 1967, *Guess* clippings file, Herrick.

67. *New Yorker*, 16 December 1967.

68. *Time*, 15 December 1967.

69. Bacon, *Hollywood Reporter*. A review in the *Motion Picture Herald* similarly posits the actor as the "deep" source of authentic emotion: "A lesser actor might have appeared to be giving a lecture; Tracy makes the words seem the spontaneous outflow of a man who feels deeply." *Guess* clippings file, Herrick.

70. When John, having just met Matt, says he cannot tell what he thinks, Joey concurs: "I don't know either. Nobody can tell when he puts on his American eagle face, except mom."

71. *Guess* review, *Daily News*, 12 December 1967 (emphasis mine), as cited in an ad for the film in *Hollywood Reporter*, 20 December 1967. Sounding a good bit like Matt Drayton, director Stanley Kramer draws a related parallel when he defends his film against "the rebel intellectual" response of certain college students. Remarking on the aesthetics of "this new unsmiling generation," he writes that "the [current] student of cinema wants to be Godard—not Wyler nor Stevens nor Ford,—nor Kramer." But he rejects "the cover-all of [counter-Hollywood] technique. The 'nouveau vague,' the 'neo-

realists' and the 'angry young men' have opened the gates to interrupted dialogue, mismatching, jump cuts, super-impositions, split screens. . . . Technique covers a multitude of sins." True to his film's faith in classical form, he concludes, "The seeds of the next revolution are planted during this one. I think there will be a massive return to utter simplicity. It remains the purest form—the most difficult to attain." Stanley Kramer, "Nine Times across the Generation Gap," *Aah'ou*, April–May 1968, 13, 12.

72. "Fiat Lux," *Hollywood Reporter*, 18 April 1967, invoking Genesis 1:3.

73. This visual restoration of the challenged racial-sexual-visual order uncannily echoes the representation of its distress, as discussed in the last chapter, in *The World, the Flesh, and the Devil*.

74. Here I refer to several kinds of theoretical and critical work, often now referred to as "*Screen* theory" and "apparatus theory," by writers like Christian Metz, Laura Mulvey, and Stephen Heath. While my inquiries of race, history, reception, and nonfilmic texts deviate significantly from these theoretical traditions, without them they nonetheless would not be possible.

75. Obviously a vast history of theory and criticism itself, indeed of intellectual thought, is also accountable.

Index